THE ABINGDON
PREACHING
ANNUAL 2012

EDITED BY DAVID N. MOSSER

THE ABINGDON
PREACHING
ANNUAL 2012

COMPILED AND EDITED BY
THE REVEREND DAVID NEIL MOSSER, PH.D.

ASSISTANT EDITOR RONDA WELLMAN

Abingdon Press
Nashville

THE ABINGDON PREACHING ANNUAL 2012

This book is printed on acid-free paper.

ISBN 978-1-4267-1018-6

ISSN 1075-2250

11 12 13 14 15 16 17 18 19 20—10 9 8 7 6 5 4 3 2 1

MANUFACTURED IN THE UNITED STATES OF AMERICA

For his dedication to the preacher's task, this book is respectfully dedicated to a first-rate human being in the realm of God whose title is nearly as large as he is: Ron Allen, Nettie Sweeney and Hugh Th. Miller Professor of Preaching and New Testament at Christian Theological Seminary, Indianapolis, Ind.

CONTENTS

❧❧❧

vii

Contents

MARCH

APRIL

Contents

Contents

Contents

Contents

DECEMBER

IV. CD-ROM (THESE RESOURCES ARE FOUND ONLY ON THE ENCLOSED CD-ROM)

Entire Print Text plus the following (see the ReadMe.txt file on the CD for instructions):

INTRODUCTION

The book you hold in your hands, *The Abingdon Preaching Annual 2012,* is a true preaching *annual* in that it follows the calendar year from January through December rather than following the liturgical year from the first Sunday of Advent to The Reign of Christ (or Christ the King) Sunday. Half of the sermons are from the liturgical calendar employed by the Revised Common Lectionary (RCL); half of the sermons are series that cover a variety of topics germane to life in the body of Christ. Some of the series are up to seven weeks long, while others are as short as two weeks in duration. One lectionary and one series sermon is offered each week. The individual preacher will, of course, decide between lectionary and series each week through creative design under the providential and attentive guidance of God.

It used to be easy to find collections of sermons in bookshops and libraries. Today, however, sermons are generally available online and (too often for my taste) not in print but in audio format. Clearly preachers produce sermons for listeners to hear, but there is an elegance and utility in reading and pondering another preacher's words. The written word can contain slices of art that we cannot hear as easily as we can see as we read. In addition one can scan, read over, or examine ten sermons in the time it takes to listen to a single homily. We hope that *The Abingdon Preaching Annual* will motivate readers to reflect on the work of our contributors who, almost without exception, preach week in and week out in fine pulpits in various denominations.

The Abingdon Preaching Annual brings superior preachers to print and continues to offer a variety of voices and types of preaching. We pray that the "preachers as readers" who profit from *The Abingdon Preaching Annual* may be both young and old, experienced and novice, urban and rural, male and female—and of every ethnic subgroup that is faithful to the gospel of Jesus Christ. Our world needs folks who can announce the good news in our time!

We also hope that as you study and return to the fine sermons in this volume, you see the wide variety of elements that comprises good preaching—logical development, clear exegetical method, and compelling illustrations.

But even more than simply preaching and sharing sacred texts for congregations, *The Abingdon Preaching Annual* provides ways to prompt deeper worship experiences. In addition to the weekly sermons on lectionary and series themes, each with Worship Aids intended to help "prime the pump," the *APA* furnishes commentary on lectionary texts not used for the primary sermon. The enclosed CD-ROM includes the full text of the print edition as well as the full lectionary text of each week's readings and offers search capabilities and hyperlinks for easy navigation. The CD-ROM also provides pre-sermon, offertory, and pastoral prayers for major liturgical celebrations, an extensive annotated bibliography of biblical commentaries to help preachers in their preparation, classical and contemporary prayers and affirmations, and a classic sermon from the past for inspiration.

As you prepare to preach, remember that God has called you to this task. Whatever tools you can get your hands, eyes, and heart on will be helpful and beneficial, but always take a few minutes to be fully in the presence of the divine, who will give you the wisdom and discernment to serve God's people. No other gift will serve you better.

David N. Mosser
6 March 2010
Feast Day of St. Basil (335)
Arlington, Texas

I. GENERAL HELPS

FOUR-YEAR CHURCH CALENDAR

	2012	2013	2014	2015
Ash Wednesday	February 22	February 13	March 5	February 18
Palm Sunday	April 1	March 24	April 13	March 29
Holy Thursday	April 5	March 28	April 17	April 2
Good Friday	April 6	March 29	April 18	April 3
Easter	April 8	March 31	April 20	April 5
Ascension Sunday	May 20	May 12	June 1	May 17
Pentecost	May 27	May 19	June 8	May 24
Trinity Sunday	June 3	May 26	June 15	May 31
World Communion	October 7	October 8	October 5	October 4
Thanksgiving	November 22	November 28	November 27	November 26
First Sunday of Advent	November 25	December 1	November 30	November 29

LITURGICAL COLORS

If the gospel can be proclaimed visually, why should it not be? Color helps form general expectations for any occasion. Traditionally, purples, grays, and blues have been used for seasons of a penitential character such as Advent and Lent, although any dark colors could be used. White has been used for events or seasons with strong christological meaning such as the Baptism of the Lord or the Easter Season. Yellows and golds are also possibilities at such times. Red has been reserved for occasions relating to the Holy Spirit (such as the Day of Pentecost or ordinations) or to commemorations of the martyrs. Green has been used for seasons such as the Season after Epiphany or the Season after Pentecost. The absence of any colored textiles from Maundy Thursday to the Easter Vigil is a striking use of contrast. Colors and textures can be used most effectively in textiles for hangings on pulpits, on lecterns (if any), for the stoles worn by ordained ministers, or for ministerial vestments.*

Advent: Violet (purple) or blue

Christmas: Gold or white for December 24-25. White thereafter, through the Baptism of the Lord. (Or, in the days between January 6 and the Sunday of the Baptism, green may be used.)

Ordinary Time (both after Epiphany-Baptism and after Pentecost): Green

Transfiguration: White

Lent Prior to Holy Week: Violet. Black is sometimes used for Ash Wednesday.

Early Holy Week: On Palm-Passion Sunday, violet (purple) or [blood] red may be specified. For the Monday, Tuesday, and Wednesday of Holy Week, the same options exist, although with variations as to which color to use on each day.

Triduum: For Holy Thursday, violet (purple) or [blood] red may be used during the day and changed to white for the evening Eucharist. Then the church may be stripped.

Good Friday and Holy Saturday: Stripped or black; or [blood] red in some churches on Good Friday.

Great Fifty Days: White or gold. Or gold for Easter Day and perhaps its octave, then white for the remainder of the season until the Vigil of Pentecost.

Day of Pentecost: [Fire] red

Annunciation, Visitation, and Presentation of Jesus: White

Commemoration of Martyrs: [Blood] red

Commemoration of Saints not Martyred: White

All Saints: White

Christ the King: White**

* James F. White, *Introduction to Christian Worship* (rev. ed.; Nashville: Abingdon Press, 1990), 85-86.

** Laurence Hull Stookey, *Calendar: Christ's Time for the Church* (Nashville: Abingdon Press, 1996), 156-57.

LECTIONARY LISTINGS 2012*
THE REVISED COMMON LECTIONARY

Sunday	First Lesson	Psalm	Second Lesson	Gospel Lesson
01/01/12	Ecclesiastes 3:1-13	Psalm 8	Revelation 21:1-6a	Matthew 25:31-46
01/08/12	Genesis 1:1-5	Psalm 29	Acts 19:1-7	Mark 1:4-11
01/15/12	1 Samuel 3:1-10,(11-20)	Psalm 139:1-6,13-18	1 Corinthians 6:12-20	John 1:43-51
01/22/12	Jonah 3:1-5,10	Psalm 62:5-12	1 Corinthians 7:29-31	Mark 1:14-20
01/29/12	Deuteronomy 18:15-20	Psalm 111	1 Corinthians 8:1-13	Mark 1:21-28
02/05/12	Isaiah 40:21-31	Psalm 147:1-11,20c	1 Corinthians 9:16-23	Mark 1:29-39
02/12/12	2 Kings 5:1-14	Psalm 30	1 Corinthians 9:24-27	Mark 1:40-45
02/19/12	2 Kings 2:1-12	Psalm 50:1-6	2 Corinthians 4:3-6	Mark 9:2-9
02/22/12	Joel 2:1-2,12-17	Psalm 51:1-17	2 Corinthians 5:20b-6:10	Matthew 6:1-6,16-21
02/26/12	Genesis 9:8-17	Psalm 25:1-10	1 Peter 3:18-22	Mark 1:9-15
03/04/12	Genesis 17:1-7,15-16	Psalm 22:22-31	Romans 4:13-25	Mark 8:31-38
03/11/12	Exodus 20:1-17	Psalm 19	1 Corinthians 1:18-25	John 2:13-22
03/18/12	Numbers 21:4-9	Psalm 107:1-3,17-22	Ephesians 2:1-10	John 3:14-21
03/25/12	Jeremiah 31:31-34	Psalm 51:1-12	Hebrews 5:5-10	John 12:20-33
04/01/12		Psalm 118:1-2, 19-29		Mark 11:1-11
	Isaiah 50:4-9a	Psalm 31:9-16	Philippians 2:5-11	Mark 14:1-15:47
04/05/12	Exodus 12:1-4,(5-10),11-14	Psalm 116:1-2,12-19	1 Corinthians 11:23-26	John 13:1-7,31b-35
04/06/12	Isaiah 52:13-53:12	Psalm 22	Hebrews 10:16-25	John 18:1-19:26
04/08/12	Isaiah 25:6-9	Psalm 118:1-2,14-24	Acts 10:34-43	John 20:1-18
04/15/12	Acts 4:32-35	Psalm 133	1 John 1:1-2:2	John 20:19-31
04/22/12	Acts 3:12-19	Psalm 4	1 John 3:1-7	Luke 24:36b-48
04/29/12	Acts 4:5-12	Psalm 23	1 John 3:16-24	John 10:11-18
05/06/12	Acts 8:26-40	Psalm 22:25-31	1 John 4:7-21	John 15:1-8
05/13/12	Acts 10:44-48	Psalm 98	1 John 5:1-6	John 15:9-17
05/20/12	Acts 1:15-17,21-26	Psalm 1	1 John 5:9-13	John 17:6-19

* This list represents one possible selection of lessons and psalms from the lectionary for Year B (January 1–December 1) and Year C (December 2–31). For a complete listing, see *The Revised Common Lectionary.*

Sunday	First Lesson	Psalm	Second Lesson	Gospel Lesson
05/27/12	Ezekiel 37:1-14	Psalm 104:24-34,35b	Acts 2:1-21	John 15:26-27; 16:4b-15
06/03/12	Isaiah 6:1-8	Psalm 29	Romans 8:12-17	John 3:1-17
06/10/12	Genesis 3:8-15	Psalm 130	2 Corinthians 4:13-5:1	Mark 3:20-35
06/17/12	Ezekiel 17:22-24	Psalm 92:1-4,12-15	2 Corinthians 5:6-10,(11-13), 14-17	Mark 4:26-34
06/24/12	Job 38:1-11	Psalm 107:1-3, 23-32	2 Corinthians 6:1-13	Mark 4:35-41
07/01/12	Lamentations 3:23-33	Psalm 30	2 Corinthians 8:7-15	Mark 5:21-43
07/08/12	Ezekiel 2:1-5	Psalm 123	2 Corinthians 12:2-10	Mark 6:1-13
07/15/12	Amos 7:7-15	Psalm 85:8-13	Ephesians 1:3-14	Mark 6:14-29
07/22/12	Jeremiah 23:1-6	Psalm 23	Ephesians 2:11-22	Mark 6:30-34,53-56
07/29/12	2 Kings 4:42-44	Psalm 145:10-18	Ephesians 3:14-21	John 6:1-21
08/05/12	Exodus 16:2-4,9-15	Psalm 78:23-29	Ephesians 4:1-16	John 6:24-35
08/12/12	1 Kings 19:4-8	Psalm 34:1-8	Ephesians 4:25-5:2	John 6:35,41-51
08/19/12	Proverbs 9:1-6	Psalm 34:9-14	Ephesians 5:15-20	John 6:51-58
08/26/12	Joshua 24:1-2a,14-18	Psalm 34:15-22	Ephesians 6:10-20	John 6:56-69
09/02/12	Deuteronomy 4:1-2,6-9	Psalm 15	James 1:17-27	Mark 7:1-8,14-15,21-23
09/09/12	Isaiah 35:4-7	Psalm 146	James 2:1-10,(11-13),14-17	Mark 7:24-37
09/16/12	Isaiah 50:4-9a	Psalm 116:1-9	James 3:1-12	Mark 8:27-38
09/23/12	Jeremiah 11:18-20	Psalm 54	James 3:13-4:3,7-8a	Mark 9:30-37
09/30/12	Numbers 11:4-6,10-16, 24-20	Psalm 19:7-14	James 5:13-20	Mark 9:38-50
10/07/12	Genesis 2:18-24	Psalm 8	Hebrews 1:1-4; 2:5-12	Mark 10:2-16
10/14/12	Amos 5:6-7,10-15	Psalm 90:12-17	Hebrews 4:12-16	Mark 10:17-31
10/21/12	Isaiah 53:4-12	Psalm 91:9-16	Hebrews 5:1-10	Mark 10:35-45
10/28/12	Jeremiah 31:7-9	Psalm 126	Hebrews 7:23-28	Mark 10:46-52
11/04/12	Deuteronomy 6:1-9	Psalm 119:1-8	Hebrews 9:11-14	Mark 12:28-34
11/11/12	1 Kings 17:8-16	Psalm 146	Hebrews 9:24-28	Mark 12:38-44
11/18/12	Daniel 12:1-3	Psalm 16	Hebrews 10:11-14,(15-18),19-25	Mark 13:1-8

* This list represents one possible selection of lessons and psalms from the lectionary for Year B (January 1–December 1) and Year C (December 2–31). For a complete listing, see *The Revised Common Lectionary*.

Sunday	First Lesson	Psalm	Second Lesson	Gospel Lesson
11/22/12	Joel 2:21-27	Psalm 126	1Timothy 2:1-7	Matthew 6:25-33
11/25/12	Daniel 7:9-10,13-14	Psalm 93	Revelation 1:4b-8	John 18:33-37
12/02/12	Jeremiah 33:14-16	Psalm 25:1-10	1 Thessalonians 3:9-13	Luke 21:25-36
12/09/12	Luke 1:68-79	Philippians 1:3-11	Luke 3:1-6	Malachi 3:1-4
12/16/12	Zephaniah 3:14-20		Philippians 4:4-7	Luke 3:7-18
12/23/12	Micah 5:2-5a	Isaiah 12:2-6 or Psalm 80:1-7	Hebrews 10:5-10	Luke 1:39-45, (46-55)
12/25/12	Isaiah 52:7-10	Psalm 98	Hebrews 1:1-4, (5-12)	John 1:1-14
12/30/12	1 Samuel 2:18-20,26	Psalm 148	Colossians 3:12-17	Luke 2:41-52

* This list represents one possible selection of lessons and psalms from the lectionary for Year B (January 1–December 1) and Year C (December 2–31). For a complete listing, see *The Revised Common Lectionary*.

II. SERMONS AND WORSHIP AIDS

JANUARY 1, 2012

New Year's Day / Epiphany

Readings: Ecclesiastes 3:1-13; Psalm 8; Revelation 21:1-6a; Matthew 25:31-46

A Story That Really Gets Our Goat!

Matthew 25:31-46

The parable of the sheep and the goats begins by emphasizing the authority of Jesus, not to mention all the angels and nations gathered before Jesus. Matthew celebrates a high Christology, and perhaps we notice—perhaps we don't—that while all the heavenly hosts above accompany Jesus (the heavenly hosts are active), all the nations are gathered before Jesus (the nations are passive). The authority of Jesus underscores the people's passivity as he separates them like sheep and goats; what was whole is divided by Jesus. We don't know what to do with that yet, but we file it away as interesting.

What do you think? Are we predisposed to think of sheep as good, goats as bad? Do we assume right to be better than left? Could it not be that the Son of Man is simply separating based on the perfectly obvious difference between sheep and goats—like the perfectly obvious difference between those who are passive and those who are active?

Jesus invites the gathered nations to action: "Come, you that are blessed [passive] by my Father, inherit the kingdom prepared for you [passive] from the foundation of the world" (v. 34). While some read into the verb tenses of this verse the idea of predestination, the blessing and the preparing of the kingdom are not separated but have been being simultaneous through time.

"For I was in need and you took care of me" (see vv. 35-36). Finally, we shut our passive file. Finally, people are active. Taking care of people who need help—not in dramatic ways, but in the most basic of ways, meeting the most basic of needs. We recognize that this isn't hard. You

3

shared some food. You spent some time with me. The text doesn't say, "'I was sick and you healed me,' or 'I was in prison and you liberated me'" (Frederick Dale Bruner, *Matthew: A Commentary: The Churchbook: Matthew 13-28: Revised & Expanded Edition* [Grand Rapids: Wm. B. Eerdmans, 1990], 569).

The righteous answer Jesus. *Righteousness* in Matthew consistently refers to the "right conduct of [people who follow] the will of God..." (Gerhart Kittel, ed., *Theological Dictionary of the New Testament: Volume II* [Grand Rapids: Wm. B. Eerdmans, 1964], 198). Righteousness has to do with what we do. The passive file remains shut. The initial response of the righteous—that Matthew didn't think was quite literary enough for his Gospel—was: "Huh?" It's not that they were surprised at the recital of what they had done. They knew what they had done. They were surprised to discover who had received what they had done.

"What you did to one of the least of these, you did to me." What a highly individual response! This is not about feeding the hungry; it's about feeding one hungry person. As a result of a simple act people have been being blessed and the kingdom of God has been being prepared; those verbs create a sense of simultaneity—almost as if the kingdom is being prepared not just *for* those who care for others, but *by* those who care for others—as if when we follow Jesus, we are helping prepare the kingdom into which we are welcomed.

"You that are accursed...." Note the passive again, but this time Jesus doesn't add "by my father." Is it implied? Or is blessing what God has to give while being cursed is simply not accepting blessing, not responding to blessing? "You that are accursed, depart from me into the eternal fire prepared for the devil and his angels" (v. 41). Beyond your present passivity, there is no past activity to distinguish you. Depart from me because you would have no part of me when I needed you.

Huh? They can't believe it. It's not that they are surprised at the recital of what they have not done. They know what they have not done. They are surprised to discover who they have neglected. "No fair!" they protest. "We would have acted if we'd known it was you. We wouldn't have been so passive."

But there comes a time, claims our story, at which the opportunity for appropriate human initiative ends, and the divine response to human initiative (or lack thereof) takes over. There will come a time at which it will no longer matter what we do or intend to do, but only what we have done.

Those who actively live a unity—taking care of others and thus taking care of Jesus—are taking care of the kingdom of God, preparing it, and bringing its blessing to themselves and others. They have, in other words, been in the kingdom. Of course, there's the flip side: those who passively deny unity—who, however active they may be otherwise, do not take care of others—are separated from the kingdom, and not just now. They have been separated from the kingdom. If we don't act to get out of that passive file, there will be nothing to distinguish us, to cause Jesus to identify us as his own.

The chaplain of the state penitentiary in Stillwater, Minnesota, took aside Bill, just then beginning work with inmates, and said, "Don't forget, Bill. If Matthew 25 . . . is right, you didn't come to bring Jesus to these guys; you came to find him" (quoted in Bruner, *Matthew: A Commentary*, 575)! Here's the thing: the very high Christology with which this text begins (Jesus with the authority of God) has integrity only when simultaneously celebrated with the very low Christology revealed throughout the text (Jesus is made incarnate in the very least of us), and our own salvation has more to do with our relationship with Jesus in the least of these than our faith in Jesus as God. Does that get your goat? (John Ballenger)

Lectionary Commentary

Ecclesiastes 3:1-13

The wisdom literature of the Old Testament typically offers insight into and lessons about God and the way of right living within the everyday details of life. The philosopher/teacher of Ecclesiastes, in his observation of life, is much more focused on ideas about that life than on any ideas or affirmations about God, and he certainly does not shy away from noting the limitations of all human endeavors. Our reading, however, does seek to contextualize the particularities of life, not in some order or pattern—certainly not in any form of justification—but within the affirmation that the whole of life is gift of God.

Revelation 21:1-6a

To trace the record of Jerusalem in Scripture is to trace, on the one hand, the great pride and the profound hope manifest in the city of God, and, on the other hand, the profound disappointment at the dichotomy between what Jerusalem was meant to be and what it turned out to be. The prophetic literature and Jesus in the Gospels all express both responses to Jerusalem: alternating words of love and appreciation with words of anger and judgment. In our apocalyptic text, we look ahead to a time when God will restore Jerusalem as it was always meant to be: God's home on earth among mortals. (John Ballenger)

Worship Aids

Unison Call to Worship

We gather this day again, before your throne, to discover what you remember about our living—to be reminded of what we have done—and not done. We entrust ourselves to your grace, even as we commit ourselves to your truth. We are your flock. You are our shepherd.

Invocation

Our God, we invoke respect for your authority and awareness of the importance of our active living. We invoke sensitivity to your presence among us and hope in the possibility of ministering to you. We invoke commitment to your way in and through our living. Amen.

Pastoral Prayer

Our God, we both prepare and enter your kingdom by meeting the basic needs of people we encounter. May we celebrate our opportunities and embrace them, and thus embrace Jesus with full and grateful hearts. This we pray in the name of the one who awaits us. Amen. (John Ballenger)

Time to Renew

First in a Series of Four on Turning Over a New Leaf: Beginning Anew

Genesis 1:1-5

The mail brings them to us, envelopes with the words "Time to Renew" printed on the outside. The magazine subscription is about to expire, and it is time to renew. The membership period is coming to a close, and it is time to renew. The warranty is ending, and it is time to renew. The calendar turns to another year. It is time to renew.

So here we are on the first day of a new year. We may be a little groggy from New Year's Eve parties, but the message for us is an exciting one: it is time to renew. What this year will bring no one knows, but the possibilities are unlimited. It is time to renew.

I suggest we live this year with a "What if?" attitude. What if we lived as though all the hopes and dreams of our lives were really going to happen? What if we approached this year with the expectation that life truly can be renewed? The gospel is about beginning again. It is about renewal. We can walk away from yesterday into the freshness of tomorrow. That is the good news I bring to you today.

"What if?' is what the sun asks every morning before pinking the sky with a new day. "What if?" is the thought of the ballerina preparing to step on stage. "What if?" ask the eyes of lovers as they see each other across the room. In the beginning, when God created the heavens and the earth, God said, 'What if?'"

The story of creation is the drama of renewal. Seasons change, time passes, and through it all the cycle of life brings forth the things that make possible the existence of life on earth. It is as if the physical world teaches us a lesson—renewal is at the heart of everything. No death is permanent; no birth goes on forever. Renewal is at the center of everything, a dynamic of endings and beginnings that never ceases.

In a sense every Sunday is an opportunity to begin again. This is why having a new year begin on a Sunday is symbolically important. We believe that the grace of Christ brings the possibility of renewal. On this first Sunday of a new year we are invited to let that grace wash over our lives so that like fresh-washed children we can begin again. After all, we are the people of Easter. We believe in the radical grace of life defeating death. We are the people who say to one another, "Hear the good news: in the name of Jesus Christ, you are forgiven!" That powerful statement applies to your life and to mine on this Lord's day. I pray that we can hear the gospel today and know that—as in the beginning, so now—God is creating, and the possibilities of that creation are unlimited.

Today is the first day of the rest of your life. It is always the first day in God's hands. Think of the moments in the life of Jesus when he was confronted by seemingly permanent dead ends. Bartimaeus, sitting blind by the side of the road, had his sight restored. He was renewed. The woman at the well, living with the burden of a past that grew heavier with each passing day, was introduced to the living water of grace. She ran back to her tormentors to tell them to come see a man who has seen her life as no one else ever had; she was renewed, restored, redeemed. "Come see this man," she says. Miserable Zacchaeus sat in a tree just to get a glimpse; Jesus goes home with him, and Zacchaeus becomes a different man.

7

Nicodemus comes to Jesus in the dark of the night and is invited to be born anew as the dawn of grace breaks over his rule-driven life.

On and on the story goes of God's grace coming to us, restoring our lives, renewing our days, recharging our spiritual batteries, giving us the chance to begin again. It is the first Sunday of a new year and the rich grace of God is given to us in such a way that we don't have to be who we were when we walked into this worship center. We can be different people. We don't have to be like snails who drag the shell of their past around with them. No, ours is a gospel of renewal. We believe in the God of second chances. We have seen God's revelation in the one whose touch is always renewing, whose word is always redemptive and whose love is powerful enough to let us begin again.

May this grace embrace you on this first day of a new year. May you live as if all your dreams can be realities. Even now God is creating a new day for you. Run to it and let it be the experience of a true new beginning for your one wild and beautiful life. It is time to renew! That is why the gospel is called *good news*.

Somewhere on the golden streets of heaven a man is grinning big. He once hung on a cross next to another man and must have thought his life was over. All he had was a prayer that went something like, "Jesus, remember me." All he had was a prayer, and it was all he needed. A con man was given a second chance. If that could happen for him, it can happen for you. In the beginning God created, and in your life God is creating. Now is the time to let that energy of renewal embrace you and make you new. It's time to turn over a new leaf, and Jesus is here to help you begin anew. (Chris Andrews)

Worship Aids

Call to Worship

We gather on the first Sunday of a New Year.
We come with expectance and anticipation.
Let us open ourselves to the possibilities of God's grace.
**Our hearts are open, our minds are ready. This is the day the
Lord has made; let us sing and rejoice!**

Invocation

Come to us, O Holy One, and bring your renewing grace to our lives. We stand ready for a new year. May we embrace the power of your Spirit that makes all things new.

Benediction

Go forth to live in the abundance of God's renewing grace. May you walk in the power of Jesus' love and have the courage to dare to live your dreams, now and always. Amen. (Chris Andrews)

JANUARY 8, 2012

❧❧❧

Baptism of the Lord

Readings: Genesis 1:1-5; Psalm 29; Acts 19:1-7; Mark 1:4-11

The Grand Overture

Genesis 1:1-5

"In the beginning. . ." is a time frame so vastly other, so immensely bigger than our own. We are, in fact, somewhat unsettlingly, taken out of our time frame. This isn't the beginning of a new year or the beginning of a semester. This is *the* beginning, the time frame that includes any and all other time frames. Our time frame is contextualized within all time.

Have you seen that graphic that takes all time—all of history—and depicts it in twenty-four hours? Would you believe the last of the dinosaurs were still alive at 11:51 p.m.? Humans didn't appear until 11:59 p.m. and not in North America until 1/7th of a second ago! Our Scripture removes us from our tiny sliver of a fraction of a second to contemplate the fullness of all the hours of history.

"In the beginning when God created . . . ," this is to say, first, in the beginning, God. God is already present, identified within time but not defined by it. This is a profound theological affirmation. Second, in the beginning, God is not just present but active. God is involved in this beginning. God initiates this beginning that eventually leads to us.

"In the beginning when God created the heavens and the earth. . . ." Added to the chronology so much longer than ours, we are also displaced from our familiar spatial context into one so much bigger. Again, it includes our own but within the largest possible conceptualization of it—the biggest frame. Like the sliver of a second in twenty-four hours, the context of all creation makes us small.

Space and time come together to affirm that this story is not our story as individuals, as members of a family or a community; it is not our national story, not even the human story. This story takes our biggest story and makes it small. Yet, in acknowledging our smallness within the largest of all possible frames of time and space, we are taken out of our moments to be a part of all time and taken out of our place to be a part of all space; we are taken as one part of creation to be placed in direct relation to the creator and thus to all that is, ever has been, and ever will be.

Some scholars suppose (no one knows for sure) that these first verses of Genesis were written in Babylon during the exile. "Such a judgment means that the text is not an abstract statement about the origin of the universe. Rather, it is a theological and pastoral statement addressed to a real historical problem" (Walter Brueggemann, *Genesis* [Atlanta: John Knox Press, 1982], 25). It may be that these verses were written at a time, in a place and circumstance in which people needed the comfort of an unsettling, displacing word that removed them from their time and place. More than a reminder of a larger context—God, God's power, God's design, and our place within God's design—an unsettled, displaced people read, "in the beginning, when God created the heavens and the earth, the earth was a formless void and darkness covered the face of the deep, while a wind from God swept over the face of the waters" (Genesis 1:1-2). Amid the threatening images of chaos, Scripture affirms God as creator of order out of chaos. When life is unsettled in exile, an unsettling word can actually be a comfort. When people are displaced, a displacing word can actually offer a reassuring sense of place.

Purpose and intent are imposed on the formless void, but note that the waters and the darkness do not go away. Within darkness, God says, "Let there be light" and there is light, and God sees that the light is good. But there is still darkness, for God separates the light from the darkness. We know that, don't we? We know the shattering truth of chaos intruding into our lives. We know the disturbing reality of darkness. Darkness and chaos maintain a place in creation.

Toward the end of our text, we get to the first evaluative statement in Scripture. God names (judges) the light as good. There is no evaluation of the darkness. It is not named good or bad. It is what it is. "God called the light Day, and the darkness he called Night." Inherent in creation is difference, separation, and distinction, but always in relationship. Difference, separation, and distinction do not deny, negate, or compromise relationship. In this case, related through a cycle—there is evening (darkness) and there is morning (light)—the first day.

"Unlike the other days of creation, which are summed up by reference to their place in sequence" (Avivah Gottlieb Zornberg, *The Beginning of Desire: Reflections on Genesis* [New York: Doubleday, 1995], 4), the first day has no meaning until there are more days. Before there is a second day, in other words, this day is not the first day, but simply *day*—evening and morning, a day. That day. This day. Any day. Today. Within the real interplay of light and darkness; within the known reality of feeling both at home and displaced, grounded and unsettled; having the memory and knowing the fear of chaos intruding on order we claim a connection to God, who is still at work, still creating. A good day. A very good day. (John Ballenger)

Lectionary Commentary

Acts 19:1-7

Acts records the spread of the gospel from Jerusalem to the ends of the earth. To this end, the author of Acts, presumed to also be the author of the Gospel of Luke, ends the Jesus story in Jerusalem. There are no appearances of the resurrected Jesus in Galilee. This version of the story does not go backwards but proceeds clearly from Jerusalem through the known world, and Gentiles are explicitly included in the story of God's great initiative of grace. So it is that in our text, we read another version of the Pentecost story, this time in Ephesus, among Gentiles. Notice the resonance with the story from the beginning of Acts with twelve (this time Gentiles) receiving the Spirit and subsequently speaking in tongues and prophesying. The story we know is the story that continues to unfold.

Mark 1:4-11

To our minds, Mark begins his Gospel in the middle of the story. Skipping any form of infancy narrative, Mark starts in the wilderness with all of Jerusalem and Judea gathered to hear a message of repentance and forgiveness. Bear in mind the importance of beginnings and ask yourself why Mark would choose to begin this way. God calls God's people out of the holy city, out of the promised land, back into the wilderness, there to encounter God again—to be led, again, in the way of God, out of bondage and into freedom. (John Ballenger)

Worship Aids

Prayer of Confession

Named children of light, we confess to living into darkness. Called to work with you in bringing your order to chaos, we confess to counting the cost and justifying chaos. Within all that you name good in blessing, we confess to being judgmental and small. Forgive us, God, we pray.

Words of Assurance

Hear the good news! The God of goodness and light forgives.

Pastoral Prayer

Speak into the darkness of our lives. Speak into the chaos of our lives. Speak words of order and purpose, words of light and intent, words of presence and relationship. Speak words of power that recreate, renew, and transform, and then bless us with your grace and with your love. Amen.

Benediction

Go from here into all the light and all the darkness that awaits you—all the chaos within your order. Go to face it with the God who consistently speaks, and creates light and order, and invites us to speak and create too. Go in hope with commitment. (John Ballenger)

The Place of Renewal

Second in a Series of Four on Turning Over a New Leaf: Beginning Anew

Psalm 73

This is the time of year when lots of people are trying out new things. Driven by resolutions designed to get life back on track, folks make early morning trips to the gym, take midday winter walks, and watch their diets. Then of course there is the resolution to watch less TV and do more reading. This culture provides so many ways to improve our lives it is a wonder that we are not all blissfully happy and content. Visit the self-help section of the local bookstore and you will find a "how to deal with any problem" book or guide for just about any life issue you can name.

There is something about a new year that pulls at us and awakens our desire to turn over a new leaf and start life over in fresh ways at all levels of life: physical, emotional, and spiritual. But the secret to all renewal is the spiritual life. If we start with it, the other dimensions of our lives will fall into place. If we neglect it, no diet or number of pushups or miles walked or run will be enough to give us a sense of well being.

A long time ago there was a man in need of renewal. He had grown tired of living in a world of contradictions and uncertainty. There was a

13

time when he had it together, when he was sailing true north, but life had weighed him down, and now he just did not know if things were worth the effort. Diets, exercise programs, self-help books—they all lacked staying power. This man was ready to give up. What was the man's problem? He had begun to doubt his faith. Have you ever done that? He looked around at his world, and things did not fit as they should. He saw all kinds of contradictions. The good people were taking it on the chin and the bad guys were getting rich. The righteous were being run out of town and the ruthless were taking over the places of power. People who played by the rules and did the decent things they had been taught to do were getting taken advantage of by the con artists who played the game with loaded dice or a stacked deck to make sure all came out in their favor.

This man was tired of trying to make sense of life, much like the psalmist in verses 4-16 of Psalm 73. These are desperate verses, a lament from a person who is ready to throw in the towel, give up, and walk away. He is tired and he is discouraged, like we are sometimes. Then we come to verse 17: "until I went into the sanctuary of God." In the sanctuary the psalmist found hope and faith came alive again because in the sanctuary he renewed his relationship with the answerer, the living God of all life.

Life has a way of stumping us. Questions come that seem to have no good answers: Why do the innocent suffer? Where is God in the face of gross injustice? What is the will of God for me? Where can I find faith that will not be shaken by the hurricanes of contradiction and disappointment that can so brutally assault life? Answers to these kinds of questions are found in relationship rather than in words. There will always be contradiction and confusion in the experience of living, but in the presence of the answerer we prevail.

Sacred space is so important for our well being. Our ancestors piled rocks on top of one another to designate a place sacred. The cathedrals of antiquity are testament to the value earlier people gave to the power of worship. The house where we sit for this worship service was created because people who lived before us knew that they needed a place to come to and put life back together again. You and I gather here for the most significant moments of life, such as weddings and funerals and baptisms, because in such moments we need to be in the place that most fully represents the sacred.

The psalmist was confused and confounded by life until he came into the sanctuary of God. We are too. You can go to the gym, read all the books, and make pilgrimages to Wal-Mart, but nothing will substitute for the sanctuary of God. In this New Year, resolve to make worship a discipline of your life. Come to the sanctuary regularly and often. It is the place of renewal. It is the place to find your way through the maze of life's questions and confusions. In the sanctuary of God burns the sacred fire of hope that is the light of the world. In the light of that fire is hope and help and truth. Do not neglect the sanctuary of God as the place to be renewed again and again. (Chris Andrews)

Worship Aids

Call to Worship

We gather in sacred space to meet the Lord of life.
We come seeking the fire of truth, the way of holiness.
In this place Christ reigns. Here love points the way.
Our hearts are open to receive the goodness of God's grace.

Invocation

Come, O Holy One, still our minds and quiet our hearts. Lead us into your presence by the power of your Holy Spirit. Bring us again to the experience of your graceful love shown forth most perfectly in our Lord, Jesus Christ.

Benediction

Go forth to live in the power of God's love. Take that love into the world and be the presence of Christ to all you meet along life's way. May the blessing of this place carry you forward until we meet again in this renewing sanctuary of God. (Chris Andrews)

JANUARY 15, 2012

❧❧❧❧

Second Sunday after the Epiphany

Readings: 1 Samuel 3:1-10, (11-20); Psalm 139:1-6, 13-18;
1 Corinthians 6:12-20; John 1:43-51

Every Breath I Take

Psalm 139:1-6, 13-18

Our lectionary text is a somewhat artificial construct; a spliced
together text, consisting of the first six verses of Psalm 139 and then
another six verses later within the psalm. So we work with what we have
but recognize that it is part of a significantly larger whole.

The psalm begins with "O LORD"—the holy, unspeakable name of
God. We are grounded from the beginning in the transcendent sacred
otherness of the mystery of God. Yet we are quick to discover that this
mystery of God searches out and knows the psalmist. After naming the
Lord, the psalm affirms God's initiative and God's knowledge in relation
to the writer. Interwoven from the very beginning of the psalm are the
transcendent and the immanent, the divine and the human, the absolute
and the relational.

As the psalm proceeds it focuses on the common, everyday activities of
the psalmist who sits down and rises up, who thinks and speaks and walks
a certain path, who lays down and follows a variety of ways, and the transcendent and the immanent are even more tightly woven together. Holy
God and the everyday life of an individual are braided together in a way
that evokes the Shema—that ancient and fundamental affirmation of
Judaism—rooted in the covenant relationship between God and the children of God (Deuteronomy 6:4-6). When you say a prayer twice daily, as
is customary with the Shema, and when that prayer refers to lying down
and rising up, those linked actions found in another text will resonate
with your experience.

16

The affirmation of the psalmist through these first six verses is an extremely thorough "God knows me." God knows all the particulars of my day-to-day living at a very deep, complete, and intimate level. God knows me inside and out. God pays close attention to me.

How comfortable are we with God's close attention? In 1983, the rock group The Police released the song "Every Breath You Take." Initially it perceived as a love song, but the more you listen, the more its intense focus seems creepy. You begin to hear it less as a love song and more as a stalker's song. There is a touch of that in this psalm. "For instance, the verb in the phrase 'hem me in' . . . can have the sense of 'besiege,' 'confine' as well as 'protect.'" (J. Clinton McCann, Jr., *Psalms: New Interpreter's Bible*, Volume IV [Nashville: Abingdon, 1994], 1236). The "watchdog God" idea has long made people uncomfortable and uneasy.

There is certainly a risk, an intimate vulnerability, which the psalmist does not shy away from acknowledging. But that risk is clearly placed within a larger affirmation and celebration of relationship, without the need or the desire to control. The first six verses end with the same awe and wonder with which they began: recognition of the vast knowledge of God. It is mind-boggling that God would know me as God does, that God would be involved in the specifics of my living as God is.

In the next six verses we will consider (13-18), we have the same structure as in verses 1-6: a movement from God's initiative to God's knowledge in relation to the psalmist. This time though, it is not God's initiative as searcher that leads to knowledge; it is God's initiative as creator. The psalmist offers us a poetic collage of images of God as maker, knitter, weaver, writer, shaper, and as the one who forms. In so doing, the psalmist both names and celebrates creator God, and links the creative activity of God with a deep knowledge of creation.

What and whom God created, God knows. Creation though can only yearn to know God. For while the infinite can comprehend the finite, the finite cannot begin to grasp the infinite. And yet there is relationship, the wonder that it exists and the awe of appreciation for the gift.

In this psalm, God's initiative first knows the psalmist (and therefore us), and then moves to God's initiative that made the psalmist (and us). We are seen first as subjects of God's search, then as objects of God's creation. Interestingly, the context of God as creator—the image of primal power—is located within the context of the God who knows individuals. The power of God is subordinated to the personal dimension of relationship with God. It is so significant that the pronouns "you" and "I" are in every line of our text, and often together in the same line.

Verses 13-18 end with the same awe and wonder with which we began. As amazing as it is, as unlikely or even as impossible as it might seem, imagine: we are known by and in relationship with the Holy One completely beyond our understanding, our knowledge, our thinking. So we work with what we know, but recognize that it is part of a significantly larger whole. We affirm that as much as we don't know and can't know, what we do know—which is more important—is the assurance of a relational reality. The truth of our covenant relationship with God is always true for more than we can possibly know; it is a truth too wonderful, too high, too weighty, and so vast. We come to the end; we are still with God. Thanks be to God. (John Ballenger)

Lectionary Commentary

1 Samuel 3:1-20

In a time of great transition, God demonstrates God's presence, God's involvement in the unfolding story of God's people, and God's willingness to use unexpected people to advance that story in ways that align with who and how God is.

1 Corinthians 6:12-20

Writing to the Corinthian Christians, Paul suggests a prioritizing life in light of the ultimate priority of God. As Christians, he writes, our actions are not to be determined by what is lawful or by what is desired. What we can do and what we want to do must be subordinated to what is best for our witness as the redeemed people of God.

John 1:43-51

In the first chapter of John's Gospel, we are introduced to one of the tensions that will run throughout. Will Jesus primarily be identified as the son of Joseph or as the son of God? Our text also locates the Jesus story within the larger story of God as it links the unfolding story of Jesus to the great and ancient stories of Moses and the prophets. Our writer also links this, one of the first stories of the gospel, to one of the last stories of the gospel, to the story of Thomas, in the process creating some meaningful resonance with the image of Jacob asleep, with angels ascending and descending in his dream. According to this Gospel, our story transcends time. (John Ballenger)

Worship Aids

Prayer of Confession

We presume to know you more than we can. We assume a familiarity that is not only presumptuous but also dangerous. We risk losing more of you in claiming less, and on top of it all, we know not what we do.

Words of Assurance

The wonderful, lofty vastness of our God's transcendence knows the limitations of our thinking and of our knowledge, even as it knows the extent of our pride. Today, we gratefully celebrate again the immense and unconditional love that cherishes our littleness within God's largesse that loves and forgives us and sets us free.

Benediction

Go from here in the knowledge of God's knowledge of you. Go from here in the assurance of God's love. This is the relationship that has embraced us from the beginning, through all our days up to this day, and that will continue to embrace us through all days yet to come. (John Ballenger)

A New Perspective

Third in a Series of Four on Turning Over a New Leaf: Beginning Anew

John 3:1-10

A little boy with an ice-cream cone gets on an elevator with his older sister. The ice cream begins to melt faster than he can eat it, and it's making a sticky mess down the side of the cone. The elevator stops, and an elegantly dressed lady in a full-length fur coat gets on. She turns and faces the door with the children standing behind her. The little guy is now struggling to keep up with the melting ice cream. He looks at the back of the woman's beautiful coat and gently begins to wipe the ice cream off his hands and onto her coat.

"Be careful, Billy," says his sister. "You will get fur in your ice cream."

That little story illustrates the power of perspective. Sometimes how we see something depends upon where we stand. In this New Year I invite us to live from the perspective of God's rich grace shown us in Jesus Christ our Lord.

One day a man named Nicodemus came to Jesus to discuss religious matters. In the conversation Jesus says something that has guided our faith ever since. "I tell you, no one can see the kingdom of God without being born from above," Jesus says (v. 3). Nicodemus is confused and questions what Jesus means. It is a fair question. Just what does it mean to be "born from above," or to use the more familiar rendering, to be "born again"?

In a word, it means to live with a new *perspective*. You see, Nicodemus had a problem, but it was not that he did not have religion. Nicodemus had plenty of religion. After all, he was a Pharisee, the most religious group in Jesus' world. The Pharisees knew all about religion. They could recite the law. Their lives were dedicated to following the proscriptions of the Hebrew faith. They were the sons of Moses, and they knew what being God's people meant. It meant walking a certain way, eating a certain way, worshiping a certain way, wearing certain clothes, and observing certain days with holy activities. Nicodemus' problem was not that he did not try to be good or religious or righteous. It was something else.

To this religious man, Jesus says, "be born from above." Poor Nicodemus does not have a clue as to what Jesus means. Sometimes we don't either. Jesus is inviting Nicodemus to live from the perspective of grace. Jesus' invitation is to discover a faith that carries you rather than a faith you have to carry. Jesus is talking about the amazing grace of God that, when we see it and experience it, makes all the difference in our lives. Do we see life as a prize that has to be won or as a gift to be received? Are our days spent trying to acquire more stuff or becoming aware that all we need has already been given to us by the gracious hand of a loving God?

Into a world caught up in keeping the rules, Jesus invited people to embrace the lessons of grace. "Consider the lilies," Jesus said. "They neither toil nor spin, yet I tell you, even Solomon in all his glory was not clothed like one of these" (Matthew 6:28). "Do not worry about your life," he counsels (Matthew 6:25). In other words, God loves you and is looking out for your well-being.

What a difference it makes to live from this perspective! We know that all we need has already been provided. We become aware that life is a gift to be received rather than a prize to be won. We are freed to live by cooperation rather than competition. In this New Year this is the perspective I invite you to embrace.

What if we lived as though everything we need has already been provided for us? We sing about this grace in the hymn, "Great Is Thy Faithfulness," that reminds us, "all I have needed his hand hath provided." What a difference it would make to live the message of that hymn. For this is the truth of the gospel. There is enough air, water, and food for all God's children. There is enough shelter, clothing, and money for all to live in comfort on this earth. Glory to God! You are rich beyond measure, for you are held every moment in the hands of a love that will never let you go. Has there ever been better news than that?

There is enough, and we don't need to hoard or be fearful. We can share; we can give. There is enough. That is the perspective of grace. There is enough. We are invited to let that perspective birth us into a new way of living in this New Year. Be born again, and again, and again until grace fills every moment, every breath of your life, so you might show the world a new way of living. (Chris Andrews)

Worship Aids

Call to Worship

Come to the living water of God's abundant grace.
We come, but we hesitate. Will there be enough for all of us?
Come and see what God has done.
**We come, for we are weary with the struggle of making life
    happen. We want to receive the gifts of God.**

Invocation

We seek your blessing, O Holy One. Show us once more that we are the beloved and that from your hands we receive all we ever need. Help us live with the confidence of children who know there is enough.

Benediction

Go forth to live as children of the Gracious Other whose love for you was shown in Jesus our Lord and who invites you to show that love to others. (Chris Andrews)

JANUARY 22, 2012

Third Sunday after the Epiphany

Readings: Jonah 3:1-5, 10; Psalm 62:5-12; 1 Corinthians 7:29-31; Mark 1:14-20

Meeting People Where They Are

Mark 1:14-20

My friend Tommy has been in ordained ministry for more than forty years and serves as a small church pastor in a town not far from my own. Tommy has lots of experience in ministry, but he is not a traditional minister. Tommy is a tall, lean man with a weathered face and hands that have known hard work. He is more at home in a pair of blue jeans and a t-shirt than in a three-piece suit. He almost always wears a pair of scuffed cowboy boots, and in cold weather, he wears a leather jacket. He drives a Harley-Davidson motorcycle and has an infectious laugh. He loves a good story or a joke better than just about anyone I know. He is not what most folks think of when they think of a Baptist preacher.

The most wonderful thing about Tommy though, and what makes him such a wonderful preacher, is his love of people. He never meets a stranger. In the years I have known Tommy, I have marveled at his ability to get to know people he encounters. It doesn't matter where we go in town—a restaurant, the dry cleaners, or Wal-Mart—Tommy can greet almost everyone by name. At some point in the past he has introduced himself, asked their names, and often learned a little bit of their stories. Tommy takes the time to get to know each person he encounters. He meets people wherever he finds them, and he offers them friendship. I have seen him visit with truckers, nurses, cashiers, and young mothers. I have heard him laugh with them and seen him cry with them. He has prayed with them. These folks hear about Jesus, and most important, they see Jesus, although many of them have never attended the church where Tommy is a pastor. He meets all of them where they are in life.

Tommy's ministry reminds me Jesus' ministry. This Gospel account of Jesus calling his first disciples is striking in its simplicity. Mark tells the story very briefly. There aren't many details about the conversation between Jesus and these potential disciples. Jesus simply gives an invitation to follow and they respond. We don't learn much information about their backgrounds, their motivations, or any questions they might have had for this itinerant preacher. Jesus speaks and they follow. We can speculate all we want to about how Simon, Andrew, James, and John came to be disciples, but the one thing we know for certain is that Jesus met them where they were that first day.

Mark tells us that "As Jesus passed along the Sea of Galilee, he saw Simon and his brother Andrew casting a net into the sea—for they were fishermen" (v. 16). I have always thought it was wonderful that Jesus found these folks as he made his way along the road by the sea. We aren't told that he made a special trip or a detour to find them. He didn't specifically hunt them down to the exclusion of any others. Jesus simply found them at their work in the midst of their daily routine, and he stopped to visit. Jesus met these men where they were in life, and he made them an offer. "Follow me and I will make you fish for people" (v. 17). What a wonderful connection Jesus made. He didn't ask or expect them to be anything other than they were when he met them. They were simple fishermen, but Jesus invited them to join him in work that would change their lives forever.

Jesus' ministry is filled with stories of people he encountered along the way. We read stories about healings taking place in homes or along the roadside. We read of how Jesus taught about the Sabbath as he made his way through the grain fields, and how he fed the multitudes as they gathered in a deserted place. He didn't seek out important people who held positions of power but spent most of his time with ordinary folks. He didn't wait in the temple or synagogue for the people to come and hear him speak of God's kingdom. He walked among them, and told stories about sowers and seeds, things lost and things found. He ate with prostitutes, tax collectors, lepers, the lame, and the blind. Jesus' entire ministry was centered on meeting people where they were in life. He went to find them, not the other way around. Jesus shared God's love with them and proclaimed to all those he encountered "The time is fulfilled, and the kingdom of God has come near; repent, and believe in the good news" (v. 15).

When I think about my hope for the church, I think about how wonderful it would be if we embraced Jesus' model of ministry. All of us encounter people in the course of a day who are hurting, alone, lost, and discouraged. They need someone to be the presence of Christ in their midst. People need someone to share the gospel of hope with them. Folks need someone to talk to them using their own language. They need someone to engage them in conversation about ultimate things. Many of these people may never darken the doors of a church or a house of worship. I confess that as a preacher, far too often, I am content to stay within the walls of the church, waiting for people to come and see me. I need to be more like Tommy, taking the church into my community. I am missing an opportunity to be like Jesus, to meet people where they are in life. (Wendy Joyner)

Lectionary Commentary

Jonah 3:1-5, 10

Jonah preaching to the people of Nineveh is a wonderful story of repentance. Jonah initially resisted God's call to preach to his sworn enemies, but once he relented and set out to preach God's judgments, the results were nothing short of miraculous. The people of Nineveh repented in dramatic fashion, and all the people believed in God. Perhaps even more amazing than the repentance of the people of Nineveh however, is God's own repentance. We are told, "God changed his mind about the calamity that he had said he would bring upon them" (Jonah 3:10). God responds to the decisions we make, and God is willing to be vulnerable in relationship with us.

1 Corinthians 7:29-31

The Apostle Paul is writing to the church at Corinth about how their faith in Christ reshapes the world around them. Everything in a believer's life is affected by the good news that Christ has come among us to usher in God's kingdom, that Christ is resurrected and seated at the right hand of God, and that Christ will come again in glory. These verses are part of a section in which Paul deals with how family relationships are transformed in light of Christ's presence. Paul argues, "the present form of the world is passing away" (1 Corinthians 7:31). All our attitudes and relationships must be re-evaluated and reshaped in the light of the coming kingdom. (Wendy Joyner)

Worship Aids

Call to Worship

Know the amazing and wonderful truth that God has redeemed us and calls each of us by name. God desires to meet us in this hour and in this place. Let us open our hearts and listen for God's voice that we might worship in spirit and in truth.

Invocation

O God, our help in ages past and our hope for years to come, we thank you for your presence with us all along life's journey. We ask for your companionship with us today. Walk beside us as our master and our friend, teaching us your way. Amen.

Benediction (Jude 24-25)

"Now to him who is able to keep you from falling, and to make you stand without blemish in the presence of his glory with rejoicing, to the only God our savior, through Jesus Christ our Lord, be glory, majesty, power, and authority, before all time and now and forever. Amen." (Wendy Joyner)

Renewal through Living

Fourth in a Series of Four on Turning Over a New Leaf: Beginning Anew

Romans 12:1-2

Let's practice a mantra for the New Year. It goes like this: it is easier to live your way into a new way of thinking than to think your way into a new way of living. Say it with me: "It is easier to live your way into a new way of thinking than to think your way into a new way of living."

Those words have particular relevance as we consider Saint Paul's admonition to the church at Rome to "Present your bodies as a living sacrifice, holy and acceptable to God" (v. 1). Ultimately the Christian faith is something we do. It is more than thought. It is a way of life. Christians live the gospel.

This is a necessary corrective for today's culture of faith. Too often people have the idea that having faith is having the right answers. Faith is more than knowledge. Faith is about lifestyle. It is about doing more than it is about thinking. In a word, the Christian faith is about *practice*.

The more we practice gospel living the better we are at living the way Christ invites us to live.

Jesus calls us to be his disciples in this world. There is something counterintuitive about what he asks of us. Remember some of Jesus' instructions: to be first, you have to be last; to be rich, you have to become poor; to live, you have to die. Forgive your enemies; love those who persecute you; be a servant. At one level none of these thoughts makes much sense. They certainly don't feel like the way to happiness and success. But on another level, the witness of the faithful, is that these instructions are the secret to a renewed life.

So we practice the faith by doing the things Jesus asks us to do. At first living like a Christian feels unnatural. It is difficult and burdensome. But the more we do it, the more right it feels until one day we find ourselves living the Christ life without even thinking about what we are doing.

Wesleyan Methodists have a term for this. It is called "sanctification." John Wesley said this was the third work of grace. It is the growing grace that moves us toward perfection until we can say with Saint Paul, "For me to live is Christ." Grace grows us as we practice the means of grace in our daily lives. As we pray, worship, study the Scriptures, give ourselves to service projects, we are shaping lives that look like Jesus for the world's redemption.

There is a football team that has a sign over its practice field that says: "You play like you practice." How true those words are. An athletic team practices and practices until the moves necessary to win a game become second nature. We Christians must live the same discipline.

The text urges us to present ourselves as a living sacrifice, holy and acceptable to God. Someone has observed that the problem with a "living sacrifice" is that it keeps slithering off the altar. Well, we all know that experience. We have all been guilty of missing the mark (the literal translation of the word *sin*) when it comes to living as a disciple of Jesus. We know what it is to say we are committed to the way of love and to have that declaration rendered useless by a flash of anger or the desire for revenge. We know what it is to struggle to love the enemy and to welcome the stranger who looks so different . We know how it is to live with gaps between the affirmation of faith and the deeds of our lives. We have done our share of slithering off the altar.

Yet we keep at this business of trying to live like Jesus' disciples in this world. We do this because we have seen in Christ the light of truth. We have been grasped by Jesus' redemptive love. In the words of Peter (John

6:68), "Lord, to whom can we go? You have the words of eternal life." So we practice, and bit by bit we find ourselves becoming different people. Little by little we are renewed until one day the world looks at us and sees Jesus. Glory to God!

Do you remember learning to drive a car? Some of us learned in automobiles with manual transmissions that required all sorts of actions done in a sequence that at first seemed impossibly complicated. You had to push in the clutch, move the shift lever to the proper place, press the accelerator, and slowly let the clutch up. Then, if the car moved ahead without stalling, you had to do it all over again with the car moving this time. Still there was another sequence to be done before the car was in third gear and ready to drive down the road. If you were like me, this exercise was at first very frustrating. Driving was an experience of starts and stops, of lurching steel and stalled engine. But you continued to do it, and one day there was a smooth start and a synchronized movement of feet and hands as you moved through the sequence of gears. You practiced and got it right until driving became second nature, something you could do without thinking about it.

The Christian faith is like that. We give ourselves to the way of Christ. We receive the church's instruction about what a disciple does. At first it seems complicated, even impossible to do. "You want me to forgive my enemies?" "You want me to give away my money to people I don't know?" "You want me to carry a cross?"

But we try to do it. We show up to carry out our part in the community of faith. Then, lo and behold, one day we're doing it. We are living the Christian life! We have shown up at the altar of faith enough times that our bodies really are living sacrifices for the glory of God.

"It is easier to live your way into a new way of thinking than to think your way into a new way of living." In this New Year let us be renewed by fresh determination to live the faith until the way of Jesus becomes so natural for us that the world will look at us and say, "There goes a Christian. There goes someone who follows Jesus." (Chris Andrews)

Worship Aids

Call to Worship
We come together as the body of Christ.
**We open our hearts and minds to the way of Jesus in the
world.**

We are here to be shaped into the witness of Jesus' love.
We have come to practice how to live as Christ calls us to live.

Invocation

O living God, our lives are often confused and full of contradictions. Clarify our thinking, consecrate our lives, and help us to be the people who show others the marvelous ways of Christ. We have come to learn again how to be Jesus' witnesses in the world. Grant that we, by the power of your Holy Spirit, may be your faithful people in all moments.

Benediction

Go forth to live as disciples of the living Lord. Be the light of Christ for the world. Let your good works shine that the way of Christ may be seen by all in what you do and in what you say. Amen. (Chris Andrews)

JANUARY 29, 2012

❧❧❧

Fourth Sunday after the Epiphany

Readings: Deuteronomy 18:15-20; Psalm 111; 1 Corinthians 8:1-13; Mark 1:21-28

Belonging to One Another

1 Corinthians 8:1-13

My father was not a real churchgoer. He was more likely to be on the golf course on a Sunday morning than in a church pew, but he taught me many valuable lessons about life and faith. My father taught me much about what it means to be in community with others, and he did so in the context of our family. I guess as the father of four daughters, he had to be able to articulate things in a way that we would remember and be able to live out in daily interactions. One of the biggest challenges we faced had to do with articles of clothing. My younger sister and I often wanted to borrow each other's clothes for a date or an outing with friends. If you were the borrower, you knew that nothing in your closet would be as great as what was in your sister's closet. If you were the owner of the clothing, you feared that your sweater would come home with a big mustard stain down the front, ruined forever. There were many lively discussions about the borrowing of clothing, and often the arguments would devolve into the simple proclamation: "No, you can't have it; it's mine." That was when my father would step into the conversation. He would ask simply, "Who earned the money to buy you those clothes?" We would grudgingly admit that he had done so. Then he would gently remind us, "I did that because I love you. What I have is yours, and what you have is your sisters'. It's not yours or mine; it's ours." It wasn't a lesson that we relished as we reluctantly handed over the desired item of clothing, but the longer I live, the more I realize the beauty of my father's lesson. It's not yours; it's not mine; it's ours. It's a radical image of life in community.

29

The Apostle Paul spent much of his time addressing issues of life in community. The church at Corinth had many problems that needed to be resolved, and they had many questions about what faith in Christ looked like for each of them. They were struggling with the balance between old and new, law and grace, freedom and restraint. The issues weren't esoteric either, but rather things that they would encounter in their day-to-day living. One of the questions the community had for Paul dealt with eating meat that had been offered to idols. Apparently, some of the community had no problem at all with eating the meat, while others still struggled with whether or not that was the right thing for them to do in their spiritual life. Paul seems to come down on the side of those who would eat the meat, but with one important caveat. He knows that eating the food in and of itself is not a sin, but he says to those who agree with him that there is more involved in making this decision. He writes, "But take care that this liberty of yours does not somehow become a stumbling block to the weak" (v. 9). Paul makes the argument that just because you don't have a problem with something doesn't mean that you should do it. He reminds the Corinthians that there are others to consider in weighing moral choices. They are always to be concerned for the family of faith. He reminds them that what an individual does has consequences for others. None of us lives in a vacuum, and we have to be careful that our words and actions do not cause others to sin against God. Paul is saying, in essence, it's not about something—a belief, an action, or a possession—being solely mine or yours; it is ours. We are in this together. As J. Paul Sampley writes in his commentary on this passage, "Over against knowledge, their definitional marker, Paul sets love. When love is at work, it can only accomplish or effect edification, upbuilding" (*The New Interpreter's Bible*, Volume X [Nashville: Abingdon Press, 2002], 896).

Paul argues for an ethic of love that is grounded in community relationships. The ethic of love of neighbor was difficult for the Corinthians to embody, and it remains difficult for us as well. We, like the Corinthians, are quick to think about what is best for us. We draw distinctions among ourselves, and worry most about our own viewpoints or needs rather than those of our brothers or sisters. We tend to privatize our faith and our moral choices. We are quick to offer the rationale that "this is between me and God; it's no one's business but my own." The truth of the matter, however, is that what we do has an impact on others. The choices I make can influence others in a variety of ways. I have to realize that the moral choices I make can cause another to be hurt, confused, discouraged, or frustrated. I could also choose to live in such a way that I influence others for the good, helping them to be encouraged in their faith, just in their own actions, and righteous in their living. That is what it means to be part of a family of faith. It's not my life or your life, but our life together in Christ.

I wonder sometimes what our families, our churches, and our communities would look like if we took seriously Paul's call to consider others before self. How would we make decisions about how we live before one another? What if one of the first things we were to bear in mind was living "so that I may not cause one of them to fall" (1 Corinthians 8:13)? I believe that if we place the ethic of love at the center of all we do, it will make a difference in our world. (Wendy Joyner)

Lectionary Commentary

Deuteronomy 18:15-20

In this passage from Moses' farewell sermon, the nation of Israel is promised a prophet. The people have made known their need for an intermediary in hearing God's voice or seeing God's holy fire. God promises that God will indeed give them a prophet and outlines not only the authority that the prophet will possess but also the responsibility that comes with the prophetic office. The prophet's words are to be heeded, but the prophet must also speak only what God would have him or her say.

Mark 1:21-28

Jesus here teaches and heals in the synagogue in Capernaum. This is Jesus' first miracle in the Gospel of Mark, and the people respond to his exorcism of an unclean spirit with amazement. Not only his actions but also his words carry great power. Jesus is identified as one who speaks God's word with great authority. (Wendy Joyner)

Worship Aids

Call to Worship (paraphrased from Psalm 111)

Let us give thanks to the Lord with our whole hearts. Let us praise the Lord with our brothers and sisters in Christ. Let us proclaim that God has done great things for us. God's work is full of honor and majesty, and God's righteousness endures forever.

Invocation

Almighty God, we have gathered here in community, that we might better learn how to love you with all our hearts, souls, minds, and strengths. We come seeking to love our neighbors as we love ourselves. God, send your spirit upon us, that we might be changed. Amen.

Benediction

Now as you depart, know that you belong not only to God but also to one another. May the world know that we are Christians by our love one for another, in the name of the Father, and of the Son and of the Holy Spirit. Amen. (Wendy Joyner)

Missions in the Name of God

First in a Series of Four on Missions with the Lord's Prayer in Mind

Matthew 6:9

"Youth mission trip," "summer service project," and "spring work-cation" are just some of the titles we have heard or used to describe organized acts of Christian mission to perform service with and for others in Christ's name. Youth and adults give up summer vacation time and college students take a "work-cation" instead of spring break in order to live out servant discipleship. There are numerous passages in the Gospels that demonstrate and speak to Christian service, but the prayer of Jesus offers us some of the most important lessons in how Christian mission is rooted in prayer and our relationship with our God.

The Lord's Prayer, or the "Our Father" as some faith traditions refer to it, is the most famous and most memorized prayer of the Bible. There are two versions of the prayer, found in Matthew 6:9-13 and Luke 11:2-4. Because not all ancient biblical manuscripts of these passages are identical, notations are included in almost all translations in order to explain textual variations that are integral to translating and applying this ancient lesson in prayer.

Luke's account opens the prayer with Jesus' words: "Father, hallowed be your name," while Matthew includes, "Our Father in heaven," as the preface. Jesus teaches that prayer begins with and is rooted in the acknowledgment of the holiness of the creator God. Judaism, from its beginnings to today, teaches the sanctity and power of a name. Genesis describes God giving to humankind dominion over the creatures and created order and God allowing Adam to name all of the creatures as an act of co-creation with God. The creation story bears witness to the Hebrew understanding that to name is to have dominion over, hence the unpronounceable name of God, YHWH, (typically translated LORD in English translations). Of course, to do missions in the name of God carries with it the highest of expectations, clearly expressed in the third commandment: "You shall not make wrongful use of the name of the Lord your God..." (Exodus 20:7). God's very name is holy.

Prayer is anchored in our holy connection with the God who first connected with us. God speaks a divine word and the mere utterance brings life into being. We offer our words in prayer to God to nurture this sacred connection. The Lord's Prayer first declares that God is the holy creator of all, and our connection with God makes us holy too.

As we are offspring of God and disciples of Jesus, what does the Lord's Prayer teach us about missions? Perhaps a better question might be, "What does it mean to do missions in God's holy name?" Certainly there is a distinction between the church's mission and the missions we undertake to fulfill our calling or purpose to serve others as disciples of Jesus.

The church's mission, according to the Great Commission of Matthew 28, is to go into the world beyond the safety of our homes and meeting places and tell of the transforming power found in a relationship with Christ. To "make disciples" is not a command to coerce people into belief in Jesus as the Christ. To do so would not engender true faith, for faith in God comes by gracious invitation and an inspiring encounter, not by means of a demanding imposition and rigid expectation. Jesus invited his first disciples, and invites us, into a relationship. Jesus did not provide a formula—"Say these words and you can join the club"—but offered an example of Christian community. The work of Christian missions is an extension of this relationship.

Missions is both an act of discipleship (following Christ's example of service and justice), and an expression of God's redemptive and unconditional love. We don't earn salvation. Neither do we earn the right or necessarily deserve to offer or receive an act of service; it is a gift derived from God and passed along by faith through God's followers.

Doing missions in the name of God requires an open acceptance of those whom we seek to serve. It demands that we start on the terms of those whose lives we strive to touch, and that means speaking in a way that all can understand. We Christians have unique language that we use matter-of-factly and presumptively, expecting non-Christians to follow along with what some might call "code words." For example, a church announcement might read:

"There will be a meeting of the confirmation class (translation: persons exploring their faith in Christ) following Sunday school (translation: Bible study classes typically held on Sunday mornings, but perhaps on other days and times as well) in fellowship hall (translation: a gathering place for Christians to enjoy each other in a relaxed social setting where food is often included). I made a reference to *fellowship* one day while in conversation with a local rabbi, and he inquired about the meaning of the word. He had never heard of fellowship. He opened my eyes to words that the Christian community often takes for granted as part of our faith language.

God's name is holy, and to do missions in the name of God requires serious and prayerful discernment coupled with selfless and humble action. Discipleship costs something. Sacrifices often must be made for something to have value. Whether building for Habitat for Humanity, helping earthquake victims on another continent, or holding the hand of an elderly woman living alone, Christian missions are our opportunity to once again make the Word become flesh. Let us do so with humility, in the name of the One who first reached out to us. (Gary G. Kindley)

Worship Aids

Call to Worship

Holy is your name, O God,
Greatly to be praised!
Your ways are far from our ways,
Your thoughts high above our greatest considerations.
In these moments of worship, we desire to draw closer to you.
Grant us the wisdom to hear and understand what you say to us this day. Amen.

Offertory Prayer

Today our currency and coin become a holy offering that is given in Christ's name. We take on the title, "Christ-followers," and give something of ourselves in sacrificial worship. In the name of the One who gave all. Amen.

Benediction

Go forth to be in Christian mission, sharing your faith, serving others, and offering grace in the name of Jesus Christ. Amen. (Gary G. Kindley)

FEBRUARY 5, 2012

❧❧❧

Fift Sunday After the Epiphany

Readings: Isaiah 40:21-31; Psalm 147:1-11, 20c; 1 Corinthians 9:16-23; Mark 1:29-39

Starry, Starry Night

Isaiah 40:21-31

Do you remember the first time you looked up into the night sky and really noticed the stars? I do. As a college student, I served as a summer missionary in a small church in Lake Tahoe, California. A native of Atlanta, I had never been west of the Mississippi River and had certainly never lived in a small town surrounded by beautiful national forest. Late one evening, some of my fellow missionaries and I walked down to the shore of the lake. We lay on our backs on the dock and looked up into the clear night sky. I was overwhelmed. It seemed as if there were millions of stars above. I never realized how much the city lights had obstructed my view, but that night out in the wilderness I felt I could see forever. I remember being humbled more than anything—by the splendor of God's creation and by the thought that the creator of all that my eyes could see knew me by name. I can't read passages about stars without remembering that night. I read about the majesty and glory of God as it is revealed in the night sky, and I remember how it felt that night in Tahoe to sense the awesomeness of God. That sense of wonder has been an important part of my journey of faith because it helps me to keep the right perspective on things, especially when faced with trouble or adversity.

The writer of today's Old Testament lesson knew how difficult it is to keep the right perspective when faced with life's challenges. The prophet was writing to the people of Israel after they had experienced a period of judgment and exile from their homeland. He was addressing people who had undergone great trials and adversity. They were so beaten down by life that they had forgotten that God was still with them. They began to

35

question whether God remembered their plight at all. Isaiah knew their situation, and he knew their hearts, and he challenged their forgetfulness. He wrote to the people and asked a crucial question, "Why do you say, O Jacob, / and speak O Israel, / 'My way is hidden from the LORD / and my right is disregarded by my God?' (v. 27)." Isaiah knew that God had not forgotten them, and he offered words of comfort and encouragement.

The most important thing for the Israelites to remember was the identity of the God they served. As Christopher R. Seitz so insightfully writes, "The issue is not God's grasp, but Israel's weariness and exhaustion" (*The New Interpreter's Bible*, Volume VI [Nashville: Abingdon Press, 2001], 344). So Isaiah calls to the Israelites and tells them to look up at the stars.

> "Lift up your eyes on high and see:
>   Who created these?
> He who brings out their host and numbers them,
>   calling them all by name;
> because he is great in strength,
>   mighty in power,
>   not one is missing." (v. 26)

Isaiah knew that the people would regain their perspective on life if they lifted their eyes to the heavens. Remember, Isaiah writes, that our God formed the heavens. Our creator knows the number of the stars in the sky, and calls them each by name. Think about this wondrous truth and sense the awesomeness of God.

If this is the God that you worship, the God that calls each of you by name, can God not help you in your time of struggle? Isaiah 40:28-29 says look at the stars and remember the power and magnificence of the God you serve. "He does not faint or grow weary; / his understanding is unsearchable. / He gives power to the faint, / and strengthens the powerless."

What a wonderful promise to a people who were discouraged, beaten down, and worn out with life—God can be your strength. God gives us what we need when we think we can't continue on the journey. So today, when you look at the circumstances of your life, what do you see? Are the problems that are facing you so overwhelming that it seems as if there will be no end to the struggle? Do the obstacles in your path prevent you from imagining what might be possible tomorrow? Do you despair of any hope for true healing to take place? Are the wrong choices of the past more than you can overcome? Are you feeling alone and powerless? Isaiah says to us—lift your eyes to the heavens.

The circumstances of your life may indeed be overwhelming. You might in fact be too weary to take another step. The good news is that you don't have to do it all alone. Isaiah reminds us that it is when we are most helpless, most despairing, and at the ends of our ropes, that we are best able to receive the gifts of God. Our God is strong, and mighty, and all-powerful love. God has not forgotten us and never will. Jesus told his own disciples in a time of great anxiety "Are not two sparrows sold for a penny? Yet not one of them will fall to the ground apart from your Father. And even the hairs of your head are counted. So do not be afraid; you are of more value than many sparrows" (Matthew 10:29-31).

Sometimes when life is at its most difficult, we lose perspective. It's easy to lose sight of the trees because of the immensity of the forest. That's when we most need to remember. Look at the world around you and rejoice that the creator of the universe knows your situation. God understands your fears, your hopes, your dreams, and your pains. God's wisdom is unsearchable, and God's power is unmatched. Remember whose you are, and rest in God's holy presence. Look up at the stars, and receive the gift of perspective. God is so big, and you are so small, and God is holding you in the palm of God's hand. (Wendy Joyner)

Lectionary Commentary

1 Corinthians 9:16-23

In keeping with the theme of evangelism that is so prevalent during the season of epiphany, the Apostle Paul here outlines his own philosophy of sharing the gospel. Although Paul had much to boast about in terms of his own background and religious pedigree, he knew that the most important component of sharing the gospel was finding common ground with his listeners. This was especially true when sharing with others who were radically different from him. Paul realized that God's call to be an evangelist would necessitate that he "become all things to all people, that [he] might by all means save some" (v. 22).

Mark 1:29-39

This passage from the first chapter of Mark's Gospel recounts the major concern of Jesus' ministry. Here we read of Jesus healing many who were sick and freeing those who were possessed by demons. Jesus also went to all the surrounding towns to proclaim the message of the kingdom of God. Already, in these summary verses, we sense the incessant demands of the crowds and the disciples. Yet we are reminded of a vital part of

Jesus' spirituality as well. We are told that in the midst of ministry, Jesus went to a deserted place to pray. (Wendy Joyner)

Worship Aids

Call to Worship (Psalm 62:5-6)

Let us be still before God our creator. Hear the words of the psalmist as we enter into worship, "For God alone my soul waits in silence, / for my hope is from him. / He alone is my rock and my salvation, / my fortress; I shall not be shaken."

Invocation

Gracious God, as we gather together in this holy place, we ask that you draw near to us. We ask that you might open our hearts and our minds to receive your word and to see your glory as it is revealed in your son, Jesus, our Savior. Amen.

Benediction

Now as you depart from this place, may you see the world around you in a new way. May you lift your eyes to the heavens. May you know that the creator of all good and perfect gifts loves you, redeems you, and calls you by name. Amen. (Wendy Joyner)

Thy Kingdom Come: What Are We Building?

Second in a Series of Four on Missions with the Lord's Prayer in Mind

Matthew 6:10

Jean Arnwine was a member of her church's mission team that flew from Texas to Port-au-Prince, Haiti, in January 2010, to work at an eye clinic for the poor that her church had built and sponsored. She was donating time that could have been spent with her husband, son, and daughter, not knowing that she would not make it home for her daughter's wedding and would never see her family again. Jean suffered internal injuries during the Haiti earthquake when the clinic walls collapsed on her. She died before she could be flown to a hospital capable of treating her injuries. Although Jean lost her life while living out the mission of her faith, in death as in life, her Christian witness continues. Perhaps her testimony is made all the more powerful by her sacrifice and its consequences for her family and loved ones.

If missions fulfill the will of God, what does the kingdom of God on earth look like? What is God's idea of the divine kingdom realized on earth? Certainly, building the kingdom of God is not merely about building an edifice, though we have plenty of those. One of my relatives from Minnesota remarked on his first visit to Texas: "I expected to see cowboys and Indians, but what I saw was so many churches!"

The Lord's Prayer was given at a time of Roman domination. At that time, it was urgent, especially for people of faith who were potentially facing persecution under pagan imperial reign, to establish God's idea of rule and order. Perhaps Jesus' words in this portion of the prayer are a reminder that we must seek to understand the nature of God's realm if our actions are to be consistent with God's design for our lives and all of creation. The biblical text repeatedly supports the observation that Jesus' intention for his followers was for them to think and act differently from others. Christians are called to look at the world through different lenses.

World famous architect Philip Johnson designed some magnificent buildings in his life. His last design was the Interfaith Peace Chapel at Cathedral of Hope in Dallas. The chapel will hold services for Jewish, Roman Catholic, and Spanish-speaking Protestant congregations. What makes this chapel unique is that it is one of the few buildings in the world designed without right angles in any of the exterior or interior walls. The interior walls are unique because they are made of a material that repairs itself from nail holes and "dings." Johnson's design is a visual lesson in the requirement for peace: think differently.

Building the kingdom of God requires much self-examination and the exploration of many questions. Is the church about membership or discipleship? We need not apologize for constructing buildings for the work of the church, since this is a practical and essential component when homes can no longer contain a growing faith community. An important question to ask when we do undertake physical construction regards the purpose of our efforts. Are we building an ecclesiastical mansion or a place for holy mission? I am not suggesting that all church architecture be relegated to the most simplistic utilitarian form, but I am asking that we consider the motive behind our efforts.

When we look to grow larger as a church, do we seek to be bigger for multiplying ministry or satisfying ego? Bragging rights can apply to churches too, as we proudly proclaim the attendance numbers at the Easter service or the new decimal place that is added in the annual operating budget. We need be honest about our true motives and desires, whether our faith community is large or small, because our devotion to Christ cannot ring true when we are dishonest with ourselves.

Small congregations may say that they welcome newcomers, but there can be mixed messages given to those who seek affiliation there. The unspoken message might be, "You can join us for worship as long as you agree with us, don't try to change anything, and recognize that you will always be the 'newcomer'!" One couple in a small town church where I once served said that they were still the "newcomers" to the congregation with which they had united thirteen years ago!

Edward Hick's famous painting, "The Peaceable Kingdom," is the artist's representation of Isaiah 11:6-9. The text paints an image of a time when the wolf lies with the lamb and the child plays near the den of the cobra without fear of harm. It is an ideal world where peace can exist among the created order. Our current natural order requires that wolves eat meat, not vegetables, and parents must protect their children from that which they do not instinctively know to fear. I believe that the kingdom of God on earth that Jesus spoke of is not an expectation of a world where everything goes our way, but rather a world where we do what is within our power so that things unfold in God's way.

Christian community is about selfless service, caring commitment, and daily discipleship that make a transforming difference in people's lives. Before we put on our "tool belt" and launch forth into whatever missions work is at hand, examining the biblical blueprints may reveal that what God requires is hardly conventional construction but transformational change. For justice to be realized it may require bulldozing previous construction (physical, social, or ideological) and starting afresh. I want to live in a world where no child must go to sleep at night hungry, abused, alone, or afraid. I think that is the sort of kingdom that Jesus had in mind too. (Gary G. Kindley)

Worship Aids

Unison Invocation

O God, we thank you for giving us this place of worship, and for those who have gone before us who have made this building possible. Today, remind us that this place is not the church; we are the church. May we have the courage to live up to that truth. Amen.

Pastoral Prayer

Holy and gentle God, who calls us into service and equips us for our call, we come with gratitude for those who serve in your name. We pray for missionaries and mission teams, evangelists and educators who take their Christian conviction into the world and share the truth of your wondrous love. Equip us for daily Christian mission and empower us to be Christ's witnesses. Amen.

Unison Benediction

We go out into the world to build the kingdom of God by being holy people of God. Grant us courage and perseverance to be reflections of the love of Jesus Christ. Amen. (Gary G. Kindley)

FEBRUARY 12, 2012

❧❧❧❧

Sixth Sunday after the Epiphany

Readings: 2 Kings 5:1-14; Psalm 30; 1 Corinthians 9:24-27;
Mark 1:40-45

What Is the Prize if I Win?

1 Corinthians 9:24-27

I admire driven people. I have a friend who is in his late sixties. Most men his age are retired. He is very well off financially and could easily retire with them, but last year he made $750,000, and he is convinced that he can beat that number this year if just a few things fall his way.

Anna, a student who works with me, is training to run a half marathon. She has run several 5k races, but she is pushing herself to the next level. I admire her too.

I have another friend from college; he's in his mid-forties like me. He keeps posting his impressive running times on Facebook. I wish he would just stop.

No, the truth is I admire all of them. As I said, I'm impressed by driven people. I'm up working on this sermon at 7:00 a.m. on my spring break. I hope you are impressed. Yesterday, I worked in my office from 6:30 a.m. to 4:30 p.m. When I got to the office yesterday, Tom's car was already there. Tom is a wealthy man in his early seventies, and his car is always in the parking lot before mine. Do you admire driven people as much as I do?

There is a fierce discipline that attends driven people. They have a commitment to push beyond the limits of the last attempt and to push for a faster time, more revenue, and heavier weights.

Golfers tell the story of a group of men at a PGA tournament who were watching one of their favorite pros hit golf balls on the driving range to warm up before his match. One spectator said to his friend, "I'd give anything to hit a 7-iron like that." The pro overheard him and walked over to where they were standing and said, "No, you would not give anything to hit a 7-iron like that. I've hit golf balls on a driving range until my hands bleed. Then, I've taped my hands and continued to hit. If you were willing to do that, you would hit a 7-iron like I hit it."

The admiration of that kind of discipline was just as fervent in ancient Greece. One great venue for athletic accomplishment was the Isthmian Games, which were held in Corinth every two years. Since they did not have ESPN, there was no overexposure to athletic triumph and the celebration of these disciplined athletes. Large crowds gathered to see chiseled bodies and disciplined minds compete with every ounce of competitive drive. The athletes called upon hours of disciplined training, and the people cheered the great drama of sport and applauded their great admiration for the discipline and sacrifice. In the end, there was only one winner of each competition, and the judges hung a wreath of dried wild celery around the winner's neck while the crowds roared in admiration.

Paul draws upon the heroic images of discipline and sacrifice and enslavement to a cause and invites us to a new vision. How do we discipline ourselves in the same admirable, driven way to serve the community instead of serving self? How do we exercise self-control and focus, so that we are not running aimlessly or boxing the air? How do we enslave ourselves to a discipline that does not hear the sound of cheering fans but offers more than a wreath of celery?

When I was a hospital chaplain intern at Emory University Hospital, I visited a man in his mid-thirties who was dying. He was attended by his two brothers from out of town. Sitting in the waiting area outside the hospital room, one brother said to me, "We stayed last night in my brother's condo downtown. He has three closets there filled with custom-made suits, and now he's in a hospital gown that looks like everybody else's. I drove over early in my brother's Jaguar. My other brother came later in his BMW. What I'm trying to say is that right now everything that was so important to my brother isn't worth a darn."

We have all known competitive people who drive themselves to see how many "toys" they can accumulate. But we have also known some Christ followers who are disciplined and enthusiastic about pushing themselves to serve others. Most of my real heroes fall into this second category. Who comes to mind for you? Who do you know who is most fiercely committed to serving as an agent of blessing to others?

I know a young couple in Atlanta with a baby just a few months old. They are living frugally on the husband's salary. They have chosen to live modestly, and they have chosen to live in one of Atlanta's most crime ridden areas so that the wife can volunteer at the elementary school. They do not have children at the elementary school, but this couple makes a deep sacrifice so that she can help children read and show them love that is motivated by commitment to Christ. The couple is disciplined and driven and certainly not boxing the air.

Paul tells us to run in such a way as to get the prize. Sacrifice and discipline your mind and body to work for others, give to the enduring glory of God's kingdom, and serve others. With fierce discipline, enslave yourself to the gospel and to the everlasting contribution of giving your life away as a blessing to others.

Or, you can just get up early and work hard to win the other prizes. You could even end up with a celery wreath. (Dock Hollingsworth)

Lectionary Commentary

2 Kings 5:1-14

Biblical power is almost always ironic. People who care about being powerful or being close to power would sidle up to the king of Aram, Naaman the commander, or the king of Israel. Yet in this story, not one of them has any real power at all. It is a servant girl who gives the prophetic word, and it is Elisha who provides the answer for healing. Naaman is angry because Elisha did not come outside to see him and honor his great standing and power. He is healed only when he listens to his (unnamed) servants and humbly follows Elisha's command. Biblical power is almost always ironic.

Mark 1:40-45

This is another story of a person with leprosy being made whole again. In this week's Epistle reading, Paul appeals for us to compete for things that matter and are lasting. In the 2 Kings reading, Elisha uses his power to heal. Now, in Mark, Jesus uses his power to heal. The lasting things, the things that matter, may always be tied to stories where we use our power to help someone else. (Dock Hollingsworth)

Worship Aids

Call to Worship

We are very busy and work hard all week because we care too much.
We build new barns because ours are already full,

**and we like to impress people with our new barns
because we care too much.**
All: Teach us not to care so much.
We neglect the relationships most dear to us
    because we care too little.
**We are too busy to see the pain all around us
because we care too little.**
All: Teach us to care more. Amen.

Invocation

We have been striving all week. God, grant us the grace to receive in this
hour what we cannot work to earn, and inspire us to work for things that
will outlast our living.

Benediction

Go in the plenty of God's love. Go in the example of Christ's giving. Go
in the power of God's spirit to be a blessing to others out of your abundance. Amen. (Dock Hollingsworth)

Bread for Tomorrow

Third in a Series of Four on Missions with the Lord's Prayer in Mind

Matthew 6:11

Norman Borlaug knew something about providing daily bread. He
lived not far from me in the town of University Park, an enclave surrounded by the city of Dallas. Norman is credited with saving the lives of
1 billion people from starvation because he developed a type of high-protein, hardy wheat that grows in almost any soil. It was a feat so significant
that he received the 1970 Nobel Prize for Peace, the Congressional Gold
Medal, and the Presidential Medal of Freedom (accomplished by only
four other people: Martin Luther King, Jr., Nelson Mandela, Mother
Teresa, and Elie Wiesel). Providing daily bread is a vital task.

"Give us this day our daily bread." What exactly does this text mean?
Is it merely what it appears to be, asking for our essential need for nourishment, or does Jesus have something greater in mind? If we continue
to consider the Lord's Prayer as both a lesson in holy living and a model
for our relationship with God, then connecting with God includes
the reminder that, in the end, our efforts alone are insufficient. We are
ultimately dependent upon divine providence for our existence. An

essential element of prayer is to remind ourselves of that divine dependence. The Lord's Prayer provides the occasion to reflect upon, and the opportunity to ask for, our needs for today.

This brief verse holds much meaning and a depth of possibilities for interpretation. Many biblical scholars suggest that this intriguing passage can also be interpreted "our bread for tomorrow." If so, such prayer gives us a chance to look to the horizon and to seek God's prevenient grace for what our future may yet hold. With that in mind, it is reasonable to believe that this text may be not only a reference to future needs but perhaps a plea to provide for the needs of all at the end of time. Prayer can also be apocalyptic and look to the ultimate conclusion of our earthly experience. I choose to focus on the needs of today rather than any apocalyptic concerns of the eschaton, because there are so many for whom there will not be a tomorrow without daily sustenance now. This truth must inform our actions and choices as Christian leaders in a world hungry for both bread and salvation.

Consider the following two disparate views of "daily bread." A church in Frisco, Texas, decided to break the Guinness world record of nacho-eating by serving up almost two tons of chips, salsa, and jalapenos as a promotion to attract teens to a new youth ministry program. Giant heat lamps from local auto-body paint shops were used to melt the heaping mounds of cheese and chips. Thanks to the hungry hoards of teenagers who showed up, they did establish a new world record. Before this, I had never thought of nachos with jalapenos as an evangelistic tool!

In contrast, a youth retreat center in central Texas established a policy that food could not be used for games unless it was to teach the reality of world hunger. The camp's director said that food fights in the parking lot and giant banana splits contained by thirty feet of rain gutter resting upon saw-horses on the sidewalk started her thinking about the message they were sending to the youth who participated. Using food wastefully did not reflect Christian stewardship when countless people sharing our planet faced starvation from famine and economic inequity. Thinking of "daily bread" is not only about sustenance but also an opportunity for prayerful reflection about stewardship and compassion.

Years ago, in my parent's home, there was a familiar framed print on the wall near the dining table. Taken by Minnesota photographer Eric Enstrom back in the troubled year of 1918, "Grace" is now the state photograph of Minnesota. Enstrom photographed Charles Wilden, an elderly seller of boot-scrapers, in a posed scene portraying gratitude for simple gifts. In the portrait, Wilden is praying with his folded hands supporting his bowed forehead. His serene face, framed by his white hair and beard, conveys both peace and wisdom as he prays before his meal. The large family Bible with reading glasses upon it and the bowl of soup and loaf of bread that adorn the table represent simple but adequate nourishment for both body and soul.

When we gather around the family table or sit in the booth of the local café and prepare to take our meal, prayer becomes an act of claiming the holy. It is a sacred moment, made all the more rich by the presence of friends or family with whom to share the meal. God is with us in that moment, and so no one ever dines alone. Daily bread provides nourishment, God's presence provides comfort, and our gratitude recognizes the blessed gift of both.

Whether our prayer is for the need of bread this day or sustenance in the days ahead, we entreat holy God not merely for the sake of our stomachs but for the emptiness of our souls. Adam and Eve walked in Eden's garden in the cool of the morning and encountered God there. They were given a place of abundance that could supply all their needs. They squandered the abundance at hand for the temptation of what God warned they did not need. Innocence was shattered.

May we be satisfied with the blessings God gives while we work to fulfill the opportunities God provides, and in doing so come to realize that this is sufficient. God gives us enough if only we ask. (Gary G. Kindley)

Worship Aids

Call to Worship
Lord God, we humbly ask; give us this day our daily bread.
Gracious God, we humbly ask; give us this day
    our bread for tomorrow.
Bread for today and bread for tomorrow both come
    from your hand, O God.
All: Guide us to fulfill the opportunities that you provide and
    remind us that even the work of our hands is possible
    because of your generosity.

Prayer of Confession
God of tender mercy, we confess that we have spent more energy satisfying our stomachs than nourishing our souls. Forgive our misplaced priorities

and selfish choices. Open our eyes that we might realize the blessing that a well-fed soul can be for ourselves and for those we love. Amen.

Words of Assurance

Hear the good news! God provides for today, for tomorrow, for all time. Thanks be to God.

Offertory Prayer

Gracious God, thank you for calling us into your circle of generosity as stewards of your world. Following the example of Jesus, we offer our gifts to your service, knowing that the greatest blessing is in giving rather than receiving. Amen. (Gary G. Kindley)

FEBRUARY 19, 2012

❧❧❧

Transfiguration

Readings: 2 Kings 2:1-12; Psalm 50:1-6; 2 Corinthians 4:3-6;
Mark 9:2-9

Lost Heroes

2 Kings 2:1-12

I tried to remember and list all my heroes, and I had a hard time determining whether Batman or Superman had a larger influence over my life. Try it. Like many, my earliest heroes are my parents. But I tried to list the others. Batman and Superman surely made the list. Don't laugh; I'm not talking cartoons I mean the real ones—Adam West against Caesar Romero as the Joker and the real black and white Superman. I ran through the house with a towel safety-pinned around my neck and jumped off the ends of the sofa.

As we mature, our heroes change a little. The next one I can remember is Henry Aaron. I think I was twelve when he hit the home run that broke the record.

Next was Bond...James Bond. Now come on, when you are a teenager, nothing is cooler than Bond. If the situation required that he know how to speak Russian, then Bond knew Russian. If it required knowing how to fly a plane, then he could fly it. If it required knowing the fox trot, then Bond could dance. He kept the world free from harm, never got his tie messed up, and ended up with Ursula Andress in the end. At age sixteen, that is as cool as it gets.

As the songs of faith and call started singing in my life, I looked for new models. I was challenged and fascinated by new heroes, among them were Martin Luther King, Jr., and Harry Emerson Fosdick. My heroes had changed again.

But I never met any of them. What would that have been like?

49

Elisha had the chance to know his hero. He walked with the greatest hero of the Jewish people in his day. Elijah, you remember, led the dramatic contest with the prophets of Baal at Mount Carmel. All of Israel remembers the contest; God answered Elijah's prayer on that day. Elijah called on God for fire, and fire came down from heaven and consumed the sacrifice on Mount Carmel (see 1 Kings 18). It was a high day. Elijah was God's prophet and the people's hero.

Here in our text, toward the end of his life, Elijah the old prophet walks along with the younger Elisha. The story has all the dramatic signs you would expect of Elijah's final scene. He tells Elisha, "Stay here for the Lord has sent me to the Jordan" (2 Kings 2:6). Elisha will not stay and abandon his hero in the last moments. A company of fifty prophets follow at a distance and watch the slow walk of the aged Elijah and his edgy young companion. They watch as Elijah takes off his cloak, his mantle, and touches the waters of the river Jordan. No longer completely amazed at the power given to Elijah, they do go silent as the waters part and the two men walk on dry land to the other side.

Elisha has a thousand questions but can only remain silent until asked, "What may I do for you?" Maybe this question is what distinguishes the truly called ones. I don't know that I could trust my answer if someone who had been given that much power asked what I wanted. Elisha answers, "Please let me inherit a double share of your spirit" (2 Kings 2:9). He asks Elijah to leave him the blessing of leadership and power that allows for continued demonstration of the goodness and power of the one true God. The request will be granted only if Elisha actually sees Elijah being taken from him.

They walk some more. Then the winds pick up and Elisha cries out as he watches the chariots and horsemen and the fierce whirlwind that take Elijah away. In grief, Elisha tears his own clothes.

Then Elisha picks up Elijah's mantle, calls on the Lord, touches the water with Elijah's cloak, and in sight of the fifty attending prophets, walks on dry land to his new role of leadership.

What a great story.

There are parts of my own story that I find throughout that drama. The loss of great leaders has led to grief for me. When great leaders retire and die I sometimes fret about whether life can ever be the same.

Also, I have found myself afraid of the mantle. God is at work in the world bringing peace and reclaiming lives. I have watched great men and women participate in that enterprise. Sometimes when I have seen Elijah's mantle in front of me, however, I have been afraid to pick it up. What happens if I pick it up and hit the water with it and nothing happens?

But the part of this story that interests me the most is actually not a part of today's text. Further along in the story, the fifty prophets insist on sending a search party for Elijah. They can't believe he is gone. Although Elisha insists that a search will be fruitless, they persist and search three days for Elijah. They just can't accept that a chapter is closed. They can't move into what God wants to do in the present and future because they are guilty of believing that God's great work belongs to a day that is over. These fifty remind me of the folks who still hang around Graceland insisting that Elvis is still alive. They can't move past an era that is over. They can't open their eyes to what is going on in the world now. Maybe this is why Elisha had to see Elijah go away. Maybe he had to know for sure that the era was over.

It is embarrassingly simple of me to think that the heyday of the church was when I was a child and churches were full and we all looked alike. I had a happy childhood, and they were good and abundant days, but my hope is always too small if it is in reverse. Is there a part of us that has given up on God doing something really big in the present?

Elijah did not represent God's final great work, although some people thought so. God was still at work redeeming the world. Later, God would come to earth as a human—a person. God is still at work today, and God's greatest work may still be ahead.

I mentioned with regret that I never got to meet any of my childhood heroes. The irony is that the great hero of my adult faith is trying to meet me! Like Elisha, I follow a hero who ascended and wants to give me a portion of his spirit. Jesus may also want me to pick up a mantle and do something important within his great drama of redeeming the world. My hero is trying to meet you too, and his greatest work may be ahead of us, if we do not miss it because we are looking behind us. (Dock Hollingsworth)

Lectionary Commentary

Mark 9:2-9

The familiar inner circle of Peter, James, and John receive another confirmation of the divine Jesus as he is transfigured. In eight short verses, the transfiguration is linked to several other parts of God's redemptive drama. This story ties Jesus to Moses and Elijah, has hints of baptismal language, and in Markan style, declares this One to be the Son of Man.

2 Corinthians 4:3-6

In each of today's texts, there has been some appeal to honor the heroes of the faith story. Elisha honors his hero Elijah. Peter wants to build shelters to honor Moses and Elijah. In 2 Corinthians 4:5, Paul is dealing with some adoration that is shining his way. There is a clear appeal to remember that "we proclaim Jesus Christ as Lord and ourselves your slaves for Jesus." (Dock Hollingsworth)

Worship Aids

Invocation

We gather in Christ, in anticipation and the hope for surprise. Even as you demonstrated your power at the transfiguration, we pray that you would surprise us in your power today. Move us toward a larger vision of your work in the world. Amen.

Prayer of Confession

God, we confess that at times we have acted rashly like Peter and inserted our own will. At times we have acted like Elisha and shown reluctance to pick up the mantle of leadership. Forgive us for doing too much and forgive us for doing too little. Amen.

Words of Assurance

Our great hero of faith continues to seek us, to forgive us, to cheer us on. Hallelujah!

Benediction

Go now, in the powerful reminder that God's redemptive story is still being told. In the days of Moses and Elijah and the earthly Jesus, God has been the author of a new way. Go in the challenge that you have a role to play in that same unfolding story of redemption. (Dock Hollingsworth)

Grace in the Name of Jesus Christ

Fourth in a Series of Four on Missions with the Lord's Prayer in Mind

Matthew 6:12-13

I think it is very appropriate that on the Sunday marking the transfiguration of the Lord, we are considering a quality of Christ that changes us and all who encounter such a powerfully transforming gift. I am speaking of the unconditional love of God that Christ exemplified and that we simply call *grace*. The Hebrew word, *hesed*, is the term that is translated in the Old Testament as "loving kindness." The New Testament simply refers to grace as God's unconditional love; it is an expression often found in the writings of Paul. In fact, it was so central to Paul's construct of the Christian message that he often opened or concluded his epistles with this reference.

The two verses that we consider today are so rich in meaning and significance that they yield both enigma and revelation. They are simultaneously profound and controversial. Forgiveness is a radical and wondrous concept. To go against the human tendency for enmity, bitterness, and grudge-holding and offer unconditional forgiveness is truly a mark of Christian character. Forgiveness is the foundation of Christian ethics and the hallmark of Christ's passion.

What is troubling about verse 12 is the latter portion, which implies— and is stated very clearly in Luke's version—that we ask God to forgive us our sins (also rendered "debts" or "trespasses"), because we already have done so for those who have wronged or are indebted to us. I prefer the translation I learned when growing up that implied it was reciprocal: if we forgive others, then God will forgive us. By contrast, if we don't forgive, then we remain without forgiveness. This seems a more reasonable transaction than stating to God, "OK, we've forgiven everyone, now forgive us!" The question remains: have we forgiven everyone and can we truly ever make that claim? In the truly unreasonable way of God, we are forgiven without ever holding up our part of the bargain.

The Lord's Prayer is a lesson about the nature of the holy relationship that humankind shares with God. There is presented here the ideal of the kingdom of God toward which we are to live. The prayer speaks to the perfect present and ideal future. It is not about ultimatum—forgiveness out of obligation—but rather reciprocity: when we live the fulfillment of the will of God, the forgiveness we offer is reflected back upon us by the One who originated the gift. This is far more satisfying and less loathsome than the thought that we may place demands upon God or declare ourselves to be as thoroughly forgiving as the divine grace that God alone can supply.

Although our focus is the grace of Christ, we cannot ignore verse 13, which leads us to end the prayer on a troubling note, pleading for God to not "bring us to the time of trial." There is also the request for salvation from "the evil one." Considering the first-century context, it again appears to be addressing the early Christians' fear of persecution. These fears would not be fully realized until two centuries later when the Roman Empire took a stand against Christians who refused to make offering to Caesar, although almost everyone else of any religious conviction was willing to do so. How ironic that those whose religious tenets were grounded in unconditional love and acceptance were also the ones most intolerant of demands to pay homage to any but the God whom Christ had revealed. The Christian community had yet to see the worst of their troubles, and Jesus' prayer prepared for the yet unknown future, whether near or distant.

Grace is easier to understand when we see it as deserved. I know an amazing musician who offers such grace in the name of Christ to "the least of these"—children who are ill, dying, or with challenging physical or emotional conditions. He is the founder of an organization with a primary mission of providing healing experiences through the performing arts for children with special needs. I have heard him tell of his touching experiences looking into the eyes of children with cancer, many of whom have wisdom and an understanding of life and death that is far beyond their years. It can safely be said that the generous offering of unconditional love that is poured out for these innocent children, whose lives have been profoundly altered or cut short by illness or circumstance, is something that would be met with almost universal approval and be considered well-deserved. Most of us would want such love to be extended to these precious little ones. Extending that same grace to incarcerated offenders of the law, however, is another matter.

Violent offenders whose actions have desecrated human decency, torn the fabric of society, and taken the lives of victims for little or no reason seem unworthy of grace. Jesus' demonstration of God's grace says otherwise. Christ's ministry was not limited to those who lived or believed a particular way but extended to all—even the most desperate and unlikely of sinners. In Jesus' last agonizing moments in human form, he extends forgiveness to a criminal who hangs crucified alongside him. What a lesson and legacy of unconditional love and forgiveness!

In the first sermon in this "Lord's Prayer Mission" series, I said that Christian mission is both an act of discipleship (following Christ's example of service and justice), and an expression of God's redemptive and unconditional love. God's grace renews the world whether or not we believe in God or accept God's divine grace. God's belief in us is not contingent upon our belief in God, and that defines the astounding nature of grace and establishes such unqualified love as the amazing offering that it is. Doing Christian missions with the Lord's Prayer in mind begins and ends with the holiness of God and the gift of God's grace. That is the greatest truth that Jesus tells us about prayer and Christian service; both are to be done after the example of Christ and in the name of God. (Gary G. Kindley)

Worship Aids

Unison Invocation (Psalm 51:1-2)

Have mercy on me, O God, / according to your steadfast love; / according to your abundant mercy / blot out my transgressions. / Wash me thoroughly from my iniquity, / and cleanse me from my sin. Amen.

Prayer of Confession

God of deliverance, we confess that we have not been gracious with others, though you have been merciful to us. Redeem us from our broken spirits and strengthen us by your Spirit. Amen.

Words of Assurance

God forgives while we are yet sinners. Thanks be to God.

Benediction

Go forth delivered, redeemed, and loved without condition! Amen. (Gary G. Kindley)

FEBRUARY 22, 2012

❧❧❧❧

Ash Wednesday

Readings: Joel 2:1-2, 12-17; Psalm 51:1-17;
2 Corinthians 5:20b–6:10; Matthew 6:1-6, 16-21

When Your Wife Fasts

Matthew 6:1-6, 16-21

I grew up in a Baptist church in Huntsville, Alabama. Like a lot of folks that I have met in other Baptist churches, we joked about how many times we gathered together as a church to eat. We ate Wednesday night suppers together. We ate at church-wide get-togethers. We went out to eat with church members. We had people to our houses to eat. We went to other people's houses to eat too. Whenever Baptist folks got together, there was food involved. Food was seen as a blessing from God, and we didn't miss out on opportunities to celebrate those blessings. We weren't gluttons, but food was an integral part of fellowship as a church family.

In our passage of Scripture today, Jesus talks about fasting…intentionally going without food. About the only fast that I can remember growing up was at children's camp one year. I don't even remember how long the fast lasted, but at one point we were allowed to eat some rice. We were hungry and complained that our stomachs were aching. Even the kids who didn't particularly like rice ate it up as fast as it was served. As a kid, I equated fasting with learning about hunger. I assumed that one fasted to learn what it was like to be hungry. Our job as Christians, therefore, was to help alleviate hunger throughout the world. Fasting helped us be more aware of the starving people in our world. As you can imagine, as I grew older, I learned that my view of fasting was a little skewed. I hadn't learned a bad lesson as a child, but there were more lessons that I could learn about fasting. I encountered others who fasted and whose faith practices encouraged fasting, but I never participated in a fast.

In January 2009, I had what I consider to be my first real experience with fasting. Not me, but my spouse, decided to fast. One day at work, one of her pharmacy technicians started talking about doing a Daniel fast. Apparently their church begins every year by fasting. The Daniel fast is akin to the Daniel of the Old Testament who ate vegetables and water instead of the royal food. In the end, Daniel and his Jewish friends were found to be healthier than the Egyptian soldiers. Therefore, Daniel and his God were praised and promoted throughout the land.

At first, my wife decided to join in the fast as an effort to lose a few of the holiday pounds, but her friend encouraged her to put a spiritual dimension to the fasting and not worry about any weight loss. She did. Sure enough, my wife started praying about some specific areas in her life and in the lives of loved ones. Over the three-week fast, it was amazing how she heard God speak.

She's convinced that God probably wasn't speaking any louder or more often, but it was just that for the first time, she was focused enough to actually listen. For my wife the absence of food, which used to be a reward or escape from the stress of life, was replaced by a dependence on God. She allowed God to take control in all areas, even the small things. She discovered that when we let God in every part of our lives, God is always looking to bring about things for our good and not our harm.

Down through the centuries Christians have employed many different disciplines to help us focus on God. I wonder how our Protestant denominations could do a better job at helping members realize the benefit of these types of disciplines. We don't have to rely on these disciplines to see God at work in our lives, but I am convinced that they can certainly help us stop and get out of the rat race that many of us find ourselves in each day.

Jesus talked about fasting by saying, "when you fast" (Matthew 6:17). In other words, he referred to it as an already assumed circumstance. When the disciples couldn't cast out certain demons, Jesus told them that some demons could only be cast out by fasting and praying. Paul told the early church to approve ourselves as ministers of God in our fasting. This discipline helps us to humble ourselves before God. We don't fast to gain attention for ourselves but to draw attention to God.

Today, a lot of people fast as an expression of showing that they truly want to see what God is saying about a specific situation. When we fast, we set aside the appetites of our body to focus on communicating with God. We deny the physical needs of our body in hopes that we will have spiritual gains. We learn that humans do not live by bread alone but rather by the word of God. When God sees the motivation of our hearts, somehow God mysteriously purifies our motivations and blesses our efforts.

For my wife, 2009 will always be a year of true spiritual renewal. Fasting truly changed her life. Her faith was strengthened and encouraged. She saw that beginning a new year with this kind of focus through fasting set the tone for the entire year. In fact, she started 2010 by fasting again. She is determined to start each year with this kind of focus and attention to God. In fact, I don't see her beginning a new year any other way. What about you and me? Are we ready to fast? (Ryan Wilson)

Lectionary Commentary

Joel 2:1-2, 12-17

Who can endure the day of the Lord? That's the overarching question of Joel. To answer it, he calls for the people to repent. When people repent of their sinful and evil ways, it is a reflection of their hearts and touches the very heart of God. When it may appear that there is no hope, God's love and mercy provide a way. God desires for humankind to move toward reconciliation, and so we often use this text on Ash Wednesday to remind us of our part in making things right with God.

2 Corinthians 5:20b–6:10

Paul continues talking about being reconciled to God and then leads into trying to be reconciled to the church in Corinth as well. Paul hopes that God will soften the hearts of the church to allow for a better relationship with them. In chapter 6, Paul writes of things that from the outside might appear as detriments to one's faith and message (for example, troubles, hardships, hunger). However, despite the difficulties that come with life and sharing one's faith, Paul has found that through the Holy Spirit and love, he has everything he needs. God provides just enough to confront whatever might come his way. Paul believes God will do the same for the community's relationship with God. (Ryan Wilson)

Worship Aids

Prayer of Confession

Lord, we are given freedom in this world and you give us commandments to help us enjoy those freedoms. But we confess that we often go outside your commandments and delve into our own selfish desires. We often deliberately go against your ways. Our actions are an indication that we don't trust your word. Help us to know your word and write it on our hearts so that it will penetrate our sinful desires.

Words of Assurance

Your word tells us that if we will confess our sins, you are faithful and just and will forgive our iniquities. Because you have confessed your sins to the Lord, hear these words of assurance: you are pardoned. Your sins are covered by the blood of Jesus, and you are made whiter than snow.

Invocation

O God of reconciliation, take our hardened hearts and begin to mold them again. Come to us even now and fill our voices with praise. Fill this sanctuary with your holy presence and help us to see ourselves for who we are and who we can become in light of your love and grace. As we gather today, may our worship send up a pleasing aroma to you and may we honor you with our lives this coming week. (Ryan Wilson)

Darkness and Ashes

First in a Series of Four on Christian Suffering in an Age of Entitlement

Genesis 3:1-7; Romans 7:14-25a

This is a day of darkness and ashes. Have you ever noticed that many Ash Wednesday services take place in the dark? They happen early in the morning when we receive ashes on our foreheads or hands or they occur in the night time. Either way, the bright sun is in hiding, and the darkness accentuates the mood of the ashes.

By nature we resist the darkness. Everywhere artificial lights battle the dark. Something in our souls struggles against the night. We even use nightlights in our homes and hallways to cast faint illumination on our sleep and to guide us through familiar spaces if we should arise in the dark.

In the Gospel of John, we find Jesus in contention with the dark. John declares early on that "the light shines in the darkness and the darkness has not overcome it" (1:5). Nicodemus visits Jesus in the dark, and Nicodemus' darkness is more than a matter of the missing sunlight. Nicodemus is lost in spiritual darkness. Jesus declares himself as the light of the world.

As we begin Lent, the time of day and the cold ashes remind us of a reality we would prefer to avoid. We like to imagine that all is well. We like to imagine that our personal problems and sins are minor and can be corrected by a bit more knowledge or willpower. Surely we are entitled to live in the light of our own merit! Surely we deserve all the best in life. Certainly, we are the good people who have earned a life relatively free of trouble and distress. We are educated and hard-working. We are law-abiding. We pay our taxes and attend our church. There is nothing seriously wrong with us. Others, perhaps, are children of the dark, but we are persuaded that we are children of the light.

Perhaps we should dispense with the ashes. They are dirty and messy. They don't belong on us. We are so careful about cleanliness and appearances. We would not dream of going out of the house with dirty clothes or even worse, dirty faces. What are we doing submitting to the out-of-date ritual of dust, dirt, ashes, and darkness?

The reality is that people stay away from Ash Wednesday services in great numbers. We won't find our sanctuaries full this day. It's just a service that runs against our normal attitudes and expectations. The trouble is that Ash Wednesday is all too real. It is all too realistic. We do walk in the darkness.

There are folks here who are struggling with a marriage in trouble. There is conflict, lack of understanding, resentment, and worse. There is no clear way forward. We may have thought that we were entitled to a peaceful and happy marriage, but that is not what we got. The cycle of doubt and recrimination seems unbreakable. Sadness and guilt are covered by anger and resentment. Worst of all, there seems to be no way out. Perhaps we can put on a good face for the neighbors, but we do not fool ourselves. The marriage is in darkness. Our naive hopes for a blissful home have been lost in the gloom. Darkness rather than light seems to be the fact of our lives.

Others among us are despairing over a child. Whatever they call the darkness: drugs, rebellion, rejection, promiscuity, underachieving, belligerence; in whatever form it takes, it is darkness. We cannot see to take the next step. Everything we try seems to blow up in our faces. Those babes that once were the chalice of our most intense hopes have grown to be a flagon of disappointments that break our hearts and keep us awake in the darkness. Surely we have been responsible parents. We did our best. Those little ones did not come with instruction manuals. There was no lack of love. We took them to Sunday school. We made them go to youth group as long as we were able to do so. It ought not to have turned out this way, we cry. It's just not right that young people with all the opportunities and advantages we provided for them should throw it all away. We deserve better and so do they.

Others here carry pain of other sorts. When we are honest with ourselves and with God, we know that though we have done our best and believe we are entitled to better results, our lives have become unspeakably messy. We have food and shelter and other outward blessings, but we know suffering.

The pastor places ashes on our forehead and intones, "Dust you are and to dust you will return." The big darkness. The fear of a painful death. The thought that the world could go on nicely without us makes us feel worthless and small.

Ash Wednesday confronts us with the fact that, though we live in an age that expects to have it all, we don't have it all. We are not automatically entitled to happiness and health. We are often Nicodemus groping in the darkness.

Does all this sound hopelessly dreary? Did the preacher just get up on the wrong side of the bed today? Perhaps, but until we can muster the spiritual honesty to confront the reality that life is not all sweetness and light, until we become spiritually mature enough to walk the journey of Lent, until we face up to the darkness and ashes of our lives, we cannot be ready for Easter when it comes. We want to be safe. We want to be protected. We feel entitled to the best. But we are not the best, and our hope must be grounded in something beyond ourselves.

We start the journey of Lent in darkness and ashes. The light comes not now at the beginning of the journey but in the end of Lent as day breaks and the women come to the tomb. There we will find our suffering, our darkness and ashes, healed in the bright light of the resurrection. Receive the ashes and hope for the light. (Carl Schenck)

Worship Aids

Call to Worship

Come to and receive the ashes.
But we do not want to be dirty.
Come and confront the darkness.
But we prefer the light.
Only as we face the darkness and ashes can we know
    the true source of light.

Then let us face the darkness that Christ might become our light.

Prayer of Confession

O Christ Jesus, we have lived in the darkness of self deception. We have sought the image of goodness. Yet we know that there is no righteousness in us, and we stand in the need of your mercy. Help us accept the reality of the ashes that we might experience the joy of forgiveness. In your name we pray. Amen.

Words of Assurance

Even in the dark night of our souls, we are not alone. Call on the One who hears and accompanies us on the journey to hope.

Benediction

Now may we begin our journey to the cross knowing our deep need and resting our hopes on God's great mercy. Go in hope. Amen. (Carl Schenck)

FEBRUARY 26, 2012

❧❧❧

First Sunday in Lent

Readings: Genesis 9:8-17; Psalm 25:1-10; 1 Peter 3:18-22;
Mark 1:9-15

All In

Mark 1:9-15

Jesus was baptized. The Greek word is *baptizo*, which means either to "dip" or "submerge." There is nothing like hooking your listener early in the introduction to a sermon by saying "the Greek word is...," but my Baptist heritage has much invested in the translation of this word. (Actually, I tricked my United Methodist colleague who teaches New Testament at the seminary and asked him to translate this for me.)

Because of my Baptist heritage, every time I have seen someone baptized, they go all the way under the water and come up drenched. Now I know that the way I grew up seeing baptism has surely had more effect on me than the Greek verbs but in either case, when I hear the verse, "And just as he was coming up out of the water...," my imagination conjures the image of Jesus coming out of the river Jordon soaking wet from head-to-toe.

That image, informed by my tradition and confirmed by the Greek verb, is also a symbol of full commitment. In a story with all of the grandeur of the opening heavens and the descending Spirit, I just can't imagine Jesus any way but fully drenched. There is something about an image of Jesus with his clothing stuck to his body and his hair matted to his face that says, "I'm all in. This is a wide-open full bore commitment to my purpose in life; this is a head-to-toe, sopping wet, full commitment to the kingdom of heaven and my part in it."

While I contend that "all in" might describe Jesus' entry into public ministry, it would not have described mine. I'm a bit more careful. I've always been a little skittish around radical folks. They scare me. I am careful, prudent, and orderly. I want to be perceived as having my act together—a person of dignity and moderation—not as some radical. People of radical commitment wear orange pants to Clemson football games, set Guinness records for the largest collection of gelatin molds. People of radical commitment drive mopeds that run on used cooking oil.

While I love to see a good radical every now and then, I have always favored balance, order, partial commitment to several worthy causes that might help the human condition a bit. To my thinking, it is better to not cause a stir, not be too sold out to anything, not to be so fully committed to any cause that I might look foolish. Then I look up and see my Lord at the beginning of his ministry, coming up out of the river Jordan soaking wet—all in.

Jesus' ministry begins with a symbol of full commitment, and the teaching in the Gospels sounds as if he's looking for other radicals to join him. In Mark's Gospel alone he says things like, "If any want to become my followers, let them deny themselves and take up their cross and follow me" (8:34). "Whoever wants to be first must be last of all and servant of all" (9:35). "You lack one thing; go, sell what you own, and give the money to the poor, and you will have treasure in heaven; then come, follow me" (10:21). I think the kingdom of heaven is looking for a radical or two!

I was a hospital chaplain intern in the Clinical Pastoral Education (CPE) program at Emory University Hospital in the late 1980s. Each week we had to present a verbatim case study to our small learning group of six people, but once I had to present to a larger group. About thirty-five folks were assembled to hear my case study, and I had poured over it and weighed every line. I did not want to look foolish. Before I started to read, one of the supervisors from another group said, "Dock, I can't sit here and listen to you with all of the slick stuff you have going on. Your clothes are crisp, and your hair's in place, and it just makes me sick. If you will loosen your tie, mess up your hair, and lower your socks, then you might have enough defenses down to actually learn something, but as it is, I don't think anything will penetrate your slick stuff."

In my hubris I said, "Jim, I did not dress to please you."

We spent the next hour talking about why I would not push my socks down to please the supervisor, and we never got to my verbatim.

I did not do what he wanted, but from a distance I now see his point. He made his point in a belligerent way, but I now see what he was getting at—"How can I protect myself from what others might think and be open to something as radical as what God is doing in the world?"

In David Halberstam's history of the Freedom Riders, *The Children*, he told the story of John Lewis and the other young students who caught a vision of a different kind of world. John Lewis is now a congressman from Georgia, but the book centers on the time when he was a seminary student and became involved in a learning community of students, professors, and pastors. A mentor, Jim Lawson, used a phrase in these meetings that jumped out at John Lewis—he talked about "the beloved community" (David Halberstam, *The Children* [New York: Random House, 1998], 79).

Some level of new commitment to the gospel and to the possibility of a beloved community took hold in Lewis and the others. The book goes on to tell the story of these young activists who were so devoted that they committed to nonviolent sit-ins. They allowed themselves to be thrown from lunch counter stools, kicked in the head, cursed at, and spit on. Lewis was living into an image of the gospel that was worthy of a soaking wet, all in, commitment. He trusted that this gospel was true enough, dependable enough, important enough, and big enough to throw his whole self into the kingdom and his part in it.

I'm not asking you to subject yourselves to beatings, but I am asking that we not avoid this question: "What would full commitment look like in your life?" When you see an image of our Lord standing in the river Jordan, with wet hair matted to his face and with pleading eyes that ask if you are "all in," what does Jesus want from you?

Some people spend their whole lives clocking in on time and preparing balanced meals at home and watching television.

But some people catch a vision. Some look into the eyes of a sopping wet Jesus and respond with their own, wide open, radical, full commitment to the kingdom of heaven and their part in it. Those people change the world. (Dock Hollingsworth)

Lectionary Commentary

Genesis 9:8-17

From the earliest verses of Genesis, we find water identified with chaos and destruction. Then, in the great flood, water is literally an agent of chaos and destruction. But, beginning with Genesis 9, God shifts the image. "Never again" will water be used to destroy all flesh. If tied to baptism, what once symbolized destruction of life now symbolizes new life.

1 Peter 3:18-22

This letter ties Christian baptism to Noah and the flood. In an odd turn from the ordinary, the writer highlights the eight people who were not destroyed by the flood. Instead, they "were saved through water." Like the Genesis 9 reading, 1 Peter reminds us that water can destroy or save. Baptism involves the water that saves us from the waters of chaos. (Dock Hollingsworth)

Worship Aids

Call to Worship

Through Noah and the ark, God provided safety for eight passengers.
We give thanks for their deliverance.
They were made safe from waters that could destroy.
We give thanks for their deliverance.
Through baptism, God has provided safety for all who will come.
We give thanks for our deliverance.
We are made safe by waters that restore.
We give thanks for our deliverance.
All: Amen.

Prayer of Confession

Today, as we remember our baptisms and remember the power of our oaths to be faithful, we confess that we have not always been true. We have waded into the enticing waters of destruction and betrayed the waters of our baptisms. Forgive us. Amen.

Words of Assurance

In the cleansing flood of God's love, we are delivered from failure and sin and called to go "all in." Hallelujah!

Benediction

Go into this world of chaos reminded of the power of your baptism. Reclaim the oath and the grace of your baptism so that you might be an agent of healing in a fractured world. (Dock Hollingsworth)

Suffering and the Bible

Second in a Series of Four on Christian Suffering in an Age of Entitlement

Isaiah 62:1-5; Romans 8:18-27

For Christians, suffering has always been a spiritual and theological problem. We cannot deny the objective reality that the world is full of suffering. At the same time, our faith, our belief, our theology, and our hearts tell us that God is love. We have a problem of irreconcilable truths. The world is full of suffering. God is love. This spiritual struggle grows if we are under the misconception that the biblical promise is one of protection from life's traumas. We often feel entitled to God's protection, comfort, and blessing, and instead life sometimes batters us.

There are no fully adequate ways to make peace with this problem, but some things can help us understand it and have a more mature, more adult, more spiritually sound and realistic way of believing in a loving God in a suffering world. We begin by acknowledging that there are different categories of suffering.

The first category is suffering caused by human beings and human societies. Many suffer because people lie, steal, cheat, and are violent. If this isn't bad enough, sometimes we unintentionally cause suffering. How many people die in auto accidents each year? Very rarely are those deaths intended, but almost always they are caused by errors made by people. An enormous amount of suffering is caused by us.

How do we reconcile the God of love with the suffering that we cause? Remember God has chosen to make us free. We are not puppets. We are not on strings. God does not control us, and so we hurt each other. It is impossible to conceive that God could make us both free and perfect. I'm sorry friends, I would like to be both free and perfect, but even more I would like you to be free and perfect!

Unfortunately, human freedom and human perfection are irreconcilable. They cannot both exist simultaneously. They're like solid objects that cannot occupy the same space. If we are free, we will hurt each other. God does not prevent us from doing so, because the only way God can prevent us from hurting each other is to make us puppets. That's the trade-off. God loves us enough to set us free, even at the terrible price of suffering that accompanies that freedom.

We want desperately for God to protect us from our own or someone else's foolishness. I wish God would protect me from you. That would be very nice. You probably wish God would protect you from me. But when

I expect God to protect me from you, I am not thinking religiously, I'm thinking magically. Magic would allow you to be both free and nice, but we are not in the magic business.

Our freedom is not incompatible with a God of love; in fact, it is God's love that sets us free. Mature Christians know free and fallible human beings will hurt us.

There is another category of suffering that is harder to understand. That is the suffering caused by the failures of creation itself. Earthquakes, hurricanes, tornadoes, terminal illnesses—all of these are part of nature. Nature wounds us deeply sometimes.

I think we make a tragic spiritual mistake when we read the first creation story in Genesis. It says God created for six days and rested on the seventh day. We sometimes see that seventh day as forever. Did you ever think that on Monday God went back to work again? The Bible doesn't say that creation is complete. In fact, the New Testament suggests that creation is still unfinished and that God is still at work. Now we may argue with God about being so slow, but the passage from Romans says, "All creation groans as a woman in labor." Creation groans and so do we.

Creation groans when earthquakes take lives. Creation groans in hurricanes like Katrina. Creation groans as if it is in labor for something not yet born. God is not done with creation. We live in the time of unfinished creation, and sometimes it will hurt us terribly. We may quarrel with God because God doesn't hurry up, but it is not up to us to impose schedules on God.

So if God is love, what's the deal? We must get over this notion that God is some kind of seatbelt or a protective cage that will protect us from all harm and sorrow. We are mature enough to know that if we climb on the roof and jump, God will not suspend gravity just to protect us. Yet we expect God to protect us from all other hurts and troubles. It's childish, really. We need to grow up.

God is not in the protection business. God is in the accompanying business. God is in the business of presence, not protection. God is in the business of walking with us through the pain and hurt of our lives. God stands beside us when the world seems to turn against us and creation itself seems to fall down upon us. God promises we will not be alone.

Look at the biblical record. Early in the Bible, the Israelites are made slaves in Egypt. That was hardly protection. When they are finally released from slavery and come to their land of promise, they discover it's not all they hoped it would be. They are surrounded by hostile people.

They have droughts and famines and storms and all kinds of problems in the land of promise, and after being there for six-hundred years or so, the Babylonians come and take them away into exile.

Protection? The Bible's not about protection. Christ is tortured and executed. The apostles all suffer and die. God is not about protection. God is about accompaniment.

Suffering is part of our lives, and a God of love does not coddle us and protect us from it. The God of love walks with us through it, and provides for us what the hymn writer called "strength for today and bright hope for tomorrow" ("Great Is Thy Faithfulness").

Not protection, but presence and hope—that is the gift of God's love when we suffer. Amen. (Carl Schenck)

Worship Aids

Call to Worship

Come and worship our Lord Jesus Christ.
He is our hope and our salvation.
Come and follow in his pathways.
He is our guide and teacher.
Follow him as a suffering servant.
O God, give us grace to suffer with him that we might also be glorified with him.

Confession

O Lord, we confess that we live too much with a feeling of entitlement. We expect life to treat us well, and we expect you to protect us from the role of the suffering servant. Forgive us for seeking the easy path and the wide door and keep us in the paths of Christ. We pray in Christ's name. Amen.

Words of Assurance

Hear the good news! We are not alone. God walks with us through our suffering into the light of hope.

Benediction

Now go into a hurting world ready to join Jesus in giving yourself for others. Go in love. Amen. (Carl Schenck)

MARCH 4, 2012

❧❧❧❧

Second Sunday in Lent

Readings: Genesis 17:1-7, 15-16; Psalm 22:22-31; Romans 4:13-25;
Mark 8:31-38

The Way of the Cross

Mark 8:31-38

Marketing firms have now learned how to make money from churches. One congregation sent a glossy advertisement describing their "casual, creative, contemporary church." They list five reasons for us to "Come and check them out": (1) jeans and t-shirts, no suits and ties; (2) no guilt. Leave your wallet at home; (3) positive messages you will enjoy; (4) awesome programs for kids and teens; (5) pop, rock, country—our band rocks. I am guessing they would think of me as a tie-wearing, wallet-carrying, guilt-feeling, negative-thinking, classical-music-loving senior citizen.

A second congregation invited the residents at the Youngers' address for four special Sundays. On the first the skit guys, "possibly the funniest guys on the planet," will provide hilarity. On the second Sunday a jazz trio will supply "possibly the best jazz on the planet." On the third Sunday they will hear "possibly the best singer on the planet." On the last Sunday Chaggy the Clown and Leno the flutist will lead "possibly the most diverse service on the planet." It was possibly the least enticing invitation on the planet.

A third church promises: we won't make you listen to organ music; it won't take more than an hour; we won't visit your home unannounced; we will let you remain anonymous; we serve espresso drinks. None of these are mentioned in the description of the early church in the book of Acts.

The cotton-candy, give me what I want, name it claim it, gain is godliness sales gimmicks might draw a big crowd, but so does Britney Spears. Selling God the way you sell cereal is not what Jesus had in mind.

71

Simon Peter was the one who understood church marketing. He recognized that entertainment is always in style and sacrifice is always out. Talking about taking up crosses is no way to sell the church. When Jesus starts preaching about suffering, rejection, and death, the disciples do not want to hear it. Peter taps Jesus on the shoulder and motions for a word in private: "Jesus, what are you talking about? Your popularity is skyrocketing. You don't need to talk about dying."

Peter has a good argument, and he has made sacrifices to follow Jesus. He and his brother Andrew left a thriving fishing business. They staked their futures on the belief that Jesus was going to make them look smart. Up to now everything indicated that they had made a wise decision. Peter watched with approval as Jesus healed the sick, fed the hungry, and told wonderful stories about God's love. Everything was going great. Now Jesus wants to mess it up with talk about sacrificing and dying. A leader is supposed to keep followers from suffering. Who wants a leader who leads them to suffering?

Shouldn't faith make us safer—"safe and secure from all alarms" (from "Leaning on the Everlasting Arms")? We come to church, in part, because we hope it will make us happier. If we are comfortable with who we are and how we live, then Jesus' words may not make much sense.

Peter took Jesus aside privately, but Jesus lets Peter have it in front of his friends. He starts by calling Peter "Satan," and it goes downhill from there. Then Jesus gathers not just the twelve, but everybody who will listen: "If any want to become my followers, let them deny themselves and take up their cross and follow me" (v. 34).

Some of the rest of what Jesus says is easier to take. "What will it profit them to gain the whole world and forfeit their life? (v. 36)" sounds enough like "You can't take it with you" to be found in a fortune cookie. But what can we possibly do with "deny self, take up a cross, and follow"? Apparently Jesus does not expect his followers to fare any better than he will.

What does it mean to follow someone who has been executed by the state? Are we expected to die for what we believe? Do we have to give up personal ambitions, forget about our own comfort, speak to people we do not want to speak to, listen to people we do not find interesting, care about people who made the mistake of being born in the wrong country, be true in those places where Christianity is not welcomed, and walk toward rather than away from people who are hurting?

Why would we follow someone who suffers and then tells us that we have to do the same? Who doesn't already have enough suffering in their lives without looking for more? What will we have left if we give ourselves away?

Why did the disciples follow Jesus? Why didn't Peter leave and go home? Because Jesus practiced and pictured the character and possibility of all of us at our best. Because Jesus gathered around himself a community and gave them the gifts to be the church through pain and joy. Because there has been no one since to match Jesus' words and deeds.

Our day-to-day decisions are not likely to lead to martyrdom, but each day we have to decide if we will give away our time and attention. Giving our lives away may mean turning the other cheek, standing with the people who are losing, doing good that will receive no applause, sitting in a home where someone has died, treating discarded people as children of God, shopping for someone else's groceries, baking cookies that we won't eat, reading stories to someone else's children, taking flowers to someone who's not our type, visiting someone else's mother in the nursing home, watering someone else's plants, washing dishes we didn't dirty, discussing current events that don't interest us, talking about faith when we would rather be silent, doing good for people who will do no good to us in return, weeping when others weep, praying not for an easier life but for strength to give our lives away, and discovering that if there's nothing for which we would die, then we don't have enough for which to live. (Brett Younger)

Lectionary Commentary

Genesis 17:1-7, 15-16

One of the amazing things about this story is that Abram is able to see his life in a way that no one else does. He sees God's place in the story. Abram's story has all kinds of twists and turns. Abram—now Abraham— imagines descendants like the stars of the sky. He thinks about how many years he and Sarah have been trying to have a baby, and how many have told him that they will never have children. When their son finally shows up, they name him *Isaac*, which means "laughter," because the very idea of it is funny—it's sort of like Medicare paying for a baby's immunizations. They laugh because instead of seeing only a gynecological fluke, they see the grace of God.

Romans 4:13-25

Throughout the letter to the Romans, Paul argues that we are justified by faith, not necessarily by our faith in God, which falters, but by God's faith in us. God has faith that we are going to make it. Paul uses theological words like *justification*, but there are moments when it is clear that Paul is writing not an academic treatise but a love letter. After several chapters of theological exposition, Paul writes: "For the promise that he would inherit the world did not come to Abraham or to his descendants through the law but through the righteousness of faith."

Worship Aids

Call to Worship
We have gathered in the name of Christ, the one by whose name we are called. We come so that Christ may strengthen our hands to serve and guide our hearts in the ways of justice and peace.

Prayer of Confession
God of the cross, it is so easy to be overwhelmed by the suffering around us that we have learned to turn our heads. Keep our eyes fixed on your hope. Teach us to live as if Christ died for us, and our life is now to be lived for Christ.

Words of Assurance (Matthew 11:28)
"Come to me, all you that are weary and are carrying heavy burdens, and I will give you rest."

Benediction
Go in the grace of God, in grateful obedience. Go in the way of the cross, knowing Jesus has walked the path before us. Go in the power of the Spirit to share God's love. (Brett Younger)

Undeserved Suffering Redeems

Third in a Series of Four on Christian Suffering in an Age of Entitlement

Luke 9:18–27
Last week we struggled with the painful fact that biblical faith does not promise us exemption from suffering. This is doubly distressing when we feel entitled to exemption from suffering. When looking at these matters, we are likely to be looking at suffering that comes from acts of nature, illness, accident, and death. This is the suffering that seems to have no purpose. It causes pain, and we find it difficult to understand or justify the pain we experience.

Yet as followers of Christ, we must also come to grips with the suffering that is embedded in our faith itself. We believe, in ways we cannot fully articulate, that Christ's suffering on the cross is mysteriously connected with our redemption. We believe the forgiveness of our sin is related to the suffering of Christ. We have no trouble believing that Christ's suffering was for us and that it did good. As Saint Paul said, it "set [us] free from the law of sin and of death" (Romans 8:2). Some suffering has meaning because it brings with it deep good.

Any woman who has borne a child understands the goodness that emerges from suffering. The pain of labor can be intense and all consuming. But when the child is born, the suffering turns to joy. The goodness of new life far exceeds the risks and pain of birth. That pain itself is redeemed by the blessing of the child.

Parents know this process in many other ways. All parents experience occasions when the pain of the parent is part of the redemption of the child. In due time, goodness in the form of a healthy, productive adult redeems the heartaches and sleepless nights of parenthood.

Some kinds of suffering can be redemptive far beyond our families and personal lives. The greatest recent Christian prophet of this truth was Dr. Martin Luther King, Jr. Dr. King maintained throughout his ministry that redemption can come through unearned suffering. Throughout the years of the American civil rights struggle, those on the forefront of the call for justice were killed, beaten, fire-hosed, jailed, spied upon, and in many other ways attacked. But Dr. King understood that there was a moral force in undeserved suffering, that it called forth the compassion and the fundamental sense of right and wrong of the general public. The way of nonviolent suffering called the nation's attention to the plight of the oppressed. It is easy to forget that this was, and to some degree remains, a long struggle. From the beginning of the Montgomery bus boycott on December 1, 1955, to the signing of the civil rights legislation July 2, 1964, was nearly a decade of continuous struggle and suffering. But this suffering awakened the conscience of the nation. Redeeming justice could come only through the wilderness of suffering.

Dr. King's philosophy of the redemptive power of unmerited suffering had its roots in the gospel of Jesus Christ. From its first days, the Christian movement believed that Jesus' brutal execution by Rome was not a meaningless or wasted death. Instead, the early Christians made the bold claim that it was this very suffering that reconciled a sinful world to a righteous and loving God. The seeds of this faith had been sown deep in the soil of the Hebrew Scriptures. In the "suffering servant songs" of Isaiah sprouted the idea that sacrifice and even suffering on the part of one person or people could redeem others.

In light of this core teaching of our faith, we must ask ourselves where we might engage in risky mission and ministry through a path of sacrifice and possible suffering that might bring redemption to others. Most ministries of Christ involve some measure of sacrifice and even suffering.

Those involved in ministry to youth know that when we love young people, they can break our hearts. When we seek to shape the lives of youth by giving our time and love to them, our efforts may not be appreciated and our love not returned. Yet a key part of most of our faith journeys would be the good influence some adult had on us when we were young. Some teacher, parent, grandparent, pastor, coach, or older friend had sacrificed their time and love to make us whole.

Those involved in ministry to the aged know the same risks. People avoid skilled nursing facilities for all kinds of reasons, but underneath them is the painful reality that if we invest ourselves in the elderly and disabled then we will grieve when they die. The relationship we build and the love we give to the elderly may cost us deeply in sorrow when they pass from our sight.

When we suffer for others in the name of Christ, redemption is possible. There is a famous prayer that was written by an unknown prisoner in Ravensbruck concentration camp and left next to the body of a dead child. The prayer says,

> O Lord, remember not only the men and women of good will, but also those of ill will. But do not remember all the suffering they have inflicted on us, remember the fruits we have bought, thanks to this suffering—our comradeship, our loyalty, our humility, our courage, our generosity, the greatness of heart which has grown out of all this, and when they come to judgment, let all the fruits which we have borne be their forgiveness. (as quoted in Richard J. Foster, *Prayer: Finding the Heart's True Home* [San Francisco: HarperOne, 1992], 224)

Let us pray our suffering will never reach this extreme, but let us never forget that unmerited suffering can be redemptive.

We come together today to worship God whom we know in Jesus Christ—the one who knew the way of suffering. Suffering chosen and accepted for our redemption. If we are to follow him, we must sometimes choose the paths of suffering, knowing that our suffering can heal and redeem others. (Carl Schenck)

Worship Aids

Call to Worship

We come to this house to find a home in Christ.
May we experience a home here that passes all understanding.

Confession

Lord, we do not expect to find blessing in suffering. Teach us again that the way of the cross is the way of blessing. Forgive us for always seeking the comfortable way and show us the way to a better life. We pray in Jesus name. Amen.

Words of Assurance

The Lord creates. Christ redeems. The Holy Spirit accompanies us through suffering to redemption. Thanks be to God.

Benediction

Now go to be transformed and to transform others down the path of redemptive suffering. Go in hope. Amen. (Carl Schenck)

MARCH 11, 2012

Third Sunday in Lent

Readings: Exodus 20:1-17; Psalm 19; 1 Corinthians 1:18-25; John 2:13-22

Foolishness and the Cross

1 Corinthians 1:18-25

Since John F. Kennedy was assassinated in 1963, conspiracy theorists have speculated that the CIA, FBI, Mafia, Fidel Castro, Lyndon Johnson, the Teamsters, and almost everyone else were involved. We have seen the Zapruder film frame by frame. The 1991 Oliver Stone movie *JFK* was nominated for best picture, but in spite of the title, it was not really about John F. Kennedy.

In December 1999, a jury in Memphis, Tennessee, concluded that James Earl Ray did not act alone in assassinating Martin Luther King, Jr. Thirty-one years after Dr. King's murder and two years after the man sentenced for the crime died in prison, the courts were still debating what happened.

The detailed investigations of the murders of John F. Kennedy and Martin Luther King, Jr., focus on facts and deflect attention away from the meaning of those assassinations. When great leaders are killed, the most important questions do not get the most attention. Shouldn't we ask: "What does a martyr's death say about our world, our society, ourselves, and the one who was murdered?"

No death has inspired more bad questions, wrong answers, and peculiar theories than Jesus' death. Paul writes to the Corinthians, "the message about the cross is foolishness to those who are perishing" (1:18). J.B. Philips translates *foolishness* as "nonsense." Much of what has been said about the cross is foolish nonsense.

This is what I learned growing up in Southern Baptist churches in Mississippi: God made humankind knowing that we would mess up. When we did mess up, God got mad. God warned us through the prophets, but we kept messing up. God lost patience with the indirect approach and sent his son to get killed for our sins. On the cross Jesus took the whipping we had coming, so that God could grudgingly forgive us. Jesus rose from the dead to prove his victory over sin, and he is coming back soon to judge us. If you are lucky enough to hear and believe this theory about what happened on the cross, then you get to live forever. If you never hear the story or the theory does not make sense to you, then you burn in hell.

If that was what I believed about the cross, then I could not believe that God is love. So much of what is said about Jesus' death makes no sense that educated people are tempted to ignore this central event in the history of Christianity. Some of the blame goes to theologians like John Calvin and Anselm. The theory of vicarious punishment is wrong, but it has been repeated so many times that people believe it. The portrayal of a bloodthirsty God who requires a terrible sacrifice because someone has to die is not true to the Bible.

Paul writes that the cross does not lend itself to easy analysis: "the discernment of the discerning I will thwart" (v. 19). If we have to have a formula for everything, then the cross will be a stumbling block.

If we were writing a story about God's love, we would not include a cross, but there is something about it that draws our attention. The cross is a picture not only of human nature at its worst but also of the human spirit at its best. How does Jesus die? He is extraordinary. In the midst of excruciating pain, Jesus makes provision for his widowed mother. When a thief asks for comfort, Jesus offers a word of hope. He prays, "Forgive them, for they do not know what they are doing" (Luke 23:34). Jesus feels the terrible absence of God, "My God, my God, why have you forsaken me?" (Mark 15:34). He dies with dignity and courage.

The people who see Jesus die are amazed. The Roman executioner, the person most used to this cruel process, is so moved by the way Jesus dies that instead of saying, "another fool eliminated," he says, "Truly this man was God's son" (see Mark 15:39).

The people who saw Jesus die thought the cross looked like the suffering of God. When they saw the Messiah crucified they understood that God suffers terribly. Seeing Jesus' pain led them to realize that God shares our sorrows.

If you were handed crayons and construction paper and were told to come up with a picture of God's love, what would you draw? Would you draw green grass and flowers on a sunny day? Would you draw a happy family at a picnic? The people at the foot of the cross came to the conclusion that God's love looks like Jesus dying.

When the disciples preached and wrote about Jesus' death they had trouble explaining the connection between the cross and forgiveness, but they were sure that if you could picture God's forgiveness it would look like Calvary. When people hurt us, we don't suffer in order to forgive them, but suffering is the shape of forgiveness.

Imagine a wife untrue to her husband. She thinks he knows what she has done, but she does not confess, and she does not stop being untrue. Her husband loves her and suffers because of what she is doing. She sees his suffering and is moved by it. He so obviously loves her. She asks for and receives forgiveness. His forgiveness changes her. His suffering grace creates a new relationship. The costly, suffering forgiveness of God looks like the cross.

Years ago, I went with a group of friends to see a film about Jesus' life. We planned to go to dinner afterward so that we could talk about what we did not like. As I watched the movie I made mental notes on the historical inaccuracies. The temple was smaller than that. The disciples were not that old. John the Baptist's dungeon did not look like Joan of Arc's dungeon. I felt like Roger Ebert going to church. When Jesus carried the cross I started to point out that victims only carried the crosspiece, but then I realized to my shame that the woman seated next to me was crying. The church is made up of people who have caught a glimpse of the suffering love and painful forgiveness of God. (Brett Younger)

Lectionary Commentary

Exodus 20:1-17

When the Ten Commandments are in the news it is usually because some judge or teacher has hung them up on the walls, where they seem like a token or an insult to people who are not Christians or Jews. The Ten Commandments do not need to be posted nearly so much as they need to be practiced. They need to be taken down from the wall and talked about, defended and argued with, but most of all, they need to be taken seriously. If we do so, then rather than see them as tokens, insults, or negative "thou shalt nots," we will see them as life-giving, joyful affirmations of a better way of life.

John 2:13-22

What makes this story shocking is that Jesus is not attacking Mafia hit men in a casino. Jesus is angry with religious people. Jesus is furious, because they have come to church and neglected to worship. Jesus' anger is directed, not against unbelievers, but against believers who have trivialized worship. This story is hard to hear, because Jesus could chase us all out of church. We sometimes forget or fail to recognize the importance of worship. What would we think if Jesus showed up and insisted that we are not taking this seriously enough? What if the table Jesus turned over was our table? In worship, God intrudes upon our complacency, overturning tables, setting wild birds loose, and clanging coins on the floor. God's presence is the sting of a whip driving us out of our smugness. (Brett Younger)

Worship Aids

Invocation

Gracious God, there is no way that we can repay you for your suffering love, for the ways in which you sorrow with us each day. In this time of worship, we offer but a small portion of who we are. Receive us as grateful children. Amen.

Prayer of Confession

Jesus was courageous;
We are careful.
Jesus trusted the unworthy;
We trust those with good collateral.
Jesus forgave the unforgivable;
We forgive those who do not really hurt us.
Jesus was righteous and laughed at respectability;
We are respectable and smile at righteousness.
Let us confess our sins to God.

Words of Assurance

Hear the good news! Because of Jesus' courage, trustworthiness, forgiveness, and righteousness, we are not alone, and we can begin again.

Benediction

Children of God by grace, disciples of Christ by choice, servants of the Spirit by faith, go with eyes to see, hands to heal, and hearts to love. (Brett Younger)

Suffering in Hope

Fourth in a Series of Four on Christian Suffering in an Age of Entitlement

1 Peter 1:3

We now reach the halfway marker in our journey from Ash Wednesday to Good Friday. We have explored how our society and our psyche encourage us to believe that we are entitled to nothing but the best. We have acknowledged that suffering is the human predicament and that there are times when the followers of Christ must choose the road of suffering in order to serve our neighbors.

But when we are in the clutches of suffering and pain, whether it is imposed or chosen, we need a shelter from the storm. Hope is that shelter. Hope does not do away with the storms of life, but it can shelter us sufficiently that we can weather the storm and sustain our faith in the face of suffering.

At this halfway point of Lent, let us peek ahead to see if there is enough light to carry us through the darkness. When we look ahead we see, in part, the looming cross. We try to clean up the cross and tame its horrors, but we cannot. Dress it up as contemporary jewelry or polish it to a high sheen on our altars, it still remains the instrument of torture and death. The cross is the human condition.

As we peer into our personal and collective futures, only denial or willful ignorance can obscure the realization that being human means to walk in darkness and to suffer. While life may be sweet today, every day carries with it the risk of injury or illness. Any day could be the day when our most loved one dies. Any day can bring divorce, unemployment, or a runaway child. The cross always looms before us, just as it loomed before Jesus.

Our age of entitlement deludes us with the picture of safety and security, but in our deepest and most honest moments, we know that to be human is to suffer. We may not suffer today, but many do. We will all bear some portion of the world's suffering. The cross is not an oddity that befell Jesus; it is the universal experience of humanity.

But in the suffering and resurrection of Christ come two promises of hope.

First, the Christian story exclaims that suffering does not have the last word. Perhaps it is dimly seen when we are in the throes of suffering, but our faith declares that the forces of suffering endure but do not prevail. We are not a Good Friday people but an Easter people. Suffering may come for a day or a season, but the resurrection of Christ is a promise in the final victory of God over the powers of sin and death—suffering at its worst.

While we are not entitled to a life without suffering, we are promised life beyond suffering. To use a boxing metaphor, suffering may win many rounds but God takes the decision. This faith gives us hope that can empower us to endure needless suffering and even to choose that suffering we take on for the sake of others. Without hope suffering destroys. When we live in hope, suffering can scar but it cannot destroy. Suffering will not endure forever.

The second promise of hope in the suffering and resurrection of Christ is the assurance that even suffering is contained within the broader sea of God's love. The cross of Christ is a thing of love. It is the final and complete incarnation. Our claim that "God was in Christ" takes its authority from the cross. If God had been in Christ only in our joys and pleasures, God would not have fully embraced the human condition. Only in suffering could Christ be fully human. Without suffering Christ could not be fully "with us."

So the cross, which begins as an instrument of torture and death, becomes in Christ love personified. In the fulfillment of the incarnation on the cross, that which is most ugly becomes a thing of beauty.

The eyes of faith must look carefully to see the love of God at work in our suffering, but we can see the love of God clearly in Christ's suffering. Those who suffer are never alone. Christ is always beside them in love. Here lies our hope. No suffering is outside of God's love.

Nora Gallagher, in *Things Seen and Unseen: A Year Lived in Faith*, tells of learning that her brother Kit was diagnosed with a terminal disease. With this news came pain for Gallagher and her family. Kit would suffer, and all those who loved him would suffer with him. Struggling to find some hope in this hurt, Gallagher writes that she found herself walking a labyrint. She describes it this way:

> I'm flooded by memories: the light fur of the palomino horse I had as a child; my father's hand on my head; my mother bringing me a low tray filled with white flour, for snow, and tiny figures—animals, men, women, and children—with which to build a village scene, a story. Kit on crutches when he was fourteen, having broken his leg skiing, playing tag with me among red poppies. Faith rises up out of ordinary days....I ask God a simple question: How will I live now, with my brother so ill, what can I do? As I walk one of the great outer rings, I

feel the purest peace. The answer comes, this thinnest of threads; everything is contained in my love, even this. (Nora Gallagher, *Things Seen and Unseen: A Year Lived in Faith* [New York: Vintage Books, 1998], 233)

For those of us in Christ understand we are not entitled to pain-free lives, but we hold firm to the faith that even suffering is contained in God's love for us. In that hope, we not only live, we overcome. (Carl Schenck)

Worship Aids

Call to Worship

We come from the hurts of a broken world.
We come from the pain of illness and death.
We come seeking a hope that is beyond our powers.
We find that hope in Jesus Christ whom we worship.

Confession

O Lord, forgive us for placing our hope in the wrong things. We are not saved by our affluence or education. We are not saved by our power or beauty. Teach us again to place our hope in you and in the resurrection of Christ in whose name we pray. Amen.

Words of Assurance

The hope of God's love endures all things, walks with us through pain and suffering, and leads us to the light of Christ.

Benediction

Now full of the hope that only Christ can give, go to a hurting world. Go in peace. Amen. (Carl Schenck)

MARCH 18, 2012

❧❧❧

Fourth Sunday in Lent

Readings: Numbers 21:4-9; Psalm 107:1-3, 17-22; Ephesians 2:1-10; John 3:14-21

Choices

Numbers 21:4-9

Do you want that for here or to go? Should we take the freeway or drive through town? Should I go to the gym or the ice cream shop? Most of our decisions do not require a lot of thought. Even the big ones—go to Mercer or some other university; keep on your present career track or consider the fast-paced world of ministry; stay in Atlanta or move some place with normal weather where people are not already mowing their lawns—even the important decisions do not seem permanent. If we do not like the college we choose, we will transfer. If we do not like our job, we will find another. If we do not like where we live, we will move. It is easy to forget that the choices we make have consequences.

We face a world of decisions every day. Choice is built into the essence of our existence. We cannot have it all. From the moment we are born it is clear that there is more to do than we can ever do.

Every time we choose a path we miss countless others. Every decision is the death of the alternatives. The power of our decisions is so over-whelming that some decide that we must be mistaken; our choices can-not be as important as they appear. It is tempting to deny any permanency to our decisions.

It is difficult to admit that some directions are irreversible. We find it hard to bring ourselves to say, "This one thing I do." We keep standing at junctures where two roads diverge and try to go down both. It is painful to decide to do "this" when we know it means we will never be able to do "that."

It is simpler to convince ourselves that all the paths end up converging, that it does not matter what anyone decides, that everything will turn out the same in the end, but that is not true to our experience. Some decisions build permanent fences.

When theologians address questions of eternity, they are understandably uncomfortable with the idea that our decisions have eternal significance. Why do you think so many people are attracted to predestination—the idea that eternal destiny is unrelated to human choice? God makes all the decisions because big decisions should not be left to human beings. In much the same way, universalism, the belief that God accepts everyone into eternity unchanged, is attractive because it lessens the significance of our decisions.

This strange, striking, scary, unsettling, unseemly, and slightly slimy story in Numbers is about decisions and their consequences. Moses is getting nothing but heartache from the Israelites. They have the gall to complain about being set free. They describe captivity in Egypt as if it were Camelot. Their impatience turns to impertinence as they grumble about the wilderness, the lack of food and water, and the food they do have. Manna was never especially appealing, sort of like a bologna sandwich, and after years of the same thing going hungry does not seem so bad.

Usually, Moses would intercede with God, who would graciously meet their needs for food or water or security or whatever they wanted. This time, however, complaining about the menu prompts God to send poisonous serpents. Now the snakes seem way out of proportion to the crime. The people were just grumbling about the food: manna yesterday, manna today, and more manna tomorrow. Who can blame them for complaining? We all like a little variety.

The Israelites, not surprisingly, scream for help. They have a change of heart. They confess their grievous wrongdoing and beg Moses to beg God to get rid of the snakes. God is eager to help, but their prayers are not answered in exactly the way they hoped. The consequences of their actions do not disappear. The dangers remain, and the people continue to suffer from the death-dealing snakes.

God does not cancel the plague, but commands Moses to make a copper snake. Moses thinks it is a strange idea, but when you are up to your ankles in adders, you do not ask questions. The promise is that everyone who chooses to take a look will be fine. It works like a charm. The snake on the pole, this distasteful sight lifted up, brings healing.

Hebrew scholars try to protect their reputations by ignoring this story. The ones unfortunate enough to have to reflect on the book of Numbers go to great lengths to say that the writer is not saying that the snake heals anybody. It is the people's decision to look that matters. The author's point is that when people look to God, they find healing.

Even if you get rid of all the bizarre stuff—the manna, the poisonous serpents, and the snake on a stick—this story still sounds peculiar to modern ears, because the difference between life and death is one decision.

God comes to our death-bound situations, but we have to decide to look up and see the life God offers. We find the outline of the snake story and the gospel reading throughout Scripture—sin, penalty, repentance, and grace. People make their own path, experience the consequences, confess their mistakes, and find their way to God's love. This is the pattern of the Christian life. We go in meaningless directions, know the penalty of emptiness, confess our foolishness, and remember God's grace.

God has given us the wonderful, painful gift of choice. When we do not have the courage to choose what is best but act as if our choices do not matter, we make no progress even on the smoothest path; but when we choose courageously, we go forward even on the roughest road.

From the first choice we make in the morning until we choose to go to sleep at night, we are making the decisions that form our lives. We choose the words we speak or refrain from speaking, the people we love, the people we do not even see, the thoughts we entertain, the ideas we hold, the deeds we do, and those we leave undone. We choose to love or ignore, heal or hurt, bless or curse. We choose death or life. (Brett Younger)

Lectionary Commentary

Ephesians 2:1-10

Paul understands despair. He points out that we have felt more dead than alive, but then Paul writes that no matter what foolishness we do or hopelessness we feel, the ultimate reality is grace. Now God has us where God wants us, with all the time in this world and the next to shower grace and kindness upon us. Saving us is all God's idea. All we do is trust enough to let God do it. It is God's gift from start to finish. It is not about what we can do. Even when we feel dead, God says we are alive. Most sermons suggest that we start doing something new, but the word Paul offers and maybe the word we most need to hear is that we can stop doing something old. We can stop carrying the burden of trying to make our own dreams come true.

"For by grace you have been saved through faith, and this is not your own doing; it is the gift of God" (v. 8), not the result of anything you have done, so do not boast about it and do not worry about it, just be grateful to God.

John 3:14-21

For Christians, Jesus is the defining revelation of God's love. That does not mean that Christians believe that no one else knows God, but it does mean that in Jesus we best see God's mercy. This verse we have known from childhood, John 3:16—the one Martin Luther called the gospel in miniature—promises that God loves the whole world, not just those who gather on Sunday, not just the religiously inclined, not just those who have heard the name of Jesus, but the whole world, so God comes in Christ to show the way of life in the midst of death, the way of peace in a violent world.

God's love has the positive and negative effect of calling us to choose. A stepping stone can also be a stumbling block. A healing presence can also be disturbing. Every light casts a shadow. We have to decide how we will respond to God's love. (Brett Younger)

Worship Aids

Call to Worship

Each Sunday when we come into the sanctuary, we have several choices to make. Do we just mouth the words to the hymns or do we sing from the depths of our soul? Do we listen intently for God's word in Scripture or do we count the bald men in the choir? Do we give a sacrificial offering or do we pass the plate like a hot potato? Do we genuinely pray or do we keep our heart out of worship?

Prayer of Confession

God, help us want to be Christians, to be like Christ. We confess that you offer renewal from above, but we are satisfied with old, earthly things. You offer healing, but we cling to that which hurts us. You shine the light, but we hide in the dark corners. Draw us to your renewal, healing, and light through Jesus Christ. Amen.

Words of Assurance

Christ, the light of the world, shines in hope and love for our healing. Thanks be to God.

Benediction

We go into a dark world to offer God's light. We go into a selfish world to live with God's love. We go into a hurting world to share God's peace. (Brett Younger)

Looking Forward, Not Backward

First in a Series of Three on the Teachings of Jesus

John 9:1-7

We often seek spiritual edification from slogans. Most slogans are shorthand for a deeper insight. When our faith needs a jump-start, we can recite the slogan and keep going. One of these slogans is "Life is hard, but God is good." The deeper insight is that things will not always go well for us just because we are Christians, yet God gives us the resources to cope. Sometimes, we need to be careful with our slogans. When we say to ourselves, "Let go and let God," we might mean that our anxiety can often block us from seeing how God is active in a problem. If we are not careful, though, we might become too passive in our attempts to "let God," and not do for ourselves what we know we need to do. One slogan with which we need to be careful is "Everything happens for a reason." Surely it is true that God sees meaning in things that seem senseless to us. We have all known situations that looked bad at first, like a broken relationship that turned out better than we thought it could. What we considered a deep grief led to a blessing. That may be the deeper insight behind the slogan, "everything happens for a reason." Still, we need to be careful with this slogan, because it can lead us astray.

When the disciples see the blind man, they seem to assume that his condition happened for a "reason." They ask Jesus whose sin lay behind the blindness, his own or his parents'. The narrator tells us that he was blind from birth, but perhaps the disciples didn't know that. How could someone sin before birth? We also have to wonder if they asked the question loudly enough that the blind man heard them. Dr. Kathy Black, a professor at Claremont School of Theology, knows that some people say hurtful things loudly enough for others to hear them. As a girl, she swam in a polluted lake, leaving her with neurological damage. She occasionally experiences episodes similar to epileptic seizures. During one of these episodes, she heard a woman remark, "There but for the grace of God, go I." We say that to remind ourselves to be grateful, but do we realize that we imply the person who faces the physical challenge does not have God's grace? Whatever the woman intended by the remark, Kathy experienced it as condescending. Again, we need to be careful. God has shown abundant grace to Dr. Kathy Black (see Dr. Kathy Black, "Why Me?" in *Patterns of Preaching: A Sermon Sampler*, ed. Ronald J. Allen [St. Louis: Chalice Press, 1998], 192–98).

The question of the disciples shows us the danger of using the slogan, "everything happens for a reason." The slogan turns our attention backward, trying to find the reason behind some painful event. God may have a purpose in some of the struggles we face, but can we really say God has a reason for everything that happens? When a child dies tragically, can we assume God had a reason? How much hurt has been caused by someone saying to a grieving parent, "it was God's will," when we don't know God's will in every situation? Nothing in Scripture suggests that God wills a young child, full of potential, to die. When we start digging around, trying to find God's "reason" for something, we can lead ourselves astray. We can begin to assume that something bad is a punishment for sin. We even run the risk of turning God into a monster that would bring a hurricane or earthquake, or the death of a child, for a "reason."

Jesus answers the disciples' question by focusing them on how God will respond. "Neither this man nor his parents sinned; he was born blind so that God's works might be revealed in him" (v. 3). Jesus turns our attention away from trying to find the reason behind a tragedy to trying to see how God is working in the tragedy. Where does God heal, reconcile, comfort, confront, open up, strengthen, renew? The man's blindness is a manifestation of the darkness in all of creation. Jesus appeared as the light to dispel that darkness. John does not spend much time explaining why we experience darkness or where it comes from. In the opening poem we simply read the words, "The light shines in the darkness. But the darkness has not understood it" (John 1:5). John does not say anything about a reason for the darkness, only that the light shines through it. John just assumes everyone knows the darkness is there. In this narrative, Jesus frees the man from his darkness when Jesus spits on the ground, makes mud, and then spreads it on the man's eyes. Jesus heals the man, and the darkness loses another battle.

What we tend to call the "reason" behind some of the tragedies in our lives, we should see as examples of the darkness. The battle between darkness and light weaves throughout the Gospel of John. Nicodemus comes to Jesus at night, symbolizing the darkness of doubt. When Judas leaves to betray Jesus, John says simply "it was night" (John 13:30). Mary Magdalene comes to the tomb after the crucifixion while it is still dark, symbolizing her unbelief. God does not have a reason behind the pain in our lives. They are examples of the darkness in all creation. Jesus is the light that scatters the darkness.

When we face some form of the darkness in our lives, let us hold on to Jesus' words here. We may not find a reason behind something that happens to us. We should not search for an undisclosed sin for which God has sent a punishment. We should rejoice that God's work could be revealed in our situation. God might teach us wisdom or strengthen our faith. God might confront our apathy or tear down our stubbornness. God might give us the grace to sustain our spirits. God might heal us or take away the pain we feel. In all of those ways God's light shines in the darkness. Let us open our eyes to see that light. (Chuck Aaron)

Worship Aids

Invocation

O God of light, we gather as those who face the darkness of the world every day. Yet we worship because we trust in your light to win the victory. As we sing, pray, and listen in this service, let us see the light shining into the darkness. Amen.

Prayer of Confession

We confess, O God, that often we skim along on the surface, content to mouth a platitude rather than search deeply for the truth. We confess that often we hide in the darkness, rather than seek the light that will expose our sin so that we can conquer it. Forgive us, O God. Teach us to seek the truth, even when it hurts, so that we can put away falsehood. Let us embrace light, truth and life. Amen.

Words of Assurance

Hear the good news! Christ is the light, the truth, and the life. Trust and follow and be made whole.

Benediction

Go out now into a world of suffering so that God's works can be revealed in your lives. Go out now to proclaim the truth in a world fascinated by lies. Go out now to spread the light in a world blanketed by darkness. (Chuck Aaron)

MARCH 25, 2012

❧❧❧❧

Fifth Sunday of Lent

Readings: Jeremiah 31:31-34; Psalm 51:1-12; Hebrews 5:5-10; John 12:20-33

What Shall We Say?

John 12:20-33

I live in a small town in Texas. If you know anything about living in Texas then you know that Friday nights in the fall are all about high school football. It is a ritual that involves whole communities. I grew up in a similar place, so I know the routine well. Of course at the heart and soul of it all is winning—you know, being number one and all of that. Through such rituals and expectations we boldly teach our children and youth that winning is important and to be valued.

Some Greeks went to worship at the feast, and they wanted to see Jesus, John tells us. Jesus hears about the request from Phillip and responds by identifying that the time has come for him to be glorified. He then begins to describe what glorification looks like in the ordinary and every day. The images he uses are neither flattering nor popular in a culture consumed with competition, beating others, working harder and smarter to get ahead, measuring how you are progressing by what you have done and where you are on the tally sheet, and sacrificing whatever you must to be at the top. In light of such cultural realities, Jesus talks instead about dying, hating one's life in the world in order to keep it for eternal life, being wherever Jesus is, and serving and following him.

This passage fits well with themes of the Lenten season. It reminds us that if life with Christ is about anything, it is about finally having the courage to let go and simply follow where the Christ dares to lead us. When will we learn that the life of faith is countercultural to most of what we are taught? Friday night lights in Texas are just one example of such teaching. There are, I am afraid, many others. As preachers who

God calls to live out a prophetic role, we are the ones who dare to voice the alternative values. In John's retelling of this moment in Jesus' life, he seeks to end Jesus' public ministry with a bold and declarative proclamation regarding what life in the kingdom of God looks like.

Jesus then goes on to live out his proclamation as he powerfully states that in this hour of his life and in this time in history, he understands exactly who he is, why he has come into the world, and what he is here to do. Jesus allows God to define him in such a way that his life is not his own, and he surrenders obediently to the will of God for the sake of glorifying God in all that he does and is. The statement is characterized by the images Jesus used earlier: he now dies to himself, hating his life in the world, being where God is, following and serving the will of God with all that he has and is.

I was at a bookstore the other day, and as I read book titles in the various sections I did not see any books on following, few on serving, none on hating one's life in the world, and very few on dying. I didn't see many titles on surrendering, being obedient, giving in, or giving up. Most of the titles I saw were on self-help, getting ahead, how to become wealthy, managing time and money, being number one at almost anything, how to stay competitive, and on and on. Try it sometime. It tells much more about life in our culture than most of us would like to admit.

After John has Jesus clearly and lucidly proclaim his sense of God and his role in the glorification of God, John has the voice of God confirm the reality and truth of all that Jesus has said. God pronounces that Jesus will indeed glorify God, and he will glorify God again. The word confirms what we already know about Jesus. Jesus has a sense of his time and place in the work and movement of God in the history of the world. Jesus then interprets for all of those who have heard that this will be a time of judgment when the prince of this world will be driven out. Jesus then predicts how he will die and gives meaning to his dying as a means to draw all people to him. In a world consumed with itself, wasting time and energy on pursuing all the wrong dreams and values, John seeks to redefine history as purpose-filled, rooted, and grounded in the glorification of its creator, redeemer, and sustainer.

When my daughter was in elementary school she entered a science fair. Her project was to answer the question as to whether cut flowers would live longer in a vase with plain water or a vase filled with sugar water. We went through the process of filling the vases with the appropriate water and placing the cut flowers in each and then documenting the process of the cut flowers and what happened to them over the next several days.

We observed that the cut flowers lasted longer in the sugar water than they did in the plain water. What also became clear over those days of observation was that neither grew and eventually both sets of cut flowers died. Neither set of flowers had soil, which helped to shape and grow them into what they were designed and created to be. Without the soil they lost their sense of purpose, meaning, and identity. John wants to be clear in this Gospel passage about Jesus. Jesus knew who he was, he understood and lived the life God gave him, and he realized his time and his place in the work and purpose of God. So . . . what shall we say in this time and place of our lives? God, glorify your name! (Travis Franklin)

Lectionary Commentary

Jeremiah 31:31-34

The Jeremiah prophecy is an appropriate one for the Lenten season. Even in the midst of suffering and death the prophet reminds the people that there is always hope with God. He dares to proclaim a new hope in a new covenant that God will author in the hearts of God's people, one that will overwrite the old covenant that has been broken. Such words in light of the sinfulness and mortality of Ash Wednesday and Lent remind us that God's hope somehow transcends and breathes new life into human history. This powerful vision and hope come at a time of crisis and transition in the life of God's people. It refers to the undeniable nature of God's love and its ability to forgive, restore, and to re-define people and history.

As the Lenten season moves us to the cross and beyond, passages like this one help us to understand that regardless of how human beings respond to the love of God in the world, God's will and movement will always have the final word. That final word is always that for which we hope and pray. Jeremiah boldly proclaims God will always find a way no matter how bad things may appear to be!

Hebrews 5:5-10

This passage helps us to remember the humanity of the Christ and the days that Jesus lived on the earth. Within the Lenten context this passage seeks to lift up the undeniable reality of Jesus the human being who chose to be obedient to the will of God, even to death on the cross. Jesus becomes an example for all of us who seek to obey the will of God. The cross becomes for the author of Hebrews the defining moment of Jesus' obedience to the purpose and claim of God on his life. Jesus as Christ lives out for us what such obedience demands of us. In this season of self-denial we too seek to take up our cross and follow wherever the will of God is leading us. (Travis Franklin)

Worship Aids

Pastoral Prayer

O God, we gather here today to be reminded that we are a people consumed by your love. Offer us an awareness that life is not about what we get as much as it is about what we are led to give. Forgive us for pre-occupation with ourselves and the idols we have created. Empower us through your Holy Spirit to surrender to your will and your purpose. Declare to us that we are not here this morning for any other reason but to glorify you and your love for a world that is lost. We thank you for loving and claiming us as your children. Use us in whatever way you would, for whatever cause you would, for whatever reason that you would. In the name and spirit of a risen Lord we pray. Amen.

Prayer of Confession

We humbly come before you today, O God, to acknowledge and admit our sin and wrongdoing. We have gone our own way, and it has led us to acts that we now confess. We are sorry for what we have done that has hurt and disappointed you. Forgive us, we pray. Take our sin away and liberate us with your divine love. Restore us to a right relationship with you. In the name of Jesus, our Lord, we pray. Amen.

Words of Assurance

The love of God forgives and restores you. May God's grace mend and heal your brokenness and heartache. Know in your heart that today, in this moment, you are forgiven and delivered in the name of God's love. (Travis Franklin)

Whose Face Is Our Face?

Second in a Series of Three on the Teachings of Jesus

Luke 16:19-31

We truly become engaged with a passage of Scripture when we identify with a character. When we see our lives in one of the characters in the text, it opens up the story for us. When one trouble piles on top of another, we turn to Job. Job lets us blow off some steam when he shakes his fist at God, demanding to know why life has to be so cruel. In better times we can identify with the psalmist who rejoices that the great shepherd has led him down all the right paths. The poet helps us disperse our fear when we are in the dark valleys. When a passage presents us with more than one character, we have to decide which character has more to teach us. We like to identify with David, making all of our problems and challenges into giants that God will help us slay. Do we ever ask if we might sometimes wear the armor of Goliath? Do we loom large in someone's life, so that our temper or our withheld approval makes us appear nine feet tall to them? If we allow ourselves to identify with a character that doesn't seem to fit at first, we might grow in ways we don't expect.

We find two main characters in Jesus' parable. Striking contrasts separate them. The first one, the rich guy, dresses better than P. Diddy or Usher and eats like a luxury cruise passenger every day. His biggest problem might be that his Armani suit isn't back from the cleaners yet or that his steak is undercooked. The other character has fallen through the cracks of life. We don't know how he ended up the way he did. Was he too sick or injured to work? Did the economy just not have a place for him? Were his sores the cause of his poverty or the result? All we know is that his life sounds miserable. He reminds us of the pictures of AIDS victims in Africa, who languish, poor, sick, and hungry with little to comfort them. The poor guy in the parable is so weak and helpless he cannot fend off the dogs that lick his sores.

If Jesus' story ended at verse 21, we would have no problem choosing which one we wanted to identify with. We would take the fancy clothes and table full of food. Who wants to be the poor, sick, hungry man trying to shoo the dogs away from his open sores? I wonder, though, if we can identify well with either man. A handful of people in the world might fit in the shoes of the rich man. Some people really and truly have more than they know what to do with. We know that many of those people end up making messes of their lives. With flashbulbs popping away they confess how sorry they are to have disappointed their spouses and their many fans. Even with all of that, they represent only a small fraction of the people in the world. Surely, Luke does not want us to identify with the rich man, the one who doesn't even have a name. If we don't identify with the rich man, are we Lazarus? Many of the people of the world live in severe poverty. Perhaps a billion people lack access to adequate food and water.

Luke could catch more people by hoping we see ourselves in Lazarus. Still, Lazarus is about as low as one can go.

Of course, by the middle of the parable, the situation of the two men reverses. Lazarus resides in a place of contentment and peace, as the phrase goes, in the "bosom" of Abraham. The rich man, however, now writhes in misery. The tongue that once savored the tastiest of food is now dry and desperate for any relief. Might Luke try to get our attention that way? Might Luke warn those who are too comfortable while offering hope to those who find life pure misery? Certainly, the parable accomplishes some of that. Nevertheless, the parable doesn't make much of the rich man's sins or of Lazarus' moral goodness. The rich man doesn't serve as much of a real warning and Lazarus doesn't serve as much of a model to follow. Perhaps Luke did not intend for us to identify with either character too closely.

If we do not fit into the role of either Lazarus or the rich man, who helps us identify with the parable? Some characters come up at the very end that might fit us. The rich man has five brothers. Luke does not describe them with nearly as much colorful detail as he does the two main characters. Nevertheless, by the end of the parable, they are the ones who still have choices to make. Their faith remains a question mark. The rich man wishes he could show them the dramatic scene of his torment and Lazarus's peace nestled in Abraham's arms. He hopes that might grab their attention. He begs Abraham to let him go back to the land of the living for just long enough to tell his brothers the way things are.

Should we see this parable through the eyes of the five brothers? Sometimes God has trouble grabbing our attention. We do not always notice God's grace right before our eyes. We see the rich and the poor and make judgments about them. Those judgments may not correspond to God's judgment, however. Our judgments may not take into account how God will act in the resurrection. Abraham responds to the rich man's request to go back to the living for just a while by saying that the brothers already have Moses and the prophets. We have them too. As an act of grace, God has spoken through the Scriptures. Those Scriptures can open our eyes to the moral bankruptcy of some rich people and the deep goodness of some poor people. Those Scriptures can feed our faith. Let us open our eyes to the ways God offers us life, faith, and hope. (Chuck Aaron)

Worship Aids

Invocation

Merciful God, as we worship, let us increase in gratitude for all you have given us. Let us increase in care and love for those who do not have enough. Let us seek your word in Moses, the prophets, and the evangelists. We are here because something has gotten our attention. Use that attention to lead us to deeper faith. Amen.

Prayer of Confession

God of compassion, we confess that we turn our eyes from those in need. We care more about how our food tastes than about those who have not tasted food for days. We blame those who have simply encountered bad luck, consoling ourselves that we deserve what we have. Forgive us, O God, and teach us to love those who suffer as you love them. In your mercy, give us caring hearts. Amen.

Words of Assurance

God hears; God cares; God forgives. Thanks be to God.

Benediction

Let us go out into the world and share with those, like the five brothers, who need to hear a word of confrontation and grace. Let us go out to live lives of generosity and charity, so that others will see the love of Christ. (Chuck Aaron)

APRIL 1, 2012

❧❧❧❧❧❧

Palm / Passion Sunday

Palm Readings: Mark 11:1-11; Psalm 118:1-2, 19-29
Passion Readings: Isaiah 50:4-9a; Psalm 31:9-16;
Philippians 2:5-11; Mark 14:1–15:47

As We Will
Philippians 2:5-11

We prize choice in this culture. We want to know what our options are related to just about anything we do. Have you tried to buy tennis shoes lately? Of course even the name "tennis shoe" is no longer an appropriate description. When I grew up that term did not mean literally shoes you would buy specifically to play tennis. "Tennis shoe" was a generalized term that designated a canvas, casual shoe that you wore to play in. When you go to buy such a shoe today you need to specify what specialty you are playing. It is basketball? What kind of surface will it be? What particular brand would you like? Do you need a low top, mid top, or high top? Do you want leather or canvas? What color do you want? On and on the choices go. Oh yes, we have made choice an idol to the point where it is ridiculous.

Paul writes to a young, new church to remind them what is at the heart and soul of their identity. He reminds them of what their attitude should be in response to whatever goes on in the culture. Paul seeks to set them straight regarding their Christology. In so doing he defines the essence of who the church is and who is at the core of the church's witness to faith in the world.

Paul begins by stating that although Christ's nature was God's, Jesus chose to make himself nothing. In verses 7 and 8 Paul boldly proclaims that Jesus Christ humbled himself and was obedient to who God was sending him to be in the world. Another translation of the word used here for *nothing* would be *poor*. Christ made himself poor, choosing to be a servant and a human being. This choice not only comes to define who Jesus is but also who the church confesses as the Lord of life.

What Paul wants this young church to remember is that there really is only one choice that matters in the community of faith. That choice is the Lordship of Jesus Christ. The church not only confesses such truth but it becomes defined by it as well. The fleshing out of this choice leads the church to claim its humanity too. This confession frees the church to be who it is as it humbles itself and takes on the role of servant. Paul wants the church to know that as Christ was obedient, even to death, so must the church become obedient to the will of God and the Lordship of Jesus Christ and what that will mean in its life and witness.

In our time, when choice has become idolized, the church needs to witness to what choice must seek to define and shape all other choices. Without our witness, people become lost in choice for the sake of choosing. Choosing becomes just another excuse for not making a commitment. Paul wants the church to powerfully and definitively proclaim obedience to the only choice there is, the Lordship of Jesus Christ. Jesus chose the will of God in his own life. Christ was obedient to the only choice that matters in life.

Paul also wants the Philippian church to realize that God will respond to such a choice with exaltation and glory. Jesus will forever be defined by his choosing, which elevated him to the highest place. Jesus chose, and God exalts the choice. This truth becomes the cornerstone upon which the church witnesses and proclaims. Today the world must choose, just as Jesus chose, who will ultimately define and shape history.

There is a story told of a wise old man who lived in a mountain village. Anytime the villagers needed advice or help they came to the wise old man and he offered them direction and advice. A young man from the village went away to school and came to pride himself on his knowledge and wisdom. When he returned to the village, he remembered the old man and the way the villagers sought his counsel. He became jealous and angry and devised a plan to prove how foolish the old man really was.

The young man caught a sparrow and held it in his hand. He went to the village square and announced that he planned to go to the old man's home and expose him and his uneducated ways. The whole village followed the young man to the old man's home. When they arrived the young man beat on the door of the old man's house and challenged him to come out and meet him. The old man came out onto the porch.

The young man told everyone that he had a sparrow clutched in his hand and challenged the old man to say if the bird was alive or dead. His plan was that if the old man said the bird was alive he would squeeze the bird till it was dead and then show the village the dead bird. If the old man said the bird was dead he would then open his hand and allow the living bird to fly free.

The two men stood on the porch. The crowd was silent. The young man held up his hand and asked, "Is this bird alive or is this bird in my hand dead?" After a long pause the old man looked at the crowd and then looked directly into the eyes of the young man and responded, "As you will, my son, as you will."

Paul wants a young church to claim its identity in witness and proclamation. He reminds them that just as Jesus chose to be obedient to the will of God and took on the role of a servant so too must each of us decide. As we will. As we will! (Travis Franklin)

Lectionary Commentary

Isaiah 50:4-9a

This text is a part of Second Isaiah and the third of the "servant songs." It is the end of the Babylonian exile, and God is doing something new. Persian King Cyrus will be the means by which God works. The power of the servant song, however, is the new understanding it offers of the painful experience of the exile and the lessons it has to teach the community. Speaking out of the humility that suffering brings, the prophet offers meaning in that suffering and shares that the suffering will be vindicated by God and God's action in history. Trusting God in the midst of suffering gives great meaning and power to our experiences.

Mark 14:1–15:47

Mark's retelling of the Passion narrative focuses on the events that happened to Jesus in an effort to display for us Jesus' complete identification with humanity. Throughout the story Jesus is alone. He continues to be abandoned by those around him and those who say they love him most. Mark wants the reader to experience the events as they happened to Jesus, with all of their cruelty, inhumanity, and horror. This Passion narrative reminds us of the humanity of the Christ and the decision Jesus makes as a human being in the midst of suffering. (Travis Franklin)

Worship Aids

Pastoral Prayer

O God, we gather here today in this sacred time and in this sacred place to give thanks and to celebrate who you are among us in this moment and every moment. Ground us in your love. May the soil of your love permeate us and nurture us that we might be the people you want us to be. Love the world and others in and through who we are and what we do in the name of your love. Forgive us when we love poorly or don't love at all. Empower us by your most loving Holy Spirit to transform the world in the name of your love always! In the name and spirit of a risen Christ we pray. Amen.

Prayer of Confession

We have failed to live our authenticity, dearest Lord. You have made us in your image, to be a genuine expression in creation of your love, and we have chosen our own way and missed the mark of who we might be in you. Forgive us, Lord, and heal us from our brokenness. Free us to be all that you love us to be. In the name of Jesus, the risen Christ, we pray. Amen.

Words of Assurance

The power and presence of the love of God in Christ pardons and delivers us from our sin. Praise be to God and glory to the love God offers that heals us and forgives us for our sins. (Travis Franklin)

Faithfully Disobeying Jesus

Third in a Series of Three on the Teachings of Jesus

Luke 17:11-19

We would feel sorry for this group of lepers if we saw them. They endured miserable lives. Besides the discomfort of the rash or skin disease they carried, they felt the ongoing bitter shame of exclusion. How awful to have to cry out the most embarrassing thing about yourself everywhere you go, just as they had to cry out, "unclean." How awful to have to eat the food your family tosses to you. We have seen people who remind us of them. We have seen the teenagers who have no friends, sitting all alone in the cafeteria. We have seen the homeless shuffling along by themselves, trying to make it through another day. We look away when we see them because perhaps they remind us of the times we have felt rejection. We may find it curious to think about the one leper who stands out in the story, the outcast among the outcasts. It is curious to think that the Samaritan leper, the one the other lepers would never have hung out with under ordinary circumstances, is the person we will come to envy. He is the one who teaches us about our faith.

The members of this sad fraternity of rejects know what is demanded of them. They follow the strict rules spelled out in Leviticus. They come just close enough to Jesus that he can hear them shout, but they stay far enough away that they don't bring any more trouble on themselves. Somehow, despite their isolation, they know about Jesus. They know he represents a desperate hope. Not only can Jesus heal their skin, but he can restore them to some kind of life. He can give them back their families and friends. Wouldn't that be worth crying out to a stranger?

Jesus hears their cry. Jesus heals them in a rather unspectacular way. Jesus tells them to go and show themselves to a priest, the only one who can pronounce them clean. Jesus tells them to act as if they already were clean. Without a word, they do just as Jesus tells them to do. As they go to a priest to hear that they are clean, they actually become clean. Luke does not describe the exact relationship between the freely offered grace of healing and their faith that creates space for the grace and healing. They act in faith and along the way, they experience healing.

Up to this point, the group acts together. They speak the same words; they do the same things. Their solidarity up to this point highlights the actions of the Samaritan. When he realizes that he has experienced true healing, he turns back and falls at Jesus' feet. Jesus praises him, even though he doesn't do what Jesus says to do. His disobedience to Jesus seems to arise out of a spontaneous joy. A feeling of gratitude wells up inside him. He seems not to think out what he does next—turning back, shouting out, and falling at Jesus' feet.

Although he endured disease and cold rejection, we envy this Samaritan leper. How long has it been since we felt so overwhelmed with gratitude and joy that we forgot where we were, who was watching, what we were supposed to do, and just cried out in exuberance? We don't feel the kind of joy we can't keep inside nearly often enough. We wish we felt just like this leper, but such a feeling usually eludes us. Even for the leper himself, we have to wonder how long this feeling lasted. Was he still shouting out and falling over in joy ten years later? Luke shows us the very moment God's grace entered his life. His life had just changed. Even in the rare times when we feel such joy, it usually doesn't last.

Who of us can conjure up joy and gratitude at will? Have you ever tried to talk someone into feeling more grateful? Parents often take on this task, without much success. We know how the conversation goes: "But look at all that you have! Don't you know other people would give any-thing to have what you have?" To which the eye-rolling response comes, "Oh, OK, I'll try to do better." Trying to conjure gratitude in someone else usually produces only guilt or grudging agreement. Joy and gratitude don't show up right on cue.

The leper noticed God's grace and healing in his life and then acted on it. He didn't have to summon the joy, it just poured through him, and then he acted out his worship. We may need to reverse the process. We may have to act in gratitude until gratitude starts flowing in us. We may need to pray our way into gratitude. We may need to sing our way into gratitude. We may need to give our way into gratitude. We may need to love our way into gratitude. Haven't we known times when we absent-mindedly opened the hymnal, only to find that the song fed our spirits? Haven't we known times when giving lifted our hearts?

Maybe we find ourselves out of touch with joy and gratitude this morn-ing. We brought our set of troubles with us today. Something we face this week keeps us up at night. Something is broken in our lives, and we don't know how to fix it. Our last clear experience of God's grace seems like a long time ago. Something that has happened to us just sucks the joy right out of us. God offers us grace and healing. God offers us strength and comfort. Let us act in praise and gratitude. We may not feel the joy come right in an instant as the Samaritan leper did. The joy may seep into us drop by drop.

If we sing when we don't feel like singing, give when we don't feel like giving, praise when we don't feel like praising, God's grace will come into our lives. We had better watch it, though. The joy might overwhelm us, so that we act like crazy fools. But wouldn't that be worth it? (Chuck Aaron)

Worship Aids

Invocation

Next week is Easter, O God. We gather as the community that you have called to experience joy. Even right before Easter, we may not feel joy.

We cannot always feel what the season suggests we feel. Our gratitude may be buried deep within us. As we worship, we ask that in your mercy you enable us to connect with the joy and gratitude you offer us as gifts. Amen.

Prayer of Confession

As we begin Holy Week, we confess that we don't act holy, O God. We neglect the seasons of the year, such as Lent, which could feed our spirits. We fail to see how and why repentance during this time is so important. We place our hope in things other than resurrection. Forgive us, O God. Clear away the grief, weakness, and rebellion that keep us from participating in the seasons of the church year. Enable us to reflect on our shortcomings, so that we know they will begin to die this week. Cultivate in us the joy that this season should produce in us. Amen.

Words of Assurance

God hears our cries. God loves and forgives. God empowers us to respond in joy. Thanks be to God.

Benediction

Let us go out as a holy people into a world that mocks holiness. Let us be a healing, purifying force in a world that wallows in greed, hate, and violence. (Chuck Aaron)

APRIL 5, 2012

❧❧❧❧

Maundy Thursday

Readings: Exodus 12:1-4, (5-10), 11-14; Psalm 116:1-2, 12-19;
1 Corinthians 11:23-26; John 13:1-7, 31b-35

A Night of Glory
John 13:1-7, 31b-35

Say the word *glory* aloud. Let it roll across the tongue and out of your
mouth. The very word *glory* contains a sense of triumph and grandeur. On
August 16th in 1976, I walked out the center aisle of the Chapel of
Perkins School of Theology at S.M.U. Holding my arm was my wife.
Looking back over three decades plus it is still a moment I glory in.

Or take another incident in American life and culture. On the night
of November 4, 2008, President-elect Barack Obama walked out to greet
the gathered crowd at Grant Park in Chicago, Illinois. It was a night of
triumph and glory for his supporters. It was night of glory in a larger sense
because the election of the first African American to the office of the
presidency represented the crashing of a racial barrier. The word *glory* in
description of that event evokes the emotions of joy and exultant triumph.

No doubt you can come up with your own experiences of glory. It may
be associated with a purely personal event such as a wedding. It may
evoke a sports triumph or great social victory. Images for glory abound but
almost all involve some deep sense of exultant, joyous triumph. As a die-
hard Chicago Cubs fan (any team can have a bad century), I still hear the
legendary announcer Harry Cary shouting, "Cubs win! Cubs win!"

Contrast those emotions with the scene reported in the thirteenth
chapter of the Gospel of John. "When he had gone out, Jesus said, 'Now
the Son of Man has been glorified, and God has been glorified in him. If
God has been glorified in him, God will also glorify him in himself and
will glorify him at once' (vv. 31-32)." Pause. Reflect. Pray. Soak in the

jarring contrast between our experiences of glory and God's glory as Jesus speaks about it. Understand that this is a night of glory, true glory, God's glory.

Typical understandings of this passage land quickly on the story of Jesus washing the feet of his disciples. It is an appealing, evocative demonstration of the depth of Christ's love. A common sermon appeal urges us to wash the feet of others, mimicking Jesus in our actions. It fits nicely with the close of the passage containing the admonition of verse 35: "By this everyone will know that you are my disciples, if you have love for one another." What is missing is the full impact of the teaching from Jesus.

The assigned text moves from verse 7, "You do not know now what I am doing, but later you will understand," to the verses of glory and glorification. In this night, this sacred meal decisively changed from a Passover supper into the Lord's Supper. Through this action we are called to embrace the glory of Christ. Biblically, glory denotes worship. To glorify someone is to worship them! The supper and the service (footwashing) are declarations of Jesus as the incarnate God. Jesus is the glory of God—God present and in action to us and for us. The act of footwashing, far from being merely an example of dedicated service that we are to emulate, reveals how God is present with us and for us. God is present as a servant among us. Glory and glorification are the revealed presence of God.

How then do we twenty-first-century people know and experience God? We encounter God in embracing God's glory. The sacrament begun this night so long ago invites us again to the table to encounter Christ. Acts of love poured out in sacrificial service for others (even and especially for those who desert us or betray us) lead us to an encounter with the gloried (revealed presence) of God in Christ.

The understanding of this text must do far more than just call us into sacrificial service for others. Faithfulness in proclamation requires an invocation of who Jesus really is. Jesus as the Christ is the revealed presence (the glory) of God. Augustine writes: "But the glorifying of the Son of man is the glorifying of God in him" (Joel C. Elowsky, ed., *Ancient Christian Commentary on Scripture: New Testament IVb: John 11–21* [Downers Grove, Ill.: InterVarsity Press Academic, 2007], 110).

Once in Sunday school a little boy was determinedly drawing a picture on a piece of paper. The teacher asked him, "What are you drawing?" Confidently he replied, "A picture of God." Kindly, with laughter in her voice, the patient teacher responded, "Oh, nobody knows what God looks like." Even more confidently the young boy retorts, "They will when I'm done."

On this night of glory we learn again what God looks like; we encounter God in the flesh at the table with Jesus. Let the faithful revel in the glory of God on this night of glory. Let us not stop at the foot-washing or rush too quickly ahead to the great verse 35. We invite our congregation to glorify God in Christ through our worship.

Then, and only then, may we properly move to the second element of the lesson. In encountering God, we come to understand the nature of God. In the example of Christ we learn again that it is God's nature to sacrificially love. "So we have known and believe the love that God has for us. God is love, and those who abide in love abide in God, and God abides in them" (1 John 4:16).

Do not be afraid to live in silence and awe in our worship and our lesson. The presence of God should bring us, like those of old, to stillness in adoration and praise. There will be time for sacrificial service later. The sacrificial love of Christ, the giving of himself, and the washing of their feet; all these may and should inspire us to action. The source of such action springs first from a recognition of God's glory, God's very presence in Christ sitting at the table with us and for us. Let this be a night of glory. (Mike Lowry)

Lectionary Commentary
Exodus 12:1-4, (5-10), 11-14

The Passover story of Exodus 12 is the story of God's redemption of God's people. The lamb was sacrificed for the redemption and rescue of the people. Ritually, the blood of the lamb marks one as a chosen child of God's. It is also the crucial background of Christian teaching about Jesus as the Lamb of God. In the sacrifice of the lamb, the sins of the people are paid. It is blood atonement; only blood will do as payment for sins and liberation from Pharaoh. Old Testament scholar Brevard Childs remarked in a speech: "Israel remains a people who have been redeemed, but who still awaits its redemption."

The early Christian writers constantly read this passage as an allusion to Christ. He is the Lamb of God to which Exodus refers. The preacher must both be sensitive to the original Passover context as offered in the Hebrew Bible and grasp the way in which the New Testament sees Jesus as a fulfillment of this passage.

April 5, 2012

1 Corinthians 11:23-26

The Apostle Paul opens this passage by emphasizing that he is passing on a core incident and conviction that the early Christian movement embraced. The institution of the Lord's Supper is not a casual accident that can be lightly dismissed; it is central to the Jesus tradition. This passage at once points us back to the Exodus Passover story and leads us forward to its completion in Jesus offering himself as body and blood at the table that night.

The faithful should take care not to jump quickly to the Lord's Supper as merely a memorial meal. The text directs us that it is an institution of the real and continuing presence of Jesus in our midst. We are commanded to do this until he comes again. (Mike Lowry)

Worship Aids

Call to Worship (Psalm 62:5-8)
For God alone my soul waits in silence,
for my hope is from him.
He alone is my rock and my salvation, my fortress;
I shall not be shaken. On God rests my deliverance and my honor; my mighty rock, my refuge is in God.
Trust in him at all times, O people; pour out your heart before him.
God is a refuge for us.

Prayer of Confession
Great and gracious God, we come to you in this night of our Lord's Last Supper mindful that we too sit at the table with Jesus. We are conscious of the times we let you down and acted out. We are aware that our hands have been with the hand of the betrayer leaning on the table and yet not following your way. Reluctantly we must acknowledge the squabbling for greatness with our own human family that you encountered at the first Communion table. Grudgingly we confess a temptation to be served over a desire to serve. Forgive us for such failures and renew in us this night a desire to follow in your footsteps of sacrificially loving others. Placing our lives at your mercy we pray. Amen.

Words of Assurance
As those who gathered at that first table for Holy Communion in a borrowed upper room receive now the love and mercy of the Lord Jesus

Christ: "Peace I leave with you; my peace I give to you. I do not give to you as the world gives. Do not let your hearts be troubled, and do not let them be afraid" (John 14:27). In the name of God you are forgiven. In the name of God you are forgiven. Amen and amen! (Mike Lowry)

With Whom Do You Celebrate?

First in a Series of Three on From Darkness to Light

Job 1:1-5

It is Maundy Thursday, and you would think I would choose anything but the epic poem about Job. Bear with me because in addition to tonight's sermon, we will follow the plight of Job on Good Friday and again on Easter Sunday.

What is the correlation between the passion and resurrection stories about Jesus and this Old Testament character? In this introductory passage from Job, we get a picture of what a great person is like, then and now.

People tend to focus on attributes such as knowledge, reputation, education, wealth, athleticism, and a handsome or pretty appearance. From what we read about Job, he was apparently blessed with some of these characteristics. It could even be argued that he had all of them. If truth be told, Job possessed many traits that most of us admire and desire.

In conventional thinking, when a person has the right car, right house, right reputation, right investments, right spouse and children, he or she makes a significant impression. What was it that Job had? He had seven sons and three daughters, and in his fields were more sheep, camels, oxen, and female donkeys than is imaginable even in our time. His home and holdings had more servants than we would dream anyone could need. In addition to that, Job was the greatest of all the individuals of the east. We measure people by dollars today, but in Job's day it was based on the number of animals and people under one's control.

The scriptural depictions of Jesus present a man without possessions, no young brides and multiple children, and as far as we can tell, the carpenter's son became the carpenter. We know Jesus studied in the temple with people who would ultimately turn against him. He wandered throughout the land seeking shelter among friends and among people the religious leaders of the time considered repugnant. We do know that Jesus possessed a direct relationship with God and that earthly riches were not part of his life. We only know for sure that he owned a desire to love and care for all people regardless of their ethnicity, gender, or stage in life.

The New Testament story that leads to the upper room meal with the disciples came just four days after a triumphant entry into Jerusalem. We read that on the day we call Palm Sunday, Jesus had to borrow a donkey, and having no servants, he sent his students to bring it to him.

In each of these stories, the characters receive the equivalent of a ticker-tape parade, recognition for their accomplishments, positive relationships with others, and great public press. After the parade and recognition has ended, both are about to meet up with adversaries most people would not consider possible for either.

The poem about Job begins by introducing the characteristics of Job that one cannot easily see: "blameless and upright, one who feared God and turned away from evil" (v. 1). A person's assessment of character is often slightly biased. But in this case we should know that this was exactly what God said of Job (see 1:8; 2:3).

Who could argue the point that Jesus was also blameless, full of integrity, and wholeheartedly pure? Like Job, he was upright, righteous, and lived according to a strong moral code. Certainly the written evidence indicates that he acknowledged God's ways and lived according to them. The stories about his constant outreach to the poor, sick, and undesirable are strong evidence of his resistance to the temptation to serve self first. The footwashing and sharing of the bread and wine on this day support the moral and ethical standards of Jesus.

The question I have to ask myself is, am I living up to the standards set by these two righteous men? Can I take the elements we will eat and drink tonight and know that I deserve them by my service and actions, and at the same time receive them unearned through the sacrifice of Jesus?

Very few people could imitate Job in his wealth, possessions, or even family size, but we all can strive to be like him in heart. The rich and poor have equal access to a godly character. Job didn't have any advantage in this area. He faced a tough world even as we do.

Although Job's immense wealth was impressive, we know that these possessions did not make him special. Job's inner qualities distinguished him despite his great wealth. With such position, he could have chosen to do many wrong things as we will learn that his friends believed. He could have gone beyond the law and managed to get away with it. Yet Job constrained his behavior because of his love of the Lord.

Job sets a great example for us as he breaks through the cheap materialistic view of the world and dares to live right in God's presence. His possessions do not make him great; his character and godly commitments shape his decisions. Job does not strive to be wealthy but to be acceptable before God and live rightly before people. As we partake of this Lord's Supper may we find strength in the lessons from Job, and may we make an impact on the world in which we live. Amen. (Ted McIlvain)

Worship Aids

Call to Worship

Darkness began on this day before Jesus died. In the dimming light Jesus knelt before his disciples to wash their feet in absolute humility and servanthood. From the example of the great Teacher and Son of God we gather in humility and servanthood tonight. Let us find comfort in the breaking of the bread and pouring of the wine so that the Lord's example will remain forever in our minds. May we remember that the greatest among us are called to be servants in the sight of God.

Prayer of Confession

We confess, dear God, that we have allowed the coming darkness to keep us from remaining vigilant in our service to your creation. We have failed to see the poor and neglected in the light of the way your Son Jesus instructed us to see. Save us from these sins of selfishness and disobedience and renew our commitment of service to you and the creatures of your doing. Let this night refresh our minds with the teachings of Jesus Christ in whose name we pray. Amen.

Words of Assurance

We will arise from the table refreshed and renewed, confident in the character and grace of Jesus the Christ who serves and saves. Amen.

Benediction

Be a shining example of the love of God to all. Be the glimmer of hope as we enter this time of darkness. Be awakened by the call to serve. Be blessed in the name of the Lord, Jesus Christ. Go in peace and be in service. Amen. (Ted McIlvain)

APRIL 6, 2012

❧❧❧❧

Good Friday

Readings: Isaiah 52:13–53:12; Psalm 22; Hebrews 10:16-25;
John 18:1–19:42

The Cross of Life

Hebrews 10:16-25

For a couple of years my wife and I have attended Good Friday services at St. John the Evangelist Monastery (an Episcopal monastery in Cambridge, Massachusetts). The quiet, contemplative service centers on an adoration of the cross. At the appropriate time, following the monks' lead, participants are invited to approach the cross solemnly kneeling and bowing to the ground three times as they move closer to the cross. The third station of adoration is at the very foot of the cross where participants either kiss or touch the cross in some manner.

There is something deeply moving about this strange and ancient service. Good Friday invites us to come to the cross. It beckons us to stand or kneel in awe before the reality of this night. The words of John Bowring's great hymn portray the essence: "In the cross of Christ I glory, towering o'er the wrecks of time" ("In the Cross of Christ I Glory," *The United Methodist Hymnal* [Nashville: The United Methodist Publishing House, 1989], 295).

The truth we know well. The cross was a cruel form of the death penalty used by the Roman Empire as deterrent. Today's equivalent is the electric chair or the syringe for a lethal injection. Yet for many, the cross is simply a nice piece of jewelry; a dangling bauble to hang on a chain. This night invites us back to the strange world of the first Holy Week and thrusts us forward into our bruised and bleeding modern world. On this night the Roman sign of cruel death is transformed into a cross of life for today.

Consider well how the teaching from Hebrews invites us to participate in the transformation from a crucifixion of cruelty to a cross of life. It begins with a quotation of Jeremiah 31:33. God acts to indelibly write the law on our hearts. Such action by God is stunning movement beyond pitiful human attempts to sacrifice, cleanse, or fix the problem of our brokenness. God's law is not a rule to keep from a dusty book but a living relational covenant of love. The additional quotation of Jeremiah 33:34 makes explicit the mercy we receive. "I will remember their sins and their lawless deeds no more." Metaphorically we approach the cross out of God's gracious action of undeserved mercy or not at all.

Many a modern reader cringes at images of blood sacrifice. We like our world cleaned up and sanitized. Yet incontestably the employment of the Old Testament image of Jesus as a "blood sacrifice" is anchored in the cross. To a world that knows bombs and IEDs, violence and heartache, a sanitized Jesus will not do. By the new and living way that he opened for us through the curtain (that is, through his flesh), we come to a cross of life. Jesus' physical death on the cross is a metaphorical tearing in two of the temple curtain (see Matthew 27:51). Previously the curtain kept the common believer separated from God. Now, on this day, we dare to call good because of our great priest Jesus, the sacrifice has been made that opens our way to God. We are reconciled to God through the cross of life. Eugene Peterson's paraphrased interpretation catches the essence: "So, friend, we can now—without hesitation—walk right up to God, into 'the Holy Place.' Jesus has cleared the way by the blood of his sacrifice, acting as our priest before God" (Hebrews 10:19-20, *THE MESSAGE*).

From this towering conviction we claim a cross of life amidst death's rubble. From here the rest of the passage unfolds as a call to faithfulness and perseverance. The faithful need to take care not to move the attention from the cross. Because we have a cross of life and not a sign of death we are ushered to (1) a reception of mercy, (2) a confession of hope, and (3) a plan of action.

The reception of mercy is explicit in the verses that follow. We can approach God not through vain cover-up but with "full assurance." Many, both outside and inside the community of faith, are convinced that mercy applies to everyone but them. Faithful proclamation invites us to remember our most unfaithful moment since last Good Friday and lay it on the altar of God with assurance of God's great mercy. The punishment we deserve is laid aside by God in and through Christ.

We think of confession as a confession of sin. The amazing truth of this night is that we are invited to confess our hope. "Let us hold fast to the confession of our hope without wavering, for he who has promised is faithful" (v. 23). Biblical hope transcends fleeting optimism. It is anchored not in our faithfulness but God's. The Divine invites the congregation to reflect on their deepest, most heartfelt hopes, and place than in the hands of God.

The plan of action comes last. It is important in our culture with the stress on human striving and accomplishment to emphasize this. The sacrifice (atonement) is Christ. The mercy is the Lord's. The hope is anchored in God. Our action comes as a natural outgrowth of the sacrifice, mercy, and hope. It is simple and straightforward. "Let us consider how to provoke one another to love and good deeds" (v. 24).

Such love arises from the worship of God and the encouragement of meeting together. Thus the plan of action properly closes with a common sense bit of advice that we are to not neglect in meeting together "but encouraging one another, and all the more as you see the Day approaching" (v. 25).

The text folds out neatly for us on this night of nights. It bids us first come and behold the true wonder of the cross. All the rest flows from that position of adoration, grace, and mercy. It comes from God's action in Christ alone. Faithful proclamation shines the spotlight on the cross. Through Christ's sacrificial, atoning love, death is transformed into life. The three acts of (1) a reception of mercy, (2) a confession of hope, and (3) a plan of action might best be used as a time of silent reflection and prayer in the body of the sermon itself. We are called to the cross of life on this night. (Mike Lowry)

Lectionary Commentary

Isaiah 52:13–53:12

This Isaiah passage is arguably the greatest of the so called "servant songs" of Isaiah. The passage opens with the triumph; "he shall be exalted and lifted up" (52:13). The victory will be not just over Israel but over the nations. Yet the rejection of the servant is real. In a deep sense this passage must be embraced as written to a nation in exile. The despair of the present is countered with the eventual triumph of God. It is further distinctive that the servant suffers instead of others. "Surely, he has borne our infirmities and carried our diseases" (53:4). Much argument can be expended on whether the servant is a person or representative of the nation as a whole. In the original context of Isaiah, the case is best made as a representative of the nation.

The earliest Christian theologians looked back on this passage and made the explicit connection to Christ. It is not so much a fulfillment of prophecy as a living out of God's eventual triumph that takes place in and through the cross. The careful reader will also note the deep element of confession in this passage. "All we like sheep have gone astray."

John 18:1–19:42

There is so much contained in these powerful chapters of passion that a simple dramatic reading invites the listener to step back into the text. The text of Jesus' arrest, trial, and crucifixion fits carefully in the context of the original Passover celebration narrative. The dialogue between power and passion is something we know full well. John is careful to show that the various prophecies are fulfilled. Nothing in the text will let us escape the real horror that happened. Nothing in the text will allow us to deny the reality of death. Don't jump ahead to Easter but dwell on the sacrifice. Reflect carefully on the public nature of crucifixion and the heartrending reality for the original disciples. Live in Good Friday spiritually, emotionally, and intellectually. Ours is an Easter faith, but Easter makes sense only in light of Good Friday. (Mike Lowry)

Worship Aids

Call to Worship (Psalm 116:5-9)

Gracious is the Lord, and righteous;
Our god is merciful.
The Lord protects the simple;
When I was brought low, he saved me.
Return, O my soul, to your rest,
For the lord has dealt bountifully with you.
For you have delivered my soul from death,
My eyes from tears, my feet from stumbling.
I walk before the Lord
In the land of the living.

Prayer of Confession

We come before you, Lord, in this night of nights not boasting of our goodness but awed by your graciousness. We confess that too often we have ignored your sacrifice of love for us. We acknowledge that we have brushed past the cross as if it did not happen. We have sanitized your love and ignored your actions. We are impoverished by our casual dismissal of the truth of this night. Bring us now in this worship, we pray, to pause before the greatness of your love and the depth of your grace. Forgive our wandering ways and arrogant pride. Humble us by your mercy and let the symbol of death become again for us a cross leading to life now and forever. This we pray in the name of the Lord God who gave himself for us, Father, Son, and Holy Spirit, Amen.

Words of Assurance

On this night of nights hear the astounding good news: "For while we were still weak, at the right time Christ died for the ungodly. Indeed, rarely will anyone die for a righteous person—though perhaps for a good person someone might actually dare to die. But God proves his love for us in that while we still were sinners Christ died for us" (Romans 5:6-8). Live in the sure and certain truth that through our Lord Jesus Christ you have been reconciled to God. Amen. (Mike Lowry)

Who Do You Blame?

Second in a Series of Three on From Darkness to Light

Job 1:13-22; 2:1-8

Reading this epic poem, the book of Job, we get the impression that the curtain of heaven is pulled aside to give us special insights to the daily work of God. It is as if we traveled some yellow brick road to heaven to communicate with Almighty God. This is not like the road that led to the Wizard of Oz, where we meet trickery and deception when the great curtain is opened by accident. In Job, we meet God, who opens the curtain for us to see. The scenes in the opening passages from Job reveal God's power and absolute authority. On this Good Friday we are standing in the presence of God to remember the treachery and angry reactions of people. We are called to remember how the masses of people struck out at the goodness we learned about last night on Maundy Thursday. We can hear the cheers of Palm Sunday change to angry cries of "Crucify him!"

It is wise for us to consider how we face adversity in our lives. It is probably even more important for us to consider how we deal with our relationship with God. And more important yet is assuring that we understand the impact of Jesus in that relationship. I have to believe that the recording of the events in heaven were written for you and me. These writings teach us to slow down so that we can reflect on who we are and why we are here.

God allows two tests for Job, and the testing is thorough. Generally we think of tests as proving times for what we have learned and how we apply that knowledge. The tests we read about in Job reveal what is in his heart. First, Job loses all his wealth and his children. Unimaginable sorrow! In the second test, Job loses his health in one quick turn of events. Reading these passages makes me appreciate that the percentage of my retirement savings that was lost in the recession was less than all of it, and the stubbed toe that I fussed about this morning is really trivial.

People try to blame God for poor health, loss of wealth, accidents, or the death of loved ones. Through Job's two great trials we learn some important truths that I believe were also taught in the trials and crucifixion of Jesus. Job and Jesus do not blame God for the pain and suffering they endure. Job wishes never to be born. Jesus' plea to let the cup pass from him is a human cry to live without trials and convictions. These are desired preferences, but unrealistic in the scheme of creation.

The author of Job focuses on the theme of bad things happening to good people. It is Job's friends who suggest that his suffering has to do with wickedness. The story reveals that God is aware of all the troubles that creatures endure. The text assures us that troubles are dispensed only as far as God judges as right and good. Based on this revelation, we sense that God is ultimately in control, not the environment and not our enemies. God's people are especially protected by the power of God.

Instead of trying to justify why we should not have pain or loss, let us be aware that God allows hardships to come our way. We have knowledge, reason, and processes for responding to suffering. With those gifts and God's grace, we can endure. "No testing has overtaken you that is not common to everyone. God is faithful, and he will not let you be tested beyond your strength, but with the testing he will also provide the way out so that you may be able to endure it" (1 Corinthians 10:13). There are no exceptions to this for God's people. How we deal with the plight of Job may say something crucial about the way we resolve our own troubled hearts.

Difficult circumstances reveal the way we love and trust the Lord. In stressful times, we can enter a process of healing through which we can understand our own hearts, dislike the harmful things we do, search for God's abundant mercy, and walk in ways we learn in the life and teachings of Jesus. Grace is abundant in times of trial.

Most of us cannot see our own sins. We simply cannot see the idols we worship, and we do not want to see them. Similar to the Pharisee who prayerfully reminded God of all the laws of Moses that he attended to weekly, the average religious person is too full of pride to think that there is any impurity in his or her heart.

Job happened to be wealthy. Take all the riches away, and he still is the same contented person. He said, " 'Naked I came from my mother's womb, and naked shall I return there; the LORD gave, and the LORD has taken away; blessed be the name of the LORD' In all this Job did not sin or charge God with wrong-doing" (Job 1:21-22).

Through all of his sufferings, Jesus never charged God with wrongdoing. Let us vow today that in our own sufferings, we will not blame God. (Ted McIlvain)

Worship Aids

Call to Worship

The suffering of Job, the suffering of Jesus, and the suffering we each face continue even after this day of passion and agony. We return to the day of Jesus' trial, conviction, punishment, and death to understand the nature of his suffering and gain perspective on our own. Let that understanding remove us from the darkness of pain, and let it advance us to peace and comfort in the hands of God.

Words of Assurance

The birth, life, teachings, conviction, crucifixion, and resurrection of the Son of God and Son of Man give new light and new hope. On this day when darkness descended on the earth for those few hours, we receive a light to share with all humanity. Carry the light as we walk in humility and service as Jesus taught us, and let it shine through our countenance and caring spirit. Let it be known that no greater light can we share than to give love, encouragement, and hope to all we meet and greet in Jesus' name.

Benediction

Go in peace knowing that out of the darkness a light shines. Be strengthened by its illumination in spirit and in truth. Go to comfort others displaying a new hope for brighter times. In the name of the Father, the Son, and the Holy Spirit. Amen. (Ted McIlvain)

APRIL 8, 2012

❧❧❧❧

Easter

Readings: Isaiah 25:6-9; Psalm 118:1-2, 14-24; Acts 10:34-43; John 20:1-18

Who Are We Looking For?
John 20:1-18

That first Easter experience is somewhat lackluster, especially in the lives of those first responders. The story involves three persons who were followers of Jesus. Mary Magdalene, Peter, and the beloved disciple are the first to the tomb that morning. John doesn't tell us why Mary comes. Maybe she is there to grieve. Maybe she comes to remember and give thanks for the life of this savior who had changed her life forever. Maybe Mary comes because she needs some time alone to think and to sort out what the past few days' events mean to her. John doesn't tell us.

As Mary arrives she sees that the stone is rolled back from the entrance of the tomb. Immediately she leaves without further investigation. Mary tells Peter and the beloved disciple. Once they know they too run to the tomb, with the beloved disciple getting there first. Peter looks in and sees the place where Jesus had been, and nothing is there. The beloved disciple looks at the same scene, and the Scripture tells us he believes. Then, they go home.

Mary now encouraged by the boldness of the other two wants to take a look for herself. She too sees the place, only now there are two angels, one sitting at the foot of where Jesus had been and the other at the head. "Who are you looking for?" asks one of the angels. Mary begs him to tell her where they have taken Jesus' body. As she turns around she sees Jesus but does not recognize him. She supposes he is the gardener and asks him if he knows where they have taken the body. If he will but tell her she will go and get the body. Jesus then calls her by name, and immediately she recognizes him. Jesus then instructs her not to touch him and to go and tell his followers, which she does.

What a strange and mysterious story. The greatest event in human history is dramatically unfolding, and the first three eye-witnesses have very strange and mixed responses at best. Mary reduces it to grave robbing, the beloved disciple sees and believes, Peter sees and nothing. After witnessing the empty tomb, Peter and John just go home. Where is all the hype, the celebration, the reality of the fact that what Jesus predicted happened—no party, no ticker tape parade, no news coverage, nothing. Isn't this just like God? It seems God has God's way of working in human history. This story sounds very familiar. Just several years earlier in the evening, the Son of God was born into the world in a stable. A few folks showed up but, in light of the magnitude of the event, not much response from the world really. Again God does what God does in the time and way God deems necessary.

Maybe the message in this Easter season is for us to allow God to be who God is, to do what God does, and in the time God deems necessary in our lives. Maybe that is the real power of this story. God acting in history to change the shape and movement of the world, and people just responding in such different ways trying to grasp all that God is doing. The older I get the more comfortable I become with allowing God to be God. I say now—more than I ever would admit when I was younger— that I just don't know. I am coming to realize that maybe knowing isn't what this faith business is all about in the first place.

Maybe what this is really about is what God is doing and the power of my just trusting it and giving it the freedom to do what it needs to do in my life and to lead where it needs to lead.

My family and I went white water rafting a few years ago in the Taos Box in New Mexico. Before we climbed in the boat, the guide gave us some instructions about what to do if we found ourselves in the water. He told us to keep our feet up, trust the buoyancy of the life vest, and to enjoy the ride. The movement of God in the world seems to be like that. God is moving and working at God's pace, in God's time, and in God's direction. Maybe our response needs to be to keep our heads up, trust what God is doing, and just enjoy the ride!

John saw and believed. Peter looked in and nothing. Mary recognized Jesus only after he spoke her name. God loves no matter what our response is. That is the good news of this story. God brings resurrection because of who God is. The reality of the empty tomb reminds us God is at work in the world doing what only God can do. In all humility, without much fanfare, and certainly not dependent on the response of people,

God goes about God's business; our lives and the life of the world will never be the same again.

Mary came looking for the Jesus who had died. Peter and John came looking in response to news of a possible grave robbing of Jesus' body. Why have we, you and I, come today? As we enter this sacred space, who is it we came looking for? (Travis Franklin)

Lectionary Commentary

Isaiah 25:6-9

This passage from Isaiah appears in the collection of Scripture known as the Isaiah Apocalypse (Isaiah 24–27). These chapters express the confident perspective that, beyond a day of judgment, God's enduring reign will be established. The form of the passage is an announcement of salvation with strong eschatological themes. The imagery is that of a banquet where one day all people will come together to a holy place for Communion with one another and with God. The text has Easter implications as it announces a new age of joy and peace that will extend to all people.

Acts 10:34-43

This is Peter's sermon immediately following the story of Peter's vision of clean and unclean food and his encounter with Cornelius, the Gentile centurion. It is an important moment in the development of Peter's theology, its powerful effect evident in Peter's words. He now proclaims that God's grace does not discriminate between nations (Jew vs. Gentile). After this, Peter and the early church join Paul in boldly opening the door to the Gentile community and accepting them into the body of believers. The sermon climaxes in the powerful proclamation of Christ's death and resurrection, naming Jesus as the eschatological Lord who rules over the hearts of all humankind.

Worship Aids

Pastoral Prayer

We gather here today, O God, in awe of your love and its work and movement in the life of the world. We give thanks and celebrate the resurrection of our Lord and all that it means for our living and our dying. Forgive us for our lack of vision and trust. Like those first witnesses of the

Resurrection, move us beyond our doubts, our fears, and our hesitation at believing the reality of your work in our lives and in our world. Empower us by the presence of your Holy Spirit, and help us to follow it as it seeks to lead us in the brokenness of the world. Equip us to be your hands, your feet, and your heart in responding to the woundedness of the world. In the name of the risen Christ we pray. Amen.

Prayer of Confession

Listen to our humble confession this day, O Lord. Accept our contrition as we confess to you our struggle to be the people you want us to be, to do the acts of compassion you call us to do. Forgive us, we pray, and restore us to wholeness and rightness of heart and soul so that we might serve you all the days of our lives. In the name of the Christ we pray. Amen.

Words of Assurance

The saying is true and worthy of our acceptance: Jesus came into the world to redeem sinners. We are redeemed and pardoned today. God's love and forgiveness cleanses us. God's amazing grace claims us! (Travis Franklin)

Who Do You Trust?

Third in a Series of Three on From Darkness to Light

Job 42:10-17

On Thursday evening, we began this series on Holy Week lessons from the book of Job. On this Easter Sunday morning, I want to talk about who we trust in difficult times. Job provides an interesting perspective on the way we deal with God in times of peril. Remaining loyal and dedicated helps strengthen our determination to overcome, even when our friends and family may question our sanity for continuing.

Many of us have not learned how to trust God in such circumstances, to trust that God is always present to help and bring us through. And so, we may try one of three approaches.

First, we may choose to isolate ourselves from the issue, but avoiding a problem will never make it go away. Over time it may feel like less of a problem, especially if it is a problem of relationship. Tempers may calm and the cause may be forgotten, but the issue still exists and will eventually flare up again. Wealth and health concerns are more persistent and generally cannot be avoided for long. Calls from collectors may be a constant reminder. Nagging pain or chronic coughing reminds us of an untended health issue. Avoidance in these cases only leads to more complications.

Jesus went to Jerusalem to engage the issues when other alternatives were available to him. Some of his disciples suggested other courses of action, but Jesus would not avoid the adversaries who were already questioning his authority and actions.

A second option that many people choose is to accept the problem as inevitable. Such resignation in relationships may be stated as, "Oh that is just the way he or she is." We come to believe that no amount of effort or new approach will bring about change, and we resign ourselves to living with unhappiness. The belief becomes more engrained, and change will not occur. Wealth and health problems are avoided in much the same way. I have heard people say, "My family was poor, and I am destined to be the same." Perhaps you have heard someone say, "I have always been a sickly person." Again, once stated, the belief becomes engrained, making change improbable.

I am intrigued by the fact that Jesus never said anything about his adversaries that would lead us to believe he accepted their behavior as inevitable. He simply persisted in living his life with integrity and offering new choices for living to everyone he encountered.

The third approach is to take some assertive action. When problems are relationship driven, one or the other has to take the first step toward reconciliation. We seem to want to wait for the other person to say "I'm sorry," but it is important for us to take the first step and start the dialogue. Some of you are saying, "You don't understand pastor, I have gone to the person I don't like, and it didn't work." My answer is to try again. Trusting God involves more than waiting for answers. It means we take an active role in finding resolution to problems.

In wealth and health situations, there are multiple avenues to help overcome problems. Financial planning courses are available from a variety of good sources. Assertive action means enrolling, adopting the processes, and following through. Beginning preventative health exams and changing eating and exercise habits is the best assertive approach toward living a healthy life.

On this Easter Sunday, we are reminded that Jesus took action. He did not wait for others to come to him but rode triumphantly into Jerusalem on Palm Sunday. He faced those who were in conflict with him and treated them with respect and kindness. On Friday he faced the earthly consequences of his actions, suffered, and died a horrible death. But Jesus' action on our behalf was not finished. On Easter Sunday he rose again and lives still.

Job's action in the face of his enormous losses was not physical, but he trusted, he hung onto hope during the agonizing times and left us with an image of the value in trusting God.

The lesson from Job is that he did not get so preoccupied with the severe testing that he lost sight of God. Some religious people don't believe God allows troubles to come to people. Others just insulate themselves from the one who specializes in caring for them in such situations. Some harbor bitterness in their hearts, upset that their "toys" have been taken away.

These narrow perspectives keep people from living in the light of eternity's hope. On this day, it is through God's grace that we can exit the tunnels of pain and poor financial conditions. On this day, it is through God's grace that we can look out and see if the storm is over and release some of the anger inside. On this day, it is through God's grace that we can begin again to believe in the goodness of God and God's creation. Only after Job forgave his friends and prayed for them did he receive the blessings that God reserved for him.

On this day, it is through the resurrection of Jesus Christ that we must resolve to walk by faith. Trials are those times when what we see does not seem to match up with what is true. On this day, it is through the resurrection of Jesus Christ that we confirm our faith and walk confidently out of the darkness and into the light. Amen. (Ted McIlvain)

Worship Aids

Call to Worship

Two women walked in sadness to the tomb
     where the body of Jesus had been laid.
Lord, we seek you on this day.
The man in the tomb said, "He is not here; for he has been raised."
He is alive?
Yes, the Lord is no longer in the tomb, for he has been raised.
Christ the Lord is risen today!
Hallelujah!
All: Hallelujah, Christ the Lord is alive today!

Prayer

God of the empty tomb, we worship you for the great mystery of this holy day. We celebrate the resurrected Jesus, and we celebrate that you have raised us from the problems of life and given us joy and peace and hope. We give you thanks for the new life and the new light that we sense today while in your presence. May our faith in you resound throughout your creation, and may the light of the Resurrected Savior be visible in us as we venture out of this place of worship. Grant a world of peace and forgiveness through our prayers and example to other people. Hear this prayer in the name of the resurrected Lord. Amen.

Benediction

Christ the Lord is risen today. Take this as a sign of personal victory and go forth lifted up, renewed, and bold. God's love has conquered all pain and sorrow and set us free. Let that sense of freedom be the light for all to see in you. Amen. (Ted McIlvain)

APRIL 15, 2012

❧❧❧❧

Second Sunday of Easter

Readings: Acts 4:32-35; Psalm 133; 1 John 1:1–2:2; John 20:19-31

A New Kind of Caring

Acts 4:32-35

A man saw his children on the front porch and asked what they were doing. "We're playing church," they answered. The father said, "It doesn't look like it." The children replied, "You came in at the end. We've already worshiped. Now we're out on the steps smoking." Many of us remember this joke as one of the first bits of church humor we heard. It was true to life.

What do people see when they look at our church? We probably wouldn't want to know. Those who look from the outside usually see us church people in less flattering ways than we see ourselves.

Today's text describes a particular church—the early church in Jerusalem. Theirs isn't necessarily a model for all subsequent Christians to follow. But in terms of time and geography the Jerusalem Church was closest to our origins. So we Christians of whatever era would do well to lean in and learn from this congregation.

In Jerusalem we see a band of Christians who are highly energized. They feel a connection to the Holy Spirit and display that energy. They are focused and determined to follow the leading of the Spirit. An immediate evidence of this energy is their boldness. In fact, boldness in witness is a key theme in the first half of the book of Acts. Our text says that the Jerusalem Church testified "with great power" (4:33).

When we compare their witness with that of the church today, there's a stark difference. Today a great many Christians are uncomfortable witnessing to their faith. Is it any wonder that our churches are declining?

Another evidence of the high energy of the Jerusalem Church is the unusual quality of their fellowship. Luke says they "were of one heart and soul" to such an extent that they held all property in common. That does-n't describe most congregations in America today. Certainly not in our materialistic, acquisitive, individualistic, pleasure-seeking society.

Something had clearly happened to these followers of Jesus in Jerusalem. They weren't living as they had before they were joined together by the Holy Spirit in love. They were fulfilling Jesus' prayer in John 17 that his followers would "become completely one" (v. 23) and would be filled with Jesus' joy.

For us contemporary Americans, Christian unity—spiritual oneness—isn't a priority. It isn't a priority within our congregations or among reli-gious groups. We prize our individualism and see religion as an individual, private matter. We believe that the work of religion is to service the needs of individuals—make them happy or successful or give them peace of mind. One modern metaphor for the church is the gas station. It's where we go to get spiritual fuel for the week. Division within or among the churches doesn't matter. If we don't get along, we'll part company. The more gas stations, the merrier!

But the New Testament has a fundamentally different view of the church. It sees things corporately, not individually. It believes that the church has a mission. When you have a mission, division hurts. It under-cuts the work of the church. Division is a sign that Christians aren't liv-ing their faith and thus have no credibility.

The first task of the church is to create a loving community in a divided world. If it's not doing this, then it's not yet the church. Community and unity are essential to the church. They aren't add-ons or extras. Thus the church must always practice forgiveness and reconcilia-tion. People can't be part of a church and live out of harmony with their neighbors.

In Chicago in 1977 Cathleen Crowell Webb accused Gary Dotson of committing a crime against her. Dotson was convicted and sent to prison. In 1985 Webb announced that she had lied. She said that she had met Jesus Christ, joined a church, and wanted to make amends based on her new lifestyle. Webb knew that she had to set things right. When people meet Jesus Christ, a change occurs. Their indifference and dishonesty are replaced with a new kind of caring. This caring isn't an option for Christians.

As we've said, one of the indicators of the high energy of the Jerusalem Church was that they held all property in common. This arrangement arose from how they felt about each other: "If you need something and I have it, why should I hold it back?"

There's a Hasidic tale about two brothers who inherited a farm. They decided to farm the land together and split the harvest. One brother married and had children while the other never married. The single brother recognized that his brother had more mouths to feed, so an equal split wasn't fair. The married brother realized that his brother had no one to provide for him in his old age, so an equal split wasn't fair. So every night each brother slipped over to the other's barn and emptied several bags of grain.

One night the brothers bumped into each other and realized what was happening. They fell into each other's arms. A gentle rain began to fall. The rain was God's tears of joy.

This story is a long way from where we are in society today. We value individualism and private ownership. Our goal is to get more and more for ourselves. A huge gap has opened up between the haves and the have-nots. Yet every day we hear angry voices of well-off politicians and commentators who want to keep the status quo. They want to retain their right to make greater and greater profits. They have little interest in helping others get out of poverty or get medical care. Their high energy is directed toward private ownership and their own consumption.

The example of the Jerusalem Church speaks to us. These early Christians were simply as concerned about their neighbors' well-being as they were about their own. Their first task was to create a loving community in a divided world. This sort of community may be a pipe dream. Or it may reflect a love into which we haven't fully grown. It's a wonderful thought that there could yet be an outbreak of this new kind of caring across our land today. If so, it has to come from us. (Sandy Wylie)

Lectionary Commentary

1 John 1:1–2:2

We have here the opening sections of 1 John, which seems more of a sermon than a letter. We hear echoes of the Gospel of John as the authors introduce the themes that they will develop. The authors try to establish the reliability of their testimony by showing that it has been amply verified by the human senses. They say that it has been heard (three times), seen (four times), and touched. The overall sensory term "revealed" appears twice. All of this sensory verification refutes the Gnostics' denial of the humanity of Christ.

Fellowship is a central concern of the text. The authors give their testimony so that their readers may have fellowship with them and may join them in having fellowship with God and Jesus Christ. This loving fellowship will bring joy to the authors just as it did to Jesus (John 15:11). All believers, like other mortals, fall prey to sin. The remedy for the sins of the whole world is in confession and the cleansing blood of Jesus.

John 20:19-31

In only five noteworthy verses (19-23) John describes the beginning of the church. First, Jesus commissions his followers to go into the world just as the Father sent him into the world. Second, Jesus gives his followers the Holy Spirit. John's chronology often differs from that of the other Gospel writers. In Luke and Acts the Spirit comes on Pentecost, but in John the Spirit comes on Easter evening. Third, the forgiveness of sins is a central feature of the church's mission. Just as Jesus embodied forgiveness in his ministry, especially in the events around Easter, he is concerned that the church embodies and carries on this vital work. (Sandy Wylie)

Worship Aids

Invocation

O God of love, we live in a world that divides us in countless ways. Yet our heart's desire is not to be separated but to be in loving community. In our worship help us to center on our oneness in Christian fellowship and purpose so that we may grow strong together. Amen.

Prayer of Confession

O God, we confess that our actions are often at odds with our intentions. We slight others when we desire to support them. We say things that discourage our neighbors when we really want to help them. We ask forgiveness for our uncaring actions and help for our growth in your love. Amen.

Words of Assurance

We thank you, O God, that in this and every hour we may call on you for help with our difficulties, for strength to overcome our weaknesses, and for forgiveness to lift the burden of our sins. For these priceless gifts we praise you. Amen. (Sandy Wylie)

Holding On . . . Letting Go

First in a Series of Three on Implications of the Resurrected Life

John 20:10-18

Mary stands outside the empty tomb. She is weeping. Her hands tremble. She shudders from immobilizing grief. Brutal pain drives her to her knees when she looks and sees not the body of Jesus but two angels who ask, "Woman, why are you weeping?" Mary responds, "They have taken away my Lord, and I do not know where they have laid him." Mary has no time for angels. She wants answers.

Turning, she sees a man standing behind her. She thinks he is the gardener. The unrecognized stranger asks, "Woman, why are you weeping? For whom are you looking?" Mary overwhelmed with grief stammers, "Sir, if you have carried him away, tell me where you have laid him, and I will take him away."

"Mary?" With the speaking of her name, awareness comes over her and terror is transformed into nascent joy. She says with great love, "Rabbouni," and throws her arms around him. Like a mother protecting her child, she holds on and has no intention of letting go. At Jesus' urging, she breaks her embrace and leaves to announce the living Lord to the disciples.

What is God saying to us through this tender story of reunion? I think in honest moments there is a terror that comes over us when we ask, "Is this story one we believe to be true?" Is it true that a Galilean field preacher was the Incarnate Son of God—the Word made flesh? Is it true that he taught as no other person taught, did what no person had done, lived as no other person had lived, died on a cross outside the city of Jerusalem, was buried, rose triumphant from the grave, is exalted at the right hand of God the Father, and one day will come again—is it all true?

Sometimes we wonder. Then, Jesus comes to us. He speaks my name. He speaks your name—Mary, John, Judy, Cathy, George—put your name there. In that moment, maybe with grief or uncertainty, confusion or brutal pain we instinctively hold on. Why? Because we say, "It is true. He is alive. He does live. He does love." When life makes us ask "Is it true?" Christ comes in a moment of revelation, and we know that it is true, and we hold on.

I wonder if this "holding on" phenomenon is not woven into all of our lives at multiple levels. For example, you are standing in a civic center or a church or a gymnasium for your child's graduation. You stand there as she comes in with her class. She has on her cap and gown. She is crowned with pride. Are you there? Do you see your daughter or your son? As she comes in and stands proudly with her class, there is a moment in which you ask, "Did I do the right thing by her? Have I done my best with her?" For just a moment, we are not sure. We are a jumble of emotions. We say to ourselves, "I need assurance and I need hope." She stands tall and you look at her and say, "Yes," and you hold on.

We hold on at other times, don't we? When a move comes and we must leave the place we call home for another place, another job, another community. The house has to be sold, the children have to be relocated; change is all around you. You have taken the job, and you know that it is the right thing to do. But there is something inside of you that wants to hold on because you are not sure.

Strange to say, but prejudice is like that. It would be a lie to tell you that preachers don't wrestle with prejudice. One of the sinister things about prejudice is our Christian faith says, "It ought not to be." But at another level of our life—parents, mentors, culture—prejudice still lives. What do we do with our prejudices? Far too often, we hold on.

Yes, grief brings this "holding on" phenomenon to life. Why do we hold on to grief so long? The Mary inside of me is saying we hold onto the pain because we fear we will let go of the person if we let go of the pain. Why is it then that, like Mary, even knowing our Lord's risen glory, we desperately hold on to our children, our grief, our memories, our past? We hold on, or attempt to do so, and then, finally, we let go and find that we still have the love, the memories, the joy of life.

I love orchestral music, particularly programs that feature a soloist. If you have been to an orchestral concert you know that as the finale of the concerto comes to its end, all the instruments are playing and the soloist is wringing all the music he or she can from an instrument. There is awesome music in the room. Then the music stops. There is a split second when the music stops and before the applause starts. Do you know what I'm talking about, that one split second of breathless silence?

Life is like that. In life, the awesome moments come and then we applaud and celebrate. But when we quit applauding the soloist and the orchestra, do you know what we do? We go home. Yet, somehow we think that the Christian experience ought to be unending applause. Jesus tells us to go ahead and hold onto the moment for just a moment. But then, go tell the story of love beyond grief and grace beyond failure.

I don't know where it may be for you, but when everything within me wants to hold on to the split second of wonder, I hear our Lord say, "Let go!" Only by letting go is there risk, faith, and the journey to trust God. Hold on... Let go! (Timothy L. Owings)

Worship Aids

Invocation

Almighty and ever-living Lord, as you met terrified disciples in risen glory, so meet us today in the power and presence of Easter life. Quicken our imaginations to joyfully worship you, gladden our hearts to generously praise you, and open our hands to faithfully serve you and others that our worship may be transformed into grace. Amen.

Prayer of Confession

Loving God, we confess our inability to fully comprehend the meaning of our Lord's death and resurrection. We are far too enchanted with trivial pursuits and meaningless activity. Our lives are full of things and appointments and demands that continually keep us from being with you and fully being with others. Forgive us, we pray. Forgive us for clutching too tightly the transitory things of life while refusing to embrace the gift that is life eternal. Hear our prayers and forgive us our sins, through Jesus Christ our Lord, Amen.

Words of Assurance

Hold on... Let go! God will bear you up and carry you in joy through the trivial and awesome moments of life.

Benediction

Now go from this gathering of believers to be the person God has called you to be in Jesus Christ. Open your hands to the poor, the confused, and the searching. Be Christ's risen presence and in so doing, fill the space you have on this planet with grace and much love through Jesus Christ our Lord, Amen. (Timothy L. Owings)

APRIL 22, 2012

❧❧❧

Third Sunday of Easter

Readings: Acts 3:12-19; Psalm 4; 1 John 3:1-7; Luke 24:36b-48

Keepers of the Flame

Luke 24:36b-48

In Sheffield, Alabama, a young man was working at an iron works plant when he was thrown onto a red-hot armor plate. Those who looked on were horrified. When the man was rolled off, it was doubtful that he would live. Someone cried, "Send for a doctor." But the suffering man responded, "Never mind the doctor. I'm dying without God. Who can help me?"

About three hundred men had gathered, but no one responded to his plea. After twenty minutes he died. One observer was an inactive church member. Later he said, "I have heard those cries ever since, and I wish I could have stooped down and pointed him to Jesus, but my life closed my lips" (Solomon Benjamin Shaw, *Dying Testimonies of Saved and Unsaved* [Self Published, 1898], 301).

How could anyone ever forget an experience like this one? Here was a human being in the greatest need of his life, and no one could help.

Few needs are this desperate, but people are walking the streets of every town, searching for some kind of help. They want friendship, they want to know God, they want to know that somebody cares. Who has a word for them?

Our text today is about this very thing. It's a story in Luke's Gospel. It follows Jesus' appearance on the road to Emmaus. Jesus comes to his disciples, reassuring them of his presence and support. Then he reminds them of their role in all of this. He says, "You are witnesses of these things. You are to tell these things to the entire world."

No word is more central to the Christian life than this word *witness*. It sums up everything that a Christian is supposed to do and be. Christians

134

are witnesses. This isn't some metaphor or figure of speech. It's simply a matter of whether a Christian is going to be a good witness or a bad witness. Some people are clear about when witnessing happens and who does it. It happens at 11:00 on Sunday morning, and somebody called the preacher does it. Sometimes even preachers get to thinking this.

Anthropologists have discovered a primitive tribe deep in the South American jungles. The most important role within the tribe is the "keeper of the flame." Since fire is so precious and takes such effort to recreate, one member is entrusted with keeping the flame alive.

Jesus called all of us to be keepers of the flame. We are to keep alive his message. He spoke about this in various ways. Jesus said, "You are the light of the world. You are the salt of the earth. If your light goes out or you lose your saltiness, the cause will be lost. These things are found only in you" (see Matthew 5:13-14)!

A minister had in his congregation a lawyer who was a skeptic. The pastor long desired to see the salvation of this man. One week he learned that the lawyer would attend worship on the following Sunday. He prepared a sermon just for the occasion. Shortly thereafter, the lawyer confessed his faith in Christ. The minister rejoiced. He asked the lawyer what portion of the sermon had especially affected him.

The lawyer answered, "It wasn't your sermon at all. I didn't hear it; I was making a brief all the while you were preaching. But afterwards as I came out, I saw old Aunt Chloe trying to get down the slippery steps. I helped her down, and as I left she looked up at me and said, 'Oh, kind sir! I wish you loved my dear Jesus.' Those words rang in my ears, and I couldn't get rid of them, until I went to my office and bowed myself on my knees and gave myself to Christ. It wasn't your sermon but Aunt Chloe's words that led me to the Savior" (adapted from Anonymous, *Anecdotes Illustrative of New Testament Texts* [New York: A.C. Armstrong & Son, 1887], 200).

Preaching is important, but the witness of lay people is more important. People expect ministers to witness; that's what they get paid to do. But when a lay person witnesses, people really listen.

When Fanny Brice, the renowned comedienne, was offered a job by Florenz Ziegfeld, she thanked his secretary politely and left. Then she raced down to the theater. She grabbed people off the sidewalk to tell them that she would soon be working there.

What would it mean if the followers of Jesus Christ left church this morning all across America with that kind of excitement... anxious to get to the sidewalks and the streets . . . anxious to invite a friend or even a stranger to God's house? Why, it would be the grandest invitation in the whole world! It wouldn't be an invitation to see a new performer or to enjoy a little entertainment. It would be an invitation to meet God and fellowship with those who love God. It could be the opportunity of a lifetime!

If we believers will just listen to the world, we'll hear the desperate cries out there on the sidewalk. We'll hear people saying, "I'm dying without God. Who can help me?" In such moments we can know no greater blessing than being the ones who know what to say. (Sandy Wylie)

Lectionary Commentary

Acts 3:12-19

This text records the response of worshipers to the healing of a lame man at the Beautiful Gate of the temple in Jerusalem. Peter and John refuse to take credit for the healing, saying that it came not through their power or piety but through the man's faith in Jesus. Peter's sermon extends to the end of the chapter, so this reading should end with v. 26 or at least v. 21. Peter locates Jesus squarely in the tradition of the astonished worshipers who are gathered at the temple. The God of Abraham, Isaac, and Jacob, whom the worshipers have gathered to praise, glorified Jesus. These worshipers and their fellow Jews rejected Jesus and killed him, but they did so out of ignorance. The good news is that God is very willing to forgive their sins if they will but repent and turn to God. All of this shows how God is able to take the evil deeds of humans and make them into something good. It further shows that the God of Israel has established the church as the divine messianic community and is at work through it.

1 John 3:1-7

As it occurs in the lectionary, this reading is divided into two parts: being children of God (vv. 1-3) and living as children of God (vv. 4-7). We are children of God by gift, not by nature. Our childhood springs from divine love and regeneration. Divine love works in us progressively to create a resemblance to God, both now and in the future; its goal is purity.

The second part of the text centers on sin. It was Christ's mission "to take away sins, and in him there is no sin." Verse 6 then makes the astonishing announcement that "no one who abides in him sins." This contradicts the authors' earlier claim that we are liars if we deny that we are all sinners. This claim in v. 6 springs from the close identification between the believer and Christ, and it follows certain logic in the dualistic world of Johannine thought. No one who is truly in Christ can be inclined toward sin. True believers incline toward doing what is right. They are the kind of people for whom sinning is ruled out. If it were not this way, something would be seriously wrong; they would be living a life of contradiction. (Sandy Wylie)

Worship Aids

Call to Worship

God calls us to this time of witness and praise.
May the Holy One make us glad and loosen our tongues.
For we have incredible good news to tell.
Let us worship the giver of this news.

Invocation

O God, you call us to be your witnesses to a perishing world. We need help in claiming our voices and shaping our messages. Come to us in this time of worship, steady our spirits, and help us to find boldness in our words as well as in our actions. Amen.

Benediction

Go forth as witnesses of God's love. Be of strong heart. Encourage others. Speak words that heal. May the Prince of Peace bless you and go with you. Amen. (Sandy Wylie)

Easter Aftereffects

Second in a Series of Three on Implications of the Resurrected Life

Acts 1:1-14

These post-Easter Sundays beg a curious question: what do we do now? What is the "more" of Easter? How about the word *aftereffects*? I did not know the word until several years ago. In an article written for *The Atlantic Monthly* titled "Post-President for Life," James Fallows interviewed Bill Clinton about what he called "the aftereffects of his presidency." *Aftereffects* are the "what now?," the "so what?" that follows anything.

OK, you have finished your degree. You graduate college. You've finished medical school. Some of your tests came back negative. You got the job. You're retired. You passed the bar. Now what? In life there will always be aftereffects. There will always be the question following the moment of euphoria. What's next? What do I do now? What will I become and what will become of me because of what happened? Aftereffects.

What are Easter's aftereffects? Luke, in the second volume of his work we know as The Acts of the Apostles, helps answer our question. The first Easter aftereffect he mentions is our need of the Holy Spirit to make sense of Easter. The Holy Spirit empowers Christians to live Easter lives. The Holy Spirit fills Christians with Easter love. The Holy Spirit reflects Easter light. To say that I am a Christian is to say that the same power that raised Jesus from the dead is the power that is ours as a gift from God.

The Spirit gives each Christian life and hope and purpose. You say, "How do you receive the Holy Spirit? How does this Holy Spirit power infuse life? How do I experience the presence and power of the Holy Spirit?" That power and presence comes to us in several ways.

Parents teach us valuable life lessons. Mentors guide us. Friends bring out the best in us. A loving church family inspires us to be all that God made us to be in Jesus Christ. At a much higher level, the Holy Spirit works that way in all of our lives. Through the Holy Spirit, God teaches and inspires us. Jesus said of the Spirit's coming: "When the spirit of truth comes, he will guide you into all truth" (John 16:13). The coming of the Holy Spirit is a powerful Easter aftereffect.

A second Easter aftereffect comes as a warning. Our text reports the last question the disciples asked of Jesus: "Lord, is this the time when you will restore the kingdom to Israel?" They hoped now that Jesus had died and risen in glory, God was going to overturn the Romans and bring again the kingdom of Israel in majesty and power.

Our temptation today and everyday is to build our own kingdoms. They may be institutional kingdoms or personal kingdoms, kingdoms of control or of might or of influence. All such kingdoms have Israel's DNA. There is only one kingdom of God, and that is the kingdom of relationships built around the love and person of Jesus Christ. We are to be "kingdom of God" people.

The third Easter aftereffect is telling the story. Jesus said, "You will be my witnesses in Jerusalem, in all Judea and Samaria, and to the ends of the earth." The word *witness* here is the Greek word *martus*. It comes into English as *martyr*. The early Christian witnesses were martyrs for Christ.

They lived their faith and at times died for their faith. The story they told was the story of Jesus and his love.

We have a story to tell. But what often happens is we tell all other stories instead of the Jesus story. We pass on and embellish and fabricate all kinds of stories, when our energies would be better suited telling the story of his life, his death, his resurrection; being living witnesses to his love. Jesus' story is the story we must tell.

The Easter aftereffect that could take hold of us and change our lives arrives when we relate how Jesus' story and our story met. Tell how his story intersected your story and changed your life and brought you into the kingdom of God. If we come to Easter and walk away from Easter and simply glory in the majesty of the moment but do not let his story become a part of our story, we miss the point. This story of Jesus is to be on our lips and in our lives. When an opportunity presents itself to us to share our witness, we say, "Could I share with you the person who changed my life and who is making me new? I'm not perfect, have not arrived, but grace is working in my life." We have a story to tell.

The fourth Easter aftereffect is community. Jesus had brought the followers together, and God was about to birth a new community that would change the world. There is a "we-ness," an "us-ness" to the Christian story. We are called to stay together, to be community under the Lordship of Christ.

One of the great truths of our faith is that once you are a Christian you are in the company of believers forever. We are going to be together for a long time in the kingdom of God. Creating community is a powerful Easter aftereffect.

The question lingers: What are we going to do with Easter? What will be your life's Easter aftereffects? Could the Holy Spirit even now be working, knocking, wooing, inviting you to say, "I must respond to the risen Christ?" It might be one or more of these aftereffects. It may be one that is not even mentioned today, but you know there is something more; there is more to Easter than one day of celebration. What is that for you? (Timothy L. Owings)

Worship Aids

Call to Worship
Christ is risen! Alleluia!
Praise God from whom all blessings flow!
Christ is risen! Alleluia!

Praise God all creatures here below!
Christ is risen! Alleluia!
Praise God above ye heavenly hosts!
Christ is risen! Alleluia!
Praise Father, Son, and Holy Ghost!
All: Christ is risen! Alleluia! Christ is risen!

Invocation

God of risen life, Lord of risen glory, we gather our lives and our dreams, our hopes and our longings to praise and worship you. Receive our gifts, we pray, and add to them the abiding and generous gift of your empowering, risen life. Through Christ the Lord we pray. Amen.

Words of Assurance

As the risen Lord met with disciples and assured them of his abiding presence, now assure us of your healing mercy; that through the grace of our Lord Jesus Christ, we may rise to serve you forgiven and gifted to be and become followers of the one who lives and reigns with you and Holy Spirit, one God, forever and ever. Amen. (Timothy L. Owings)

APRIL 29, 2012

❧❧❧

Fourth Sunday of Easter

Readings: Acts 4:5-12; Psalm 23; 1 John 3:16-24; John 10:11-18

Laying Down Our Lives

1 John 3:16-24

In 1831, Alexis de Tocqueville came to the United States to study American democracy. He discovered a network of social service agencies that was supported voluntarily by the citizens. In Europe and elsewhere the government took almost sole responsibility for the welfare of the people, but Americans felt a personal responsibility for their neighbors. De Tocqueville believed that this ethic came primarily from America's churches. This ethic said that people ought to be kind to one another, love one another, and be devoted to one another. It even said that Christians ought to lay down their lives for one another. De Tocqueville was amazed.

The freedom and abundance that we Americans enjoy today were made possible by the hard work and sacrifice of those who came before us. I think of the struggle that my father went through to become the first person in our family to get a college education. I could never repay what he handed on to me. Every family has stories like this.

Sometimes the sacrifices of one person affect the course of an entire nation. In 1960, a girl in New Orleans named Ruby Bridges turned six, and it was time for her to start school. Those were the days of segregation, and Ruby's father didn't want her to go to an all-white school because of the danger.

But Ruby's mother thought differently. She'd had a tough time in her life. The day before Ruby was born, she had to carry ninety pounds of cotton on her back. She wanted something better for her daughter. So Ruby attended the all-white school in the face of much anger and intimidation.

141

When Ruby graduated, she became a travel agent. She enjoyed a life that wasn't available to her parents. More important, she helped open a door for people of color all across the nation (see www.rubybidges.com).

At the center of the Christian faith is a power called sacrificial love. It's rooted in God's nature and is the strongest, most enduring power in the world. Jesus came into this world to make that love real for us by laying down his life for us.

Jesus' example of sacrificial love calls for a like response from those who follow him, and John states that response in the first verse of our text: "We know love by this, that he laid down his life for us—and we ought to lay down our lives for one another." Any response less than this can empty love of its meaning and power. Sacrificial love requires that we put others first. It requires that we lay down our lives for them just as Jesus laid down his life for us.

Laying down our lives for others can take many forms. The most extreme form is martyrdom. Tertullian said that the blood of the martyrs is the seed of the church. Without martyrdom the church would never have taken root and grown. Beginning with Stephen in the New Testament (Acts 7), many Christians have paid for their witness with their lives. Christianity has met opposition and persecution in every continent. Its spread has been possible only through the blood of martyrs.

In our text, John mentions another way in which believers can and should lay down their lives for one another, and that's through the sharing of material resources. Love always demands that we help a brother or sister who is in need if we are able to do so.

We can also lay down our lives for one another through service. In a church that I served, a family had a precious boy named Michael. Michael contracted meningitis, which left him unable to do many tasks. The only remedy was an activity called patterning. Someone had to work with Michael around the clock to help him move his limbs in prescribed ways. This someone was his mother, who became totally exhausted.

Others in our church family found out about this. We trained teams of volunteers who gave the mother relief. It was hard work, but we could all see how we were growing in our love for one another.

What John is telling us in our text is contrary to the spirit of our culture today. We Americans are into individualism, competition, materialism, and consumption. We think of religion as being personal—as being a private individual matter.

But the New Testament doesn't believe that the church is just a collection of religious individuals. The church is a community that's bound together in love. It shares in Christ's love and is called "the body of Christ."

About the year 200, Tertullian recorded a widespread impression that outsiders had of the church: "See how they love one another!" The church of that day was as diverse as it is today. But they lived as "brother and sister," terms that still linger in some small town churches as words of personal address.

Today American society is very different from the world of the church. It lives according to the Super Bowl. It creates winners and losers. It's all about competition, power, fierce partisanship, and bragging rights. Some of our citizens are incredibly rich and some are very poor, some enjoy great privilege and some are permanently disadvantaged, some have health care and some don't. Sharing is a weak value.

Jesus wanted the church to be very different, more like the Special Olympics, in which everybody is valued and everybody wins. When someone in a race falls, the leader and others stop and help that person up. Then they take one another's hands and run to the finish line together—for a better victory!

The church is rooted in God's love. Because we know one who laid down his life for us, we're committed to laying down our lives for one another. Our witness to God's love is our most sacred and vital trust. For us and for our world this love is our only hope, our only salvation. (Sandy Wylie)

Lectionary Commentary

Acts 4:5-12

In this text we're still dealing with the fallout from the healing of the lame man at the gate of the temple. It's the first recorded defense of Christianity before religious authorities. Peter's speech, which is empowered by the Holy Spirit, is typical of the bold witness given by the followers of Jesus in Acts. It immediately follows an address through which Peter and John won 5,000 converts!

The real issue quickly becomes the Resurrection. The priests who customarily controlled the temple were the Sadducees, who didn't believe in resurrection. Their interrogation of Peter and John is thus an effort to establish blasphemy. Peter and John hold their ground, claiming that the healing of the man didn't come by magic or healing potions or special powers of the disciples or spontaneous natural healing. It came "by the name of Jesus Christ of Nazareth." His resurrection is the new reality that has entered the world and that demands a response from every person.

John 10:11-18

The image of Jesus as the good shepherd has brought great comfort to believers through the centuries. It has inspired much art, especially the images in our stained glass, and it's a common theme in our sacred music. The Hebrew Scriptures held the promise that God would come as a shepherd to the people (Isaiah 40:11; Jeremiah 23:1-6; Ezekiel 34). This was a very tender, comforting, and reassuring promise. Thus it's shocking to many readers of John's Gospel to see that Jesus' words in this text were met with division and derision and violent opposition.

Today's epistle reading from 1 John unfolds and reinforces the meaning of this teaching of Jesus, so the preacher can easily put the two texts into conversation with each other. (Sandy Wylie)

Worship Aids

Call to Worship

The risen Christ is with us!
The Lord of Love is in our midst!
Our neighbors are here, too—
Those who share our lives.
Let us raise our voices in celebration.
Let us worship God with gladness.

Invocation

O God, you have called us into fellowship with you and our neighbors. We look for guideposts on this journey. We search your Scriptures and feel your presence. In our worship guide us onto your paths and direct our spirits. In Jesus' name, we pray. Amen.

Benediction

Go forth to serve others in all that you do. Lift the fallen. Greet the stranger. Comfort the suffering. And may the God of all peace bless you and go with you. Amen. (Sandy Wylie)

The Awkward Commandment

Third in a Series of Three on Implications of the Resurrected Life

John 15:9-17; 1 John 3:18-24

It's just awkward. "This is my commandment," said Jesus, "that you love one another as I have loved you" (John 15:12). It is awkward for a number of reasons. I'll mention three. It is awkward because we cannot obey a commandment to love others until we first know that we are loved. Jesus said, "Love one another as I have loved you." It is awkward to love another person if first you do not know how much you are loved. Here is our Lord's gift to all of us: he loves us so, but that love must penetrate our crusty hearts.

Second, this commandment is awkward because the words *love* and *command* simply don't go together. We love because we feel deeply and passionately desire another. We love because something inside of us—a longing, a need, a desire—wells up and we act on that.

A baby girl was born into a family already blessed with two little boys. Coming home from the hospital, the proud father announced to his pre-school sons: "God has blessed us with a baby girl. You have a sister, and your mom and I command you to love her!" How absurd! Love and command do not go together.

There is a third reason. The commandment is awkward because we still have trouble connecting our love for God and our love for others. We love Jesus. We sing about our love for Jesus. We learn as children we are to love him, and he loves us. Loving Jesus is not difficult. The difficult part is translating our love for Jesus into loving others.

So the question is: how do we transform this awkward commandment into an awesome commandment? The texts give us two clues. In both John 15 and 1 John 3 the key word is *abide*. Jesus said, "As the Father has loved me, so I have loved you; abide in my love" (John 15:9). The writer of 1 John 3:24 put it this way: "All who obey his commandments abide in him, and he abides in them." The word *abide* is the Greek word *menao*. It means to dwell in, to stay with, to be connected to, to draw life from. To abide in another reality is to find your life coming from that reality.

Just as branches draw life from the vine, we are to be joined, grafted to Jesus Christ who offers us the ability to love others as he loves us. This awkward commandment becomes powerfully awesome when we realize deep within our being we have no life in ourselves without Jesus Christ.

We may involve ourselves in all manner of church life, but if we are not abiding in Christ this commandment is forever awkward.

There is something else here. We must deal with the word *commandment*. You cannot command another person to love. How do we move from awkward to awesome? Simply put, we must decide to act ourselves into loving even when we don't feel like it. It is easier to act your way into a new way of thinking than to think your way into a new way of acting. And most of us have that backwards.

We believe that if we think about loving another person long enough, we will behave in loving ways. That is not true. In fact, in many circumstances, the more you think about the situation the more distance you create from the other person. If you dwell on what a person did or said you may never act in loving ways toward them.

"A new commandment I give you, that you love one another as I have loved you." We must decide whether we are going to obey the commandment, not because we feel like it or it is convenient. No, we must love regardless. We must move from awkward to awesome by simply acting in loving ways.

In the little book, *Tuesdays With Morrie*, Mitch Albom records tender moments with his beloved college professor Morrie Schwartz. In a scene from the film version of the book, Mitch tries to comfort Morrie by rubbing salve on his feet. He says, "Morrie, we must love one another or die." Morrie realizes that the student really doesn't believe it so he says to him, "Do you really believe that? I don't think you really believe that. There is something you find suspect about the spiritual reality of life. You think it is just syrupy sentimentalism, just gooey sentimentality. But we must love one another, or we die" (New York; Doubleday, 1997).

That could not be any more profound were it spoken over the entire Christian faith. We must love one another or we die. Here is the central reality of the whole Christian story. Take the entire New Testament and sum it up. It is right there. "Love one another as I have loved you," and move from awkward to awesome. (Timothy L. Owings)

Worship Aids

Litany

Jesus said: "No one has a greater love than this, to lay down one's life
    for one's friends."
Teach us to lay down our lives for others.

Jesus said: "Love one another as I have loved you."
Teach us to love others as you have loved us.
Jesus said: "I am the way, and the truth, and the life."
**Teach us to follow your way, embrace your truth,
and celebrate your life.**
Jesus said: "Follow me, and I will make you fish for people."
Teach us to follow you.
Jesus said: "I am the resurrection and the life."
Teach us to live in your risen life and walk in your risen way.
**All: Lord of eternal and risen life, teach us to be and become
the people you are making us to be. Open our hands to
love, free our lives to serve, and empower our wills to love
others as you have loved us.**

Pastoral Prayer

God of death and life, the grave and the empty tomb, we have careers and calendars, families and friends, work and worship, and we ask that you grant us grace to rest in your nourishing love. We especially pray for all who grieve the loss of loved one or friend, who know the sting of death and the loneliness of sorrow. Grant all who mourn the gift of your comforting mercy. We pray for those who find life confusing, even cruel. A son has walked away from his faith, a daughter has forgotten the power of faith, a spouse has abandoned all sense of companionship. Be to all who are lost in the fog of confused and confusing life the gift of your abiding love. God of death and life, the grave and the Resurrection, hear our prayers and open our lives to your presence, through Jesus Christ, the ever-living One, we pray. Amen.

Benediction

Christ is risen! So go now in the power and grace of the risen Lord. Choose to love even when you find no feeling to do so. Choose to be Christ's living presence to others. Choose life over death, grace over judgment, and above all, love over all that is and will ever be, through Jesus Christ, risen and living Lord. Amen. (Timothy L. Owings)

MAY 6, 2012

❧❧❧

Fifth Sunday of Easter

Readings: Acts 8:26-40; Psalm 22:25-31; 1 John 4:7-21; John 15:1-8

Abide in Christ

John 15:1-8

Jesus' disciples were always being surprised, delighted, shocked, and humbled. Every turn, every new day with Jesus was a holy adventure. Jesus called them, they followed; he taught, they listened; he guided, and they stumbled along behind and beside him, sometimes faithful, sometimes clueless. They were like us, following Jesus wherever he might lead. As they journeyed together Jesus often would have intimate conversations with them, just the disciples and maybe Mary or Martha and a few others. He would call them aside to share something of himself with his closest friends, something that would help them along their way.

One day Jesus gathered his followers around him and began to teach them the words in our lesson today. We might imagine Christ saying something similar to us as we journey together as the church. If we ask him what he would have us do, what should shape and define our life together as the church, he might remind us that we are called and set apart as God's gift to the world and that through our life together—through our witness as the body of Christ, God is redeeming and renewing all of creation. Through us the ministry of Jesus continues because we have been given his ministry of reconciliation. Through us God is healing the sick, feeding the hungry, clothing the naked, sheltering the homeless poor, reclaiming the lost, offering hope to the hopeless, making peace, proclaiming resurrection. It is not that God cannot do these things apart from us, but that for some strange reason, God has chosen to work through the broken, messy, limited nature of our lives as the church.

God's kingdom, God's beloved community is like a vine lovingly planted by God who is the vine grower. That vine is a sign and a foretaste of God's kingdom pointing to the renewal of all creation. That vine is Jesus, the first fruit of a renewed creation, the source of life and healing and renewal for all the nations. In the midst of a world of death and decay, Jesus, the vine, is a sign and source of life. All who come to him, abide in him, and make their life in him will find the fullness of life. So as long as we remain attached—connected to the vine through prayer, worship, study, fellowship, and service—so long as we are friends of Jesus we will grow and thrive and bear much fruit. But if we seek our own way, if we follow our own individual agendas, if we make church about the pastor or about the members and attach ourselves to people and ideas, anything or anyone other than the true vine, we will be like deadwood which is cut off and used for kindling.

Because of our inflated sense of self-importance, Jesus' words are an important reminder to the church that he is the vine, the source of our life together. He is at the center of the church, not you and not me, Jesus is the vine and we are the branches. If we remain intimately and organically connected to the vine, if we stay in love with Jesus, if we dwell in God's love, and make our home in the heart of God, then we will grow, and run, and flourish, and bear much fruit for God's kingdom. You see the church exists not for itself but for the life of the world, for the healing of the nations. We are merely the first among the redeemed and are the means whereby God the vine-grower is tending and renewing the garden of creation. To that end Christ Jesus has called us his friends and has invited us to join him in kingdom work. But this is only possible in as much as we respond to Christ's gracious invitation to abide in him.

Perhaps Jesus had this conversation with his disciples because he knew them and us so well. He knew our tendency to abide in all the wrong things; to make career, or family, or our superficial desires, or even our anxieties and fears our home. So if we find that our life together is not producing the kind of fruit we'd like then perhaps we need to look at where and with whom we are abiding. Where are we spending our time? To whom are we devoting our attention and energy? To whom or what have we given our hearts? Perhaps we need to ask ourselves what part of us, what part of the church, needs to be pruned? Where is the deadwood in our lives, in our fellowship, and in our witness that needs to be removed and thrown into the fire so that there is room for something new to grow in its place?

To abide with Christ means spending time in the presence of Christ until that relationship becomes our natural condition. Abiding with Christ means that we give him our time, our energy, our attention, our prayer, our worship, our hearts, minds, and souls, all that we are—not occasionally, not when it is convenient or fits into our schedules—each and every day. Jesus says to us, the church, "Abide in me as I abide in you. Just as the branch cannot bear fruit by itself unless it abides in the vine, neither can you unless you abide in me" (John 15:11).

Here in this season after Easter, the season of resurrection, the promise, the good news for us, the church, is that because of Easter we are not alone. Christ has come even to us, has made his home with us and offers us life on the vine, an opportunity to share in the life-giving fellowship that exists at the very heart of God. So where, O church, are we abiding today? Abide in Jesus, as he abides in you, so that your joy may be complete. (David Hockett)

Lectionary Commentary

Acts 8:26-40

Up until this point most of the action in the book of Acts has taken place in Jerusalem. Here, however, Luke moves us out of Jerusalem and south into Gaza where he reports Philip's missionary work and the conversion and baptism of an Ethiopian eunuch. Perhaps the geographical shift is meant, in part, to remind us of the universal nature and scope of the good news. Here we see the church beginning to enact the companion gospel's claim that "...repentance and forgiveness of sins are to be proclaimed to all nations, beginning from Jerusalem" (Luke 24:47). While the inclusion of the Ethiopian eunuch points to the universal reach and appeal of the gospel of repentance and forgiveness, he is probably a Jew and thus the shift to the mission to the Gentiles is not yet fully underway. One can only imagine what happens when the eunuch arrives in Ethiopia as a newly baptized convert to the way of Christ.

What is also clear is that as important as Philip and the other apostles are to the work of proclaiming the gospel, the work of salvation is God's. The apostles are not the primary actors in the story, and neither are those who are responding to the good news. God is the primary actor and agent. The Spirit of the risen Christ was at work in Jerusalem, in the wilderness of Gaza, and presumably in far flung places the apostles had yet to travel. The apostles are merely to join the one who has gone ahead of them to prepare the way. The writer tells us that it is the angel of the Lord that drives Philip out into the wilderness of Gaza. It is the Spirit that instructs Philip to approach the chariot and to interpret the scroll of the prophet in light of the life, death, and resurrection of Jesus of Nazareth, and it is the Spirit of God present at the eunuch's baptism that removes Philip to Azotus where he continues to proclaim the good news. This is Luke's way of reminding us that the work of salvation, the renewal of all creation that began in Christ and now continues in Christ's body, the church, is the work of God. The work of salvation is something in which we are graciously invited to share but not something we initiate or control.

1 John 4:7-21

In the epistle reading for the day the writer of 1 John defines the nature and character of the Christian life as being the way of love as it is manifest in Jesus. In the beloved community of the church we are to love one another because love is from God. The writer suggests that we know that God is love and that God loves because of the atoning work of Christ. Thus it is not that we loved God but that God loved us. But we should be clear, love as it is understood here is no mere sentiment or emotion, as our culture often defines love. It is less about how we feel and more about how we live. Christian love is a way of being and living that has its origin in the radical love of God as it is embodied in the life, death and resurrection of Jesus. The way of love is now the vocation of all who abide in Christ, a vocation made possible by the gift and presence of the Spirit. "Love one another" is the peculiar way of those who define themselves as disciples of the crucified and risen Lord. This means that the preacher must take care not to sentimentalize or moralize the call to "love one another" as it is less about what we do and more about how we align ourselves with the peculiar way of God in the world. The reader will recall that this text is appointed during the season of Easter as the church continues to consider the theological and practical implications of the Resurrection. That is, the cross and resurrection call for a radical reorientation of life so that the church comes to reflect or mirror the nature of its Lord whose nature and name are Love. In as much as our life together is shaped and defined by the radical, other directed love of the Son, the church becomes an icon of the beloved community of the Trinity and the ongoing embodiment of the love that is the source of creation itself. (David Hockett)

Worship Aids

Opening Prayer

Gracious and merciful God, source of our life and well-being. In your presence is beauty and truth and life. We, your church, come to this time of worship to abide in your glorious presence and to offer you a sacrifice of thanks and praise. Grant us grace that we might cling to you, love you, and abide in you, so that our life together might come to resemble the beloved community of Father, Son, and Holy Spirit, to whom be blessing and honor and glory forever and ever. Amen.

Prayer of Confession

God of perfect and perfecting love, we say that we love you. But far too often we abide in our own selfish and narrow desires, and your word does not become flesh in the way we live in the world. We say that we love our neighbor, but too often that means only those neighbors that we believe are worthy of our love. We claim to be your people, but we trade discipleship for mere religion. Forgive us and spare not your love from us. Come and fill our hearts with your love. Come and refine us and make us new. Cast out our fear and perfect us in love that we might worship and serve you in newness of life, through Christ our Lord. Amen.

Words of Assurance

The Lord who is Love fills us, refines us, and calls us to new life. Thanks be to God.

Benediction

Beloved of God, "in this is love, not that we loved God, but that he loved us..." (1 John 4:10). Go in peace to abide in Christ and to love and serve God and your neighbor to the end that the beloved kingdom may come upon the earth. Amen. (David Hockett)

The Skeletons in the Family Closet

First in a Series of Four on Christian Perspectives on the Modern Family

Matthew 1:1-17

A friend of mine is an avid if amateur genealogist. He spends hours in the local library and newspaper archives, at the records deposit of the county and university libraries in distant cities, all to uncover not his own family roots but the heritage and legacy of soldiers who fought in the Civil War. He is always ready, even eager, to share the latest minutiae he has discovered. I say this with affection: a quick way to derail your afternoon plans is to ask my friend about his most recent discoveries.

153

Recently he said to me, "There is lots of good stuff just in the lists," and by "lists" he does not mean the mere names of a certain lieutenant's progenitors and progeny, but what you might find on tax rolls and such: how many pigs and chickens the lieutenant had on his farm before the war and whether he had animals (or land) left when he returned home from the war. "Those kinds of lists are the untold history," my friend delights to say, "and that kind of history is what really connects our time to the past."

Our most recent conversation happened during Advent when I was preparing a sermon for Christmas Eve. While I have long followed the advice of my homiletics professors who warned us off the lists ("Not much meat on those bones! Nothing bores a congregation more than a sermon full of names or places or "begats." No one cares about the begats, so avoid the lists!"), after talking to my friend I looked at the genealogy of Jesus with a new perspective.

Matthew was very concerned about the "back story" of Jesus as it is represented in the long list of "begats" with which the evangelist begins his account of the good news. Some of the characters are unknown to us outside this index; some are names we know quite well, patriarchs and kings whose exploits are found in the Hebrew Scriptures. And intermixed here and there are not only Gentiles, but also four women. And not just any four women, but four women whose stories are less than pristine. The genealogy of Jesus, as conceived by Matthew, is in no way immaculate!

In Matthew 1:3 we find Tamar, whose story is told in Genesis 38. Tamar's husband was Er, a son of Jacob's son Judah. Er died before Tamar had children, leaving Tamar with neither husband nor offspring and, therefore, with little hope for the future. Judah suggested she "remain a widow" in the house of her father till another of Judah's sons was old enough to provide for her. Tamar did not wait, however, but took matters into her own hands.

After Judah's wife died, he sought comfort with a woman he took to be a prostitute. He left her with his "signet and cord" as pledge until he might send her proper payment—a kid from his flock. The woman was not a prostitute, however; it was Tamar, who had dressed herself as a harlot in order to seduce Judah. When she was found to be pregnant, Judah was ready to have her killed as an adulteress. Then she showed him the signet and cord, and Judah was forced to admit his own sin. She bore twin sons who, along with Judah and Tamar, are in the genealogy.

In verse 5 of Matthew 1 we find Rahab—the prostitute of Jericho who helped the Israelite spies escape and later gave birth to Boaz, whose wife

Ruth is also mentioned in verse 5. Boaz was a kinsman to Naomi, who like her daughter-in-law, was a widow, their husbands having died in Moab. Naomi's other son also died, but his widow returned to her own country while Ruth determined, famously, to stay with Naomi as she returned to Bethlehem, the hometown of her late husband.

These two unattached women, without resource or recourse, would have been easy prey for the worthless fellows in town as they gleaned from the fields after the regular harvest. But Boaz, the son of Rahab, took notice of how Ruth cared for Naomi, and instructed the harvesters both to grant her safe passage in the fields and to leave extra so that her gleaning would be less strenuous. He also shared food with Ruth, which Ruth shared with Naomi.

When the harvest was finished there was a great celebration. Naomi instructed Ruth to wait until Boaz was spent from both work and festivity—and also full of wine—and then to sneak, as it were, into his sleeping bag. Next morning, Boaz claimed her as his wife and soon she bore a son: Obed, who was the father of Jesse, who was the father of David.

The last woman mentioned in the genealogy is not mentioned by name, but by the name of her faithful husband, Uriah. As scandalous as the stories of Tamar, Rahab and Ruth are, each in their own way, the story of David and Bathsheba is so shameful that Matthew only alludes to it.

Is this the Bible or Jerry Springer? How surprising is all of this unholy stuff, these unholy alliances that we find in our Holy Bible? And what does any of this have to do with a Christian perspective on "the modern family"?

Only this: God is ever bringing divine purpose out of human scandal and sin. Families in the Bible are just as fragmented, just as torn, just as suitable for daytime TV as anything we can imagine. That is at least part of the story we find in this list. How hopeful to proclaim that God can use our families, too, such as they are, to work the divine purpose in the world. What wonderful good news that is! (Thomas R. Steagald)

Worship Aids

Call to Worship (adapted from Ephesians 3:14-15; 1 Peter 2:10)
Once we were not a people, but now we are God's people.
**Once we had not received mercy, but now we have received
   mercy.**

For this reason we bow our knees before the Father,
**From whom every family in heaven and on earth takes its
name.**
**All: God has made us a family, a people, a priesthood
proclaiming God's mercy to all generations.**

Collect

O God, whose habitation is among your children and who continually
brings order from chaos. Grant that as we bring the disorder of our lives
to the throne of your mercy we may be granted clarity of vision, serenity
of spirit, and singleness of purpose to praise you for your life in the midst
of our lives, and your Spirit's work to accomplish your will in and through
us. Through Christ our Lord. Amen.

Invocation

Come among us, O God, and give us a strong sense of your presence that,
as we confess our failures to be all we had hoped to be, we might find that
you are and have always been more than we imagined, and able to bring
your purposes to life in and among us. Amen. (Thomas R. Steagald)

MAY 13, 2012

✤✤✤✤

Sixth Sunday of Easter

Readings: Acts 10:44-48; Psalm 98; 1 John 5:1-6; John 15:9-17

Friends of Jesus

John 15:9-17

Today, Jesus surprises us by lifting up the image of friendship to describe his relationship with us. "I do not call you servants any longer... I have called you friends" (v. 15). Jesus, the Christ, the very Son of God, Lord of all creation, calls us friends. This means, to borrow from our Quaker brothers and sisters, that the church is a society of friends united by the love Christ has for each of us. Yes we are called to be servants and apostles but we are also, by God's grace, friends of Jesus.

Following the Resurrection and prior to his ascension Jesus shared with his disciples his vision for their life together, telling them that the love that united him with the Father now unites Jesus with his disciples and his disciples with one another.

"I've called you friends." In calling us friends Jesus has given us a new name, a new story, and a new identity, not that we've chosen, but one that has been chosen and given to us. Before we are anything else—husbands, wives, sisters, brothers, white, black, American, Republican, Democrat, employee or employer, tea partiers or teetotalers, we are friends of Jesus—we are Christians. We have been caught up in his story. By God's grace we have been written into the story of Jesus and his church. "I've called you friends," he said. One of the interesting things about life in the church is that as we come more and more to abide in Christ, to develop a relationship with Christ that is intimate and organic, we also come more and more to share life with others who are friends of Jesus. As a colleague once remarked, "Jesus makes strange friends."

We typically think that our friends are those we choose because we share something in common or we like each other. But Jesus clearly

157

reminds us that the basis for Christian friendship is much deeper. "You did not choose me, but I chose you" (John 15:16), he said. From a disjointed and unlikely group of tax collectors, fishermen, women, sinners, and religious zealots Jesus forms a society of friends whose life together is rooted in and grows out of their friendship with him. This society of friends is then called to embody the kind of radical, self-giving love that is seen in the life and death of Jesus. Being friends of Christ means that we are graciously chosen—chosen not because of any inherent quality we may possess and chosen not for reward but for the responsibility of being obedient to Christ's commandment of love. By calling us his friends it is clear that the invitation to share in friendship with Christ and in the fellowship of his church is Jesus' invitation to give. He decides with whom he will be friends. This is a radical notion for many congregations where sharing in the fellowship of the community seems to be often defined by life interests or family ties, rather than an intimate relationship with the one who makes strangers friends.

Finally, being friends of Jesus means that we are commanded by Jesus to love. Love is not a choice; it is the way of life for those who are friends of Jesus. Christian friendship is not so much about what we feel toward one another as it is about our willingness to follow Christ's example in considering the needs of the other before we consider our own. We are to love by laying down our lives for our friends (see v. 13). We discover what it means to be commanded to love one another in Jesus' sacrificial death. It is Jesus who demonstrates for us what it means to lay down one's life for one's friends. We don't always have to like one another, but we do have to love one another, because even when we were unlovable Jesus extended the love of God to us and made us who were once strangers—friends.

The surprising thing about being friends of Jesus is that the closer we draw to him the more friends we discover we actually have—even some we would have never counted among our friends and others that perhaps seem quite unlovable. We often romanticize and sentimentalize Christ's invitation to friendship with him. But it can be a radical thing. The world says, "Keep out those who are different, build fences and secure your borders." Jesus says, "Welcome and befriend the stranger." The world says, "Kill your enemies." Jesus says, "Love your enemies and pray for those who persecute you" (Matthew 5:44). The world says, "Only certain kinds of people are worthy of our friendship." Galatians 3:28 says that in Christ "there is no longer Jew or Greek, slave or free, . . . male or female; for all of you are one in Christ Jesus." The world says, "Maintain clear distinctions between the good guys and the bad guys." But Jesus once said to a group of former fishermen, tax collectors, religious zealots, betrayers, and saints, good and bad alike, "I have called you my friends."

What a profound gift we have been given—friendship with God. But make no mistake; this gift is also a command. We who were once strangers, far off from the promises of God, have been brought near because Jesus made us his friends and invites us to be his friends in the world. Our lives are forever redefined because of our friendship with him. Our vocation, our calling, our way in the world, is now to befriend any and all who are friendless, who themselves are lost and alone, estranged from God, from themselves, and from one another. As a society of friends the church points to the beloved kingdom of God where all are invited to gather around the table and share the feast of love in the name of the one who calls us his friends. (David Hockett)

Lectionary Commentary

Acts 10:44-48

This brief passage from the book of Acts is a portion of the larger narrative of the conversion of Cornelius found in Acts 10:1-11:18, which depicts the early church wrestling with the impartial nature of the gospel. That the gospel first took root within Judaism is not surprising considering the disciples were observant Jews. However, if the gospel is for all people, what is the relationship between Jew and Gentile, and who can be baptized and share in the table fellowship of the church? These are not merely practical questions, they are important theological questions that go to the heart of the nature of God, salvation, and the church.

The gift of God's Spirit was poured out on the church at Pentecost; now Peter and the "circumcised believers" witness an outpouring of the Holy Spirit on this group of Gentiles who had heard the proclamation of the good news. It is ultimately the gift of the Holy Spirit to these Gentile converts that convinces Peter and others that "... in every nation anyone who fears God and does what is right is acceptable to God" (Acts 10:35). This passage from Acts is a bold reminder that faith in the gospel and even the reality of the church itself are ultimately gifts of the Spirit of the risen Christ. The "Spirit blows where it will" (see John 3:8), the resurrecting God is unpredictable and uncontrollable; God the Father of our Lord and Savior Jesus Christ shows no partiality.

1 John 5:1-6

Here the epistle writer defines who we are as Christians. Those who believe, who place their trust in Jesus as the Christ, have been born of God. Their lives are defined by a new kind of existence in which their behavior is marked by obedience to the commandments of God. Given what John has said elsewhere about the commandments of God we can assume that a Christian's obedience to the commandments of God is characterized by love of God, love of one's fellow Christians, and love of neighbor—friend and enemy alike. It is by the church's faithful obedience to Christ that the kingdoms of this world are overcome—not by violence or coercion, but by the radical, self-giving, sacrificial love of God. (David Hockett)

Worship Aids

Call to Worship

Jesus said, "As the Father has loved me, so I have loved you."
So we come to abide in Christ's love.
Jesus said, "Love one another as I have loved you."
So we gather remembering that we are brothers and sisters in Christ.
Jesus said, "You did not choose me, but I chose you."
All: Lord, grant us grace to be friends of Christ, loving God and neighbor, and bearing fruit that will last.

Opening Prayer

Great and glorious God, we come into your presence this day making a joyful noise and praising your holy and beautiful name. You are a God of mercy who welcomes all. We come, not by any merit of our own, but by your gracious invitation. We come, male and female, rich and poor, black and white, sinner and saint, knowing that Christ Jesus laid down his life for us and called us friends. As his friends, may our lives come to resemble his life, so that in our life together we might become a living sacrifice of praise unto you. Amen.

Benediction

Brothers and sisters, you are the baptized, those who have been born of God. Go in peace obeying all the commandments of God and conquering the world with love, in the name of the Father, and of the Son, and of the Holy Spirit. Amen. (David Hockett)

Family as Pastoral Prophecy

Second in a Series of Four on Christian Perspectives on the Modern Family

Jeremiah 29:5-7

When it comes to what we might call "traditional values," the Bible seems locked in a family feud. On the one hand, there are passages that would appear to offer non-negotiable templates for familial and even social relationships. Of particular note in this regard are the household rules found in Colossians 3:18–4:1, Ephesians 5:22–6:9; and 1 Peter 2:13–3:7. These texts are sometimes regarded uncritically and wielded gracelessly as weapons against the perceived decline of family and the so-called "assault on marriage." As these "maladies" are perceived as eroding the "foundations of our way of life," these texts serve—for some—as prophetic defenses of a Christian view of both gender and role differentiation.

It can be argued, however, that there is nothing uniquely Christian about these patterns at all. In fact, the household rules may represent a kind of capitulation to the hierarchical social ethic of Roman society that valued the traditional family as a lynch-pin of the *Pax Romana*. Moreover, as these same texts endorse slavery as an acknowledged, unchallenged, and accepted social convention, the whole index is brought into serious scrutiny.

On the other hand there are passages that, to be frank, discount the value of families as we traditionally know them, and not least in the Gospels. Did Jesus not say, "Who are my mother and brothers?" and "Whoever does the will of God is my brother and sister and mother" (Mark 3:34, 35). Jesus also said, "Whoever loves father or mother or son or daughter more than me is not worthy of me" (Matthew 10:37)?

We might argue, however, that despite such statements, marriage and family are important threads in the fabric of the gospel. It is of no little importance that, according to John's account, Jesus' first "sign" took place at a wedding in Cana of Galilee. Exegetical and theological issues sometimes distract us from considering the context of this miracle as carefully as we might, but the episode itself—as well as our insistence (and persistence) in referencing it during services of Christian marriage—suggest it has abiding, pastoral importance for marriage.

Likewise, among Jesus' last words on the cross was a reconstituting of the beloved disciple's family to include Mary, and of Mary's family to include the beloved. Much as Jesus paired his disciples for their missionary work, he pairs the beloved and the blessed virgin Mary as a last act of care for them. Their new bond will bless both and provide for them the prospect of experiencing his continuing presence. After all, Jesus himself said "where two or three are gathered in my name, I am there among them" (Matthew 18:20). As one expression of Jesus' desire that his disciples become and remain united in the face of the fragmentation of the culture and its shearing forces, marriage and family have an abiding prophetic purpose.

Still, because the Bible gives an ambiguous witness as regards to marriage and family, it is no surprise to hear selective readings and conclusions from preachers or teachers with prior agendas. Specifically, if some segments of the church have failed to see that simply applying the templates found in the Epistles is wrong-headed, other segments of the church are just as mistaken to suggest that the templates are all the Bible has to say about marriage and family. In either expression the prophetic and pastoral dimensions of marriage and family are thrown out with the baby's bath.

Caught in the crossfire between "This is what a real 'Christian family' looks like!" and "These passages have no value to us!" are faithful men, spiritual women, and their children listening for a redemptive word, that while the shape of marriages and families may change with time and circumstance, the function and purpose of families do not.

As Genesis affirms, it is not good for us to be alone. Indeed, God proposes to place us in communities and families, there to find havens of faith, hope, and love. In continually bringing us together for the good of each and all, God's unifying work and word takes on flesh among us and offers powerful testimony against the rending forces of the culture.

In Jeremiah we most clearly see how family can be both a haven of blessing and an alternative to a culture's forces of fragmentation. In other words, Jeremiah demonstrates how marriage and family have both pastoral and prophetic power.

The context is the siege of Jerusalem, after the first but before the second exile. Many Hebrews have already been deported to Babylon, and false prophets have arisen to proclaim that the Jews' return to the homeland will occur very soon. Jeremiah sends a letter to them saying that by God's decree their exile will be long, their return is a somewhat distant occurrence. In the meantime the word of the Lord is that the exiles should ". . . build houses and live in them; plant gardens and eat what they produce. Take wives and have sons and daughters; take wives for your sons, and give your daughters in marriage that they may bear sons and daughters; multiply there, do not decrease. But seek the welfare of the city where I have sent you into exile, and pray to the Lord on its behalf, for in its welfare you will find your welfare" (Jeremiah 29:5-7).

Pray for Babylon! And live as if Babylon is your home—which of course it is. In the same way that Daniel and the three young men kept kosher as a way of maintaining identity in Babylon (see Daniel 1), the Hebrews were to do what Hebrews do best as a way of enacting hope in a desperate situation. Marriage, family, gardening, prayer—even political involvement, as much as was possible—were and remain daily ways of both guaranteeing identity and enacting hope in the time of exile. Such "pastoral" duties were about as prophetic as could be. (Thomas R. Steagald)

Worship Aids

Call to Worship

The Lord is the strength of his people;
God is the saving refuge of the anointed.
O save your people, and bless your heritage;
Be their shepherd and carry them forever.

Collect

O God, who has set the solitary in families and believers in community. You have made us who we are and have ordained that we should not live alone. Grant, therefore, that as we love and serve one another, our unity might be testimony to your Son Jesus Christ, who with you and the Holy Spirit lives and reigns, one God in glory everlasting. Amen.

Invocation

Come among us today, we pray, and make known to us how your will might be done in and through us so that all the families of this church, to the end that all the families of earth, might praise your name with unending song. (Thomas R. Steagald)

MAY 20, 2012

Seventh Sunday of Easter

Readings: Acts 1:15-17, 21-26; Psalm 1; 1 John 5:9-13; John 17:6-19

Let Us Pray...

John 17:6-19

What a powerful image this text offers; what a hopeful image for those of us who try to be faithful to the gospel, to serve the risen Christ, to be the church in the world. Jesus prays for us. Jesus prays for us that we might be faithful and well in a world that can be a frightening and dangerous place for those called to live and proclaim the gospel. Jesus prays for us.

Prior to his arrest, trial, and crucifixion, Jesus gathers his disciples and offers his final instruction concerning what is to happen to him and how that will shape and define their life together as the church. Following his instruction, with the disciples still gathered, Jesus prays for them. "I have made your name known to those whom you gave me from the world.... Holy Father protect them in your name that you have given me, so that they may be one, as we are one" (vv. 6, 11). More than likely it is not the first time Jesus had prayed for his disciples; it certainly is not the last. But here, in his most difficult hour, when they should have been praying for him, Jesus looks up to heaven and prays for his disciples. He holds the church up to God and asks for the continued well-being of those who have followed him. Given what is awaiting him, Jesus understands the reality of evil and the hostile nature of the world. He knows that his followers are likely to face persecution and great peril, even death, because of their fidelity to his name. Nonetheless, just as God sent Jesus into the world, so now Jesus will send his followers into the world to continue the work of the gospel, that they should be one, even as Jesus and God are one.

Now we should be clear, the point here is not some kind of sentimental unity and superficial lack of dissension within the church so that our lives can be free of conflict. No, the issue is the unified witness of the church to the gospel. In asking God to protect the disciples following his death and resurrection, Jesus is not promising the church a life free from hardship or suffering. Rather, Jesus demonstrates that although the world might hate us, the presence and power of the Holy Spirit and the church's intimate relationship with God and with one another, through Jesus, will enable and empower us to persevere in faithfulness. Jesus prays for us so that we might be something that apart from him would be impossible: the church. Jesus also asks that his followers be sanctified in the truth for continued growth in godliness and righteousness. He prays that our lives might each day come to resemble his own. He prays that our hearts might be one—one with him and one with one another.

I once had the privilege of attending a gathering where Mother Teresa was the honored guest and speaker. As she reflected upon her ministry with the poor, she remarked that she often prayed to God that she would not lose her grip on the hand of Christ. How comforting to know that a saint of the faith needed to pray that prayer. Even more, it is comforting to know that Jesus prays that prayer on our behalf as he asks the Lord to keep us united in love with him.

In praying this prayer Jesus invites us to join him in the unique way of life we know as Christian discipleship. What might it mean for pastors to pray this prayer on behalf of those who have been entrusted to their care? Of course we cannot pray the prayer as Jesus did because we are not to equate who we are and what we do with who he is and what he has done on behalf of the church and the world. But what if Jesus' words and way with his disciples became the way we live among those whom we serve? What might our ministry look like if we spent as much time holding the church before the Lord and asking God to protect and sanctify the church as we do complaining about what is wrong with the people we are supposed to love and serve? Not to focus all of our attention on pastors, what if, as members of the body of Christ and fellow followers of Jesus, we devoted as much time and energy to praying for one another and asking God to support, protect, and sanctify one another as we do gossiping, back-biting, and complaining? If the church commits itself, laity and clergy alike, not only to praying this prayer but to living it as well we just might, by God's grace, come to resemble the beloved community we are called to be.

As I pray and read Jesus' words I am mindful of the mystery and beauty of the Holy Trinity—one God in three persons. I am mindful of the holy communication, the intimate and eternal bond of love that exists among Father, Son, and Holy Spirit. In Christ we are invited to share in the relationship, the community, the fellowship, that exists at the very heart of God. In Christ we are caught up in the divine life. God has given us to the Son in and through the power of the Holy Spirit. We belong to Christ and thus we belong to one another. The church is an icon of the Trinity in as much as our relationships, our fellowship, our holy communication points to the life of the blessed and Holy Trinity. So in praying this prayer Jesus says, "This is who you are."

What good news—Jesus prays for us. Through his prayer, his unceasing intercession on our behalf, we become more than we would otherwise be. Through his prayer we become the church, God's gift for the life of the world. (David Hockett)

Lectionary Commentary

Acts 1:15-17, 21-26

Here, at the beginning of the book of Acts, Luke briefly recounts Judas' role as one of the disciples, his subsequent betrayal of Jesus, and the role his betrayal played in the larger work of salvation. Luke does not attempt to explore the psychology of Judas, nor does he seek to resolve the problem of evil or how one among the twelve would try to undermine the ministry of Jesus. Luke simply recalls Judas' betrayal of Jesus and the void left by that betrayal in the early church.

With the scene set in this way Luke quickly moves the action forward to the central matter at hand—the church's proclamation of the Resurrection. Judas must be replaced by one who was a witness to Jesus' ministry beginning with Jesus' baptism. We are told that the disciples then propose two individuals, Joseph and Matthias, as suitable replacements for Judas. The story is very matter of fact. The disciples pray, they cast lots, the lot falls on Matthias, and Matthias joins the eleven. With the selection of Matthias the "acts of the apostles" continue, and in the very next scene the Holy Spirit is poured out upon the church at Pentecost, Peter proclaims the gospel of the Resurrection, and the ministry of the gospel continues.

1 John 5:9-13

The writer of the epistle lays out the argument that the most significant and powerful testimony to the truth of the gospel is the internal witness of the Spirit of God bearing witness to our spirit that Christ Jesus is the Son of God. The writer asserts that those who believe are the very ones who have experienced in the depth of their being, in their hearts, the testimony of God or the witness of God's Spirit. This Spirit-initiated belief in Christ then shapes how the believer lives. Belief in Christ is more than intellectual assent to a set of propositional truths, and it cannot be reduced to mere feelings. Belief is both an affirmation and confession of the truth of the gospel of the Resurrection and an unwavering obedience and trust in the gospel of the risen Christ that shapes the life of the one who believes so that they come more and more to resemble the life of the One in and through whom they have come to believe. (David Hockett)

Worship Aids

Call to Worship

Almighty and everlasting God, your testimony is far greater
     than any human utterance.
Our delight is in you, O Lord.
You have given us life, and that life is in your Son.
Our delight is in you, O Lord.
In him our joy is made complete.
Our delight is in you, O Lord.
Come let us worship.
All: Give thanks to the Lord, for God is good.

Prayer of Confession

God of truth and grace, your testimony alone is worthy of our full acceptance. You alone have the words of truth and life, and in your word made flesh you have offered us the gift of eternal and abundant life. But we have been unwilling to listen. We confess that we have placed our trust in the empty speech of those who promise life but whose words are powerless and deceiving. Have mercy on us and forgive our unbelief. By your grace, grant us ears to hear and the will to respond that we might delight in your word and be counted among the congregation of the righteous, through Jesus Christ our Lord. Amen.

Words of Assurance

Hear the good news! Through the power and prayer
     of Jesus the Christ, you are forgiven.

**Through the power and prayer of Jesus the Christ,
you are forgiven. Amen.**

Benediction

Go in peace to bear witness to the eternal word of God in whom there is life and life eternal. Go in peace, delighting in God's law and filled with God's Spirit to serve the risen Christ wherever he may be found. Amen. (David Hockett)

The Holy Family

Third in a Series of Four on Christian Perspectives on the Modern Family

Ephesians 3:15-19

A book-touring author of my acquaintance, whose therapeutic practice is concerned mainly with marital and family counseling, was asked this question: "How many families are dysfunctional?" Without drawing a breath or batting an eye she replied, "All of them."

There was laughter all around before she proceeded to explain that marriages and families, like individuals (and congregations and institutions) labor against strong cultural currents that overwhelm our experiences and indeed sweep away many of our expectations (and illusions!) about what it means to be family. We sometimes work against ourselves and one another, and also against the purposes of God, by making assumptions about individuals, couples, and families.

Many years ago I worked in the youth division of a religious publishing house. I was up for a promotion and, at the same time, entering the final, painful phases of a divorce. My soon-to-be-ex-wife and I had no children, so the break would be as clean as any divorce could be—and even then it was horrible. I have heard it said that marriage is like gluing together two pieces of poster board; that divorce, conversely, is like trying to separate them again, and no matter how carefully it is done, there will remain tattered pieces of one on the other.

I had made it clear before I was hired that my marriage of six years was in trouble, that separation and divorce seemed imminent. The interviewer, who ultimately hired me, offered compassion and condolence—but he did not in any way suggest that my marital situation was problematic.

When he suggested the promotion, however, which would include some travel and public speaking in addition to writing and editing—my "situation" was suddenly a problem. His supervisor took us both to task and curtly said to me, "I cannot hold you up as an example to the young people of our denomination! They might conclude that divorce is OK!"

He was right in at least this way: I was no fit exemplar. Nor did he have to tell me I was a failure. I left his office wondering if I had forever excused myself from God's service.

That was a long time ago, and while I would not wish divorce on anyone, I have come to see that divorce does not automatically disqualify one for ministry, anymore than marriage (or celibacy) automatically qualifies one. Even if there was some merit on a practical level in the supervisor's position, at least at that time in that place, he was more than wrong theologically. His assumption was that my failure irreparably damaged me as an instrument of God's work. The unstated corollary is that only the pure and pristine are worthy to be in ministry.

If that were true, most of the characters in the Bible would be disqualified from ministry, and certainly would not be held up as exemplars, for fear the people might "go and do likewise" (Luke 10:37).

Throughout the Bible are descriptions of individuals, couples, and families that have gone out of whack due to jealousy, greed, adultery, revenge, unplanned pregnancy, even murder. That can be an embarrassment for folks who assume a too-easy association between rectitude and righteousness. The good news is that God works in and through the mess and muddle to bring about the divine purpose.

That is not to say that, knowing the value of David and Bathsheba's second son, Solomon, we are to commit adultery and murder—by no means! We do not sin that grace may abound. But when we sin, we can be sure that grace abounds as we repent. Seemliness is no closer to godliness than cleanliness, and it is a comfort to know that no failure, no sin, no wound can separate us from the love or purposes of God.

Even the holy family—Mary, Jesus, and Joseph—were beset by intrigue and rumor. Mary and Joseph were not yet married when she became pregnant. That is not to suggest that, as I heard one preacher say, unwed pregnancy is "OK," only that in and of itself unwed pregnancy does not disqualify us from serving God.

Joseph disappears from the scene sometime after the family's visit to Jerusalem and so Mary is, for a while anyway (and maybe a long while) single mother. That is not to say that single-parenthood is optimal, but only that we may not assume that nothing good can come out of such circumstance.

Jesus was referred to as "Mary's son," an insult in that you never, ever identified a Jewish boy by his mother's name unless you were unsure who his father was. Which is to say that, at some point, Joseph was lost not only to Mary and Jesus (and whatever other children or kinsmen there may or may not have been) but also to the memory of those who knew Jesus before he began preaching the good news. But if Joseph was not part of the equation anymore, God was and always is so that the redemptive work of the kingdom may be accomplished, social prejudice notwithstanding.

When we read the Bible with care, we soon discover that dysfunction abounds in most of the families we encounter. But there is also a sense in which the families of the Bible are groaning for a redemption they never quite experience, reaching for a reality beyond their ability.

If no family is entirely holy, then it is still worth proclaiming and trusting that all families, whether traditional, blended or non-traditional, are or can be instruments of holiness in the world. As we love one another, as we shelter one another and take shelter in one another, as we will what is best for one another and serve one another with gladness and self-denial, we do in fact become an example of God's love and grace, held up for all to see as an invitation to "go and do likewise." (Thomas R. Steagald)

Worship Aids

Invocation

Come among us, Triune God, that as Father, Son, and Holy Spirit are forever joined in mutual embrace, the ways in which we embrace one another might become a parable of your life, love, and purpose. Amen.

Call to Worship

O give thanks to the Lord, for God is good;
God's steadfast love endures forever.
Let the redeemed of the Lord say so,
**Those God gathered together from the east and the west,
the north and the south.**

Collect

O Lord our God, who has made us for one another, let your grace and our faith find expression in our mutual love, that our abiding bond will be the unity we know in Jesus Christ, who prayed that we might be one as you and he are one. Amen. (Thomas R. Steagald)

MAY 27, 2012

❧❧❧❧

Pentecost

Readings: Ezekiel 37:1-14; Psalm 104:24-34,35b; Acts 2:1-21;
John 15:26-27; 16:4b-15

Where's the Fire?

Acts 2:1-21

A young pastor served his community as chaplain to the local volunteer fire companies. One night, his first call came, and he jumped into his car and sped off into the night. A police cruiser, lights flashing, pulled him over, and the police officer sauntered up to the driver's side window, leaned in, and asked, "Well, sir? Where's the fire?" Without hesitation, the young pastor replied, "2116 Sherman Ridge Road!" Caught off guard, the police officer stammered, "Oh, well, OK then, follow me."

"Where's the fire?" is a common euphemism used in three different ways. In the case of the police officer, it meant, "What's the big hurry?" Others use the phrase to ask, "What's all the excitement about?" Another approach uses the saying to inquire, "Where's the passion and energy?" Any of these three questions is appropriately asked this Pentecost morning of anyone claiming to be a member of Christ's church.

The story of Pentecost in the second chapter of Acts—what is considered by theologians throughout the ages as the "birth" day of the Christian church—challenges us with the "Where's the fire?" question in all three different uses. Tongues, as of fire, descended upon the gathered disciples, and each was transformed—able to preach in foreign tongues with such fervor and passion that some thought they might be drunk. There was urgency in the message they shared. There was authority and power in their proclamations. There was deep, intense passion in their words. It causes one to pause and ask, "But where is the fire now?"

Where today is our sense of urgency? Do we still believe that our beliefs and deepest values are matters of life and death? Do we have a hope of

172

eternal life? Do we believe that there is a God who wants the very best for the human race? In the early church, believers expected an immediate return of the Christ, and there was immense pressure to get "right with God" as quickly as possible. The Christian faith truly was a matter of life and death. Today we do not hold a belief in an imminent return of Jesus the Christ, but we do live in a world that is a far cry from the kingdom of God promised in our holy Scriptures. There are gross injustices, economic inequity, widespread poverty, disease, hunger, and terrorism. We live in a violent and unpredictable world. There is incredible need in our world for love, kindness, peace, compassion, healing, forgiveness, and reconciliation. These things are not nice ideas that can be put off into some vague, distant future. The world needs the healing love of God in Jesus Christ right now. Today. There is no time to wait. The urgency of God's message of forgiveness, redemption, healing, and love is as great today as it has ever been. Where's the fire?

Why are so many people who love God with all their heart, mind, soul, and spirit so quiet about it? Where's the fire, the excitement? We call the stories of Jesus contained in the Bible gospels—good news. But it can't be that good if people aren't sharing it. When we get good news, we can't wait to share it. We love to tell people good news. Good news is exciting. Good news is compelling. Good news transcends mere information to touch people's emotions. Good news makes people feel good.

So what's the problem? Why aren't we telling people about God and Jesus Christ? A growing portion of the population in the United States has little or no church background, and even among churchgoers, a growing number of people have no basic knowledge of the Bible. We actually do have a story to tell to the nations, beginning with our own. We don't have to be scholars to tell the story. Nor do we need to cram it down people's throats. We merely need to be willing to share with others what our faith means to us and be able to describe some of the miraculous and marvelous stories from Scripture. We need to see the stories of our faith as gifts that we can share with others. We have the opportunity and privilege of introducing others to the God of love and light and life that gives our own life meaning. Where's the fire?

What about the passion? What about the energy and vitality and excitement that gets us up and moving and seeking others with whom to share this amazing faith? Think for a moment about something you absolutely love to do. No one has to ask you twice if you want to play your favorite game or go to your favorite restaurant or visit your best friend.

When you are passionate about something, it shows. We may show our passion and excitement in different ways, but it's there. It doesn't take much to tap into it.

So where is our passion when it comes to our faith? What moves us up out of our pews and sends us flying out into the world to put our faith to good use? What motivates us to get involved and to do for others, as God has done for us? Where is the fire?

As the early disciples were witnesses to the grace of God incarnate in Jesus Christ, we are the modern day equivalents. On this Pentecost Sunday, perhaps our prayer should be that the mighty wind of God's Holy Spirit would rush through this sanctuary and fill each and every one of us with a sense of urgency, real excitement, and a consuming passion to share the good news of Jesus Christ with everyone we meet. Of course, we need to be careful what we pray for, because God just might take us seriously. We could end up with more than just a warm, comfortable feeling. We could end up blazing brightly, witnessing to the world that Jesus Christ is Lord, and hearing again and again, "Oh, there's the fire!" (Dan R. Dick)

Lectionary Commentary

Ezekiel 37:1-14

There are times in our lives when we feel like giving up, when things have gotten so bad that there is no hope. But this passage from Ezekiel reminds us that God is greater than any problem. There is no such thing as an insurmountable obstacle or a hopeless situation. If God can reanimate dry, desiccated bones and give them vitality, then God can enter our desperate circumstances and give us a new beginning. God's Holy Spirit can work miracles. If we don't give up on God, God will not give up on us. No matter how bad things might appear, God might not be as ready to give up as we sometimes are.

John 15:26-27; 16:4b-15

Wouldn't it be wonderful to have been one of the original disciples, to have known Jesus when he walked the earth, to have heard him teach and seen him perform miraculous healing? The passage from John's Gospel reminds us that even though we are not in the physical presence of Jesus the Christ, God's Holy Spirit is with us, to guide us, to comfort us, and to help us witness to our faith. (Dan R. Dick)

Worship Aids

Pastoral Prayer

Take comfort in the knowledge that God is with us all, through the power and presence of the Holy Spirit. The Spirit energizes us and fuels the fire of our passion to share the good news with everyone we meet. In all ways, God is with us.

Invocation

We enter God's presence in the assurance that God is with us. We seek to experience God's grace and the love of Jesus Christ, through the blessing of the Holy Spirit. Open your hearts and minds to the transforming power of God. Amen.

Benediction

The Holy Spirit works within us that we might become the body of Christ for the world, able to teach as Jesus taught, to care as Jesus cared, and to serve as Jesus served. Go forth to honor and glorify God in all that you say and do. Amen. (Dan R. Dick)

Water Is Thicker than Blood

Fourth in a Series of Four on Christian Perspectives on the Modern Family

Mark 6:7

Gene (no real names used) is dying, but he is not alone. There is sadness but also hope. Gathered around his bed are not only his wife and two adult children—the only near blood-relatives he has—but also his pastor and members of his congregation. There is a greater circle around Gene's deathbed than the biological one, an unbroken circle of faith and hope, of grief but glad expectation—an outward and visible sign of that great family circle, the church expectant, which awaits his arrival.

Zachary is to have surgery, a very serious operation he may not survive. Zachary is only three weeks old, but there is no time to wait; his heart is malformed. The doctors have promised to do all they can, but they have warned his unwed, teenaged mother that the risks are great and to pray hard. Her immediate family, so recently upset and embarrassed at the revelation of her pregnancy, sets every emotion save love aside and begs their friends and congregation to pray for Zachary's well-being. A month ago they might not have dared to speak of the situation in polite company. Now all pretense and prejudice is dropped in light of the need of this poor child's poor child.

Their pastor suggests that Zachary be baptized at the hospital on the Sunday before the operation. He brings the font and Pascal candle from the congregation's sanctuary into the ICU. He expects to see four or five people other than the mother and immediate kin, but when he arrives the most of his 11 o'clock crowd have crammed themselves into a small room on the floor, along with members of the hospital staff. The preacher takes the frail newborn into his arms as he leads the gathered in the baptismal covenant. The sacrament makes the room full of friends and strangers a congregation; the hospital becomes a tabernacle of fellowship, of faith, hope, and love.

Richard and Dee Dee are getting married. The pastor reminds them how Jesus has promised that where two or three are gathered together in his name, Jesus is there with them. He says that their two will in all likelihood become three or four or more, and that they should always set a place for Jesus at the dinner table since, as people of faith, their wedding is an act of worship, their every meal a kind of Communion. Their every bath time may be a reminder of their baptism—all because their home will be a kind of congregation.

I believe it was Martin Luther who said something to the effect that a congregation is but the largest of families (and just as dysfunctional!), while families are but the smallest of congregations. During the wedding ceremony, before the vows that are at once something old and something new, the pastor reminds Richard and Dee Dee of an unusual text for a wedding, Mark 6:7 where Jesus "called the twelve and began to send them out two by two, and he gave them authority over unclean spirits."

The passage appears near the middle of Mark's Gospel. Already Jesus has done many miracles, and already the authorities are plotting to kill him. Already Jesus has called disciples, students, special friends, whose first task is simply "to be with him" (Mark 3:14). Before they ever do a disciple-type thing, they have to listen and learn, have to spend time with the Lord. And already they have done that.

In fact, they have spent enough time with Jesus and have learned enough of what he has to teach them, that Jesus is willing to send them out as his representatives. But before he turns them loose, he does two really important things.

Jesus pairs them up. That is one thing. It is interesting how in the Gospels about the only time the disciples get in trouble is when they are alone. Maybe you too remember a time when you got into trouble and you might not have if a friend, or wife, or child, a buddy or sponsor or member of your church had been with you. We are, it would seem, prone to trouble when we are alone (remember the garden of Eden?), and Jesus knows that about his friends. And so he pairs them up, sends them out two by two. They are better together than they are alone.

And then, after Jesus pairs them up, he gives them power over "unclean spirits." Now that language offends modern ears but we need look no further than the newspapers or Internet, the TV or silver screen, we need listen to nothing other than talk radio to know that there are some pretty unclean spirits out there. But together we are less susceptible to the seduction of those spirits than we are alone. Together we can remind one another of who we are and whose we are, of whom we serve and the purpose of our lives.

Bob and Ginger are getting divorced. It is a terrible moment for each of them. Neither took their vows with the thought of breaking them, but now there is not only hurt but shame and recrimination and terrible division of their formerly blended families—all of whom are members of one congregation. The daughter-in-law is set against her mother-in-law, and the husband is set against his father who does not approve. But somehow the congregation manages to gather around this dying marriage, keeps faithful vigil, and keeps the kids in the circle of their loving attentions. The water of baptism proves thicker than blood as the sacrament has made them all a family. Sad, yes—all deaths are sad. But they are hopeful too that even in the midst of this disintegration God can affect some good, can accomplish some unifying purpose.

Circles are formed, broken, and reformed, while all the families of the earth await the final consummation, when God's dwelling will be among his people, the Father among his children, and there will be no more weeping or mourning ever again. (Thomas R. Steagald)

Worship Aids

Call to Worship (Revelation 21)

Then I saw a new heaven and a new earth,
For all the former things had passed away.
And I heard a loud voice saying,
**God dwells among his children and he will wipe every tear
from their eyes and death will be no more.**

Collect

O God, whose son Jesus became flesh and dwelt among us, grant that in our lives and relationships we might incarnate the gospel of peace and love through the same Jesus. Amen.

Invocation

Pour out your Spirit on us, O God, who have gathered in this place as a family of faith. Help us to hear what you say, learn what you teach, live as you have lived, and die in glad hope of eternal life. Through Christ our Lord. Amen. (Thomas R. Steagald)

JUNE 3, 2012

❧❧❧❧

First Sunday after Pentecost

Readings: Isaiah 6:1-8; Psalm 29; Romans 8:12-17; John 3:1-17

Lip Service

Isaiah 6:1-8

The story of Isaiah's vision of God's presence is so compelling because it is so honest. In the presence of God's majesty, one can only imagine how inadequate and unholy one might feel. Although it is an unusual phrase, we can immediately relate to Isaiah's cry, "I am a man of unclean lips, and I live among a people of unclean lips . . . !" (v. 5). In the presence of purity and holiness and grace and light, it isn't hard to imagine every base, unkind, inappropriate, insulting, and coarse word a person has ever spoken coming back to mind in an instant.

"Unclean lips" is an evocative phrase, and it covers such a wide range of behaviors. Jesus challenged the Pharisees with the notion that it isn't what goes into a person that makes them unclean but what comes out that can defile. Insults, rumors, gossip, lies, unkind comments, thoughtless remarks, prejudicial statements, and putdowns all qualify. So do making promises we don't keep, telling people what we think they want to hear, making excuses, and blaming others. Of course, there's cussing, cursing, name-calling, and taunting, but it is hoped that we keep these activities to a minimum. No, in big and small ways, we are people of unclean lips, as well as unclean thoughts and not always sparkling behaviors.

The scriptural solution seems a bit extreme—searing away dirt, guilt, and shame as well as a healthy bit of flesh and blood—but it is worth exploring metaphorically. Short of cleansing fire, how can we become a people of clean lips—guilt-free, sin-free, redeemed, and renewed? Simply stated, we can't do much of anything . . . except receive the free and loving grace of God that makes all things new.

A young homeless woman happened into a United Methodist church in St. Louis on Sunday morning. Not a churchgoer, this woman felt she had run out of options. With nothing left to lose, she decided to try God. She quietly crept into the rear of the church and sat huddled by herself. She listened to the service, not fully understanding what was happening, and panic mounted as she heard the preacher talk about something called "Holy Communion." She listened to the invitation and the Great Thanksgiving and decided that it was not for her, that she was not worthy or welcome to get the bread and juice. She liked the ideas she heard, but she knew in her heart of hearts that she was an unclean person and that Communion wasn't for people like her. As she thought her thoughts, she was startled and alarmed to see a man and a woman heading toward her with bread and a cup. She gripped her hands together and shook her head from side to side.

"What's the matter?" the woman asked.

"I've never been here before. I don't belong here. I don't know what's happening," the young woman stammered.

Both the man and woman smiled. Then the man said, "You don't have to belong here. Holy Communion is for everyone."

"Not for me," the visitor replied. "I'm not a good person. That's not for me," she said, nodding at the bread and cup.

"This is especially for you," the woman said. "No one here deserves it. It is a gift to us from God. You don't have to get ready for Communion; Communion makes you ready to feel God's love."

The young woman sat with tears in her eyes, speechless. Still clutching her hands together in front of her, she clenched her eyes shut and opened her lips. The woman dipped a piece of bread in the cup and placed it in the young woman's mouth. As the sweetness of the juice and the rich flavor of the bread mingled on her tongue, the young woman broke down, sobbing, "Thank you, thank you," over and over.

This is what it means to be a person of unclean lips. We're not evil, we're not broken, and we're not mean or hateful. We are merely human. We are as God made us, desperately in need of love and forgiveness and second chances. Not one of us is worthy of the grace of God, but it is denied to none of us. It is a gift that cleanses us and changes us and makes us the people God wants us to be.

But this isn't the end of the story. One week later, the young woman returned to the church with five of her friends. She caught sight of the woman who had served her the week before, and she waved her over. "When's Communion?" she asked.

"Oh. Well, we only serve Communion the first Sunday of the month," was the reply.

Eyes wide, the young woman said in a shocked voice, "But we need it. I haven't felt anything so good in years, and I want my friends to feel it, too!"

Communion is God's gift to us, but it is not a luxury gift—we need it. It makes us "one with Christ, / one with each other," and it also makes us "one in ministry [and service] to all the world" (*The United Methodist Hymnal* [Nashville: The United Methodist Publishing House, 1989], 10). We are redeemed and renewed, but for a much larger purpose than our own comfort and delight. We are transformed as Isaiah was transformed, and when Isaiah heard God ask, "Whom shall I send?" his immediate response should be our immediate response, "Here am I, send me!" (v. 8).

Forgiveness, acceptance, healing, and love—we all need these things, and we should not be denied them simply because we are people of "unclean lips living among others with unclean lips." We need these things *because* we are people of unclean lips, and by God's loving blessing, we have been given enough love, healing, kindness, acceptance, and forgiveness that we can share it with everyone we meet. We offer nothing of lasting value if we waste our time judging who is worthy and who is not. None of us truly deserve, but all of us have been deemed worthy by God. (Dan R. Dick)

Lectionary Commentary

Romans 8:12-17

Truly we are brothers and sisters of Jesus Christ, children of God, led by the Holy Spirit. We enter into the Holy Trinity, made one with Christ. There is no stronger declaration of our adoption as children of God and joint heirs with Jesus the Christ than this powerful passage. If we take up the cross of Jesus Christ and suffer with him, we will also reap the reward of being glorified with him.

John 3:1-17

There is possibly no more often quoted and better known passage than John 3:16—which is perhaps unfortunate since it overshadows the grace-filled follow-up verse 17: "Indeed, God did not send the Son into the world to condemn the world, but in order that the world might be saved through him." So often we spend our time worrying about what we have been saved from instead of celebrating what we have been saved for. The heart of the Christian life is not condemnation but salvation. We need to guard against obsessive focus on sin, and shift our vision to the glorious redemption God offers to all. (Dan R. Dick)

Worship Aids

Prayer of Confession

Forgive us, O Lord, when we allow ourselves to doubt. We sometimes forget that you are with us, present through your Holy Spirit. Remind us that there is nothing impossible to those who hold fast to their faith in you. Amen.

Words of Assurance

"We know that all things work together for good for those who love God, who are called according to his purpose" (Romans 8:28). We love God, and we are called to do God's will. God will bless us and provide everything we need to fulfill God's purpose.

Benediction

Let us go into the world with confidence that God's Holy Spirit goes with us. We leave this place to share God's good news with everyone we meet, to share love and kindness and forgiveness—a witness to God's grace and power. Go in peace. (Dan R. Dick)

An Investment Strategy For Troubled Times

First in a Series of Three on Preaching to People in Exile:
Isaiah, Ezekiel, and Jeremiah

Rationale for the Series

The writing prophets of the Old Testament are often discussed as if the interpreter had a crystal ball, and moreover, as though all of the interpreter's predictions pointed to either the coming destruction of Israel or the birth, life, death, and resurrection of Jesus. This series attempts to emphasize the preaching of the prophets, and specifically their messages after the exile began, after their visions of destruction were realized. How could they offer words of correction and hope to an Israel who thought that life was over? How can pastors of today—preachers to the exiles of another era—re-interrogate these texts to speak words of encouragement, correction, and hope in the twenty-first century?

Jeremiah 29: 1, 4-7

One reason that I love coming to worship each week is that I get to be reminded of the "old, old story." Every Sunday, no matter what has happened over the course of the preceding six days, I am afforded the opportunity to plant two feet, bask in a familiar time and space with a familiar set of people, and together we say yes. We say "yes, this is true," and "yes, I'm going to try and embody this faith," and yes to a whole lot of other things.

The prophets remind us that this was difficult for the folks who had been carried off into exile. Remember, that fearsome and powerful empire from up north, Babylon, had conquered Judah and in 587 B.C.E., had hauled back to their country all the leaders in the community. They didn't take everyone, but they took those who had special talents and people who might be threatening to Babylon if they were left alone.

The Babylonians' strategy was twofold: not only would they deplete the fallen country of any leadership to foster a rebellion but also they would increase the human resources back home. They hauled these folks off, apparently with families and communities intact. They were taken away from their homes, away from their spiritual headquarters in Jerusalem. In brief, they were driven away from all that they and their ancestors had loved.

Imagine the disposition of that exiled group. Psalm 137 captures it rather pointedly: "By the rivers of Babylon, we sat down and there we wept . . . we hung up our harps . . . for there our captors asked us for songs." You can almost hear the Israelites asking, "Whoever heard of singing in captivity? And why should we build anything? Why marry, who would want to raise kids in this country anyway?" Some really good songs came out of this era, the kind in which the depression and anger come through, and the songwriter just lets it all hang out toward the end. Oppression does that some times. *Godspell*, the contemporary musical, had one musical piece that translated these feelings: "On the willows there, we hung up our lives" (Stephen Schwartz, "On the Willows" [Quartet Music, Inc., 1971]).

Of course, they hope this captivity is short lived. They probably even have some prognosticators, so-called and self-appointed "prophets," who tell them what they want to hear. "It won't be long now!"

There is never a short supply of preachers who will tell you what you want to hear. Jeremiah, of course, has a different approach. Rather than succumb to the easy messages of the day in order to make friends and gain listeners, he simply tells them what is. "You're going to be there a while folks—seventy years. So this is what God says, 'You need to build some houses and settle down. Quit living in this tent village under the bridge or in some van down by the river. Plant a garden and eat from it. Nurture yourself and quit worrying that Babylonian soil is contaminated. You can even drink the water. Get married and have babies. Grow your families, your communities, get involved relationally.'"

"Seek the peace and prosperity of Babylon." Now there's a stretch. "Help the Babylonians, work with them. Pray for them." Even crazier: "God is their God, too. Get spiritually involved in this culture. Live your lives. If you're a builder, build. If you're a singer, sing. If you're a parent, parent. If you're a farmer, grab a hoe."

"Invest in this now"—that's the word from this prophet. Invest in what you can never possess. Give yourself—your time, your talent—although you'll never take complete ownership of this place. These are important words, and they are meant for us too. Our sanctuaries, our buildings, our campuses, our friends—these are not ours, and yet God invites us to give ourselves to all of it.

Perhaps you are a young adult, and you attend a church in your college town. You feel a little exiled from your home, and you dream of it (maybe no one here makes sweet tea like your mother, or you're from the hills where there's a real fall, and you never run an air conditioner on Thanksgiving Day). But you find yourself here, a transient. Jeremiah says, "Invest yourself in what you cannot possess."

For senior adults who say, "I've done my time—one Sunday per month in the church nursery and one VBS per year for the last thirty years." No, this is not your eternal home, but hear Jeremiah saying, "Invest yourself in what will not be yours."

It's a good word for all of the middle-agers, too. Churches, after all, can change before our very eyes. Perhaps you wanted church growth at one time, but now you look around on Sunday and see more unfamiliar faces than familiar ones. You used to own this place, and now you can no longer be close to everybody and every decision. Jeremiah says, "Invest in what you cannot possess."

The church belongs to God. Remember that. And remember that even when you feel most at home, you are not. Rather, you are enjoying a gift from the source of all good things. Jesus said, "Where two or three are gathered in my name, I am there among them." (Matthew 18:20). All the things that we think make us happy are not really it at all. The beauty of your sanctuary? It's not God. It is good but not God. Those familiar faces? Those decisions of which you once took ownership? Not yours, but God's.

This Sunday, as you hear or tell the "old, old story," remember the source of your healing. It will be hard, especially when you feel something new and wonderful coursing through your body, and you want to deify your minister of music; and it will be hard if you are miserable in a new town or a new place of ministry and want to "go back home."

It is just difficult for humans to avoid confusing the source of our healing with the instrument of it. So, even as you give thanks and celebrate your church and your surroundings, remember who the source of your healing is. If you are experiencing some new life or perhaps seeing the relevance of the faith a new way, know that it is not simply because of a pretty place or some temple. It's not that you are hanging out with nicer or friendlier people or folks who "have it all together." It is because God is finding you and touching your life and knowing you. The instruments are finite and limited, and you cannot get from them what you need most: life.

That's the word from Jeremiah in this text. All of God's creation belongs to God. The church belongs to God. Even if you have been carried away into something new this day—perhaps even to exile—plant yourself there. Invest in what is not yours. Amen. (Scott Bullard)

Worship Aids

Responsive (Psalm 137)

By the waters of Babylon, we sat down and wept, when we
    remembered you, O Zion.
We hung up our harps. We hung them on the trees in the
    . midst of the land.
How shall we sing the Lord's song? We tread upon alien soil!
If we forget Jerusalem, our hands will lose their dexterity, our
    tongues will cleave to the roofs of our mouths.
All: Remember the day of Jerusalem, O Lord! Remember the
    day of Jerusalem!

Prayer for Guidance

All-knowing and ever-present God, even as we enter uncertain times, help us to worship you. Let us trust that your thoughts are indeed higher than our thoughts, that we may enter into new life even as the world around us says that our struggles are in vain. In the name of the Father, and of the Son, and of the Holy Spirit. Amen.

Benediction (Ephesians 3:20-21)

Now to him who by the power at work within us is able to accomplish abundantly far more than all we can ask or imagine, to him be glory in the church and in Christ Jesus for all generations, forever and ever. Amen. (Scott Bullard)

JUNE 10, 2012

❧❧❧

Second Sunday after Pentecost

Readings: Genesis 3:8-15; Psalm 130; 2 Corinthians 4:13-5:1; Mark 3:20-35

Unbinding the Strong Man

Mark 3:20-25

The title of this sermon is a nod to Ched Meyer's fabulous commentary on Mark's story of Jesus, *Binding the Strong Man* (Maryknoll, N. Y.: Orbis, 1988). Early in Jesus' ministry, in Mark's Gospel, Jesus is immediately a figure of controversy and concern. By chapter 3, he is already in trouble—with his family, his followers, and the political and religious leaders. Jesus challenges tradition, flaunts authority, and dishonors the family. Mark sets up the dynamic tension of the story very quickly—a story that promises to be an epic battle. Mark is widely acknowledged as the earliest of the written Gospels we have, so this author is following no one else's script. In this early encounter, Mark raises the question, "Who has true authority?" Does authority come from tradition and religion, or does true authority come from God? Mark says that the authority from God in Jesus the Christ trumps the authority of the established faith. The established authority of the day—the scribes—confront the new authority—Jesus—and attempt to discredit him by accusing him of being possessed by demons. Jesus deflects their accusations deftly, saying that Satan wouldn't destroy his own handiwork. The message here is fairly clear—evil doesn't cast out evil; good does. The author of Mark then employs a cryptic and somewhat confusing statement from Jesus, "But no one can enter a strong man's house and plunder his property without first binding the strong man; then indeed the house can be plundered" (v. 27).

Some scholars believe this statement means that Jesus has already taken care of Satan for the time being, and that the prince of darkness won't be much of a problem while Jesus is around. Others believe that Jesus is putting the religious leadership on notice—that he will "tie up" the establishment and usher in a whole new church. There is a third perspective that has significant merit, especially in our day of a "house divided" within mainline Protestant Christianity. Rather than a threat, perhaps Jesus is offering a word of caution—if the strong man, defined as our faith, is "tied up" in senseless debate, red tape, endless discussion, non-productive planning, power plays, institutional preservation, and political maneuvering, then virtually any "thief" can sneak in and plunder the house. In other words, all kinds of silly and simplistic alternatives to serious faith can attract people while organized religion isn't paying attention.

Spend a few moments in a book store or online at Amazon or Barnes and Noble and scan the titles in the sections on "religion," "spirituality," or "new age." What do you see? On any given day, you will see a wide variety of titles on prosperity gospels, praying your way to health, contacting spirits, "secrets" to success, encounters with angels, encounters with demons, "Christian" reincarnation, earth spirituality—you get the picture. One thousand and one options, from the ridiculous to the sublime, all aimed at a culture that says it is "spiritual, but not religious." The strong man of organized religion may very well be tied to its own ecclesial throne, while pretenders pillage and plunder the spiritually hungry and seeking.

We may be bound, but we're certainly not gagged. Part of our problem is that we are engaged in never-ending disagreements about who is right and who is wrong, who is good and who is evil, who is righteous and who is sinful. We are not seeking unity, harmony, reconciliation, or justice. We are merely adopting the secular culture's passion for competition and winning at any cost. Forget grace and forgiveness, ignore love and mercy, disregard patience and tolerance, and label justice and generosity as socialism and communism to put "those people" in their places. Turn religion from life-affirming, joy-producing, divine blessing into legalistic, authoritarian, proof-texting moralizing and no one has to break in and bind us—we'll do it ourselves.

Jesus goes on in Mark to say that any sin can be forgiven us except one—blaspheming the Holy Spirit. Blasphemy is one of those widely misunderstood concepts that get thrown around a lot by the people who understand it least. Contempt for God and the Word of God in thought, speech, or action is the essence of blasphemy, and judging other Christians is a primary form of blasphemy. Much of what we call "religious debate" is nothing short of blasphemy, and any time one "God-group" points a finger at another and disrespects or devalues the work of the Holy Spirit in the other's faith, it is an unforgiveable sin. Yet we keep right on doing it. We stick labels on people we disagree with—like fundamentalist, conservative, liberal, progressive—heaping contempt on their heads as a way to "prove" our own superiority. The time has come to unbind the strong man.

Religion has fallen on hard times. Once religion was worn as a badge of honor, but today virtually no one wants to be thought of as *religious*. Too many people equate religion with the worst possible behaviors associated with the church—self-righteousness, judgmentalism, condemnation, prejudice, intolerance among them. Sects, factions, denominations, splinters, and divisions send a message to the world that Christians can't get our own story straight. Petty bickering and conflict within congregations reinforce the impression that being Christian offers nothing of greater value than any other club or association.

So what can be done? While the answer is simple, it won't be easy. The time has come to set aside differences and focus instead on what we share in common. Jesus says in today's Gospel lesson, "But no one can enter a strong man's house and plunder his property without first binding the strong man; then indeed the house can be plundered." Let's begin here. Let's acknowledge that we believe different things and value different things and seek different things, but at our heart and core we are all one family, children of God, and brothers and sisters of the Christ. It won't change anything overnight, but one thing is certain. If we're all on the same side, there won't be any of "those people" left to dislike. (Dan R. Dick)

Lectionary Commentary

Genesis 3:8-15

Our entire Jewish and Christian history is a cycle of making and breaking covenant with God. We are claimed as God's people; then we take matters into our own hands and reject the holy and unconditional blessing of God. When will we learn? Time after time, God promises to be our God if we will simply agree to be God's people. Yet, each time we fail. This is why we need redemption through Jesus Christ. What is impossible to us is possible only through the miraculous grace of God.

2 Corinthians 4:13–5:1

Confidence, assurance, and trust—these are gifts we receive from our relationship with Jesus Christ. Sometimes, though, it is difficult to live with such trust and assurance. We forget that God is with us, that God will provide, and that the same Spirit that gave strength and guidance to Jesus Christ resides within us as well. This is our "blessed assurance"— Jesus Christ is with us in all that we say and do. (Dan R. Dick)

Worship Aids

Call to Worship

Enter the presence of the Lord.
We come seeking God's will.
God calls us to be Christ's body for the world.
By God's Holy Spirit, we can serve today
    as Christ served long ago.
Fill us, O Lord, with your Spirit.
And use us as you will.

Prayer of Confession

Forgiving God, we confess that we do not always trust in your promises. We are distracted and preoccupied by so many things. We forget to believe. We lose faith. We seek to handle things on our own. Help us, Lord, to remember who you are and to live in the confidence of the power of your Holy Spirit. Amen.

Words of Assurance

It is all too easy to focus on what we lack and don't have. But our Lord is a God of abundance, not scarcity. Our God is a source of providence and grace. No matter what happens, God will provide, and we can live in the assurance that we are God's own children. (Dan R. Dick)

The Words of the Watchman

Second in a Series of Three on Preaching to People in Exile:
Isaiah, Ezekiel, and Jeremiah

Ezekiel 33:1-11

The Old Testament prophets were both foretellers and "forthtellers." That is, they were often known for having a knack about what the future held for Israel, but it is important to be clear that this future was always tied to the ways in which the Israelites handled their relative freedom. We need look no further in order to gain a sense of this than Israel's experience in the monarchical era. Throughout periods of

190

apparent prosperity, Israel ignored God's call to them through the prophets that their increasing laziness, greediness, and refusal to take care of the poor would land them in big trouble. We saw this last week through Jeremiah.

In Ezekiel 33, we encounter a "watchman" who is to "look out" for Israel, keep an eye on the horizon for approaching enemies, and warn the people if danger is near. It is up to the people to listen to him or not. The watchman image has already been offered by Ezekiel in earlier chapters, and yet here—with the Israelites firmly entrenched in exile—we are tempted to ask, "What good is a watchman when you're already in trouble?"

Will the Israelites ignore this one, too? Israel didn't listen to the watchmen (or watchwomen) before—that's why they are in exile in the first place, isolated from their land of promise, their freedom, perhaps even some of their family members. *Ex*, by the way, is Latin for "out." The *exit* sign over the doors in your place of business say to you "this is the way out." Your *ex*, in contemporary terms, is someone you used to date or be married to. Or—to use a more theological example—to be *excommunicated* is to be kicked out of the church, or at least to be barred from taking Communion with fellow Christians.

Have you ever been in any sort of exile? Have you ever been suspended from school as a student—*ex-pelled* (there's that Latin word again)? Maybe some of you have taken a job in a place far away from home. The job wasn't exactly what you wanted, but you hoped that it might lead to another job closer to family or maybe to a better-paying job. Maybe your company transferred you, and you had to accept in order to keep your job.

What does something like this do to you? Perhaps your reaction to the exile is a better indication of your character than the actions—yours or someone else's—that got you placed in exile. The problem with being preached to when you are in a situation like that, however, is that you can't see what is in it for you. You are at the bottom of the well and, it's a long climb to get out of there. Besides, bottoms of wells can get comfortable in a strange sort of way.

I don't know about you, but if I were Israel, I would be tempted at some point to give up, to say to the watchman or the people listening to the watchman, "You know, who cares? I mean here we are, taken captive by the Babylonians, far from home . . . it can't get any worse. Let whoever is out there come over that horizon and wipe us out." Listening in exile is hard. Listening is similar to times when your parents sent you to your room when you were a child, and then came in later and preached to you about being nice to your brother, and you were just sort of expected to say "Yes ma'am."

Or maybe you feel like the watchman this week. Like it or not, you are preaching to those in exile, whether you are aware of it or not and whether you are doing it with your lips or your actions. You are around those who are missing out on the best that God's promise holds. Sometimes the problems are of their own making. Sometimes people—perhaps even people in the church—exclude them. Thus, whatever your "job" happens to be, your vocation is relatively straightforward (although not without complexities): to be present to those who need to hear a word from God, whether it be a word of comfort or a word of correction. Although they might not want to hear it or see it, their responses are not within your control. Yet you must be watching and waiting, acting and re-acting.

That's what Ezekiel was for the people: the watchman, standing guard day and night. And if Ezekiel saw something moving on the dark horizon—or heard the sound of soldiers moving or an errant sword or two clanging together—he would stand up for his people. The faithful watchman doesn't say "Oh, the Myers Briggs says I'm a classic conflict avoider; I'm just going to keep my mouth shut." The faithful watchwoman doesn't ask, "Who am I to say, 'Wake up?' ... I wouldn't want to appear bossy," or "What if I'm just imagining things?" That would be like a New Orleans meteorologist seeing the satellite image of Katrina and saying nothing. There's too much at stake to sit idly by.

The church is here, and as even Cain learned in those first few pages of the biblical story, we are our brother's keeper, our sister's keeper—not only as we model and bear witness to what can be, but perhaps even more as we let loose in this world the energies of God's grace and love. What we do impacts everyone—from those who know they are in exile to those who walk around believing themselves to be free.

The watchman was appointed because God knew. God knew that although Israel was in exile and perhaps thought it was there to stay, the future of the world was at stake. Do we? Wake up! Salvation is near! Put aside darkness and put on the armor of light. Clothe yourselves with Christ. Amen. (Scott Bullard)

Worship Aids

Prayer for the Bulletin

Am I on the lookout? Give me vision. Have I seen the enemy? Give me a sure mind and tongue, that I may sound the warning with clarity. Have

I been warned? Help me to suppress my prideful inclinations and flee to divine safety.

Prayer

O Lord who slumbers not, give us the vision, courage, and wisdom to be pastoral watchmen and watchwomen by day, and aid our brothers and sisters in protecting all from the enemy when the night falls.

Benediction (see 1 Thessalonians 5:6-10)

This week, "let us not fall asleep as others do, but let us keep awake and be sober; for those who sleep sleep at night, and those who are drunk get drunk at night. But since we belong to the day, let us be sober, and put on the breastplate of faith and love, and for a helmet the hope of salvation. For God has destined us not for wrath but for obtaining salvation through our Lord Jesus Christ, who died for us, so that whether we are awake or asleep we may live with him." (Scott Bullard)

JUNE 17, 2012

❧❧❧❧

Third Sunday after Pentecost

Readings: Ezekiel 17:22-24; Psalm 92:1-4, 12-15;
2 Corinthians 5:6-10, (11-13), 14-17; Mark 4:26-34

Kingdom Seeds

Mark 4:26-34

Jesus taught the crowds using parables. In our parables today, we see that Jesus used everyday agricultural language to talk about God. In the first parable, he speaks of someone scattering seeds and watching them begin to grow. If you have ever planted a vegetable garden, you know how amazing it is to watch how the seeds come up, begin to grow, and eventually produce a harvest. We don't know exactly why it grows or how it grows, but somehow the earth produces the harvest, and we are able to reap what was sown.

In the second parable, Jesus speaks of a mustard seed. It is the smallest of all seeds on earth, and so some might expect that the harvest from the smallest seed would be very small as well. However, Jesus says that from the smallest seed, the mustard bush becomes one of the greatest of all shrubs. It puts forth large branches and all of the birds of the air make nests from its shade.

Verse 33 tells us that Jesus spoke the word to them using many similar parables, and that he shared "as much as they could understand." But then, don't you wish you could have been one of the disciples for the private times when Mark says Jesus "explained everything" (v. 34) to them? Wouldn't we all love to get that commentary? If we could have access to the private explanations Jesus gave to the disciples, surely there would be less confusion and more understanding. If we could just have a private tutoring session with Jesus, wouldn't we understand God's hopes and dreams for us just a little better?

Since we don't have access to the private meetings where Jesus "explained everything," we simply do our best with the help of the Holy Spirit. Pentecost suggests to us that the Holy Spirit is present and active in our world. God does not abandon God's people, and the Holy Spirit is always available to us. The Holy Spirit gives us power to do ministry in Jesus' name and to speak the truth about God's love. In these two seed parables, we learn about that which seems to have been the most important topic for Jesus, the kingdom of God.

First we learn that there is mystery to the kingdom. Some of us do not like mystery in our lives. We want order and structure, and we want to be in control. However, we are reminded that God is sovereign and works in God's own way and timing. While we may see in other teachings that God desires for humanity to join in God's efforts, this particular parable suggests that even if humanity is oblivious to what's going on around them, God is still at work. This is good news!

A second thing we can learn about the kingdom of God is that God's workings may appear to be small and insignificant, but like a mustard seed, the kingdom will grow in significant ways. When we sing Handel's "Hallelujah Chorus," we affirm that the kingdoms of this world will become the kingdom of God. God's kingdom will reign supreme, and we will experience life as God intends.

When I came to be a pastor in Seneca, S. C., I was quickly invited to a meeting to talk about a possible homeless shelter for the county. I found out that there had been talks about a shelter for years, but most of the talks had died down and nothing had been done. As a good friend of mine once told me, "Sometimes when all is said and done, more is said than done." The need, however, was still there.

At first, only a few people met to talk about the need, but as the months went on, we eventually had eight churches gathered in the effort. After creating a board and getting 401C3 status, more and more people began to join us. City government, police, lawyers, doctors, churches, businesses, and other individuals began to catch hold of the need and possibility. In 2009, Our Daily Rest opened its doors and has had a significant impact in many people's lives. I see this as one example of how kingdom work can start small but can grow to wonderful proportions. As the birds of the air perch in the big branches of a mustard tree, so now many homeless people are finding shelter in our county.

Finally, we also learn that Jesus doesn't force feed us. Instead, he gives us as much as we can understand at this point in our lives. That is good news for humans, who are not perfect and who often are slow to understand. God gives us just what we need for each day and situation. Though we may not get the full picture or the deepest understandings that day, we catch glimpses of God's kingdom and that is enough. The Israelites had to learn that lesson over and over as they wandered in the wilderness. God will provide for our daily needs. We just have to trust and be open to receiving that blessing.

Here in Seneca, the impact is already showing evidence of God's handiwork. On the surface, people at the shelter are discovering a God who provides food, clothing, and shelter. Internally, they may also see that God grants us things beyond our physical needs—like grace, comfort, and peace. How thankful we are for a God who provides just what we need through kingdom seeds! (Ryan Wilson)

Lectionary Commentary

Ezekiel 17:22-24

The imagery of the cedar shoot growing and prospering so that birds will nest in its branches is one of hope for a people questioning their place in the world. Although Israel may feel small and insignificant now, every nation will come to know of Israel's God through the reversal of fortunes. Ezekiel affirms Israel's God as sovereign over all, and he wants to reaffirm God's promise to David's line.

2 Corinthians 5:6-10, (11-13), 14-17

Paul writes about living by faith and not by sight. One component of that faith is the work of reconciliation. Because of what Christ has done for us, we are new creations. Paul is less concerned about what is happening around us and more concerned with what God is doing within us. That's where the true changes are made and where God wishes to dwell. One question for us might be, "Are we hardening our hearts or are we like clay, ready to be molded?" (Ryan Wilson)

Worship Aids

Call to Worship

O God of the seed, come and dwell in us. Plant us in the good soil, and water us with your love so that we will be productive and useful for your kingdom.

Prayer of Confession

Dear Lord, we confess that we often try to take the mystery out of our lives and simply rely on ourselves rather than on you. We also judge things by the standards of the world rather than by your standards. Help us to know your word and obey your commandments. Forgive us when we think that life is simply about us and forget that our purpose is to be fruitful and multiply your kingdom.

Litany of Assurance

We do not always know how.
But the soil produces grain.
We try to produce things in our own time.
But God harvests when the time is ripe.
We judge things by their size.
But God begins with a mustard seed.
We do things for our glory.
But God grows us to benefit others.
(Ryan Wilson)

Homeward Bound

*Third in a Series of Three on Preaching to People in Exile:
Isaiah, Ezekiel, and Jeremiah*

Isaiah 45

When Jesus, in Luke 15, tells the parable about the lost brothers, we all nod when we get to the part about the younger of the two asking for his inheritance and then wandering off into a far country to squander it. And yet, perhaps as a sign of our tendency to overlook mistakes that people make when they are young, we smile—or perhaps even shed a tear— when he comes to himself and rushes home to his father, who greets him with a kiss and throws a party.

This connects with us because, as we've been saying for the past two weeks, we all know a little about exile—chosen or not chosen—and about not being home and that sense of being made for more. As Joni Mitchell once wrote, we all think "we are golden. And we've got to get ourselves back to the garden" ("Woodstock").

Today's text, in one sense, is the beginning of the trip back to the garden. It's the payoff for this tour through the Old Testament prophets. It is different from the other texts in that, not only is there some hope for a return to Jerusalem, there is a name associated with that hope.

But before we get to the name, let's remember the backdrop from the last couple of weeks. The people have been in exile under the Babylonian empire after possessing the Promised Land for a time, and that came only after centuries of enslavement in Egypt. All of this, of course, came after God promised the land to Abraham and Sarah.

Really, then, the backdrop for this story isn't just the Babylonian exile but the entire Bible! After the sermons about why the people were in exile and the encouragement to invest in where they had to be, let us assume that the Israelites were really trying, doing their part. They were fasting, working without too much complaining, and worshiping. There is textual evidence for this, and the Israelites added determination to keep up the good work if they ever got back to Jerusalem.

But when Isaiah hints to them that they will eventually return home, he begins with an allusion to Cyrus, not the Jews; not an Israelite king, but a Persian king. God tells this foreign ruler that God will "subdue nations before him and strip kings of their robes to open doors before him" (v. 1). Sure enough, we know now that Persia came and defeated the oppressor of the Israelites, those Babylonians, and became ruler over Babylon and Israel. We also know from the end of 2 Chronicles that as one of his earliest acts as ruler of this part of the world, Cyrus told the Israelites that they could go home.

Whether this is a savvy political move to keep the subjects happy and motivated, or whether Cyrus does this because he is a genuinely benevolent ruler has been debated for centuries. But this question subverts the meaning of the text, for the title given to Cyrus in Isaiah 45:1 is *messiah*. The text clearly calls Cyrus God's "anointed." His decree will send Israel packing for home.

Although we cannot underestimate the relief or sense of hope this text might have instilled in God's people, Isaiah's description of Cyrus would have raised more than a few eyebrows, to say the least. "'Messiah,' you say? Messiahs only come from David's line!" Perhaps you are even out there in the congregation. and you are thinking, "Well, since the birth, life, death, resurrection, and ascension of one particular member of David's family in the first century A.D., we have reserved that title for one man, and one man alone, lest we commit blasphemy." Perhaps God's people found some comfort, however, in some of the lines that follow. This is all "for the sake of my servant Jacob, and Israel my chosen."

So the Jews will be homeward bound. There will be joy, of course, but there is that heavy reminder that will accompany it, that this good thing is not their doing but the work of a foreigner. Moreover, we're going to begin calling foreigners messiah? "Thanks for the vote of confidence, Lord...just when we thought we were 'back'!"

The truth of the matter is that this is not a story about the Jews or even about King Cyrus, but about God. The text includes several direct proclamations of "I am the LORD" (vv. 5, 6, 18). We might do well to read, "Israelites: I am the Lord, not you and not Cyrus." In brief, it is God who has freed the Jews. Perhaps they believed they could work enough to earn their way back home. Perhaps they believed someone would lead them back home through military coup or political power. But these will not save them and, as many of the prophets point out, reliance on their own political machinations rather than on God is what trapped them in the first place. "Remember that trick that Egypt played on you, O Israel? Why don't you go reread Hosea 7?" Sure enough, God shows them that just as God employed an "outsider," the Babylonians, to enslave them, God could use another one, the Persians, to liberate them. God is God, and humans are not. So much for our plans!

Well, what can Israel learn from this experience as the exiles journey toward home? Israel is headed home to Jerusalem, not Eden. What about us? Wherever we are headed—perhaps you've been eyeing a patch of grass that appears a little "greener" and now it is finally accessible—there are humans waiting on the other side. If humans are there, we will experience joy, but there will also be struggle.

I recall, when I was resigning from my first youth ministry job to move to a church closer to the seminary I was attending, the pastor said to me that "the faces there will be different, but the problems will be the same." There is no Eden, no Promised Land here on earth—at least in the sense that we normally think about these kinds of things. If we are honest, we know that the human condition always includes tests—even if we find our beloved, land that dream job, or retire to the Hamptons. The question is what are you learning on the way there? What are you consuming so that you may be consumed with the things of the living God and God's call to you—and to Israel—to proclaim God's glory "so that they may know that I am the LORD, and there is no other" (v. 6)? The word from Isaiah, and indeed all the prophets, seems to be that we must remember who we are, even if we are jettisoned to some place that we do not wish to be. May we do that today and everyday—whether we are on the way to some lonely outpost, firmly entrenched in exile, or on the way home. Amen. (Scott Bullard)

Worship Aids

Quote for the Worship Guide

"You have made us for yourself, O Lord, and our hearts are restless until they rest in you." (Augustine of Hippo, *Confessions*, 1.1.1)

Responsive Reading (Psalm 146)

Praise the Lord!
Do not put your trust in princes, in mortals,
   in whom there is no help.
When their breath departs, they return to the earth,
   on that day their plans perish.
Happy are those whose help is in the God of Jacob."

Prayer

God, we ask for your strength and continued communion as we emerge from this place today and carry the gospel to our homes, to our neighborhoods, and to our places of business. As we minister to others, help us to remember our own periods of exile and that you alone, O Lord, are our true home. Amen. (Scott Bullard)

JUNE 24, 2012

❧❧❧❧

Fourth Sunday after Pentecost

Readings: Job 38:1-11; Psalm 107:1-3, 23-32; 2 Corinthians 6:1-13; Mark 4:35-41

When God Finally Speaks

Job 38:1-11

When people hear the name Job, it's amazing to me how many talk about his patience. Maybe they have read the book of James in the New Testament and taken his interpretation of Job's perseverance and patience. When I read the book of Job, I definitely get a sense of Job's perseverance, but I'm not so sure about Job's patience. In fact, his words to his friends and to God seem anything but patient to me. Job's words seem direct, demanding, accusative, and questioning.

As we approach chapter 38, we must remind ourselves of everything that has happened to Job. Although he was blameless and upright, his whole world has fallen apart. Everything you can imagine in Job's world has been taken away. His children have all died. His possessions have been plundered. Job's health has become unbearable. Job's friends have come to try to ease his pain, but all they have done is accuse Job of sinning and tell him that he needs to get right with God and all will be well again.

Eliphaz has told him that the world is just . . . you reap what you sow. The righteous will prosper, and the wicked are punished. In the end, don't worry, because all will be okay. If you want to be prosperous again, agree with God and return to the Almighty. Zophar has said that the world works. God is just, and sometimes God's ways are too complicated to understand. Trust in God and turn back to God. If Job will direct his heart rightly, then God will bless him again. Bildad has said that the wicked will be punished. We may not always think so, but they will. If you want to be prosperous again, seek God. We assume that all of these suggestions come from well-intentioned friends to help Job deal with his suffering and unfortunate situation.

Job has denied that he has sinned and feels that his friends have white-washed the truth. Through his suffering, he has lamented to God and now wonders why God hasn't answered. Job wants his friends to stop talking about him and to look at him and see the truth of his situation and suffering. Job complains that God is absent and that God's silence suggests that God is Job's enemy. The lack of God's response means that God is acting in a sinister way.

Job vows that the problem is not with him, but rather, the problem is with God. In chapters 29–31 Job begins to put God on trial. He talks about the past when he always loved God and was a leading citizen in the community. People came to him for help and advice. But now his entire world has fallen apart, and Job sits on a manure heap with sores all over his body. Finally, Job takes an oath of innocence and subpoenas God to answer. If God doesn't answer, Job says, then it means that God is guilty.

Although Job has asked and even demanded that God speak, God hasn't spoken in thirty-six chapters. Although Job has taken God to trial and demanded an answer, God hasn't mounted a defense. Although we often want quick and pat answers from God, more often than not, we find that we cannot pressure God into answers. But finally, in chapter 38, God speaks! God speaks at length! Basically for almost the rest of the book of Job, God has lots to say. The silence of God is broken with a dramatic entry, and God comes speaking out of a whirlwind with a force that would blow anyone away. Instead of giving specific answers to issues of justice, however, God takes a different approach. God asks how Job can speak words without knowledge.

Do you know people who speak words without knowledge? People who are full of hot air? Have you ever encountered someone claiming to have the truth, when in fact, their message is far from the truth? Have you ever thought you had something all figured out, when in fact, you had only part of the information and needed to get the full story? Have you ever needed a larger perspective than the one that you possessed?

In chapter 3, Job cursed creation; here, God begins to give Job a different perspective of creation. Job goes on a God-guided tour of the cosmos! In our passage, Job is shown the first two corners of the cosmos...the foundations of the earth and the waters of the sea. Job has limits, but God's role in creation is vast and limitless. God is architect and builder. Everything has a role and a place. It's as if God says, "OK Job, you've asked me lots of questions and accused me of certain things; now you stand up and be accountable . . . take a new look and see if you have the same questions or opinions."

Job cursed creation, but God doesn't answer Job in kind. God has something to teach us and can sometimes overwhelm us with new perspectives and new insights. Instead of making statements, God asks questions (Who? Where? What?). Instead of giving answers, God puts the ball back into Job's court to make a new opinion. Instead of resolving questions about justice and injustice, Job is overcome with a new vision of the grandeur of God. God offers Job something more valuable than answers. Job meets the answerer, and that is enough. (Ryan Wilson)

Lectionary Commentary

2 Corinthians 6:1-13

Can you tell what matters are important and what matters are indifferent? That's really what Paul is asking the church in Corinth to think about. Learning what God values helps us differentiate between the two and gives us a glimpse at what is of value for our own lives. One thing Paul wants the Corinthians to value is reconciliation. Paul wants to work with God and with the Corinthians in a cooperative effort, and Paul suggests that reconciliation must be at the heart of life and faith.

Mark 4:35-41

Each of us must answer Jesus' question to his disciples, "But what about you? Who do you say I am?" (Luke 9:20). It is the question of discipleship. It is the question of identity. To say in faith that Jesus is the Christ, the Messiah, ultimately is to put all one's trust in him. The question of Jesus' identity appears throughout Mark's Gospel. When hard times come and when doubts arise, we often panic and wonder if God cares. But here in our lesson, Jesus reaffirms that we can put our trust in Jesus; God calms the raging storms of life. We have not been abandoned, but rather we find that Jesus is right here in the boat with us all the time. (Ryan Wilson)

Worship Aids

Call to Worship

We cry out to God for help. We cry out to God for answers. But when God speaks, are we ready for God's voice? Prepare your hearts, minds, eyes, and ears for what God would have you hear.

Pastoral Prayer

Lord, when we look at the world around us that you created we realize that we are small. Sometimes that makes us think that we are unimportant or insignificant. Yet you tell us to stand up and be who we are created to be. You made us a little lower than the angels, and you know the very number of hairs on our heads. We are made in your image, and you value us as a parent values a child. Help us to live into that value. May we see our significance, and may that self-image help us to know who we are, whose we are, and what we are about. We pray in your Son's name, Jesus Christ, our Lord. Amen.

Benediction

Now may the God of the universe answer your prayers. May God's voice not overwhelm you but give you insight into the vastness of creation. May you know that you are valued beyond all measure. Amen. (Ryan Wilson)

"I Am the Light of the World"

First in a Series of Seven on the "I Am" Sayings of Jesus

John 8:12; 9:1-12

For seven Sundays this summer we are going to explore the "I am" (*ego ami*) sayings of Jesus. These sayings tell us who Jesus is for the church and believers (Christology). One example of an "I am" saying is when Jesus tells the crowd, "I am the bread of life" (John 6:35). Many note the relationship between Jesus speaking these words and the revelation of the name of God in the *theophany* (manifestation of God) to Moses at the burning bush (Exodus 3:14). We will go in the order of the seven "I am" sayings in John with the exception of reversing the first two, since on the first Sunday of the month many traditional churches celebrate Holy Communion: thus first the light and then the bread.

As a precursor to the story of the man born blind, John puts the words, "I am the light of the world" (8:12) into Jesus' mouth. After foretelling John's death and teaching about Abraham, John tells the story of the blind one [Read applicable portions of John 9:1-41]. I have even seen youth groups share this story as a drama in seven acts: (vv. 1-5) the disciples and Jesus walking and talking; (vv. 6-7) the healing; (vv. 8-12) the neighborhood scene; (13-17) the first questioning by the Pharisees; (vv. 18-23) the Pharisees question his parents; (24-34) the second questioning by the Pharisees; (35-41) Jesus returns.

The first question raised is why Jesus healed the man on the Sabbath? After all, this blind person may have been blind for twenty, thirty, or even forty years. Why not wait just one more day? The answer is, of course, that John wanted to underline what the New Testament tells readers in another place: "Then he said to them, 'The Sabbath was made for humankind, and not humankind for the Sabbath; so the Son of Man is lord even of the Sabbath'" (Mark 2:27-28).

Second, John reveals that Jesus' work creates conflict and division. Righteousness has a way of doing this. The neighbors cannot decide whether or not the one healed is the one who was formerly blind. The blind man's parents are pitted against the leaders of the synagogue, and the Pharisees contend with one another over the meaning of this healing and the one who has done it. When people do the right thing, it often creates conflict.

Third and last, John raises the question of who is truly blind. It seems that the only one who sees begins in the narrative as blind, and the ones who seem to be sighted are, in reality, blind. This is an intentional irony that John does not want us to miss. He even has the Pharisees ask the foolish question, "Surely we are not blind, are we?" (v. 40) at the very end of the story.

We would do well to look carefully at each of these three issues because these are the questions that the writer wants us to explore. But I want to focus on a simpler issue never mentioned directly in the story. I believe it is where John is leading us.

Verse 32 tells us, "Never since the world began has it been heard that anyone opened the eyes of a person born blind." Jesus has just performed a wonderful miracle! A person who has seen nothing his entire life can now see clearly. Does anyone congratulate him or say a kind word? No!

Not one person in this whole story says a word of congratulations or thanksgiving for God granting sight to this blind one. I find this odd. Of all the responses to this miracle that could have been narrated, John suggests not a word of amazement. All the people do in response to the blind one's good fortune is pick his experience apart and disparage and criticize his healing.

How often does this happen in our lives? How often do we protect our religious turf rather than thank God for the simple and good things that God gives us? In a country that complains about its inability to say prayers in public schools, how often do we in our own families stop to say grace before meals? Many Christian families have raised a generation of children who pray neither at school nor at home. Celebration is missing in this story of the man born blind, and often it is missing in our own lives.

I heard a colleague relate an incident that happened during a bride's trip down the aisle for her wedding ceremony. It seems that a person who was hard of hearing leaned over to a neighbor and said quite loudly, "I read that over fifty percent of people who get married are divorced within only a few years." Some folks can't set aside even an hour to celebrate the joy of another. By not mentioning any celebration in this story, I think John reminds us of how petty and irrelevant we look when we forget to say thanks or to celebrate life.

Today is a good day for all of us to remember that celebration is one of the keys to a real life of faith. Perhaps knowing how to celebrate is a key to true sight. Celebration of a great healing is worth our time and attention. Amen. (David Mosser)

Worship Aids

Call to Worship

Gracious God, as we gather to praise your holy name, remind us that as we glorify you this day, you created us in your image. Give us a sense of worth as children of a heavenly parent. May we join our voices as those whom you have brought from death to life. Hallelujah! Amen.

Prayer of Confession

O God of an infinite number of acts of forgiveness, because you have called us to be your people, help us confess that we have strayed like lost sheep. We put our heads down and eat as we move along until twilight; then we look up and know we are lost. Be our light and give us hope. Amen.

Words of Assurance

Hear the good news. God will not abandon even one lost sheep to the wilderness. Thanks be to God!

Benediction

Carry the light of Christ into the world and then be the light as God's very own people—in the name of the Creator, Sustainer, and Redeemer. Amen. (David Mosser)

JULY 1, 2012

❦❦❦❦

Fifth Sunday after Pentecost

Readings: Lamentations 3:23-33; Psalm 30; 2 Corinthians 8:7-15; Mark 5:21-43

The Right Kind of Giver

2 Corinthians 8:7-15

I have learned as a parent that generosity is not a gift with which everyone is born. In my family, for instance, my oldest child has always shared easily, loves giving gifts, and on more than one occasion, cleaned out her piggy bank to give to a missionary, her church, or some charitable cause. My second child, on the other hand, reluctantly shares, is generally bothered to the point of misbehavior when others receive gifts, and can be downright stingy with his own money. Myself a joyful giver, it has been eye-opening to see the lack of desire and even struggle some have in regard to giving. For many much older than my young son, the idea of giving causes stress and discomfort. In church ministry, I've witnessed people squirming in their pews during stewardship sermons and building campaigns. Yet the concept of giving has always been an important one in God's relationship with humanity. Throughout Scripture, not only the importance of actual giving but of the attitude behind giving is emphasized over and over. In 2 Corinthians, Paul addresses this issue with the church in Corinth.

The act of giving is exemplified as an important human response to God's blessings and grace early in the Bible. In Genesis 14, Abraham demonstrates his thankfulness for the Lord's aid during battle by giving God a tenth of everything. Deuteronomy 12 instructs the Israelites on their tithe to the Lord. Proverbs 28:27 describes the importance of giving to the poor. Perhaps one of the most well-known scriptural words regarding giving is found in 2 Corinthians 9:7, as Paul writes of God's love for a joyous giver. Even Jesus taught of the importance of giving. His, however, was a lesson in attitude, which would be increasingly important in the first-century church. In Luke 21, Jesus praises the generosity of the poor widow who gave all she had even though it was just two small copper coins. As the early church struggled to survive and thrive, giving was an integral part of the church system. Not only was financial support needed for the churches and their leaders, Acts 2 describes the belief of the early church that they should share with one another all that they had, even selling their possessions to care for one another.

As Paul writes to the Corinthian church, he encourages them in their generosity as they follow this model of the early church. As a group of believers removed not only geographically from the earliest followers of Jesus but culturally as well, the Corinthian church struggled with some of the early Christian theology and practice. A church about whom Paul obviously cared greatly, he communicated with the congregation a number of times in regard to the practice of their faith and their own struggles with differentiating their new lives in Christ from their Greek, and largely pagan, culture. In 2 Corinthians 8, Paul encourages them in their generosity. He first shares with them news of the generosity of the Macedonian churches who were giving, even out of extreme poverty and need. Paul then encourages the Corinthian church to pursue excellence in their giving just as they have excelled in other areas of their Christian lives. It is unclear whether this was an area of struggle for the church, or if they were perhaps merely behind in their yearly pledge (possibly suggested in v. 11.) For whichever reason, Paul here begins teaching on generosity and giving that continues through chapter 9.

Chapters 8 and 9 deal with the giving of the Corinthians, but more specifically with their generosity. Although the two seem to go hand-in-hand, Paul emphasizes the importance of giving out of willingness and joy. Throughout these verses there seems to be some suggestion that the Corinthian people may have been experiencing some type of financial hardship that was making it difficult to complete their gift. Paul encourages them to give with the same love and sacrifice exemplified by Christ who gave up his heavenly riches in order to bring us our spiritual poverty (utter dependence on God). Paul goes on through chapter 9 encouraging and admonishing the Corinthians in their attitude of giving.

It's perhaps important to clarify what Paul was really after in this text. Although the churches and ministry did rely on financial support, Paul himself seemed careful not to rely personally on their funding. He wasn't simply trying to collect money from the church at Corinth; he was concerned about the effect of their generosity, or lack thereof, on their spiritual lives. Paul didn't want their fear or lack of faith to prevent them from completing their gift. He also wanted the Corinthians to embrace the equality that the early church leaders tried to foster. In striving to be more Christlike, Paul knew that if the Corinthian's were unwilling to sacrifice their money, real sacrifice would be unlikely.

Financial sacrifice is hard. God knows that. God also knows our circumstances and attitudes. While God doesn't want us to be irresponsible financially, I think God wants us to be careful in our priorities. God also wants our trust that the creator God of the universe is more powerful than our finances and will faithfully meet our needs even if our wants are unanswered. God wants more than just our tithe, God wants to be our number-one priority and for our lives to be spent sharing God's love in whatever ways we can. If God is our priority, our generosity will be evident and our giving complete. It doesn't mean that giving will be easy, especially to those generosity-challenged, but it does mean a shift from a grueling task of sacrifice to a precious act of love.

Dear God, open our eyes to the needs around us and accept our offering of generosity as we seek to share with others. Amen. (Tracey Allred)

Lectionary Commentary

Lamentations 3:23-33

The Lamentations of Jeremiah, the weeping prophet, is not a feel-good text. Exactly as it is entitled, it is the lament of one who suffered greatly in his service for the Lord. It is, however, full of hope. This passage extols the never-failing compassion of God, the compassion that is new every morning. Suffering is a part of the human life. Not one of us will be exempt. There are times when we, like Jeremiah, will feel desperate and woeful. This passage reminds us that there is always hope in the Lord, hope that is a renewable resource.

Mark 5:21-43

Our lives are often busy. Sometimes, our "busy-ness" is task oriented and meaningful, and sometimes it's just busy. At times busy-ness can feel like a treadmill going faster and faster without really getting anywhere. For me one of the worst things to happen when I am busy is interruption. In this passage from Mark, Jesus is very busy. He is teaching and healing. In this particular story, he is presumably about to teach a crowd by the lake when he is interrupted by a man with a sick daughter. Jesus stops what he is doing and follows the man to his home to see his daughter. While en route, Jesus is interrupted again. This time, a desperate, chronically ill woman stops to touch him in hopes of being healed. He stops, heals her, and blesses her before continuing on to the home of Jairus. While this story has much to say about faith, I think the way that Jesus embraces each of these interruptions is powerful. Jesus' compassion for people was so great that he welcomed the interruptions as opportunities to serve. May we live our lives in that same way, moved by our compassion for the world around us. Lord, interrupt our busy-ness and use us to touch those around us. (Tracey Allred)

Worship Aids

Call to Worship (Psalm 66)

Shout with joy to God, all the earth!
Sing the glory of God's name; make God's praise glorious.
Say to God, "How awesome are your deeds."
All the earth bows down to you;
    they sing praise to your name.

Prayer of Confession

Eternal God, we are aware today of your perfection and holiness. We thank you for your love and mercy during all the days of our lives. We ask your forgiveness for the ways we have failed you and your creation this week. (*Pause for silence.*) We ask you forgiveness for the hurtful words, actions, and even thoughts we have had. (*Pause for silence.*)

Words of Assurance

O God, you are the perfect giver. Thank you for your gift of forgiveness that we so humbly accept. Amen. (Tracey Allred)

"I Am the Bread of Life"

Second in a Series of Seven on the "I Am" Sayings of Jesus

John 6:24-35

Last week we began our summer's seven Sunday sermon series exploring the "I am" (*ego ami*) sayings of Jesus. These sayings tell us who Jesus is (Christology). An example from last Sunday is when Jesus tells the disciples, "I am the light of the world" (John 9:5). We also noted a relationship between Jesus speaking these words and the revealing of God's name to Moses at the burning bush (Exodus 3:14). We will proceed in John's ordering of the seven "I am" sayings, except we have reversed the first two because many churches celebrate Holy Communion on the month's first Sabbath: thus first the light and then the bread. Today we survey Jesus' declaration, "I am the bread of life."

John 6 reports two miracles, the feeding of the 5,000 and Jesus walking on the water. Our lesson today takes up where the feeding left off. The crowds look for Jesus, and when they do not find him, they then "[go] to Capernaum looking for Jesus." [Read John 6:24-35]

In John 6 we recall that Jesus feeds about 5,000—and even has "leftovers" (John 6:10). The people follow Jesus and go from place to place simply to hear Jesus speak and perform miracles. Later, after the feeding, Jesus walks on the water as he approaches the disciples' boat as they row across "the sea of Tiberias to Capernaum." The previously fed crowd eventually finds Jesus and asks: "Rabbi, when did you come here?" (v. 25). As this crowd—and every crowd—will soon discover, Jesus is not easy to keep up with. In fact his answer belies that Jesus is onto them: "You are looking for me, not because you saw signs, but because you ate your fill of the loaves. Do not work for the food that perishes, but for the food that endures for eternal life, which the Son of Man will give you" (v. 26-27).

When Jesus speaks to the crowd about bread, we might assume they understand the connection between bread for physical survival and bread that nourishes the soul. While it is true that human beings do not live by bread alone, it is also true that we do not live long without it. But spiritual nourishment is now what Jesus offers them.

As is often the case in John's Gospel, Jesus makes the theological distinction between the physical and the spiritual—in this case bread. Jesus even uses the illustration of wilderness manna to make his point to his Jewish listeners. It is God who provides this bread, and they ask Jesus to "give us this bread" (v. 34). Bread represents the hospitality of God, and when Jesus tells the crowds that "I am the bread of life" in v. 37, Jesus suggests that he is the gracious bread of God's grace. God gives Jesus to sustain us spiritually as authentic bread sustains us physically. If human hospitality is a blessing, think of the value of divine hospitality.

In the late 1970s, I lived in Liberia, West Africa. Liberia has existed at the poverty level for decades, even though it became the first African democracy in 1847. A morning newspaper reports that Liberia's unemployment rate sits at 85 percent. Yet my Liberian year amply taught me about the stewardship of hospitality, grace, and welcome—which often was taught at a table and involved bread.

When my African students took me to preach at their "bush churches," the people received us foreigners as royalty. Each village hut expected us to dine inside—and sumptuously! I have never eaten so much food in my life. These blessed people offered us much, yet possessed little. Even with little to share, the gifts of hospitality and welcome were always ready at hand. They emulated the grace God had shown them in their lives. What they had, these African villagers saw as God's gifts. Therefore, they only thought it natural to share their bounty.

As believers, we receive more than grace in Jesus as the bread of life. God also gives us sacred memory through the shared table. The church provides wonderful and compelling connection to our Savior, Jesus Christ—all through sacred memory. Whenever we celebrate Holy Communion, it is an act of both remembrance and anticipation. We experience Communion as anticipation because the holy meal is, in a sense, "bread for the journey."

As we enter the uncharted waters of change and the future, we need the sustenance that only God provides. In the Exodus story, God provides for the people by furnishing a day's worth of manna. "The Israelites ate manna forty years, until they came to a habitable land; they ate manna, until they came to the border of the land of Canaan" (Exodus 16:35). God did not provide it for two days or a week at a time. Rather, God provided the manna only a day at a time. This reminds the people (and us) that believers are in the hands of providence day by day.

Jesus taught his disciples to pray: "Give us this day our daily bread" (Matthew 6:11). Thus, we anticipate our future with God as we remember God's past providence. As we remember the important days of our lives, we know that just one day makes all the difference. No matter how much we encourage one another by saying, "May we never forget," we are people, and people do forget. Each time we break bread and recall Jesus' words, "I am the bread of life," we remember—and it is sacred.

We come to the Lord's Table today [if the church in fact celebrates the Eucharist on this Sunday] because each of us senses, or wants to believe, that somehow in the breaking of bread we will see Jesus. In a sense, each loaf of Communion bread is a miracle loaf because for us this bread represents the miracle of God's love coming into the world and entering our mortal bodies. This bread we break is Jesus, the bread of life, broken for the world. Why? Because Jesus said: "I am the bread of life." (David Mosser)

Worship Aids

Invocation

O God, we gather here as if before your heavenly throne. May our worship today be inspired by your Spirit. May our singing, praying, and preaching be not only faithful to the truth but also pleasing in your sight as we celebrate Jesus, "the bread of life." Amen.

Words of Assurance

As the Lord cares for the entire created world, so God cares for you as a beloved child. Arise and go with God's peace as God hears the confession of your heart.

Benediction (Micah 6:8)

O God, we have eaten of the bread of life and tasted your goodness in our worship this day. May we carry your charge to "do justice, and to love kindness, and to walk humbly" with you, our God. Amen. (David Mosser)

JULY 8, 2012

❧❧❧

Sixth Sunday after Pentecost

Readings: Ezekiel 2:1-5; Psalm 123; 2 Corinthians 12:2-10; Mark 6:1-13

Called by Love

Ezekiel 2:1-5

The love of God is abundantly clear throughout the Old Testament. From God's initial covenant with Abraham, God desired a relationship with the Israelite people. The majority of the Old Testament is the story of God's relationship with Israel and their journey together. God delivered Israel from famine, slavery, and its enemies. God provided for both physical and spiritual needs. God restored the people to their Promised Land, making them a strong people. God was repeatedly faithful to the people of Israel, and yet the people struggled and failed. Anyone but God might have given up on the faithless group, but God continued pursuing them, even in their rebellion. It is out of that very love that God called Ezekiel and many other prophets to deliver a word to the Israelite people.

Like most of the Old Testament prophets, little is known about Ezekiel or his life prior to God's call to prophecy. He is the son of Buzi and is a priest or at least in the line of priests (v. 3). He is among the Israelite exiles in Babylon. Ezekiel's first encounter with God occurred during the fifth year of the exile of King Jehoiachin, who was in exile thirty-seven years before being released (2 Kings 25:27). According to 1 Kings 25, Jehoiachin would have been in exile for about nine years when Jerusalem fell, so Ezekiel's initial call came when the Israelites were still in a state of partial exile. The book of Ezekiel includes prophesy spanning about eighteen years. (The last date given is in Ezekiel 40, which is stated as fourteen years after the fall of Jerusalem.) Although there are few personal details about Ezekiel other than the fact that he is married (ch. 24), Ezekiel's is one of the more colorful ministries of the prophets, as God spoke to him not only through dreams and visions, but God also instructed Ezekiel more than once to include an object lesson in his message. For instance, once Ezekiel was instructed to lay on his sides for more than a year to represent the number of days Israel had been in sin.

The passage we study today deals with Ezekiel's call by God. Ezekiel's calling begins by the Kebar River in a complex vision that concludes in chapter 1 with Ezekiel seeing a figure he believes to be God surrounded by fire and light. God then speaks to Ezekiel and gives him instructions. Ezekiel's story is similar to other call stories in Scripture. God speaks to him, raises him to his feet, and directs him on what he is to do and say to the rebellious people of Israel. Interestingly, and uncharacteristic for many of those God called, Ezekiel does not argue, and other than being a bit overwhelmed by all that he is experiencing, is obedient without complaint.

Experiencing a call by God is a powerful thing, so powerful stories of call fill the Bible. At times, those being called are ready and willing, like Abraham and Ezekiel. Other times, they are fearful and reluctant to follow, like Moses and Jeremiah. The call stories are important, not just because of the narratives of which they are part but also because they represent our human nature in relationship with God. Although it's easy to relocate "God's call" to those who are called into vocational ministry, this is not what Scripture presents. God calls each of us, every believer, to serve God and humanity in the way that we are gifted. Our reactions are often like those in Scripture. Sometimes we are elated and willing, eager to start God's work for us. Other times we are scared out of our minds and unsure of our abilities. Many times we are somewhere in between, willing but anxious. This is one of the great things about Ezekiel 2:1-5. As God calls Ezekiel to deliver God's word to the rebellious people of Israel, God does not promise that it will be easy or even that the people will listen to him. God doesn't lay out a timeline or five year plan for Ezekiel. God doesn't provide him with an army battalion or a police escort. God simply reassures Ezekiel that God is sending him and that Ezekiel is to be God's prophet. It is the same kind of assurance that God gave others, including Abraham and Sarah, Jacob, Moses, David, and Jeremiah. It is the assurance that God is the one who has called and that God will be with them.

I can still vividly remember the night as an eighteen-year-old that I felt God's call. It was very different from Ezekiel's; no fire, lightening, or heavenly vision. There was no burning bush or audible voice. It was, however, so clear. It was unmistakable, and although I wasn't sure exactly what God was calling me to do, I knew without a shadow of a doubt that God was going to be with me and would lead me to and through whatever was ahead. Through the years, the ups and downs of life and ministry, I have often remembered that night. In dark moments of doubt and frustration, I remember my call, and the assurance I felt of God's abiding love. I think that's the power of a call story. That's why it's important to experience that first moment with Ezekiel, Moses, Jeremiah, and others. Although we all have different specific callings, God's love and support are the same. It is a love so great that it pursued the rebellious Israelites for generations; and it is a love that promises to be with us, even when the road ahead is difficult. Thanks be to God! (Tracey Allred)

Lectionary Commentary

2 Corinthians 12:2-10

I remember one of my seminary professors suggesting that deep relationship with God really comes only through suffering. As a twenty-three-year-old recent college graduate and one-year veteran of ministry, I was quite sure of myself and my relationship with God, and I was offended that my professor would suggest that something was missing. He of course was right! It took a few years, some humbling, and even a little sadness to realize that indeed we do experience God in a whole different way when we are weak or suffering. I think Paul would have had the same struggle as a young man, even as a young Christian, as I did with my professor's comment. As a matter of fact, in 2 Corinthians 11 and 12, Paul gives all the reasons that he has to boast in his life and faith. Then in 12:7, he writes about a thorn in the flesh given to him by God to keep him from becoming conceited. This weakness helped him see that God's grace was sufficient, and that our power in God is made perfect in weakness. I do not think that Paul is suggesting here that all suffering comes from God. Paul is suggesting that in our weakness, we recognize God's strength and our need for God's grace.

Mark 6:1-13

Growing up with Jesus must have been quite an experience. Other than a few mythical accounts, there is really not much known about his childhood, but one would imagine that there must have been something a little different about him as the perfect Son of God. In the one story we do have from his childhood, twelve-year-old Jesus is teaching a group of people in the temple. Yet years later, when Jesus' ministry actually began, some of his biggest doubters were those in his hometown. Those who should have known him best and had probably even experienced more hints of his "Godness" rebuked him and were offended. It is easy to judge their lack of faith and shortsightedness. I wonder what our reaction would have been. I know, for instance, that I don't always recognize Jesus' or God's hand in the world. Even as a believer, I sometimes completely miss those Christ moments, opportunities to catch a glimpse of Christ at work. Sometimes, we think we know so much about Jesus that we miss Christ at work in our midst. It was the same problem he had in Nazareth, and one that we might be careful to avoid in our own spiritual lives. (Tracey Allred)

Worship Aids

Prayer of Confession (from Psalm 123)

Eternal God, I lift my eyes to you, hear the words of my heart today. Forgive me for my sins of commission. (*Pause for silence.*) Forgive me also for the things I overlooked or failed to do. (*Pause for silence.*) Have mercy on us, O Lord, have mercy on us.

Words of Assurance (from Psalm 138)

I will praise you, O Lord, with all my heart. When I called, you answered me. Amen.

Benediction

Now, go into your world embracing all that God has called you to do and knowing that the God of Abraham, Moses, and Ezekiel is with you every step. Amen. (Tracey Allred)

"I Am the Gate"

Third in a Series of Seven on the "I Am" Sayings of Jesus

John 10:1-10

My spouse is a kind of mini-rancher or farmer. She regularly receives agricultural catalogues in the mail. I look at them when I occasionally eat alone. Recently a catalogue for fencing, of all things, intrigued me. I learned there is deer fencing to keep deer off of your putting green—if you have one. There is chain-link fencing, and wooden plank privacy fencing, wrought-iron fencing, and many more types. Of course, where there are fences there are gates—stairwell gates, home security gates, child safety gates, and gates to protect swimming pools.

Recently I discovered that fencing has many laws written for clarity in the legal disputes about property and livestock. For example, "Wyoming was considered an open range state. Today, the Wyoming livestock industry is the state's second largest industry" (http://wlsb.state.wy.us/LE/fencelaw.htm). The website further explains the origin of legislation about fencing in Wyoming. Since Jesus' time, fences and walls have been topics of great land use interest.

Out West, people even today ask the question: "Are you fencing in or fencing out?" I suppose this means that animal owners are either keeping their livestock together and protected within the boundaries of a fence, or they are protecting the livestock from outside predators like coyotes, wolves, and mountain lions. Fences in this respect are self-evidently good things; but what about fences and walls and other barriers between people? What if the people on one side of the barrier are for us like a "thief and a bandit" (v. 1)? What is Jesus trying to tell us by saying that "I am the gate for the sheep?"

If we carefully read this lesson, we see that it is an extension of John 9—the story of the man blind from birth. If so, then Jesus is still indirectly addressing the "blind" Pharisees. On occasion the artificial divisions of the biblical text into chapters and verses can work against our understanding of the overall narrative context of the Gospel.

It is most important for us to see the idea of the good shepherd who enters into the sheepfold by the gate as the same one who gave sight to the blind man. Ironically, as the Pharisees try to protect the integrity of the Jewish faith by their inquiries into the blind man's circumstances, the Gospel of John divides people into those who belong to the sheepfold (and thus to Jesus) and those who climb "in by another way" (v. 1).

When Jesus speaks of the gate, he also implies the fence metaphor (a gate without a fence or wall or other barrier would be pretty absurd). We see fences all around us. In his poem, *Mending Wall*, Robert Frost tells readers that "Good fences make good neighbors." Many have speculated about his meaning, but for our purposes we can certainly see fences or other barriers as lines of differentiation between people or as ways that define us. Some people suggest we should obliterate these divisions, but at times they are necessary for us to identify ourselves.

An entrance, entryway, or portal into something protected or privileged concerns Jesus in today's lesson. The one who duly enters through the gate is the shepherd of the sheep. Next week we will explore more fully the image of Jesus as the good shepherd, but for now we note that the shepherd is the rightful leader of the sheep or the people.

Today's lesson reminds us that sheep sometimes need protection from thieves and bandits. One way to know the legitimate shepherd is not only because the sheep know his voice but also "he calls his own sheep by name and leads them out" (v. 3).

In the second half of the text Jesus also talks about those who are saved as those who enter the sheepfold through him—the Messiah. Jesus comes to offer abundant life, and this surely is a gift of God.

How does the gate of the sheepfold work? It is simply the portal through which the legitimate leader of the sheep enters and through which the sheep exit when they go out to pasture each day. As an enclosed space, the sheepfold offers protection and safety. Could the church be like the sheepfold? We must take care not to carry John's imagery too far, yet this designation of the church is a possibility. The church is led by Jesus and the Spirit, but it is not a place of coercion or force. Rather it is a place where we may abide in peace and from which we may receive "life, and have it abundantly" (v. 10).

Jesus said once, "Come to me, all you that are weary and are carrying heavy burdens, and I will give you rest" (Matthew 11:28). When Jesus bids us come to him it is always by way of a gracious invitation. God in Christ goes no further with us than to invite us into the sheepfold where Jesus is the good shepherd. (David Mosser)

Worship Aids

Call to Worship

O Lord our God, cleanse our hearts and purify our lives before you. As we come before you in worship today to consider Jesus as the gate to the sheepfold, make us those who love you enough to share our praise. Amen.

Pastoral Prayer

O Divine Spirit, we celebrate in a community of faith, and for this we give you thanks. As those who are part of Jesus' holy flock of disciples, help us listen for the sound of his voice and heed his offer of security for our common life together. We pray this in the name of the Good Shepherd. Amen.

Offertory Prayer

God of unlimited mercy and abundance, help us reflect on our wealth, which comes from your generosity. Give us the wisdom to treasure our opportunities to be generous toward others. In Jesus' name we pray. Amen. (David Mosser)

JULY 15, 2012

❧❧❧

Seventh Sunday after Pentecost

Readings: Amos 7:7-15; Psalm 85:8-13; Ephesians 1:3-14;
Mark 6:14-29

Measuring Up

Amos 7:7-15

I recently observed a kindergarten teacher attempting to photograph her class at a special event. She instructed them to line up by height, which was apparently typical instruction for the class. I watched as the group of five-year-olds attempted their queue. There were of course a couple of standouts, the obviously tallest and smallest, but overall the lineup was an assortment of tipped toes and craned necks, as each boy and girl tried to out-measure his or her classmates. Whether we like it or not, even from a young age, we as human beings care a lot about how we measure up. It is why adolescent boys pray to grow taller, and women of all ages and shapes slip their shoes off before they are be weighed. Even when we realize our limited control of our genetically predisposed measurements, most of us spend a significant part of life wishing we were taller, shorter, slimmer, or broader. As a matter of fact, God is also concerned about our measurement, albeit not our physical growth but our spiritual. Amos 7 illustrates God's concern with the measurement of God's people, both the chosen Israelite people and all of creation.

Amos was a prophet of God about whom we know little. He was a shepherd called by God to deliver a word of prophecy to Israel from Tekoa, which was in the land of Judah, south of Bethlehem. His ministry took place two years prior to the earthquake when Uzziah was king of Judah and Jeroboam was king of Israel (see Amos 1). While God's word to Amos was initially a series of charges against the neighbors and enemies of the Israelites, the bulk of Amos' prophecy dealt directly with the sins of the Israelites. They failed in their relationship with God and

221

forgot God's many instances of deliverance. God's judgment of the Israelites in Amos was thorough, addressing both their flagrant sin and their perhaps even more disturbing complacency.

Amos 7 includes three visions of God's message and intention for the Israelites. In the first two instances, Amos cries out to God on behalf of Israel, and God relents. In the third vision, God shows Amos a wall that has been built true to plumb and a plumb line. God says God will set a plumb line among the people of God and spare them no longer. Verse nine of chapter 7 describes God's plan to destroy the high places of Isaac, the sanctuaries of Israel, and the house of Jeroboam, wicked king of Judah (see 1 Kings 13; 2 Kings 14). This prophecy gets Amos in a bit of trouble with the local priest, who reports him to the king for conspiracy. Amos is not deterred, however, and further delivers God's plan for God's people.

The plumb line metaphor is a powerful image, and perhaps one of the most well-known in Amos. A plumb line was used much like a level would be used today, ensuring that whatever is being built is straight. It is a small tool that makes a huge difference in construction. It would have been an image that was easy to envision for those hearing Amos. The simple image however takes on a different meaning when God applies the same metaphor, a plumb line, to measure the straightness of the Israelite people. Without need for further explanation, it is clear that the Israelites will not pass the kind of straight and narrow measurement God illustrates with the plumb line. The Israelites failure to meet plumb in their lives brings their destruction.

As readers removed by several thousand years from the Israelites, it is easy to relocate this plumb line passage as a harsh but necessary judgment of a group of people chosen and blessed by God but callous and forgetful in their relationship with their Creator and Redeemer. As a matter fact, we live in a world where we tend to measure life, ethics, even theology with more of a sliding scale than a plumb line. Sliding scales, however, do not build solid, effective structures. That takes precise measurement, even in the most seemingly insignificant parts of construction. This word of judgment for the Israelites is a word of instruction for us as well as to how we are to live in regard to others and God.

What does living a "plumb line life" look like? First of all, we must know God's expectations for us. Throughout the Bible, there is instruction about how God intends for us to live with God and others. But simply knowing the expectations is not enough. We must be willing to follow God's instructions for our lives. God's instructions are not arbitrary or outdated. God's word for us timelessly describes the human experience and God's expectations for us. Living a "plumb line life" means understanding God's desire for us to follow and obey. The great news is that if we allow ourselves to be measured by God's plumb line, the structure of our lives will be straight, strong, and effective. Although life lived on a sliding scale may be easier and even more popular, the result is weakness, even failure.

God knows our human fascination with measurement. God knows who among us wants to be taller, shorter, thinner, or whatever our desired measurement is. God also knows that the only measurement that really matters is our spiritual measurement. God's desire for us as God's children is life in alignment with God's ways and Word. Oh God, help us to measure our lives in the way you intended. Help us to be aware of your plumb line for our lives. Amen. (Tracey Allred)

Lectionary Commentary

Ephesians 1:3-14

It feels good to be chosen. It is a lesson we learn early in life. It feels good to be chosen for a team or as a partner. There were of course times in their history that the Jews remembered what it meant to be chosen and lived up to their part of the covenant. Other times, however, they completely overlooked what it meant to be chosen by God. They sometimes took their chosenness for granted. But still, they were chosen. No doubt, many of the new, non-Jewish believers struggled with what their relationship with God was. In his letter to the Ephesians, Paul addresses this issue of God's choosing. It is a text that has challenged many theologians. On the most basic level, the passage validates our choosing by God even as non-Jews. Through Jesus Christ we are adopted into God's family, making us children of God in the truest sense.

Mark 6:14-29

There are no "do-overs" in real life. Of course, there are times we would do anything for a chance to change the past, whether to change our actions, our words, or just to get out of a bad situation altogether. I think King Herod probably experienced quite a bit of that after the execution of John the Baptist. It was Herod's guilt that first caused him to arrest John, and Herod's pride that led to John's death. It was apparently an event that haunted Herod so greatly that upon hearing about Jesus, he was convinced that John had risen from the dead. In our world, we often

223

minimize sin. As a matter of fact, we can justify pretty much any act, behavior, or attitude. This text in Mark reminds us of the long-reaching consequences of sin. Herod's sin tormented him, just as ours does at times. As we encounter sin at the crossroads in our lives, may we have the strength to walk away before we feel the need for a "do-over." (Tracey Allred)

Worship Aids

Invocation (from Psalm 84)

O Lord, we enter into your house today with hearts of praise and love. "How lovely is your dwelling place", O Lord Almighty. We thank you for the opportunity to dwell in your house. As we enter this time of worship, join us, hear us, and accept our offering of worship. Amen.

Pastoral Prayer

Almighty God, we are thankful for your presence and abiding love. We are thankful for the ways we have seen you at work this week. (*Pause for silence.*) We are thankful for the new things we have learned about you. (*Pause for silence.*) We are mindful of the hurt around us. We lift it up to you. (*Pause for silence.*) O God, we also give to you our burdens and concerns, those things that distract us from you. (*Pause for silence.*) Continue with us through this time. Amen.

Benediction

Leave this place today with the realization of God's plumb line in your life. Seek to be measured to God's standard for life. Amen. (Tracey Allred)

"I Am the Good Shepherd"

Fourth in a Series of Seven on the "I Am" Sayings of Jesus

John 10:11-18

A decade ago, I attended a worship service where a distinguished bishop was to preach. He had a fine preaching reputation, but in the experience I learned that many things distract from hearing the Word preached. I am ashamed to admit it, but on this particular day, I focused on the wrong thing. The bishop processed into the church's sanctuary and carried a crosier—a staff that represents a bishop's pastoral functions.

Throughout worship I could not shake the question: if the bishop was a shepherd then what was I?

Surely we love the twenty-third Psalm and the shepherding imagery. We also recognize the power of the Bible's shepherding image in an agrarian culture. The pastoral picture of the Good Shepherd is a valid one, no doubt. Still, being likened to sheep is not exactly flattering. Do we embrace the sheep comparison? No! Yet if we understand Jesus as the good shepherd, then we also realize that we are like sheep. No doubt we have mixed feelings about the analogy despite its value as a biblical image.

[Read John 10:11-18] Today's lesson from John's Gospel is one of many texts that use this striking shepherd/sheep image. Perhaps few of us ever see or spend time with sheep to any noteworthy degree. Yet today, as in biblical times, food and other products from sheep are among the chief sources of human survival.

Our Bible relates many stories about sheep and shepherds. The Exodus narrative hinges on the story of Passover—Hebrews slaughtering a lamb to give the angel of death a sign to pass over their houses. I do not suppose that any well-versed Jewish person could imagine hearing *passover* and not picture an unblemished lamb. Many pastors' stoles display an emblem of the Lamb of God. Biblical writers employ this symbol to the end of Scripture where Revelation depicts the lamb as a sign of apocalyptic fulfillment.

The psalms include a multitude of allusions to sheep and shepherds: sheep being scattered or led to slaughter (for example, Psalm 44:11). Scripture employs the imagery in Numbers, Samuel, Chronicles, the Major Prophets, as well as many New Testament passages. For example, Nathan's disapproving parable concerning the sordid "Bathsheba affair" begins innocently enough:

> Nathan said to David, "There were two men in a certain city, the one rich and the other poor. The rich man had very many flocks and herds; but the poor man had nothing but one little ewe lamb, which he had bought. He brought it up, and it grew up with him and with his children; it used to eat of his meager fare, and drink from his cup, and lie in his bosom, and it was like a daughter to him." (2 Samuel 12:1-3)

Still, no matter how much the Bible refers to them, sheep are smelly, stupid, and unmotivated. Above all, they are utterly helpless creatures. My most vivid memory of sheep was on a lazy, hot summer Texas afternoon. I was driving from Austin to El Paso and decided to take a scenic route on less traveled roads. In Menard I pulled off the highway near a vast holding pen of thousands of sheep. There they all stood in the hot sun, like the proverbial lambs led to slaughter. These sheep were absolutely helpless. Standing and waiting to die, with no realization whatsoever of what awaited them. Are people really like this?

And if this were not enough, in biblical times the shepherding vocation was not high on any self-respecting social climber's agenda. Shepherding relegated persons to the bottom of the socioeconomic hierarchy. Many non-land-owning peasants raised sheep to survive. This fact was, I suppose, the great scandal in the birth narrative of Luke. The angel announces Jesus' birth to a bunch of grimy hillside shepherds outside suburban Bethlehem. What is even more astounding is that Jesus would call himself the "good shepherd" (John 10:11, 14). To the first listeners in Jesus' day, this was a flagrant contradiction in terms—a first rate oxymoron.

Why is it we bristle so when we consider the analogy of people to sheep? Do we resent God—or anybody—identifying us as smelly, lazy, stupid, and oblivious? I imagine we do.

In our most honest moments, we may admit we resent the implications of this analogy because it is so true. Sheep separate themselves from a flock, not by some nefarious plan to escape, but simply by keeping their heads down and grazing from grass clump to grass clump. They graze for hours at a time without regard to anything except the grass beneath them. Suddenly, looking up, they realize there are no other sheep around them. They have literally eaten their way into a state of "lostness." I do not know if they panic, but I suspect they are anxious.

Perhaps we are like this. Most people, left to their own devices do not want to "have erred and strayed from thy ways like lost sheep... [following] the devices and desires of our own hearts" (Church of England, *The Book of Common Prayer* [Oxford: University Press, 1868], 49). And yet we do. Most of us are neither good nor bad. We simply forget what is in our self-interest. We all need what Scripture calls "shepherding." It takes a great deal of courage, ego strength, and self-knowledge to face the truth of our need.

The good news is this: although the scriptural analogy may be unflattering, we are all in need of a shepherd. Accordingly, God provides Jesus for us—the Good Shepherd. In the words of Hebrews 12:2, God has provided for us a "pioneer and perfecter of our faith." Jesus comes to us as a good shepherd to bind up our wounds, protect us, and lead us to green pastures and still waters. This Good Shepherd restores our souls. This is one biblical image we simply cannot do without. (David Mosser)

Worship Aids

Invocation

God, who gives us the Good Shepherd, gather your people today as the sheep of your meadow. Give us a sense of what it means to be in a covenantal relationship with you. Rescue us from danger and guide us into the sheepfold. In Christ's name we pray. Amen.

Prayer of Confession

O God, you know we possess much more than we need, and so this day we confess our greed. Help us consider those in our own community who endure financial adversity through no fault of their own. Make us a congregation willing to extend our faith in tangible ways to those who need our assistance. In Jesus' name. Amen.

Words of Assurance

Hear the good news! Even in our sin, even when we are lost, the Good Shepherd seeks us out to forgive us and call us to new life.

Benediction (Numbers 6:24-26)

The LORD bless you and keep you; the LORD make his face to shine upon you, and be gracious to you; the LORD lift up his countenance upon you, and give you peace. (David Mosser)

JULY 22, 2012

Eighth Sunday after Pentecost

Readings: Jeremiah 23:1-6; Psalm 23; Ephesians 2:11-22;
Mark 6:30-34, 53-56

Where Compassion Leads

Mark 6:30-34, 53-56

After moving to a new city several months ago, my family made a sobering observation. In our new town, there are lots of panhandlers. Perhaps it is a sign of the changing economy or maybe just the differences in geography, but my family, particularly our children, were disturbed by those they saw on the sides of the road holding signs. We decided to do a family mission project. After raising money at a yard sale, we made bags of supplies, food, gift cards, and money. We then gave the bags to those we saw on the sides of the road holding signs. While I imagined giving out our bags at the intersections we often frequent, my children began searching for people as we traveled. Before long, we were making u-turns and searching people out. I learned through that experience the beauty of childlike compassion. As adults, our compassion is often hampered by judgment and cynicism. What I saw in my children, however, was the strong desire to help the hurting, even if it meant going out of our way. It is exactly the kind of compassion we find in Christ. Throughout the Gospels, Jesus' compassion is everywhere. He is constantly healing and helping. Mark 6 is an excellent example of Jesus' love and compassion even as he himself is exhausted and in need of rest.

Jesus had been quite busy healing and teaching. He has called his twelve disciples. He has calmed a storm and attracts large crowds wherever he travels. He has even returned to his hometown only to realize that those who knew him best are not going to receive him. Mark 6 is action packed. In addition to visiting his hometown, Jesus sends out his disciples in pairs to minister, and his cousin, John the Baptist is executed. As verse 30 begins, Jesus and his disciples reunite to talk about all that has transpired, including presumably the death of John the Baptist. As they attempt to get away to a solitary place to eat and talk, a large crowd finds them. Although Jesus is probably in dire need of retreat to process all that is going on with his disciples, he feels compassion for the crowd and teaches them, eventually performing one of his greatest miracles by feeding more than 5,000 people with only five loaves and two fish. Following the feeding of the 5,000, Jesus again attempts retreat, sending the disciples ahead to Bethsaida so that he can be alone and pray. He joins them later by walking on water to their boat, an act that totally amazes the disciples even after all they have seen. When they arrive at the other side of the lake and anchor their boat, they are again encountered by people seeking Jesus for healing, which even in his exhaustion, he does.

There are three great lessons to be learned, I think, in this passage. First of all, ministry is tiring. Obviously the pace of ministry that Jesus kept is not something that we will ever experience in our lives. Whatever the pace, however, following God's call for your life and serving with all your heart takes a lot of energy. Even Jesus was tired sometimes and needed to be recharged. Often in our lives, we allow ourselves to be discouraged by our exhaustion. Instead of taking the chance to recharge ourselves physically and spiritually, we often just continue to attempt service with depleted energies or just give up altogether. In this passage, we see demonstrated by Christ the importance of caring for our physical and spiritual selves.

The second lesson we learn from this passage is about the depth of Christ's compassion. Even in his spiritual and physical exhaustion, and probably emotional anguish over the loss of John the Baptist, Jesus was moved to help those he encountered. He could have simply retreated, or even told them to come back later, but he was so moved by their desperation that he stayed and taught and even fed them. Although Jesus had valid reasons not to help, he helped because he had so much compassion for those around him. In our lives, we rarely allow compassion to move us to that degree. Most of us, even the most compassionate, pretty successfully compartmentalize our ability and willingness to help to times that we are ready and willing. Jesus' compassion for the crowd motivated him to stay and be with them, even when the timing wasn't right. Our compassion should so lead us. As we have said, we are not Jesus, and we must occasionally rest from our labors, but we must not use that as an excuse to turn away from those in need just because it is inconvenient or distasteful to us.

There's one more thing we learn from this passage, perhaps implied instead of explicit. It's easy to read this story and wish that in our suffering we could see Jesus as the people during his life on earth did. The great news is that same compassion Jesus displayed for the people in his life on earth he has for us. How powerful to realize that Jesus could not just walk away even in his exhaustion. How much more Jesus' compassion for us must be! Just as he did for the crowds, Jesus cannot stand to encounter our suffering without helping. Whatever our situation, whether we are going through a temporary struggle or something more serious, like illness or poverty, like many of those we encounter holding signs on the side of the road, Jesus is moved by compassion for us. Jesus is there for us just as Jesus was there for the people in Mark 6. Thank you, God, for your love and compassion, and for never ignoring our needs. Amen. (Tracey Allred)

Lectionary Commentary

Jeremiah 23:1-6

God does not forget. It is a consistent theme in the Old Testament, particularly in the Prophets. Even when God's people give God every reason to forget, or at least just ignore them, God remembers and cares for them. It is the reason that God calls Jeremiah. God wants Jeremiah to deliver God's word to the people in order for them to repent and return to God. In Jeremiah 23, God speaks out against those like the false teachers and leaders who are leading the Israelites astray. God then says that after driving out the false ones, God will gather the remnant of God's people and bring them back together, raising up godly leaders to lead them. In verse 6, God promises to restore God's people. What a powerful promise of restoration! After all the Israelites have done and all the ways they have failed God, God is willing to fight for them and restore them. Isn't it wonderful to realize that God does not give up on us? God desires to defend us and restore us. Thanks be to God for never forgetting us!

Ephesians 2:11-22

Division was common in the first-century church. As more and more people became believers, more and more differences emerged. There were differences in culture, religiosity, socioeconomics, geography, and faith experience. Perhaps the biggest difference was between the Jewish Christians, who were still practicing the laws of God, and the Gentile Christians, who found those laws unnecessary to their faith in Christ Jesus. Paul addresses these differences quite often in his letters. In

Ephesians 2, Paul addresses "one new humanity," created by God through the death of Jesus on the cross. Through Christ, both Jews and Gentiles are joined together.

In the modern day church, division can be common as well. Although the specific reasons may be completely different, the clash of a group of believers, particularly as a church grows, is common. This passage is a great reminder of the common bond we share. We are believers in Christ. Christ died for all of us. The things that make us different are really not that important. (Tracey Allred)

Worship Aids

Call to Worship

Enter God's gates with thanksgiving and God's courts with praise.
**O Lord, we rejoice as we enter your house and excitedly
    assemble to glorify you this day.**
Worship the Lord with gladness.
We leave our burdens behind, and joyfully worship you, O God.

Invocation

O God of our joys and sorrows, of our today and tomorrows, of our highs and our lows, we enter your presence with thanksgiving and joy today. Join us here. Meet us as we seek this opportunity to worship you and bring you praise. May we bring you honor today. Amen.

Benediction

Now go in the peace that passes all understanding and the compassion shown so lovingly through Christ. May we be moved to action by the needs around us. Amen. (Tracey Allred)

"I Am the Resurrection and the Life"

Fifth in a Series of Seven on the "I Am" Sayings of Jesus

John 11:17-27

To set the context for this lesson, we know that Mary, Martha, and Lazarus live in Bethany close to Jerusalem. Lazarus is ill, and his sisters send word to Jesus to come. But Jesus, contrary to our expectations, "stayed two days longer in the place where he was." [Read John 11:17-27.]

We know how the story ends. Jesus greets and speaks with Mary and then goes to the tomb of Lazarus. At the tomb Jesus prays to God and cries for Lazarus to "come out," which Lazarus does. It is a miracle, and the story tells us that "Many of the Jews therefore, who had come with Mary and had seen what Jesus did, believed in him" (v. 45).

Jesus asks Martha "Do you believe this?" and perhaps today Jesus asks us this question too. Let's examine three of the key features that this story reveals.

First, God's timetable is different from our timetable. Luke's Gospel introduces us to the family in Bethany. In Luke's story, we read that, "'Martha was distracted by her many tasks; so she came to Jesus and asked, 'Lord, do you not care that my sister has left me to do all the work by myself? Tell her then to help me.' But the Lord answered her, 'Martha, Martha, you are worried and distracted by many things'" (Luke 10:40-41). The word translated here *worried* is the Greek word for *anxious*. Jesus says that Martha's problem is an anxiety that distracts her. She cannot focus. Martha is like me—like us!

In Africa in the 1970s, missionaries warned us not to photograph indigenous people because they had seen Polaroid cameras and believed that all cameras could give them instant pictures—what they called "sudden service." They expected that if one took their picture, then they would immediately receive a copy. This caused problems and conflict if the photographer needed to send the film off somewhere to be developed.

We modern Americans are much like this as well. In a world of "sudden service"—from banks to coffee to microwaves to relationships—most of us are not used to waiting. We want things to happen, and we want them to happen quickly. Yet in this story of the raising of Lazarus when Jesus tells those assembled that "I am the resurrection and the life" (v. 25), we see here (and in the whole of John's Gospel) that Jesus moves according to his own sense of timing. For this reason, Jesus' two-day delay in coming to the tomb of Lazarus makes us, like Martha, anxious. We expect God (and in this story Jesus represents the divine) to act upon our wants and desires at once. But on the contrary, God is God, and Jesus moves at God's own speed and pace (*kairos* time). In this story things turn out well for Lazarus and his sisters, but too often in life people must wait to see the mysterious ways of God revealed. We do not always have our prayers answered in the twinkling of an eye. Most things that are good for us happen in *kairos* time and not our time.

A second key learning from this story is that we, like Lazarus, are each in our own sort of tomb. What is it in your life that speaks death to you? Is it your anxiety to control events and people? Is it the nagging fear that somehow things are going to happen to you that you could not anticipate? The German philosopher Goethe once said, "A useless life is but an early death" ("Iphigenia in Taurus").

People do this by trying to control the things around them. Control simply means "to exercise a dominating influence over." We each know people whom we might describe as "control freaks"—persons who try to exert absolute control over everything, people so entombed by their own issues of control that they might as well already be dead.

We all face situations that entomb us. For some it is a marriage that we do not know how to fix. Or the entombment comes from a job we hate but have to keep because it feeds our family. For others it is the Hades of living up to other's expectations—even when we know that these people will never, ever be satisfied. The good news is this: Jesus offers us a way out of the tomb.

The third key learning is that in Jesus Christ, God always has the last word. We can imagine no more hopeless situation than the Lazarus story. The text paints the despair: "Lord, already there is a stench because he has been dead four days" (v. 39). Martha imagines that the situation is so desperate that even Jesus is helpless. Yet Jesus' reply then is as potent as it is today: "Did I not tell you that if you believed, you would see the glory of God?" (v. 40). In Jesus, God reveals a power stronger than the last enemy—death.

What does this mean for us? As a campus minister I led a study about John. On the night we studied John 11, a thoughtful new student joined us. He said nothing until he asked, "If Jesus raised Lazarus, then wouldn't Lazarus just die again anyway? Dying once is bad enough, but twice seems cruel. Why?" Leave it to a college student who never attended church to ask a devastating question. It is a good question, which I have thought about for thirty-one years of ministry. Here is my best guess at an answer: according to the Gospel, dying a second time is easier. Why? Because Jesus said: "I am the resurrection." Amen. (David Mosser)

Worship Aids

Call to Worship

Lord, we need your help today, this week, and all our days. Too often, we are overcome by a sense that we cannot even attempt the small things you ask of us. You ask us simply to feed the hungry, give drink to the thirsty, and clothe the naked. Infuse us with your Spirit to act on behalf of the least among us. Amen.

Pastoral Prayer

O gracious Lord God, when your Son Jesus tells us that he is the Resurrection and the life, may our hearts leap within as we celebrate the newness of resurrection life all about us. Send your Holy Spirit to fill us with the passion to grow into the people you created us to be. In Jesus' name we pray. Amen.

Benediction

May God's grace enfold you; may Christ's peace be upon you; may the Holy Spirit's encouragement guide you, all your resurrected days. Amen. (David Mosser)

JULY 29, 2012

❧❧❧❧

Ninth Sunday after Pentecost

Readings: 2 Kings 4:42-44; Psalm 145:10-18; Ephesians 3:14-21; John 6:1-21

What Does It Take to Be Strong and Powerful?

Ephesians 3:14-21

Eyes are set on London. Families from all over the world are gathering around televisions, radios, and computers to follow the 2012 Summer Olympic Games. Thousands of the world's best athletes are competing on the field or in the pool for one of those elusive medals. In the next two weeks, these athletes will compete in 300 events across 26 sports. All of them will demonstrate their great skill and strength, and some will reveal dominance. The victors will be heralded as the most powerful forces in their respective sports.

Our world values strength and power because it gets things done. It creates winning athletes. It makes for fast sports cars. It controls politics. We value power because we want to be strong. We want to be in control of our lives, make our own decisions, and control our own destinies. Independence and autonomy are valued, but if we're not careful, we begin worshiping these values rather than God. When we behave in this way, we act as if we are calling the shots by demanding things from God, but this isn't how we should pray, and it's not how we should live.

Paul's prayer for the church in Ephesus is instructive. He prays that they will become more mature in their faith in Christ by being more loving people, but they cannot achieve this on their own. This is why Paul prays that God will give them the power to comprehend more clearly the love of Christ. This love will fill them "with all the fullness of God" (v. 19) and make them strong. Through this same power, the Lord is also "able to accomplish abundantly far more than all we can ask or imagine" (v. 20).

But do we really believe this? Do we really believe that God can do more than we ask or imagine? We pray for lots of things, yet if our prayer lists begin and end with names of people with health problems and go no further, then perhaps we are not trusting God with our deepest desires. Perhaps we are afraid to pray for the absurd, for God-sized events, which explains why we do not consistently pray for peace in the Middle East or the end to world hunger or even reconciliation between husbands and wives. We are afraid to pray for the absurd because it is easier for us to pray for small things like our favorite athlete getting a gold medal or being nice to an unpleasant neighbor.

Jesus would have us move out of this comfortable place by having us pray for big things, which is what we do when we pray, "God's will be done on earth as it is in heaven." This begins, of course, with having our eyes open so we can see the needs of our world. Perhaps we see opportunities for starting new ministries at our churches or in our communities, but because resources seem so limited, we fear failure and do nothing. Our non-action, therefore, communicates a lack of faith in God, for it suggests that God doesn't have the power to do something big.

Paul confronts this fear by telling us God can accomplish far more than we can ask or imagine. For that reason, we should pray for God-sized events and then act upon those prayers. When resources appear to be limited and the path is unclear, we can live faithfully by taking the proverbial "leap of faith." No doubt this is risky because of the potential to fail, but it is better to fail than not try at all. Taking one step forward keeps us from getting paralyzed and demonstrates our belief that God is working even when we cannot see that work. Furthermore, it expresses our willingness to lean on God for guidance and strength.

Taking a risk for God reminds us that we are not in charge of the world. We cannot control every part of life, even if we tried. So when we make that leap of faith, we begin to trust in God and rely on the Lord's power, not our own. When a great crowd of 5,000 followed Jesus to hear his teachings, the disciples wanted to send them all away when evening arrived so that they would have time to buy their own food in nearby villages. Yet Jesus had a different plan. He instructed the disciples to feed this enormous crowd. They thought he was out of his mind because they only had five loaves of bread and two fish—very limited resources—but at the end of the day, it was the Lord's power that accomplished abundantly more than the disciples imagined was possible.

God cannot be limited because there are no places off limits to the power of God. The Lord can do things we can't even imagine. So instead of worrying about limited resources, we should pray for God's will, and then we should celebrate the ways we witness the Lord's power at work. This may be evident when God gives us patience to relate with that unpleasant neighbor. It may be evident when we see justice spreading throughout a city or a corporation. The power of God is at work in the world, whether or not we see it. It is visible in small and mighty ways. This power is present with us through the Spirit of God, who gives us strength and power when we need it most, lest we forget that God knows what we need.

Yes, we want to be strong people, and God wants to build us up, but in our desire for power and strength, we must proceed cautiously, otherwise we might lose sight of God. We can become so focused on asserting our own will and independence that we get in the way of God's work. Paul's prayer speaks to us, for it invites us to grow strong in our faith by joining in God's work of love, and when we do this, we bring glory to God. (Mark D. White)

Lectionary Commentary

2 Kings 4:42-44

Elisha is presented as a miracle worker in the fourth chapter of 2 Kings, where he performs four miraculous acts. In the last two miracles Elisha provides food for his people, though in two different contexts. In the first verses 38-41, Elisha encounters a famine in Gilgal. He orders his servant to "make some stew for the company of prophets," (v. 38), but the stew is inedible and downright disgusting. Those who eat it say it tastes like "death." To remedy this problem, Elisha adds flour to the stew, and all the hungry happily feast.

The second food miracle is set in a much different situation (vv. 42-44). Instead of encountering famine, we encounter a man who comes sharing his first fruits with Elisha. He generously gives "twenty loaves of barley and fresh ears of grain," which Elisha instructs him to use to feed one hundred people. At first glance, it appears to be not enough food for such a large group, but God miraculously turns a small number of provisions into abundance with food left over. Both of these food miracles invite the preacher to explore the connection between God's providential care and human responsibility. Specifically, how might we trust in

God's care for us when we are living through a time of famine, and how might we give generously in times of abundance so that others might enjoy God's good gifts?

John 6:1-21

John 6 includes two familiar miracle stories—the feeding of the 5,000 and Jesus walking on water—both of which speak to the identity of Jesus. The first miracle is recounted in all the Synoptic Gospels (Matthew 14:13-21; Mark 6:32-44; Luke 9:10-17) and in each account, a young boy is the source of two fish and five loaves of bread, 5,000 people are fed, and twelve baskets of food are leftover. After feasting on fish and bread, the witnesses acknowledge Jesus' true identity when they say, "This is indeed the prophet who is to come into the world." The disciples, however, remain in the dark because Jesus "had not yet come to them" (v. 17). After boarding a boat and rowing "about three or four miles" they see Jesus walking on the water and "they [are] terrified." Unlike the crowd who recognize Jesus as the prophet, these disciples are afraid and unable to acknowledge his identity. As followers of Christ, we may not always understand the ways of Jesus, but we are called to follow and learn more about the One whom we call the Son of God. (Mark D. White)

Worship Aids

Call to Worship

We praise your name, O gracious and wonderful God.
Great is the Lord and worthy to be praised.
We praise your wondrous works and proclaim your awesome deeds.
Great is the Lord and worthy to be praised.
We celebrate your goodness and sing of your righteousness.
Great is the Lord and worthy to be praised.
The Lord is gracious and merciful. The Lord is good to all.
All: Great is the Lord and worthy to be praised.

Invocation

O God, we have gathered to give you all honor and praise. We celebrate the gift of this holy day, and now we pray that you would draw us to you in this time of worship so that your presence might strengthen us for the journey ahead. Speak to our hearts and minds by inspiring us with your words of grace and love. In the name of Christ we pray. Amen.

Benediction

Go forth with the Spirit of God as your guide. Go forth sharing love, grace, and mercy with those whom you meet. Go forth with the power of God to live and act courageously in the midst of great need. Amen. (Mark D. White)

"I Am the Way, the Truth, and the Life" (14:6)

Sixth in a Series of Seven on the "I Am" Sayings of Jesus

John 14:1-7

Not long ago a new member of our church—a new believer too—asked me, "What is salvation?" It is a good question and one that we Christians struggle with. Our lesson today is part of Jesus' farewell discourse that begins in chapter 13 and continues to the end of chapter 17 in John's Gospel.

The farewell discourse is an influential style of ancient writing; Moses' farewell discourse comprises most of Deuteronomy. Plato's dialogue *Apology* is also a type of farewell discourse. However, no one uses "the farewell discourse" as explicitly or as well as John. In this teaching, Jesus offers great comfort and promise to the disciples, whose lives are about to fall in shambles at their feet.

In this last speech of Jesus to his disciples, he tells them many things, but for our purposes today he offers them one of his seven "I am" (*ego ami*) sayings. Today our reading centers on "I am the way, the truth, and the life" (14:5). Jesus first promises the disciples that they can be assured that even after Jesus leaves them, "where I am, there you may be also" (v. 3). But Thomas asks: "How can we know the way?" (v. 5). Jesus' response to Thomas is our subject today.

Often in Christian theology this *way* is taken to mean simply a set phrase or doctrinal formation that states that "we (our group) are going to heaven and everyone else (other groups that believe differently than we do) are going to hell." Yet what this text may really mean is that Jesus, as the tangible manifestation of God, is the relationship and manner by which God receives people into Communion or association. Jesus is the particular and special revelation of God, not a statement that God has exclusive claim on only those who know some secret, or "Gnostic," knowledge. Salvation is all about being in relationship with God and about love and charity with neighbor.

In Matthew's Gospel, some of the "greatly astounded" disciples heard Jesus talking about how difficult it would be for a rich person to get into heaven. When Jesus employed the image of "a camel" going "through the eye of a needle" these disciples asked Jesus, "Then who can be saved" (Matthew 19:25; see also Mark 10:26; Luke 18:26)? In some senses this is the Christian question. The short answer is that everyone can be saved if only because salvation is a gift from God, and God gives as God will. Christian theology layers requirements and preconditions on God's gift. Therefore we simply remember that God can and perhaps will save anyone whom God decides to save.

Clearly, most Christians would confess that salvation or going to heaven is the aim of the Christian life. Yet in today's world the ways we understand salvation and talk about it sometimes keep us from grasping any understanding of salvation from a biblical perspective. Rather than a scholarly exploration, let's look at some fundamentals of salvation.

On May 24, 1738, John Wesley's Journal narrates that he "felt" his "heart strangely warmed." Wesley then writes, "I felt I did trust in Christ, Christ alone, for salvation; and an assurance was given me that he [Christ] had taken away my sins, even mine, and saved me from the law of sin and death." Salvation concerns God's assurance to us that our missteps (trespasses/sins) have been blotted out by God's grace (the unmerited favor from God to people).

Jesus said, "I am the way, the truth, and the life" and "Come, follow me" (Matthew 19:21). If we are honest, we would admit that most of our troubles surface from our character, our obsessions, and our choices. Our choices influence other aspects of our well-being, our health, and relationships. We each suffer from our bad choices, and Paul reminds us that sin leads to death.

We might suggest that suffering is sometimes the journey between sin and death. Yet Paul also points out that "The law of the Spirit of life in Christ Jesus has set you free from the law of sin and of death" (Romans 8:2). In other words, if people want to get spiritually healthy, they will choose God's salvation offered in Jesus Christ.

My friend, Rev. Karen Siegfriedt, an Episcopal priest in California writes helpfully: "Salvation is the healing of the human race; the process by which we are transformed into the likeness of Christ. *Salvation* comes from a Latin word which we translate "salve," which has the meaning of healing" ("Salvation means Healing," http://www.saintjudes.org, Aug. 22, 2004). Salvation is a spiritually healthy way to save our lives, even physically. God offers us a path to abundant life—and wants us on it—and frees us to make a healthy choice.

We miss the opportunity to testify for Christ when we remain silent. Those who need to hear the gospel may conclude that salvation is not important enough to talk about. We old-line Christians profess the historic Christian faith in God, incarnate in Jesus Christ for our salvation. We believe that salvation is ever at work in human history in the Holy Spirit. Living in a covenant of grace under the Lordship of Jesus Christ, we participate in the first fruits of God's coming reign and pray for its full realization.

Salvation is nothing less than God's gift of unmerited favor. When we look scornfully at another's spiritual state, we do violence to Christ's spirit. Rich or poor, none of us gets to heaven by our own merit. We only arrive in God's realm by God's grace. We fall into spiritual pride when we look at other people's salvation with suspicion.

How can we know the way? We know the way because Jesus told us: "I am the way." (David Mosser)

Worship Aids

Invocation

In this worship hour, bring to our consciousness the astonishing life and ministry you have provided us in the one who said: "I am the way, and the truth, and the life." Make us worthy of sharing Jesus' mystery of abundant life.

Let us keep faith alive in our society of believers, so all will know by our love we are Christians. All this we ask in Christ's holy name, enlivened by the Holy Spirit. Amen.

Offertory Prayer

God of unbounded benevolence, as you shower your blessings on us, create in our way the truth of generosity for others so that they may have life. In the name of Jesus, our risen Savior and Redeemer. Amen.

Words of Assurance

"As a father has compassion for his children, so the Lord has compassion for those who respect him" (Psalm 103:13). Know that God loves you even more deeply than you love your own kin. Amen. (David Mosser)

AUGUST 5, 2012

Tenth Sunday after Pentecost

Readings: Exodus 16:2-4, 9-15; Psalm 78:23-29; Ephesians 4:1-16;
John 6:24-35

Food Battles

Exodus 16:2-4, 9-15

Mornings at my house are always hectic, but one day my wife left early
for work, and pandemonium broke loose with complaints spilling out
from everyone. The dog was barking, whining, and even fighting with my
three-year-old daughter. My daughter was screaming at the dog and fussing about being awake at seven in the morning. So I thought turning her
attention to breakfast would have a calming effect. I asked her if she
wanted toast or cereal. She protested, "I don't want either. I want to eat
pancakes. Mommy wouldn't give me pancakes!" From this point forward,
the complaints multiplied, and it became clear that there was no way I
could compete in her mind with what mommy might have done.

We are not at our best when we complain. We act irrationally. We may
even act like spoiled rotten children. Perhaps that is the image that
comes to mind when we read about the grumbling of the Israelites. Yet
complaining is not altogether bad. When we make our complaints to
God, we are in effect hoping that God will respond to our needs and our
suffering.

At the time the Israelites aired their complaints to God, they had been
walking in the wilderness for more than a month after they had been
delivered from Egypt. They were obviously hungry, thirsty, and even
threatened by any number of dangers. The Israelites were in a difficult
spot. They were vulnerable in the wilderness, but all their grumbling
implies they did not trust God, and as a result, "The whole congregation
of the Israelites complained against Moses and Aaron" (v. 2). They were

convinced life was better in Egypt where they had enough food, and thus their past seemed far better than their present.

When we romanticize the past, we forget about all of the problems and hardships, and recall only the good. The past becomes the golden age to which nothing else can compare. This happened to the Israelites, and it can happen to us. When the Israelites made their complaints, their memory acted in a highly selective way. The only thing they could remember was the food; they had forgotten about the brutal conditions of their slavery. When the church grumbles about its present condition being far worse than its past, it has committed the same error. Many congregations will remember a day when the sanctuary was packed and the offering plates overflowed, and yet, the accuracy of that memory may or may not be on target.

It is tempting to let the past serve as a golden age. Yet when we do this (accurate or not), we deny the full truth of God's creation. God is creating a bright future that leads us to the Promised Land, but when we idealize the past, we fail to trust in God's future goodness. We deny that God has good plans in store for us, and we become blind to the love and redemption God offers to us in the present. When we live in the past, we deny the gift of life God offers for today.

Our faith affirms that God is with us in the present. Our faith also calls us to follow into the future where we are invited to enter new places of service, ministry, and witness. The good news is that we are not alone in fulfilling this call because we are sustained by a life-giving relationship with the Lord who feeds us with bread from heaven. God provides for our needs wherever we are sent. When Jesus was led into the wilderness, where he fasted for forty days, the devil tempted him to turn stones into bread, but he wisely responded, "One does not live by bread alone, but by every word that comes from the mouth of God" (Matthew 4:4).

The gift of manna, the bread from heaven, reminds us that God is our provider. God told Moses, "I am going to rain bread from heaven for you, and each day the people shall go out and gather enough for that day" (v. 4). We are sustained by God's gifts that nurture our bodies and spirits. The Lord assures us that we will have enough to survive as we follow our call, but we do not always trust in God's care. We worry that there may not be enough food or resources or whatever to fulfill our call. When the people of Israel had been graced with the bread from heaven, they acted confused. They said, "What is it?" They were not ready to respond and trust in God's promise, even though they were desperate for food. They had trouble believing God would really rain bread from heaven on them because they were full of fear, and it was fear of the future that kept them from initially embracing God's providence.

Learning to trust God requires that we let go of our fears and believe God will sustain us. My daughter thought pancakes were the only tasty breakfast food that could satisfy her needs, which is why she put up such a fight. But after she smelled the jelly toast I had made, she came around to the idea that there are other good things to eat. She even realized her daddy would not let her go hungry.

We may not be our best when we complain, but we are at least being real and authentic, which shows we trust God will hear us. The Israelites grumbled about their hunger and romanticized their past. They resembled spoiled children, but their complaints did not fall on deaf ears. The Lord recognized their need for food, and thus sent quails for meat and manna for bread. The Israelites received enough food to survive in the wilderness. Likewise, God provides for our needs. Our responsibility is to set aside our fears and trust in the Lord. (Mark D. White)

Lectionary Commentary

Ephesians 4:1-16

What is expected of the church? Ephesians 4 offers an answer to this question by telling the church to live up to its calling. According to the text, this calling principally seeks unity and oneness, for there is one body, one Spirit, one Lord, one faith, one baptism, and one God. This unity is not conformity, as will become clear with the list of gifts, but it is rather a commitment to building up the church. A familiar image used here and in other Pauline epistles to describe the church is that of the body of Christ.

Within the body, there are many gifts. The list of gifts mentioned in Ephesians sounds like a job list for any church. The church needs to be gifted with apostles, prophets, evangelists, pastors, and teachers. A second list of gifts found in another Pauline letter (1 Corinthians 12:4-11) looks more like a list of talents: utterance of wisdom, knowledge, faith, healing, working of miracles, prophecy, discernment of spirits, various kinds of tongues, and the interpretation of tongues. Both lists, however, speak to Paul's hope that the church would seek oneness and unity by employing all of its diverse gifts. What bearing does this have on present day Christians? Today's church is highly fragmented where Christians congregate around preferences for worship styles, hymnal choice, and many other hot-button issues. So how might today's church pursue unity?

John 6:24-35

The crowd mentioned in this Gospel text is evidently the same group who had been fed the previous day when Jesus miraculously fed 5,000 people from five loaves of bread and two fish. The following morning they wake up and discover Jesus and his disciples have quietly left town. Though they are surprised by his quick exit, they are eager to see Jesus again and go in search of him. However, the crowd is not interested in building a relationship with Jesus; they merely want another free meal. Are we any different? Do we follow Jesus because of something we get in return? Do we pursue food that perishes? If so, Jesus invites us to seek "food that endures for eternal life" (v. 27), which is offered by the Son of Man to satisfy our deepest hunger. (Mark D. White)

Worship Aids

Call to Worship (Adapted from Psalm 34)

I will bless the Lord at all times, and God's praise
    shall continually be in my mouth.
We praise the Lord and exalt God's name together.
In our seeking, God answers our prayers and delivers us
    from our fears.
We praise the Lord and exalt God's name together.
The Lord is good, and happy are those who take refuge in him.
We praise the Lord and exalt God's name together.
Let us bless the Lord at all times.
All: God's praise shall continually be in my mouth.

Invocation

Gracious God, we have wandered into this house of worship from many different places and with many different needs, yet we come with the common desire to be in your presence. We pray that you would draw us close to you and feed our hearts with the gift of your Word so that we might be more like Christ. Amen.

Benediction

May the grace and love of God lead you through the wilderness and through times of hunger. Now go forth in the name of the Father, Son, and Holy Spirit. Go forth to trust and follow the Lord our God. Amen. (Mark D. White)

"I Am the True Vine"

Seventh in a Series of Seven on the "I Am" Sayings of Jesus

John 15:1-11

In our last of seven sermons on the "I Am" sayings of Jesus may we explore the idea of connection? This idea occurred to me while reading about my denomination. United Methodist church historian Russell Richey wrote: "Connectionalism is a uniquely Methodist vision of and way of ordering the church" (*Methodist Connectionalism*, [Nashville: General Board of Higher Education and Ministry, 2009]). Richey fully outlines how Wesleyan-rooted churches spotlight connectionalism as part of their church polity. Not all churches organize this way of course. Some churches celebrate an unqualified congregational independence and the resulting autonomy it provides. My church conversely is one that exists in one organic piece—like a vine, for example. Hear Jesus' word about being connected via the illustration of a vine: [Read: John 15:1-11]

Jesus provides a superb image. Vines create an organic unity—from root to tip, vines are connected. As far back as Isaiah the idea of *vineyard* represented God's people—Israel and Judah. In Isaiah 5 we have a poem, song, or hymn about the "unfruitful vineyard," and Jesus may be alluding to this circumstance when he says: "Whoever does not abide in me is thrown away like a branch and withers; such branches are gathered, thrown into the fire, and burned" (John 15:6). If we read the text closely, we can see that those who abide in Jesus as Jesus abides in the Father are symbols of faith; those who do not abide might as well burn as fruitfulness itself seems to be a characteristic of abiding. What connects abiding and faithfulness appears to be keeping God's commandments and abiding in Jesus' love.

Connection is vital in plant life. Roots carry water and nutrients to the leaves. Sunlight on the leaves begins the process of *photosynthesis*, in which the plant generates its own food and releases oxygen as a surplus side-effect. Connection is vital in church life too. Like vines, there are many things that connect us in the church. The United Methodist Church structures of connection are local congregations, districts, annual conferences, jurisdictions, and the general church.

Another example of interconnected structure is the U.S. national highway system. Sometimes I like to think of my little church as a section of the whole. Perhaps I can illustrate this by seeing a fragment of U.S.

Highway 40 and thinking that is all there is. Let me explain. As a child in the 1950s in Independence, Missouri, Highway 40 was the "big road." This massive highway separated Independence from Raytown. Bev's Root Beer Stand, The Blue Ridge Mall, and a local drive-in movie theater were all on Highway 40. It was a most important highway in my judgment. My dad said it was an important link to the rest of the world. At eight years old, however, I had no idea what he meant.

Later I discovered that U.S. Highway 40 was the first American coast-to-coast highway. It began in Atlantic City, New Jersey, and traversed to San Francisco, California. If you drove this magnificent road from end to end, you would pass: New Castle, Maryland; Wheeling, West Virginia; Independence, Missouri; Denver, Colorado; Salt Lake City, Utah; Reno, Nevada; and finally, San Francisco, California. This highway links two oceans and fourteen states along the way. I would have never guessed that one highway could have linked me to all that!

U.S. 40 is an example of what it means to be connected. It reminds us that what we see today, "in our seventy years, or perhaps eighty, if we are strong" (Psalm 90:10) is not all there is. God links us to our past and to our future and to our present through saints who were and saints who are to be. This is the great line of splendor in which we stand. God connects us all in ways we can scarcely imagine.

Surely connection is grand, and God grafting us into the vine as those nourished through Jesus is an inspirational image. Yet sometimes the connection and the system break down. A friend told me how foolish he felt when he made a big deal about his family vacations, driving from Florida to Denver. The trick, he said, was that they were going "against the grain" of the highway system. He said it was easy to travel from the Southwest to the Northeast, but not so easy to travel from the Southeast to the Northwest. The roads are much more difficult to negotiate, but his family wanted to see small-town America.

He told me everything was fine until they drove to the Mississippi River in Wickliffe, Kentucky. He had planned to take the ferry across the mighty river but could not find the landing. The map clearly marked the spot until "a good-natured local" said that the ferry had closed down forty years ago. Also, he told my friend, "Your map is a little dated." A little dated? Sometimes people or institutions or other circumstances break our connections. Yet good systems have the ability to self-heal, as the body of Christ does via God's grace and forgiveness.

In the Christian church, it is the love of God in Christ that allows that healing to commence. One way that believers help the process of healing is by making promises or sacred vows—we call them covenants—with one another and keeping them. Jesus said: "Just as the branch cannot bear fruit by itself unless it abides in the vine, neither can you unless you abide in me" (John 15:4). We are connected with one another because Jesus holds our system, our community, our church together.

We help hold the church's connection together by our covenant. In chapter 11 of Romans Paul talks about natural branches that are "broken off" (v. 17), which "will be grafted back" (v. 24). This means in part that although human beings continually break connection and covenant with God, grace can graft us back and heal us again. (David Mosser)

Worship Aids

Invocation

We ask as we open our worship today, O Divine Redeemer, that once again you shower us with your Holy Spirit. We are an anxious people and need your promises of joy, hope, and assurance as those who worship the Christ revealed in Scripture. Give us the ardor to heed your holy word and be your people. Amen.

Prayer of Confession

We confess our sin today, O God of compassion, in the name of Jesus. May the holy vine of heaven connect us with one another and with the Lord of divine grace. May it be like an umbilical cord that connects child to mother. We confess that we have not heeded our call to witness and ministry, but today we ask for forgiveness. Set us on the excellent path toward you. We pray this in the name of Creator, Savior, and Mighty Counselor. Amen.

Words of Assurance

Though we may be broken branches, God will yet graft us back into the tree of life and love. Hallelujah!

Benediction

Sanctify now your church, O God, as you disperse us to serve our Christ, the true vine. As you graft us into Jesus' ministry today, tomorrow, and forever, fashion us as an extension of your will for the whole of creation. In the name of the Father, Son, and Holy Spirit, we pray. Amen. (David Mosser)

AUGUST 12, 2012

❧❧❧❧

Eleventh Sunday after Pentecost

Readings: 1 Kings 19:4-8; Psalm 34:1-8; Ephesians 4:25–5:2; John 6:35, 41-51

The Food Rule

John 6:35, 41-51

Many churches operate by an unspoken rule, which is employed for one reason above all others. This unspoken rule, when used, brings people together. We call it the covered-dish-dinner rule, the catered-meal rule, or the coffee-and-donut rule. We Christians understand that the presence of food can make the difference between high and low participation because it not only fills our tummies but it evokes our passion. We enjoy food, and we are more likely to attend a congregational meeting when fried chicken and chocolate pie are part of the agenda.

Food is a source of great passion, which means it can also incite arguments and complaints. Waiters and waitresses handle more than their fair share of grumbling about entrees that did not meet expectations. People on diets fuss about foods they are not supposed to eat. My three-year-old daughter complains that the healthy food we serve her at dinnertime is "yucky" because she would rather feast on a platter of candy than eat her fruits and vegetables.

We are highly critical of our food, so what can truly satisfy our hunger? In our nutrition-conscience society, no one answer would please every age group. Infants desire a milk diet; active teenagers crave an unlimited calorie diet, and some adults live for a high-protein, low-carb diet. Our different ideas about nutrition will occasionally lead to arguments about what foods should and should not be eaten. Even faithful churchgoers mirror this behavior by arguing about the kinds of spiritual foods that will satisfy our deepest hunger, which perhaps best describes the grumbling crowd who followed Jesus.

Jesus had already claimed that whoever comes to him "will never be hungry" but now, when he professes to be the "bread of life," the crowd loses their patience with him. They begin complaining and grumbling because they had been around Jesus. They watched Jesus grow up in their neighborhood. They knew his mother and his father. There was no way, they thought, he could have come down from heaven as the bread of life, and so they conclude that his claim is preposterous and arrogant, if not blasphemous. But their self-confidence prevents them from recognizing the truth that stands right in front of their eyes. It keeps them from seeing Jesus as the one who can satisfy their hunger.

There is nothing wrong with confidence until it inhibits trust. My daughter is confident that a large bag of candy will satisfy her hunger. She will argue, "I'm not hungry for chicken. I want to eat candy," but her self-assurance obscures the truth about candy. Eating a bag of candy for dinner has little nutritional value, and it would most likely make her sick. As virtually every other parent on the planet, I wish she would trust that her mother and I know what is best for her.

Developing this kind of trust takes faith, and yet faith is mysterious. It is not a choice we make, but it is the work of God. Jesus says, "No one can come to me unless drawn by the Father" (v. 44). God is the one who draws us in. God is the initiator, the one pulling us toward faith. We can discuss every possible way to satisfy our deepest hunger, but we can't accomplish this work on our own. Therefore, our best course of action, according to John 6, is to place our trust in God who will satisfy our hunger through Jesus Christ.

Unfortunately, this is easier said than done because we are an independent kind of people who seek to take care of our own lives and provide for our own needs. We would rather trust in our own capabilities than rely on outside assistance, but discipleship calls us to follow Jesus and *following*, by definition, involves trust. When we place our trust in Jesus, we are saying that we trust that the Lord will lead us to green pastures and still waters, which will satisfy our deepest hunger.

A major shift in the way we live occurs when we place our trust in God. For starters, we worry less and begin to enjoy the journey of life more. We begin to notice more of God's gifts that meet us along the way, like fresh summer vegetables and the joy of family and friends. When we trust that Jesus is leading us toward an abundant life, our hungers are put into perspective; we become less focused on what we desire and more grateful for God's gifts. As a result, we are more willing to share our blessings and more willing to offer help to those who are hungry. In more or less words, we are sharing life, which is doubly beneficial for it not only helps the person we serve but also satisfies our hunger. By placing our trust in God, the words of Jesus become a reality for "whoever comes to [him] will never be hungry" (v. 35).

Our world tempts us to hunger for many things that will take us off the path of abundant life and will instead lead us down a path of dissatisfaction. It is for this reason that we need to hunger for the right things. Jesus once said, "blessed are those who hunger and thirst for righteousness" (Matthew 5:6) and thus, we should hunger for a deep and intimate relationship with Jesus who is our bread of life. After all, Jesus invites us to feast on his body. Jesus is our source for survival, and when we nurture this relationship, our hungers are put in a proper perspective so that we will indeed hunger and thirst for the right things, which will ultimately satisfy us with the gift of eternal life. (Mark D. White)

Lectionary Commentary

1 Kings 19:4-8

In the previous chapter, Elijah defeated the prophets of Baal in dramatic fashion on Mount Carmel. When Ahab reports this news to Jezebel, she becomes so outraged that she threatens Elijah's life. The prophet evidently feels as if he is in grave danger, and so he flees into the wilderness. He is in such despair that he wishes for death. But then, on two separate occasions, Elijah has an encounter with an angel of God. He is woken up and given a miracle meal of bread and water because this angel knows that Elijah will need all the strength he can muster for the forty days and forty nights ahead of him as he journeys to Horeb. As we see with Elijah, life and ministry can leave us weary and tired, if not burned out; but we can find strength for the journey ahead by turning to God and seeking sustenance from the bread of life found in Jesus Christ.

Ephesians 4:25–5:2

Ephesians 4:17–5:20 comprises a unit of ethical instructions for the church, yet it is often thought to be a post-Pauline addition to the text. Prior to this section, Paul addressed broad theological concepts, but verse 17 marks a significant shift toward rather everyday matters for Christian living. Although this may seem unexciting, it does provide an important contrast between Christian and "Gentile" ways of living, or rather the difference between living in the light and living in the dark. Specifically, the Ephesians are instructed to avoid sinful behaviors like lying, stealing, and slander, and instead be "kind to one another, tenderhearted, [and] forgiving" (4:32). Resisting sin can be a first step in becoming "imitators of God, as beloved children" (5:1). Like children imitating their parents, we can replicate the ways of God to the best of our abilities when we do so with a sense of joy and discovery. (Mark D. White)

Worship Aids

Call to Worship

Jesus said, "Whoever comes to me will never be hungry, and whoever believes in me will never be thirsty." Let us come. Let us come to the Lord and give thanks for the gift of life. Let us come together to worship in Spirit and truth. Let us lift our voices in praise and adoration. Let us worship together!

Invocation

Eternal God, we hunger and thirst for many things; help us to hunger for that which gives true life. Share your presence with us. Feed us with your Word and fill us with your Spirit so that we may in turn reach out to a hungry and thirsty world. Amen.

Benediction

Go forth to enjoy the gifts of God. Feast on the bread of life. Drink from the cup of salvation. Share life with the world. And may the grace of Jesus Christ be with you always. Amen. (Mark D. White)

Just Breathe

First in a Series of Three on The Dog Days of August: Life in the Holy Spirit

John 20:19-23

I couldn't have been more than five or six years old the first time I went to a Pentecostal worship service. The majority of my prior experience of church happened in a family chapel where the congregation was comprised of half a dozen family members and, sometimes, the preacher's wife (we never had a female pastor). The most excitement we managed to conjure up in worship was to swat away the occasional honey bee that ventured away from the hive and that had settled in the wall of the old church. In the Pentecostal service, the worship seemed relatively "normal" until about a third of the way into the evening. The movement began. People shifted from pew and chair into the aisle. The response to the worship leader was no longer a low buzz of chatting. Voices raised. Tones shifted. Words became babbling syllables. One voice accumulated a multitude of prayers throughout the building. All at once a contented gathering was poked into a teeming hive of activity. I found myself not swatting away a meandering bee but swatting at a swarm of uncomfortable emotions as the Holy Spirit stirred up the congregants. I have no trouble imagining the day of Pentecost with tongues of fire and the chaos of many languages. I may not have had a clear understanding at such a tender age of the definition of drunkenness, but I did experience fear and awe in response to those Spirit-filled adults behaving in unexpected and inexplicable ways. However, my memory is an Acts 2 kind of experience with the Holy Spirit.

As inspiring and dramatic as the Acts 2 story of Pentecost is, many mainline Christians find it difficult to apply an understanding of that same Holy Spirit to everyday living. The church at large seems both fascinated and fearful of Pentecost, which might explain why many congregations open up the door and invite in the Holy Spirit on a particular Sunday in late spring only to quickly escort the same Spirit out the door until Pentecost Sunday the following year. Such a combination of fascination and fear leads Christians to view the activity of the Holy Spirit through the thick glass walls of exhibit cases rather than opening ourselves to an immediate experience and continual relationship with God's Spirit. By primarily understanding the gift of the Holy Spirit through the lens of Acts 2, the church perpetuates the angst of believers in relationship to the third person of the Trinity.

The church has been so shaped by Acts 2 that we find it difficult to embrace what John is telling us. In the evening of the first Easter, having received the news from Mary that Jesus lives, the disciples are still gathered in the house behind locked doors in fear of what the Jews might do to them if they are found. The risen Christ shows up on the disciples' doorstep, reveals his wounds, and breathes a little harder than normal. Did I miss it? What just happened? "Receive the Holy Spirit," Jesus says. The translation doesn't even have an exclamation point! This scared, beleaguered, motley crew of disciples now carries the Holy Spirit. That's it? That's all that happened? No wonder the church is enthralled with Acts 2! Where is the high drama? Where is the intense situation? How can we Christians be both attracted to and reject a story such as this? What will we do with a Holy Spirit that passes from one person to another as easily as a common cold?

In the last year or so, some preacher friends have begun collecting illustrations for Sunday sermon through status comments on Facebook. The theme for the upcoming Sunday is highlighted in the preacher's status, and then she issues an invitation for response. I am quite surprised at the number of people who do respond. These ordinary people respond to the ways in which God's grace is at work in their ordinary lives. These ordinary people give witness to the ways in which they experience Christ's suffering in those around them. These ordinary people voice the guidance of God in their everyday living. My spouse and I have frequent discussions about what illustrations are most helpful for the average person in the pew. We discuss the pros and cons of highlighting the stories and quotes of such notable Christians as Mother Theresa, Martin Luther King, Jr., John Wesley, and Saint Augustine. The lives and experiences and words of such great Christians as these may sometimes create for people in the pews the same sense of fear and fascination as the story of Acts 2. The church family remains in awe of God's work in these well-known brothers and sisters, yet we are intensely aware that we are just ordinary people in ordinary lives. Maybe God has worked wonderful and unique signs in the lives of these great saints, but rest of us are just worker bees.

In the dog days of August, the church does well to guard against the lethargy and apathy that would set in from a perception that life in the Holy Spirit is reserved for only those Christians whose mystical and profound experiences with God mirror the chaotic and inscrutable events of Acts 2. John 20 offers an understanding of life in the Spirit that attempts to demystify the Spirit's origin. Life in the Holy Spirit is rooted in the living, resurrected person of Jesus Christ. Although the church may often wonder about the origin and intent of those tongues of fire and the multitude of languages, John leaves little doubt as to the source of the Holy Spirit that is breathed on the disciples. To clarify, the intent is not to domesticate the Holy Spirit but to offer an accessible embodiment of the Spirit in Jesus. As one who lives in the fullness of the Holy Spirit, yes, Jesus performs extraordinary signs. He turns water into wine; he knows the intimate details of a woman's life; he heals a man paralyzed for thirty-eight years. However, as one who is full of the Holy Spirit, Jesus equally responds to life events in ways that are fully accessible to his modern day disciples. Jesus meets and engages an enemy of his people with respect

255

and honor; he participates in civil discourse with those who hold radically different views than his own in regards to issues of theology and praxis; he frequents places of worship, praying among and celebrating with many who don't understand him or his ways. This life in the Holy Spirit reminds us that all Jesus did was breathe on the disciples. By this same divine, holy breath of God, we too are sent forth. (Amy Persons Parkes)

Worship Aids

Call to Worship

We desire a life free from fear.
Breathe on us, breath of God.
We yearn for a peace that abides.
Breathe on us, breath of God.
We want to be equipped for kingdom work.
Breathe on us, breath of God.

Prayer

Holy God, whose breath hovered above the waters of creation and enlivened our bother Adam and sister Eve, may we share your life-giving ways. Let us breathe words of love where words of hate have suffocated your people. Let us exhale songs of peace and so stifle chants of war. By the power of your Spirit that sends us forth. Amen.

Benediction

As ordinary people with ordinary ways, may you go forth accompanied by the extraordinary gift of God's Spirit, the same Spirit that turns water into wine, wine into blood, and blood into eternal life. Amen. (Amy Persons Parkes)

AUGUST 19, 2012

❧❧❧

Twelfth Sunday after Pentecost

Readings: Proverbs 9:1-6; Psalm 34:9-14; Ephesians 5:15-20;
John 6:51-58

Bread from Heaven

John 6:51-58

There is nothing quite like the smell and taste of fresh homemade bread. I hope that sometime in your life you have had a chance to taste some. The warm bread melts in your mouth, and you really don't need anything on it. I hope someday to be able to bake fresh bread for Communion so that as you enter the sanctuary you will smell it. My wife and I make bread in our food processor. It mixes and kneads the dough, but we have to let it rise and beat it down once or twice before baking it. Today there is a bread-making machine that can take care of the whole process for you. You simply put in a package of bread mix, add water, and set the timer. Although the loaf does not look like a traditional loaf of bread, it still smells and tastes wonderful. A dear friend at one of our churches made sourdough bread. She gave away jars of the starter that had to be kept for the start of the next loaf. The fermentation process could be mighty powerful, and we heard stories of people leaving the starter in a hot car during the summer and the jar exploding and leaving a mess in the car that had a strong smell like beer that was hard to eliminate.

As I read through the Bible, I notice that there are often recurring themes. Water is one of those. The creation story mentions water; Noah builds an ark to survive the Flood; the children of Israel pass through the Red Sea; Moses calls water from a rock; the children of Israel enter the Promised Land through the Jordan River; Jesus is baptized in the Jordan River; Jesus visits a Samaritan woman at a well and offers her living water; and the list goes on. Bread is another recurring theme in the Bible.

257

Bread is a staple of life around the world, and it comes in a great variety of forms. People of all nations and races can relate to stories about bread.

One of the greatest celebrations of the Jewish year centers on bread. The celebration of Passover is also called the feast of unleavened bread. The children of Israel were in such a hurry to leave Egypt that they did not have time for the bread to rise, and so they ate unleavened bread. This bread is still a part of the Passover celebration today. As the Israelites wandered through the desert, God provided bread for them called *manna*. In John 6, we find Jesus speaking about manna. "Very truly, I tell you, it was not Moses who gave you the bread from heaven, but it is my father who gives you the true bread from heaven" (v. 32). Jesus goes on to say that this manna is a foreshadowing of the bread God will send down from heaven that will give life to the world; indeed Jesus is that very bread (v. 33).

Bread is part of the sacrificial system in the Old Testament, including "showbread" (or "bread of the Presence") placed before the Lord continually. It was this showbread that David ate with his companions when he was fleeing from King Saul (see 1 Samuel 21:1-6).

Later in the Old Testament, the prophet Elijah would meet a widow woman and ask her to make him a cake of bread. This was during a time of deadly famine, and the woman had only enough for herself and her son. Still she obediently did what the prophet asked, and she was rewarded with oil and flour that did not run out until the famine was over (1 Kings 17:8-16).

When Jesus was tempted in the wilderness following his baptism by John at the Jordan River, we are told that Jesus was starving, and the devil tempted him to turn the stones into bread. Jesus responded, "It is written: 'One does not live by bread alone, but by every word that comes from the mouth of God'" (Matthew 4:4). Later in his ministry, Jesus would multiply bread on two different occasions and feed thousands with only a few small loaves of bread.

In today's Scripture passage, Jesus states that he is "the living bread that came down from heaven. Whoever eats of this bread will live forever; and the bread that I will give for the life of the world is my flesh" (v. 51). I am amazed at the fact that Jesus was born in Bethlehem, which is not only the city of David, but which literally means "house of bread." Now Jesus says he is "living bread." This statement, "whoever eats my flesh and drinks my blood has eternal life," is difficult and awkward for us as it seems to imply some kind of cannibalism, eating human flesh and drinking human blood. But Jesus speaks to us about spiritual food, not physical food.

Jesus compares himself to the manna God gave the Israelites in the wilderness. This manna gave only temporary physical strength and sustained life for a limited time. The people who ate this manna still died. Jesus, the true bread from heaven, offers himself so that we might have eternal life. Jesus satisfies the deepest need of the human heart, but we must partake or we forfeit this benefit. It amazes me how many people still settle for the bread that perishes.

God invites us to partake of the true bread from heaven. We are invited to draw near with faith and receive the body and blood of Christ, true food of the kingdom of God that nourishes us to eternal life. What are you waiting for? Receive this bread from heaven today. (Neil Epler)

Lectionary Commentary

Proverbs 9:1-6

We receive invitations all the time. We are invited to birthday and anniversary celebrations. We are invited to baby and bridal showers. We are invited to graduations and recitals. In Proverbs 9, wisdom invites us to come eat and drink with her. We are told that she has prepared the food and drink and the table is set for us. She has sent out her servants to call us to come. If we accept the invitation and come to the meal, we are told that we will live. Let us hear and respond to wisdom's invitation to leave our "immaturity" and "walk in the way of insight."

Ephesians 5:15-20

In this passage we find a comparison and contrast of wise and foolish living. Paul states that we must be careful how we live, especially because we live in evil days. It is not enough to give lip service to what we believe, but we must be sure to live it. One aspect of foolish living is not to understand God's will for us. How can we hope to live the life God wants for us if we do not understand God's will? How can we hope to do God's will when we cannot comprehend it? Another aspect of foolish living is becoming drunk. Being drunk does not lead to wisdom but causes us to do things that are evil, things that we would not normally do if we were sober. Wisdom comes from being filled with God's Spirit. This causes us to worship God and to speak to one another with "psalms, hymns, and spiritual songs." A Spirit-filled life gives us grateful hearts and helps us to realize that in all things we can give thanks to Almighty God. (Neil Epler)

Worship Aids

Invocation

God of us all, we celebrate your presence among us this morning. We ask you to bless us as we partake of the bread of life. Help us never to be satisfied with the bread the world offers. May we remember and be thankful for the bread of heaven that you sent to us, even your Son, Jesus Christ. Amen.

Offertory Prayer

We give you thanks for all the blessings of life and especially for providing our daily bread. May we be reminded of our need for both physical and spiritual bread and of that need in others. Bless our gifts, our tithes, and our offerings and multiply them just as you multiplied the loaves you used to feed the thousands. In the name of Jesus the Christ. Amen.

Benediction

Now Lord, dismiss us with your peace. Fill us with your living bread. May we go forth to share the Good News that we have found the bread that satisfies our every need, and may we share this bread with others. May it sustain us to eternal life. In the name of the Father, the Son, and the Holy Spirit. Amen. (Neil Epler)

Birth Plans

Second in a Series of Three on The Dog Days of August:
Life in the Holy Spirit

John 3:1-9

During the months leading up to the birth of my first child, I couldn't stop watching birth stories on TV. While intellectually I understood that no two birth stories are exactly the same, my inexperience with giving birth and my indescribable need to have a sense of control over what would happen to my body and to the precious little one I carried compelled me to watch story after story of families expecting babies. Eventually, I developed the best-case scenario for my own birth story. Wouldn't you know that not much went according to my plan?

Interestingly enough, although the birth of my first child didn't go as I hoped, I was not the least bit dissuaded during my second pregnancy from similarly developing scenarios for that birth as well. Maybe I simply "nest" this way.

Nicodemus approaches Jesus in the dark of night and affirms Jesus' identity as one "who has come from God" (v. 2). In Jesus, Nicodemus senses the work of God that cannot be performed apart from God's presence. Many people, including Nicodemus, watched the signs of Jesus with great interest (see John 2:23). In our text, Jesus does not respond to Nicodemus with a sign to prove his divine connection or with a plan for how Nicodemus too can achieve this same relationship with God. Instead Jesus invites Nicodemus to consider that the Spirit of God might also claim him. Nicodemus can be born of God's Spirit even as he has been born of his mother. Early in the Gospel of John, we hear the author offer the same insight, "But to all...he gave the power to become children of God, who were born, not of blood or of the will of the flesh or of the will of man, but of God" (John 1:12-13). In Jesus' offer to Nicodemus, he qualifies this movement of the Holy Spirit by comparing it to the courses of the wind. "The wind blows where it chooses...you do not know where it comes from or where it goes" (v. 8).

Living life in the Holy Spirit means understanding that the Spirit will not be bound by our expectations and our desires. The Holy Spirit will not be managed, manipulated, or co-opted by our human agendas. Nicodemus is interested in the final product; he desires a life aligned with this Jesus who performs signs and wonders of God; but is he willing and available to be born of the Spirit? Will Nicodemus give himself over to a power at work in the realms of the spiritual and physical world that will birth him into new existence? While we might ask the question of Nicodemus, we realize the question is also one we must answer.

The birth stories in my family are not the only ones that haven't conformed to a family's expectations and birth plans. The miracles of modern medicine allow humanity to create and to dream a birth plan, giving a voice of empowerment to women's desires that have long been ignored, overlooked, and undervalued. Even as I am grateful for such possibilities, as one who has given birth, I am well aware that the primordial forces at work in giving birth are beyond any human control despite modern medicine and well-prepared, experienced birth families. To be born of the Spirit implies many of the same notions. As much as the Holy Spirit is rooted in the person of Jesus Christ, whose life, death, and resurrection bear witness to known factors of God's Spirit, we acknowledge Jesus' own testimony about the movement of the Holy Spirit. We "do not know where it comes from or where it is going." Those born of the Spirit will conform to no preconceived notions of holiness or righteousness. As the wind is free to blow where it chooses, those who wish to be born of the Spirit are invited to submit themselves to miraculous forces at work in birth. The one being born has no real choice in the matter. Which one of us decided whose womb we would be created within? Which one chose the date and circumstances of our birth? Who among us remembers the conscious decision to proceed forth from the womb to a new existence? None of us did. Not one of us. To live life in the Holy Spirit indeed questions whether or not we are willing and able to participate in the life of God that calls us to become vulnerable to God's Spirit that "blows where it chooses."

To live vulnerably alongside God's Spirit is to choose life characterized by listening, by receiving. In the end, we recognize that the Spirit is not grasped by our infantile hands. Indeed, the Spirit rests upon us. The Holy Spirit lifts up tiny strands in our hair and causes our clothes to billow up and ripple down. The Spirit alights upon our impatience and whispers soothing nothings to our cranky souls. The Spirit envelops the painful burdens we bear and shifts the load on our weakened heart. But the Spirit is not caught and held and restrained by misled notions of our self-importance.

In the dog days of August, many are searching for pools, lakes, and oceans to find a respite from the oppressive heat. The younger ones (or maybe younger at heart) are more tempted to actively pursue the gifts of water—swimming, snorkeling, diving for shells, turning flips under water, playing games of chicken sitting precariously on slippery wet shoulders. The more mature ones among us relish the opportunity to float upon the water, to be borne up by the water. Weary bodies hoping for a bit of relief from the summer sun, from the burden of carrying our bodies, we cast ourselves upon the water. We receive the gift of floating. As we float, we feel the shift of wind and the direction toward which we glide. We remember the words of Jesus, "no one can enter the kingdom of God without being born of water and Spirit. What is born of flesh is flesh, and what is born of Spirit is Spirit" (vv. 5-6). (Amy Persons Parkes)

Worship Aids

Call to Worship

One comes by night
One is the Light in the night.
One places hope in signs.

One is the Sign of hope.
One must be born first.
One is the First Born.
**All: Come let us worship Jesus, the Light, the Sign,
    the First Born.**

Prayer

O Water of Life, in these hot days of a waning summer, may we take a dip in the cool pools of your grace. As ones shaped by your Holy Spirit, may we be borne upon the waters that will wash away our sin and lead us to life eternal. May this time of worship quench a thirsty yearning for an outpouring of your presence. In your name, we pray. Amen.

Benediction

May the wind of God's Spirit blow you where it will, so it is with all who are born of the same Spirit. The grace and peace of Christ keep you as you yield yourself to the Spirit's power. Amen. (Amy Persons Parkes)

AUGUST 26, 2012

❧❧❧❧

Thirteenth Sunday after Pentecost

Readings: Joshua 24:1-2a, 14-18; Psalm 34:15-22; Ephesians 6:10-20; John 6:56-69

Putting on Our Spiritual Armor

Ephesians 6:10-20

Every morning when I wake up and get ready for work I go through a routine. First I make some coffee for me and some hot tea for my wife. I let the dogs out and get the morning paper. I look through the paper and check out the weather on the Weather Channel. Next I get our vitamins and other daily medicines to take. As I prepare to shave and shower, my wife looks for the clothes I am going to wear so she can iron them. Now I'm not real fussy about wearing wrinkled clothes, but my wife sure is. She believes that my wearing wrinkled clothes reflects' on her ability to run a tight and clean home. Someone suggested that I iron my own clothes and I tried, but I only managed to iron in the wrinkles.

It is important to have a morning routine to get ready for work and other daily activities. It is just as important to have a spiritual routine as we begin each day. I find this passage in Ephesians, about the armor of God, helpful in this regard. It is important to have our clothes and other things ready for the day ahead. Paul reminds us that it is just as important to put on our spiritual armor and prepare for the spiritual battles that we will face today. Paul states that it is essential that we put on the full armor of God so that we can "stand against the wiles of the devil" (v. 11). He reminds us that the battles we will face today are not just in this world, but our struggle is against "the spiritual forces of evil in the heavenly places" (v. 12). We must put on the full armor of God so that we will be able to stand firm, and I am guided in doing this as I dress and get ready for the day.

As I put on my pants and belt, I am reminded that I am to have the "belt of truth fastened around my waist" (v. 14). I cannot feel remotely secure without my pants and a belt to hold them up. Putting on my belt gives me a sense of security and readiness. If my pants fall down, I can't hope to do anything. This belt reminds me of the belt of truth of God in Christ and in the Holy Scripture. Jesus stated, "I am the way and the truth and the life. No one comes to the Father except through me" (John 14:6). As I buckle on my belt, I remember the truths about God's love, and I know that he will not leave me or forsake me.

When I put on my shirt, I remember that I am to have "the breastplate of righteousness in place" (v. 14). My shirt, like the breastplate, is crucial because it covers all my vital organs. It covers my heart, my lungs, my liver and stomach, everything that keeps me alive. As I button my shirt, I am reminded that my righteousness comes from God. It is not something I can earn or deserve. Earlier in this letter to the Ephesians, Paul reminds us, "For by grace you have been saved through faith, and this not your own doing; it is the gift of God" (2:8). I accept this righteousness and work with God through the Holy Spirit to be perfected in righteousness every day.

Slipping on my shoes, I am reminded that my "feet are fitted with whatever will make you ready to proclaim the gospel of peace" (v. 15). My shoes are important because they protect my feet. They provide me with balance and prepare me to move and take action. I can go out in any kind of weather knowing my shoes will keep my feet dry and give me traction so I can move. With God's peace in my heart I can be assured of my salvation, and I can cast aside my anxieties knowing that God will work all things for good (Romans 8:28). I can have peace with God, peace with others, and peace with myself.

Now the "shield of faith" (v. 16) is not something we wear, but something that we take up. When I pick up my brief case, backpack, or computer case, I think about this shield. I know today the devil will be firing missiles at me—temptations, evil thoughts, fiery trials—and I will need a strong shield to defend myself. My faith points me to a power higher, stronger than myself, so I can deflect and extinguish the devil's flaming arrows.

I do not normally wear a hat, but I am reminded of the "helmet of salvation" (v. 17) when I put on my glasses. You may wear a hat every day, and this is a perfect reminder of this powerful helmet. If you don't wear a hat or glasses, perhaps you can think about putting on this helmet when you put in your contact lenses or when you brush your hair. The helmet is crucial because it covers our heads and the vital organ of our brain. I remind myself that I have been saved through the death of Jesus Christ and not anyone or anything can take this salvation from me. I know that I am saved, that I am being saved, and that I ultimately will be completely saved.

The "sword of the Spirit" (v. 17) is again not something you wear but something to be grasped. It is the only offensive weapon we are told to use. As a minister, I am usually carrying a Bible with me, and this is my sword. Perhaps you could begin to carry a Bible with you to work or school in your briefcase, your backpack, or your purse. Just as Jesus used this mighty sword, the word of God, to defend himself against the temptations of the evil one, so we can use this sword to defend ourselves and even attack the devil's evil intentions.

This week, as you practice your daily morning routine, won't you consider adding the routine of putting on the full armor of God? (Neil Epler)

Lectionary Commentary

Joshua 24:1-2a, 14-18

The most familiar sentence in this passage is the ending to verse 15. Joshua has assembled all the tribes of Israel and Shechem (v. 1) and he asks them to consider whom they will serve. Will they serve the gods their forefathers worshiped or will they serve the Lord? Joshua says, "As for me and my household, we will serve the LORD" (v. 15). The Israelites respond that they too will serve the Lord, and it seems like an easy answer. The difficulty comes in living this choice out day by day. It is easy to choose to serve the Lord when it is the popular thing to do and we are surrounded by other believers, but what happens when following the Lord is not the popular thing to do and people begin to mock and criticize us? Do we fall away and begin to follow the ways of the world and the current fads and trends?

We may not have to worry about the same gods that the ancient Israelites worshiped beyond the Jordan and back in Egypt, but there are still plenty of other gods in this world. Are we following the gods of materialism, wealth, prestige, appearances, power, and popularity? Do we choose to follow the Lord when we must decide between telling a painful truth and telling a lie? Do we choose to follow the Lord when we see someone in need, or do we look the other way? It is easy to say that "as for me and my household, we will serve the LORD," but it is a far different thing to live out that choice every hour, every day. May God give us the strength to reaffirm this choice every day and to live it as well.

John 6:56-69

What do we do when we are given a difficult task? Perhaps we are asked to do something that seems beyond our skill level. We may not even understand the task or know where to begin. Jesus has just shared that he is the living bread that came down from heaven. He tells his followers that they must eat his flesh and drink his blood if they are to have eternal life. Many of the disciples respond, "This teaching is difficult; who can accept it" (v. 60)? Jesus continues to teach them about the Spirit that gives life and the importance of believing his words (vv. 61-64). He also shares that no one can follow him "unless it is granted by the Father" (v. 65). After this, many of his disciples turn away and stop following him (v. 66). Jesus asks the Twelve if they also want to leave (v. 67). Peter's response is powerful: "Lord, to whom can we go? You have the words of eternal life" (v. 68). Peter then reaffirms his belief that Jesus is the anointed one sent from God just as he did at Capernaum when Jesus asked them, "Who do you say that I am" (Matthew 16:15)? When life gets hard, when we have things to accomplish that seem too difficult for us, remember Peter's strong words. Jesus has the words of life, and he will see us through. (Neil Epler)

Worship Aids

Prayer of Confession

Dear Lord, our lives are so very busy. There always seems to be more that needs to be done. We never seem to have enough time. We live our lives at fever pitch. We confess that we do not spend as much time with you as we need to. We do not prepare ourselves for the battles that we have to face each day. Forgive us we pray, and help us to find ways that we can stand firm against the wiles of the evil one. Help us learn to put on the strong armor of God every day. In Jesus' name. Amen.

Words of Assurance

We are never alone. God has provided for our every need. God sent his Son into the world to show us the way. God has poured forth the Holy

Spirit to empower us and guide us in our daily walk. God will clothe you with holy armor to protect you from all evil. Thanks be to God.

Benediction

Now go forth, standing firm in the full armor of God. Fasten on the belt of truth, put on the breastplate of righteousness, shoe your feet with the gospel of peace, take up the shield of faith, put on the helmet of salvation, and grasp the sword of the Spirit. May God bless, defend, and keep you from all evil now and forever more. Amen. (Neil Epler)

The Slow Reveal

Third in a Series of Three on The Dog Days of August:
Life in the Holy Spirit

John 16:12-15

Timing is everything. Saying "I love you" on the second date may not be such a good idea. A career move in the wake of a loved one's death could be reconsidered. Think twice about shifting the worship time in the first year of ministry with a church; as a professor joked with our seminary class on church administration, "Don't change anything but your oil and your underwear in the first six months of a new pastorate." Timing is crucial. The message might be true and good and right, but is this the moment at which the message will be heard? Will your spouse be able to hear you ask for more time together as she struggles with the final details of the biggest presentation of her career? Can your supervisor grasp the gravity of your work concerns when he pops into the office to take care of essential items before heading back to the bedside of his dying father? In some cases, the right time requires a bit of engineering. The perfect surprise birthday party presupposes circumstances in which the person to be surprised is completely unaware of the goings on; such an endeavor demands planning. However, in other situations the timing of a fitting revelation is not contrived, organized, or planned; the opportune occasion is simply sensed or evolves as we become aware of what converges in the present. In the church, we often struggle to ascertain the timeliness of an event, a revelation, a conversation, an opportunity, a change; what we seek is *kairos*, the God-moment immersed in perfect timing.

These three Sundays in August, we take a broad view of life in the Holy Spirit. At base, life in the Holy Spirit is accessible and available to all Christians; the Spirit is not simply some wild, unknowable, otherness of God that highjack's any intelligible interaction with God, ourselves, and others. To live a life in the Holy Spirit is to embrace communion with a resurrected Jesus; the Holy Spirit as one person of the Trinity has a face and body and real-life, ordinary interactions as witnessed in Jesus. The Father, Son, and Spirit are one. Second, life in the Holy Spirit reflects a willingness to be moved about by God's desires and designs. One whose life resides in the Holy Spirit will not be ruled by the fear of losing control over how and when the Spirit responds and moves in one's life. Although made approachable through the witness of Christ, the Holy Spirit remains a free and independent person of God. Finally, life in the Holy Spirit is shaped by an awareness of God-moments. As revealed in these last words to the gathered disciples before his arrest and death, Jesus speaks of the Advocate (John 16:7), the Spirit of truth, who will at the right time "guide you into all the truth." As we offer ourselves to life in the Holy Spirit, we acknowledge the Spirit who is able to discern the truth we can bear at this time. We embrace a God who desires that we know the whole truth, who willingly shares all that is God's own—when the time is right, *kairos*.

Jesus says, "I still have many things to say to you, but you cannot bear them now" (v. 12). I sometimes wonder if the twenty-four-hour news channels care about how much people can bear. Granted, the distinctions of news and facts and truth are often lost on a media-overwhelmed culture. Nonetheless, journalism is marketed as the truth, the bottom-line, the real story. Who are we kidding? We want the real story. We crave the facts. We desire the knowledge. We find ourselves addicted to the possibility of comprehending what is actually going on in the world. We must have the truth. And we must have it now. So computers stay on all day and night. Phones stay charged and ready; MP3 players are loaded with the latest podcasts. TVs put us to sleep and wake us up—all this because we are afraid we will miss the truth. Jesus' statement is not intended to deny the disciples access to the truth. Instead, Jesus' desire is for the full revelation of all truth, all that God knows, to his followers. The Holy Spirit is in the business of revelation, and life in the Holy Spirit is distinguished by one's willingness to embrace the often "slow reveal" of God. The revealing work of God through the Spirit senses the ripeness of a moment and the openness of a soul. The wisdom of God through the perception of the Spirit also recognizes a hardness of heart and an inability to hear. In the goodness of who God is, the Holy Spirit offers gracious limits to humanity, asking, "What can she bear now?" Bit by bit, revelation upon revelation, the Spirit of truth discloses more and more of the mystery of God to the one who is willing to wait for the *kairotic* moment. Timing is everything.

As a parent, I often find myself wondering how much truth about birth and death and relationships I need to share with my young children. How much truth will overwhelm these beloved youngsters? How little truth will send them searching for answers from someone else? As a minister, I struggle to discern when to challenge the truth of a parishioner's understanding of God. Will questioning a particular belief send this sheep running away? Or will remaining silent be the equivalent of not clearly marking the ledge of a steep cliff? And if I care so much, how much more of a loving parent and attentive shepherd is God? God's revelation of truth through the gift of the Holy Spirit can be trusted. Timing is everything. (Amy Persons Parkes)

Worship Aids

Call to Worship

Holy Spirit, breath of Jesus,
Whisper wisdom, peace, and forgiveness.
Holy Spirit, wind and water,
Blow through us and baptize us.
Holy Spirit, Spirit of Truth,
Speak what you hear and declare what is to come.

Prayer

Spirit of truth, we confess our struggle to bear with your timing. In times of sorrow, we desire truth that comforts. In need, we beg for truth that sustains. From the great storehouse of your mercy, reassure our weakened spirits of your desire to fully reveal all truth to your children that we might be one with you, Father, Son, and Holy Spirit, forever and ever. Amen.

Benediction

Timeless God, grant an extra measure of your grace as we are sent forth into the world awakened by alarm clocks and guarded by time clocks. May we be sustained in the knowledge that these clocks will never time the Spirit's work on our souls. Go forth in peace. Amen. (Amy Persons Parkes)

SEPTEMBER 2, 2012

❧❧❧❧

Fourteenth Sunday after Pentecost

Readings: Deuteronomy 4:1-2, 6-9; Psalm 15; James 1:17-27;
Mark 7:1-8, 14-15, 21-23

The Power of Words

James 1:17-27

What are the most powerful things you have seen in your life? I have
seen a Saturn Five Rocket at a museum, and I have seen a space shuttle
launch. The power of these machines makes the earth shake as giant
flames and smoke propel these crafts into space. I have seen two United
States battleships, and I have heard the report of their giant guns. The
power from the gun's recoil makes the ship crab sideways. I have experienced the power of an F-15 fighter jet and the roar of the engines at a
stock car race. I have been to Niagara Falls and to Alaskan glaciers.
Maybe you have experienced the power of a volcano or an earthquake.
Or perhaps you have felt the power of a tornado or a hurricane.

There are other things of great power that are not as tangible. Think
about the power of prayer or the power of love. Jesus stated that if we
have faith the size of a mustard seed we can move mountains and uproot
trees (Matthew 17:20; Luke 17:6). Today I invite you to consider the
power of words.

Words have tremendous power to hurt and to do harm. Do you remember the little saying we learned as children? "Sticks and stones may break
my bones, but words can never harm me." While words cannot do physical harm to our bodies, they can do a lot more damage than sticks and
stones. Most bodily injuries heal. Sometimes it will require some medical
attention, a bandage, stitches, or maybe even a cast or surgery. But eventually, if we are healthy, we will heal. Words that are spoken in anger, or
hatred, or without thought can do damage that may never heal. Most of
us have been called a derogatory name or have had someone speak things

271

that were not true about us. The pain is very real. Most of us have also been on the other side, calling others names or joining in berating someone. In James 3:10, the author reminds us that our tongues, with which we praise God, should not be used to harm others. "From the same mouth come blessing and cursing. My brothers and sisters, this ought not to be so."

Another way that words can do tremendous harm is through gossip. Again, each one of us has probably been affected by gossip, and we probably have participated in it. I am reminded of the dandelion plants that grow in my yard. When the yellow flowers go to seed and the wind blows that ball of fluff, there is no way you can go and gather back those seeds. In the same way, there is no way to gather gossip once it has left our lips and been shared with another. The words are irretrievable, and the harm is difficult to stop.

Words also have a wonderful power to heal. The book of Proverbs shares several insights about the power of words to heal and build one another up. "Anxiety weighs down the human heart, but a good word cheers it up" (Proverbs 12:25). "A soft answer turns away wrath" (15:1a). "Pleasant words are like a honeycomb, sweetness to the soul and health to the body" (16:24). When I have a bad day and wonder if anything I do really makes a difference, I begin to question my vocation and calling, and I wonder if I am doing what God wants me to do. Then the phone rings and someone shares a kind word about how they were touched by a sermon I preached or a class that I taught. Maybe they let me know how important a visit was at just the right moment. Their words bring healing and encouragement.

Think about those three precious words, "I love you." When these words are spoken at the right moment they can lift our spirits and make us forget our anxieties and difficulties. Think about some other phrases like: "I care about you; I have been thinking about you; I have been praying for you." These words have a wonderful power to heal and lift broken spirits. And don't forget the power in giving a compliment or words of encouragement. Words have tremendous power to heal.

In today's passage, James reminds us that it is not just the speaking and hearing of words that are important, it is also important that we live them. Jesus not only spoke powerful words he also lived them. He didn't just speak about showing compassion and reaching out to the poor, the needy, and the sinners, he actually did it. Jesus shared with us an example, and he calls us to follow. Jesus saved his harshest words for the religions leaders of his day. He did not have a problem with their teaching, but he had a problem with the way they lived out their teaching. Jesus said to the crowds and to his disciples: 'The scribes and the Pharisees sit on Moses' seat; therefore do whatever they teach you and follow it; but do not do as they do, for they do not practice what they teach'" (Matthew 23:2-3). At the end of the Sermon on the Mount Jesus told his audience that those who heard his words and put them into practice are likewise builders who built on the rock, and those who heard his words and did not put them into practice are like foolish builders who built on the sand (Matthew 7:24-27). James also tells us, "But be doers of the word, and not merely hearers who deceive themselves" (James 1:22). There is tremendous power in God's word when we hear and live it.

Let us remember there is great power in words. May we avoid words that hurt and do harm and instead speak words that heal and edify. May we not only be hearers of the word, but doers of the word as well. (Neil Epler)

Lectionary Commentary

Deuteronomy 4:1-2, 6-9

This passage reminds us how important it is that we understand God's laws and commands. We not only need to know them but we also have to live them. By following these commands, the people of other nations will see and know the wisdom of the commands. This may cause them to draw near to our God. In verse 2 we are warned not to add or subtract from these decrees and laws. God made these laws complete. How can we, with our limited knowledge, have the ability to add or remove laws that God has given? Yet we often do this. We follow traditions as if they were laws. In Jesus' time the religious leaders elevated their man-made laws to the same level as God's. Jesus rebuked them for this. Let us be careful that we are not rebuked for adding laws and rules to God's or removing others as irrelevant. In verse 9 we are reminded to watch ourselves so we do not forget the things that God has done for us or forget his teaching. We are told to "Make them known to your children and your children's children" (v. 9). May we be diligent in sharing our faith stories with our own family members and passing on the torch of our faith.

Mark 7:1-8, 14-15, 21-23

How do we become followers of Jesus? By learning Jesus' teachings and following them. In these passages we find instructions for how to follow Jesus and live out our faith. Jesus warns us about judging others and cautions us that we will be judged in the same manner we judge others. He gives a rather comical illustration of a person with a plank in his or her eye trying to remove a speck of sawdust from someone else's eye. This is often how we judge others, looking for their small mistakes and imperfections while ignoring our own huge ones. To follow Jesus means to enter through the small gate and follow the narrow path that leads to life (v. 14). It is always easy to follow the well-worn path and the broad way, but as Jesus' followers, we know this leads to death. We need to stay on the narrow path and help others find their way to this path as well. When we claim that we are followers of Jesus, it is important that we live each day following his example. Just saying we belong to Jesus is not enough. "Not everyone who says to me, 'Lord, Lord,' will enter the kingdom of heaven, but only he who does the will of my Father who is in heaven" (v. 21). Let us strive to be true followers of Jesus in our words and in our actions. (Neil Epler)

Worship Aids

Call to Worship (John 1:1-3, 14)

In the beginning was the word,
And the word was with God,
And the word was God.
He was in the beginning with God.
All things came into being through him,
And without him not one thing came into being.
And the word became flesh and lived among us,
**And we have seen his glory, the glory as of a father's only son,
full of grace and truth.**

Prayer of Confession

Lord, we confess that we have used words to hurt and to harm. Forgive us we pray. Lord, we confess that we have shared gossip and things we knew were not true. Forgive us we pray. Lord, we have withheld words that could have brought healing and hope. Forgive us we pray. Help us Lord to be persons who are not only hearers of your word, but doers of your word. In the name of Jesus Christ, the Word made flesh. Amen.

Prayer of Pardon

In the name of Jesus the Christ, you are forgiven.
In the name of Jesus the Christ, you are forgiven.

Benediction

Now, may God the Creator, who called all things into being; God the Redeemer, Jesus, the Word made flesh; and God the Sustainer, the Holy Spirit, who empowered the apostles to speak words of understanding in different tongues, bless, preserve, and keep you. Amen. (Neil Epler)

Remember Who You Are!

First in a Series of Two on Back to School/Back to Church

Deuteronomy 4:1-2, 6, 9

By the time our first child was ready to leave for college I understood Mark Twain's advice about putting all twelve-year-olds in a pickle barrel, feeding them through the hole in the barrel, and when they are sixteen, closing up the hole. More than once my son and I had both said, "I can't wait until. . . ." On the day he was to leave for college, a fully packed, new red pickup sat in our drive-way. But there he stood—on the front lawn for a full thirty minutes—unable to move. Instead of seeing a defiant, independent, and determined adolescent, I saw that little boy who held my hand as he crossed the street for the first time. As he stood on the threshold of his future, he began to remember home. As I watched him stand anxiously on our front lawn that August, I remembered the first time I let him cross the street by himself, hoping that he always remembered to look both ways.

I remembered the summer I left home. Dad shook my hand and simply said, "Son, remember who you are." He had always said that when I went out anywhere. Not once did he suggest that being a P.K. (preacher's kid) held any extraordinary expectations, but being a part of our family held high expectations and responsibilities. Dad was saying to me, wherever you go, remember what your family has taught you. At the bus station, mother gave me her tearful farewell and a four-page handwritten letter. She reminded me of my childhood, her joy at my birth, her pride in my growth, and her optimism for my future. "Remember who you are."

Labor Day Sunday became a "back-to-school" tradition years ago as summer vacations came to an end and the school year unfolded again. While most school sessions have already begun, this weekend is a transition Sunday for most churches. Saturday college football has begun and households savor one last mini-vacation before the serious school work begins.

Every year, as our children prepared for school, we stood each one against a special wall and measured their height progress. With excitement, each turned to see how much he had grown. A mark, date, and name marked the progress. The same thing occurred at the end of each quarter. Report cards came back, and the progress was noted. Each time the report cards came in, our family expected progress. We didn't ask, "So just how much have you shrunk this year?" Nor at report card time said, "So how poorly you have done this year?" In our families we always expect growth and improvement.

This text from Deuteronomy lays out the Lord's expectations for God's people. This was the graduation moment for the Hebrew children. Forty years of wandering in the wilderness had come to an end. God is giving the last little instructions, a reminder to hold fast to God's teaching so that life can be full and whole and healthy. One can hear God as a parent saying, "Remember who you are."

God gives two important commands. The first is to remember what you have been taught. Four generations of Old Testament kings illustrate this principle (see 2 Kings 18–23). Hezekiah holds the honor of being one of the faithful kings of Israel. As a result, Scripture reminds us that God honored that leadership. His son Manasseh was only twelve years old at the time of his father's death. For the next fifty-five years Manasseh used Judah for his personal purposes. Having missed the benefit of his father's teaching, he is described as doing evil in the eyes of the Lord. His son, Amon, succeeded him for two years and followed Manasseh's example until his death. The whole Hebrew nation suffered as a result. Amon's son, Josiah, only eight years old when he became king, ruled more like Hezekiah, quite an accomplishment for a young child. He rehabilitated the old, discarded temple—ignored for more than sixty years, and discovered a copy of the Law (a portion of Torah). Upon hearing it read, he ordered a national time of repentance, worship, and renewal. Judah went on to a time of spiritual and national health. The moral of this story is that we cannot know how to live unless we know who we are. The church seems to be in a period of "Christian amnesia." We are in danger of forgetting who we are.

The second command is to teach this to our children. The story of Josiah paints a painful picture of what happens when we lose our heritage. It has been said that the church is only one generation from extinction. There is hope, however. Josiah restored the heritage of a nation by turning back to God. We can do the same.

The North American church is in danger of losing younger generations. For years the church could depend upon the community to reinforce the biblical message. Schools read from the Bible and even offered prayer. Media held reverence for the biblical story. This is no longer the case. Neither can we assume that a little bit of Christian education is enough for our children. This is a time for a new commitment to pass the faith along to our children. Sunday school is not enough!

I met Charles and Laura (not their real names) while attending their small church. Having lived near this small farming community since they were newlyweds, this couple, each nearly ninety years old, were the last members. Still, Charles opened the church each Sunday. When asked why, they merely told their story. The church had helped teach their children, and the faith was passed to their grandchildren. They were given a treasure that must be passed to others. Every Sunday they had church because someone might walk through the doors. When the church hierarchy offered to help them "close the doors," they reminded us the doors of the church were open because, even if the community had changed, God's word had not. (Guy Ames)

Worship Aids

Call to Worship
"Faith is the assurance of things hoped for and the confidence of
    things not seen" (Hebrews 11:1).
**But we long for more than hope and want to see
    our unseen God.**
"Without faith it is impossible to please God" (Hebrews 11:6).
We believe; help our unbelief (see Mark 9:24).
"Don't worry about tomorrow; today has enough worries of its own"
    (Matthew 6:34).
How can we live unless we plan for tomorrow?
With all these questions how can we worship?
If you want to see God's kingdom you must have the eyes of a child.
Let our worship be an act of faith, an act of trust in God.
In faith we worship our God and affirm:
    Though the fig trees do not blossom
    and no fruit is on the vines,
    ....

yet [we] will rejoice in the LORD,
[we] will exult in the God of [our] salvation.
GOD, the Lord, is [our] strength (Habakkuk 3:17-19a).

Prayer of Confession

Eternal God, we live as though we are the center of the universe. Our prayers cry out demanding attention and expecting that we should be your exception to all rules. While we hope you will look after others, we sincerely wish that we are at the top of your list. We confess to you that most of the time we don't believe we are in real need of forgiveness because we think better of ourselves than we really ought to think. We want you to give us the benefit of the doubt, but demand much of others. Forgive our unwillingness to offer grace to others. We demand that the rules be bent for our loved ones, but are unwilling to bend for those who have wounded us, who disagree with us, or those who have offended us. Like spoiled children, we want to believe that we are exceptional. Forgive our arrogance, O God. We know that your Word declares that you oppose the proud and give grace to the humble. Humble us, Lord, so that by seeing our true nature we might better grasp your great grace.

Words of Assurance

Hear these words of assurance, comfort, and forgiveness: "Remember, if anyone is in Christ there is a new creation, the old has passed away and the new has come" (2 Corinthians 5:17). (Guy Ames)

SEPTEMBER 9, 2012

❧❧❧

Fifteenth Sunday after Pentecost

Readings: Isaiah 35:4-7; Psalm 146; James 2:1-10, (11-13), 14-17; Mark 7:24-37

Honest Waiting

Isaiah 35:4-7

I appreciate the truth. I especially appreciate hearing it the first time I ask for it. Please do not beat around the bush and give me answers you think I might want. That is a waste of our time.

Our passage for today is honest and relevant for our time. There is fear in our hearts. There are calamities throughout our world. Disabilities limit the physical abilities of some. There are people who are blind and deaf among us; there are those who have no voice. We are reminded that we are all limited in some capacity—no one is perfect. The earth shares its imperfections as well. What good is burning sand, deserts, or wilderness? What do they produce or bring forth? These verses address the fact that we need healing; we need redemption; we need salvation.

We need to be prepared and alert: "Here is your God. . . . He will come and save you" (v. 4). Regardless of how great our limitations or how wide the wilderness we face, salvation is coming. God will come and make all things abundantly good.

First, physical salvation comes: the blind see, the deaf hear, the lame leap, and the speechless sing. This gets our attention; it is personal. Physical healing is at the top of many of our prayer lists when we are hurting or suffering. We are not ones to suffer quietly. We like and desire wholeness, and to some extent, physical perfection. We spend billions of dollars on research to cure diseases and "correct" physical limitations and imperfections. Our text asserts that God provides. Within God's salvation, God reverses the ailments that cause physical suffering and makes everyone well. Physical wholeness is restored.

279

Then, quickly, God moves from the personal to the corporate. God turns what we would deem as hopeless into springs of hopefulness. Waters come from the wilderness and streams flow in the desert. What was barren becomes fruitful and in abundance. Nothing that we would consider trash is left with God's salvation; all is now treasure. The redemption God brings is all encompassing, perfect, and complete.

What a relief this word should offer to us. Isaiah acknowledges that life is not always easy, that there are difficult and challenging struggles before each of us—physically and environmentally. I think the metaphor can be stretched to all categories of struggle: emotional, spiritual, and psychological. Life is hard, but salvation is assured. God comes with a promise of redemption that heals all that ails us and our world. Hope is on the way, a new life and a new way of being is coming forth.

This is indeed good news for humanity and the world, but a question lingers. When? When will God come and save us? When will we be redeemed? How long do we have to wait? The passage begins, again, in an honest way. "Say to those who are of a fearful heart" admits that it is scary to wait in the wilderness or with no voice. We are further encouraged to "be strong" and not fear, which is easier said than done. Do you know how it feels to be blind in a world where everything is based on vision or to be mute and have no voice in a crowded room? What good is it to have ears if they have nothing to hear or a tongue that cannot communicate? What is a farmer to do in a wilderness where she cannot grow crops? Burning sand serves no purpose but to chafe the feet of the shoeless and sting the eyes of the desert traveler. We are supposed to not fear and be strong in the midst of all this?

The only answer lies in the hope offered in the salvation of God. Who else can give sight, or voice, or hearing, or life to lame legs? Who else can bring fruit from dry land? The promise of what is to come is great enough to sustain us, for who else can provide in this way? No one but God can fulfill the earth in this way, and in that there is good news. We have learned time and time again that God keeps promises. We are encouraged to have singleness of mind and heart as we wait, without fear and with strength, until the day of restoration arrives. It is coming, it is promised, and it will come to pass.

But until then we are to do our best to live in the imperfect, what we might view as a wasteful and unproductive world, until the good and right and just arrives in abundance. As we wait for this promise to be fulfilled, we should strive to live as in hope, but with a clear view of what is around us. This world may not be the way we want it to be or the way God intends for it to be. We find hurt, disability, injustice, and wastefulness, but redemption is coming. We need to be alert and in tune with our surroundings as we work toward what we know God will put into place when the day of redemption comes. We can do our part to begin to usher God's work into this world as we continue to "be strong" and wait to hear those triumphant words, "Here is your God." Amen. (Victoria Atkinson White)

Lectionary Commentary

James 2:1-10, (11-13), 14-17

With the opening words of verse one, we know something is wrong in the fellowship among these brothers and sisters. Those who are professing a faith in Christ are not following their faith with actions that reflect their beliefs. James even anticipates their possible response to his condemnation by bringing up the law. Faith is important, and keeping the law is important but in the end, actions speak louder than anything. Our faith is to be organic, constantly changing and moving with the needs before us. If someone is hungry, we should feed them; if someone needs clothes, we should clothe them. Those without basic necessities cannot hear the good news, but they can feel its embrace. James asserts that our actions should speak for our faith rather than our words or our interpretations of the law. Words and rules are often what cause the problems that are crying out for action. James' words echo the message and mission of Christ himself. "Love your neighbor as yourself." In this case it means get up and act!

Mark 7:24-37

Jesus' reputation precedes him wherever he goes. He tries to keep his arrival in Tyre a secret, but his attempts at secrecy are no match for the determination of a mother with a sick child. Most of us have witnessed this kind of persistence. A parent with a sick or injured child will stop at nothing to get a cure or treatment for his or her little one. Parents can be fierce, almost to the point of obsession, in getting their children in front of the right people to get the medical attention they need. This is the framework of the woman who approaches Jesus. She doesn't care that he wants privacy, and she disregards the geographical and class status that should separate them from even being in conversation. She has heard he has the ability to help her, and so she clings to that faith with all she has. In the end, her determination pays off, despite the barriers that should have kept her from receiving such a blessing.

Similarly, the people bringing a deaf man before Jesus beg for healing. They too are desperate for his health to be restored. I wonder how often we come before Jesus with the same determination and passion. Do we approach our faith as if it is our only hope, the only thing that can save us? Or do we come to Christ with assumptions of acceptance and salvation? Those who truly received Christ in these stories received because they had nothing left to lose; Jesus was their only hope. Their faith was rewarded because of its purity and sincerity. What are we holding back that keeps us from this kind of pure and almost reckless faith? Might it also be keeping us from the blessings or healing we seek? (Victoria Atkinson White)

Worship Aids

Call to Worship

I will praise the Lord as long as I live.
Praise the Lord! Praise the Lord, O my soul!
I will lift up my voice in this new day and every day.
Praise the Lord! Praise the Lord, O my soul!
I will sing praises to my God all my life long.
Praise the Lord! Praise the Lord, O my soul!

Invocation

God, we come to you in this time of worship knowing that you are present with us in good times and bad. We ask that you call our hearts and minds to be at one with you, the one who seeks to make all things new and right. May our hope rest in your faithfulness. Amen.

Prayer of Confession

God, we know that too often we let our words speak for our faith rather than letting our actions show our faith to others. Silence us when we need to act instead. Guide our actions so that our words might follow. Amen.

Words of Assurance

Christ is the Word made flesh! Follow him to new life in Spirit and in truth, in word and in deed. (Victoria Atkinson White)

Only One Generation to Go: A Legacy of Faith

Second in a Series of Two on Back to School/Back to Church

John 1:1-18

This Sunday can serve as a Sunday school emphasis day, a day to cele-brate the teaching ministry of the church and recognize teachers, and also to encourage the congregation to invite persons to join them in Sunday school, small group ministry, or other learning opportunities.

Every year my preacher father declared one Sunday in September as Sunday School Rally Day. Classes received attendance goals, and every effort was made to be in Sunday school on that Sunday. We crowded in the sanctuary for introductions, awards, and inspiration. The classes with the best performance received special note, and school-age children were finally promoted to the next level. In the midst of that great gathering, we were reminded that we have no greater priority than teaching and raising up the next generation of Christians.

Sunday school has lost much of its importance in the contemporary church. We need to remember why earlier leaders instituted this tool for disciple making. John Wesley insisted on teaching all new Methodists. Any Methodist in good standing had to be committed to a weekly small-group session called a class meeting. About the same time Robert Raikes, a layman, advocated teaching impoverished children to read, using the Bible as curriculum. He called these classes Sunday school. Within fifty years more than 1.5 million children were enrolled in these schools! For the next 150 years Sunday school provided biblical training for much of the Western world and served as the entry point for millions of persons into the Christian faith.

No longer, however. Not only do folks avoid Sunday school, but the conversation of faith seems more difficult. How can we pass along the faith to this generation in the "post-Christian" era? We cannot even assume an "inherited faith." More and more we see our own children and grandchildren not only dropping out of church but denying the faith alto-gether. Can we pass along the faith to future generations?

[Read John 1:11-13.] Who are God's children anyway? They are those who receive and believe. We may inherit a religious tradition, but one cannot inherit faith. We don't become part of God's family through birth. This is a spiritual family; each one is a son or daughter. God has no grand-children. The Apostle Paul uses the analogy of adoption to more clearly underline this point; God has chosen us to be part of God's family and has received us into the family in the way one might be adopted into a new home.

Take some time to be present for a new citizen swearing-in ceremony and you will get the picture. Immigrants spend years learning the language, American history, and our Constitution before taking a test for citizenship. While not being born in America, these new citizens have chosen to become part of our American family. In the course of their choosing, we have chosen to make them part of our family as well, with all the attendant rights, privileges, and responsibilities.

How are we passing our faith along to the next generation? Have you ever wondered how Judaism has persisted after thousands of years of persecution and even Holocaust? After forty years of wilderness wanderings Moses stood before the Hebrew children on the eve of their crossing into the Promised Land and charged them to keep the faith. Read the words from Deuteronomy 6:4-8. If you walk into the home of any practicing Jewish home today you will see nailed to the doorpost a small cylinder or *mezuzah*. Inside are these words, the *Shema*. For more than 3,000 years Jewish families have been careful to pass along the faith. No wonder Israel exists today.

What is your spiritual heritage? Do your children know your spiritual story? Will your grandchildren know your story of faith? What about the children outside your family? How will they learn the faith? One father, refusing to allow his children to participate in a neighborhood Bible class, explained that he didn't want to overly influence his five- and six-year-old in their religious decisions. How naive.

How did you come to faith? Name the people who helped you take hold of the faith. Somewhere along your journey there have been witnesses and teachers who have encouraged you and challenged you. God has placed in your path numerous persons who have taken up the calling to teach someone else.

Mildred (not her real name) grew up underprivileged and abused. By adulthood, she enjoyed telling others that she could out-swear any sailor and drink the whole crew under the table. In mid-life Christ captured her heart. Never having her own children, she gave the rest of her life to teaching children and youth in hope that they might avoid her heartaches. Mildred was anything but a magnetic youth leader, but her love and persistence drew hundreds of teens to her Sunday school class. Mildred touched hundreds of young lives through her prayers, her love, and her witness and helped scores of young people to consider the joys of full-time Christian service. Once I asked Mildred why she did this. She answered simply, "I want to give to these young people what I never had. Growing up I never had a Christian influence in my life, so I followed every tempting voice that came along. I just hope that maybe I can make a difference in one life."

Long before the African proverb "it takes a village" was heard, Jesus said, "Go therefore and make disciples...teaching them to obey everything that I have commanded you" (Matthew 28:19-20). Our future is at stake! (Guy Ames)

Worship Aids

Call to Worship

Scripture calls to us, "the word of God is living and active, sharper than any two-edged sword, piercing until it divides soul from spirit...it is able to judge the thoughts and intentions of the heart" (Hebrews 4:12). As we worship today, may we be learners, hearing what God's Spirit is speaking to us, God's church. The Apostle Paul calls out, "I appeal to you therefore, brothers and sisters, by the mercies of God, to present your bodies as a living sacrifice, holy and acceptable to God, which is your spiritual worship" (Romans 12:1). Let us worship together.

Invocation

We invite you, O God, to lead us as we worship today. Our prayer is that all who have joined with us might sense your welcoming spirit. In the midst of our confusing and diverse lives we seek to know you. We long for a sense of your presence leading in our lives. We ask that you center our thoughts on you and this time of worship. We pray that our children might be in tune with your presence and Spirit, so that in this time of worship we all might know we have met with the living God. In the name of the resurrected Christ. Amen.

Benediction

Now as you have received, so may you give away. Keep God's words close to your heart. Teach them to your children and talk about them when you are at home and when you are away, when you lie down and when you rise. Bind God's truths as a sign on your hand, fix them as an emblem on your forehead, and may they be written on the doorposts of your homes, your gates, and your lives. Amen. (Guy Ames)

SETEMBER 16, 2012

❧❧❧❧

Sixteenth Sunday after Pentecost

Readings: Isaiah 50:4-9a; Psalm 116:1-9; James 3:1-12; Mark 8:27-38

Called to Teach

Isaiah 50:4-9a

Who are the people who have influenced you? Who helped you get where you are today? Upon whose shoulders have you stood to be the person you see in the mirror each morning? What is it about these people? What puts them on your list? More than likely, they taught you something valuable along the way. They offered more than a simple, quick fix to help you out of a difficult situation. They instilled a value in you that you continue to hold to this day. They taught you something about how to be the person you are now.

Teachers, whether by training or by circumstance, take center stage in today's text. To have the tongue of a teacher is a gift from God. With mere words, one is able to lift up those who are down. That is a pretty powerful statement, and one that should not be taken lightly. It assumes that others are willing to listen to teachers and change their attitudes based on what they hear. However, the writer is quick to note that the tongue is not to be the only organ teachers use. Each morning God wakens teachers to listen "as those who are taught" (v. 4). One does not suddenly become a teacher one day. Rather, teaching is a process of daily learning so as to be constantly ready and up to date with a word from God for the weary.

The text also carries a warning for teachers. Much to students' dismay, often a teacher's word is not always what one wants to hear. The same applies when God instructs teachers. It might feel safer to turn and run from God's instruction or to rebel and teach another way, but Isaiah's author stands strong and endures the abuse that comes with being one who listens to God. The abuse is pretty intense and humiliating; there is physical violence along with disrespect and even spitting. Listening to following God carries a high cost.

It is worth the cost, however, because the Lord stays by the faithful, the listeners, the teachers. They know their final fate lays with God, and so no person can truly confront or judge them. The disrespect and abuse is merely temporary, like a garment, and will not have lasting impact on the fate or work of the faithful.

Do Isaiah's words sound familiar to you? Have you heard this message before? In a snapshot, Isaiah's words are the instruction we are given in living a Christian life. While the object of his message is teachers, one could easily replace "teachers" with "Christians." Do you see it? We are not born teachers, just as we are not born Christians or followers of God. We become that which we are, not because of whom we are but because of whom God is. We become that which God wants us to be for God's glory and to bring others into like relationship. Likewise, just as teachers do not wake up being teachers but grow in their abilities and strengths with each day, student interaction, and experience, we too grow closer to God as we daily seek to be more in right relationship with God and others. The road is not easy for teachers, just as it is not for disciples. We should not expect it to be so. But we, as the teachers, have been told that our work on earth matters because it has rewards and repercussions in heaven; therefore, our eyes should be on that which is ahead rather than the hardships we might temporarily endure now.

Isaiah's words, while they may seem grim and discouraging at times, can be read hopefully. We are not the first to endure persecution and confrontation on God's behalf. God remains faithful to those who are faithful to God, and especially those who endure persecution on God's behalf. God "wakens" (v. 4) our ears for instructions in how to proceed in seemingly difficult situations so that others may look to us for hope, teaching, discipleship, and growth. We are never alone in our faithfulness; there will always be those who stand with us against the adversaries, which is comforting news. The temporal nature of the hardships to be endured is also comforting, because in the midst of difficulty and challenge, we need to know that relief is coming.

Few gifts come without a price. The gift of being a teacher of God has the price of earthly persecution and abuse. The reward, however, is great and eternal. As the text says, let us then stand together against those who confront us because we know where our treasure lies. For now we give our ears and tongues to God to complete our tasks and wait while we teach and follow God's message for us. Amen. (Victoria Atkinson White)

Lectionary Commentary

James 3:1-12

What an interesting text to stand beside the selected Isaiah text for this Sunday. Both passages address the great weight that falls upon the responsibility of being a teacher. This one, however, takes on a harsher and more immediate tone. The tongue is seen as a tool of danger and evil that can lead people astray and cause great damage. Warnings abound throughout these words, particularly in the idea of blessings and curses coming from the same source—the mouth. Just as salt water cannot yield fresh water or a fig tree yield olives, a mouth yielding blessings cannot also yield curses. As teachers, we are urged to keep our tongues in check, knowing just how perilous they can be when used for the wrong reasons.

Mark 8:27-38

At first glance, Jesus' behavior is quite strange in this passage from Mark. He asks the disciples who others say he is, then who they say he is, and then he tells them not to tell anyone. Then Jesus reveals an incredibly dire message regarding his future betrayal, suffering, death, and resurrection. When Peter tries to challenge this disturbing message, Jesus calls him Satan! You can sense the tension growing as the narrative progresses. You can also sense the disciples' confusion with such strange behavior. But then Jesus ironically clarifies all of this with an even stranger statement. The entire Gospel message is about being countercultural; it is not supposed to make sense according to our standards of what is normal. In order for a life to be saved, it must be lost; in order to truly gain, one must lose everything. Accordingly, Jesus' behavior, and thus our behavior, should be strange, out of the ordinary, and different from what is expected. The gospel is meant to rock the status quo and bring about a new way of living and growing in relationship with God. (Victoria Atkinson White)

Worship Aids

Call to Worship

I love the Lord because my voice has been heard;
   my requests have been made known.

I will call upon the Lord as long as I live.
I love the Lord who is gracious, righteous, and merciful.
I will call upon the Lord as long as I live.
I love the Lord who delivers me time and time again.
I will call upon the Lord as long as I live.

Pastoral Prayer

Lord, sometimes we can become introspective and think that things are all about us. Pull us out of our selfishness and open our eyes to see that which is around us. We need to be reminded of how small we are in your grand world while, at the same time, feeling your intimate and overwhelming love as if we are the only ones. Amen.

Benediction

Lord, guide and protect us as we leave this time of worship with you. May we feel your presence even in the face of persecution and abuse. Strengthen us as only you can, and remind us of your steadfast love and commitment to us. Amen. (Victoria Atkinson White)

Passionate Worship

First in a Series of Four on Vital Elements of Christian Worship

Isaiah 6

Worship, very simply, is not for us. Worship is a gift that we give to someone else. Worship is for God. The origin of our word *worship* is similar to the word *worth*. We think about what something is worth, its value. In Revelation, one of our great sources of teaching about worship, we hear the refrain: "You are worthy, our Lord and God, to receive glory and honor and power, for you created all things, and by your will they existed and were created" (4:11).

Worship is for God. But we can lose sight of this truth. Sometimes a new person will come up to me after the service and will say, "We're church shopping." What I hear is the refrain from the old fairy tale: "This soup was too hot. This soup was too cold. This soup was just right!"

We form opinions about all of life; we are comparison shoppers, and we make most of our decisions in this way. This has spilled over into worship over the past two decades. Some observers have described this as the "worship wars": contemporary versus traditional, my favorite style versus your favorite style, and music often becomes the scapegoat in all of this.

Now there is profound worship in any style, but going down the road of style leads us to the wrong place, because it places everything in the context of my preference or your taste. Worship is unique in that it is not about your preference or mine. It is something else altogether.

It's not for us. It is for God. It is the offering of our very best selves to God. There is a deep biblical tradition of worship, of giving our best offering, our first offering, the first fruits of the harvest, to God. Christians worship on the first day of the week. Sunday is the first day, not the last day. God's people were instructed to give of their first fruits to God. Worship is an offering of our best selves, our real selves, to God.

We see a rich picture of what worship looks like in the sixth chapter of Isaiah. Isaiah is in the temple, overwhelmed with the beauty and glory of God, and he hears the voices singing, "Holy, Holy, Holy is the LORD of hosts; the whole earth is filled with his glory" (v. 3).

This is nothing other than an experience of praise. Then something happens. After praise, if it is authentic worship—an experience of the holy—we see ourselves in a different way. Isaiah makes a confession, an acknowledgment, a true statement about himself. "Woe is me, I am lost. I am a man of unclean lips and I live in the midst of a people of unclean lips" (v. 5).

When we worship God, we are somehow changed. This is not the purpose of worship; it is not about us, but by experiencing God we are transformed. Then there is good news, an intervention: "our guilt is taken away, our sins are forgiven." The God of the Bible is powerful and mighty, holy and beyond us, but at the same time gracious and merciful, abounding in steadfast love. Our guilt is taken away, our sins are forgiven.

But that is not the end of worship. Worship is more than a relationship between God and the individual. When worship is authentic, when it is an experience of the holy, there is unfinished business. God has our attention.

"Then I heard the voice of the Lord saying, whom shall I send, who will go for us?" Isaiah responds: "Here am I, Lord. Send me."

If we have entered into the world of the Bible we are a long way from church shopping; we are a long way from sizing up the deity that matches our temperaments and tastes, our styles, and status. The roles have been reversed, the world has been turned upside down, and all of a sudden we are a part of someone else's agenda. Worship is all about praise, confession, and forgiveness, and from worship there flows the desire and the call to reflect God's glory beyond the temple, outside the sanctuary into the world, and so there is the invitation: "Whom shall I send, and who will go for us?" Then there is the response: "Here am I; send me" (v. 8)!

Worship is not about us; yet when we have worshiped the biblical God, we are transformed, we have begun to experience the new creation, and we are filled with a deep desire to reflect God's glory in the world.

Without worship, everything else is threatened. We see our gifts as our own possessions, the world as a resource to be used, our neighbor as competition for the goods that we would seek for ourselves, and the truth as whatever spin we can put on it. Without worship, we easily deceive ourselves and ignore others. Without worship, we can wander off into all kinds of places, and none of them is the destination that God wants for us.

Passionate worship changes all of life. I will confess to you that I consider worship to be something of a miracle. Sometimes someone will make a comment like "our attendance was a little down this morning." My thought is usually "I am just amazed that anyone comes to worship." Why would anyone leave the comfort and warmth of their bed on a Sunday morning, put expensive gasoline in their cars, search for a parking place that sometimes is some distance away, drink coffee that may not be as good as you make at home, sit in a room that is usually either too hot or too cold, sometimes next to people you don't even know? Why would people do this?

It makes no sense, unless there is a God who is real, who is above us and beyond us but also beside us and within us, who created and sustains all things, who is worthy of our worship. (Kenneth H. Carter Jr.)

Worship Aids

Call to Worship
Holy, Holy, Holy, is the Lord of hosts.
The whole earth is filled with God's glory!
Let us worship in spirit and is truth.
All: To God alone be the glory!

Words of Assurance
God's ways are not our ways, and God's thoughts are not our thoughts; and yet in Jesus, God has come near to us in the beauty of creation, in the Word made flesh, in the indwelling Spirit. Thanks be to God.

Benediction

Now to the one who is worthy of our worship, who is above us and beyond us and among and within us; to God alone be the glory, in the name of the Father, the Son, and the Holy Spirit. Amen. (Kenneth H. Carter Jr.)

SEPTEMBER 23, 2012

❧❧❧❧

Seventeenth Sunday after Pentecost

Readings: Jeremiah 11:18-20; Psalm 54; James 3:13–4:3, 7-8a; Mark 9:30-37

Childish Behavior

Mark 9:30-37

Having sat with family members at the bedside of a dying loved one, I have witnessed and participated in many conversations about death. Some are beautiful and peaceful, as you watch the dying bestow blessings and affirmations on the ones they are leaving behind. Family members will often sit and hold the hands of the dying while they cry and silently take in the moment and the blessing being offered. They may not understand all that is happening right then, but they know it is a time like none other in their lives and so they are quiet. They are open to what is happening, and they soak in all that their dying loved one is offering them. Perhaps things will make sense later, perhaps not, but they are in the moment.

Then there are other families who approach death and dying in a dramatically different way. A dying loved one will try to explain things to their family or let them know the gravity of the moment, while the family tries to quiet the dying person as if not saying the words will keep death from occurring. They may try to pass it off as saving energy or strength for recovery, but it is a disguise of fear and misunderstanding. These families mean well, they want more time, more memories, and restored life for their dying loved one. Unfortunately, they are so focused on what they want that they miss the pivotal moments happening before their eyes. And sadly, too often they miss incredible opportunities to be present and help usher their loved one from this life into the next.

The disciples are met with an "end of days" conversation with Jesus in our text for today. It is an intimate time between Jesus and his closest friends, and he takes the opportunity to share something deeply personal with them. I will be betrayed. I will die. I will rise again. This is one of those moments when the disciples should be hanging on Jesus' every word, struggling not to miss anything. This is one of those life-changing moments. But the disciples do not get it. They miss the moment. They do not understand. They are afraid. So they do not attempt to truly be present with Jesus in this revealing and crucial conversation.

The disciples, in a sense, act like children, and in their fear, turn to bickering and lose focus on the significance of the time at hand. In a matter of moments, they go from hearing Jesus reveal plans for his death and resurrection to arguing about who is the greatest among them. How much more childish could grown men act?

To their credit, they know they have behaved badly. When Jesus questions them about their conversation, you can almost picture them sheepishly avoiding eye contact, kicking the dirt, and mumbling. They know they have been caught by Jesus not only doing something he would not approve of but disrespectfully moving from a conversation as significant as his upcoming death to an argument about their greatness and who outranks whom. They are embarrassed and ashamed, so they stand in silence with nothing to say.

Jesus takes advantage of the teachable moment and calls the disciples to him. Jesus also, ironically, considering their childish behavior, brings a child into their circle of conversation. In a most calm manner, Jesus tells them how truly wrong they are, not just for engaging in the greatness conversation but also for how they went about measuring each other's greatness. The great one, the first one, in Jesus' words is not one who will be measured by merit or valor, but rather by service to all. It is a countercultural message that undoubtedly got the disciples' immediate attention. Again, I can almost picture them moving from a stature of slumped shoulders, probably still avoiding eye contact and drawing lines in the dirt with their feet, to looking up in surprise, leaning forward to make sure they hear Jesus right. This just cannot be so, greatness awarded by service?

Then to really drive the message home, Jesus references the child in their midst. Here stands an innocent boy or girl representing the ways the disciples have behaved and looking to them as adults, role models, Jesus' closest companions. Jesus embraces the child to show how serious he is about caring for the little ones and explains his message to the disciples in a way they cannot ignore. "If you welcome a child in my name, you welcome me and also the one who sent me" (see v. 36). It doesn't get much simpler or clearer than that. Greatness is not about grandiose deeds or adhering to the letter of the law. Greatness in the eyes of Jesus is about welcoming the small, the often ignored, the insignificant. Greatness is about taking notice of those who are often slighted or misunderstood.

How sad and ironic then is the beginning of this text. Jesus foretold his death and, because of the disciples' confusion and fear, his words were ignored and unacknowledged. Then the disciples had the nerve to argue about greatness? Can you imagine how they felt? For those who truly grasped the transpiring events and understood where true greatness lies, it must have been humiliating and yet also a revealing moment of hope and clarity.

We have the benefit of learning from the disciples' childish behavior through their stories. We are able to learn from their mistakes and hopefully strive for true greatness, the kind Jesus challenges all to live, as those who embrace servanthood, as those who notice the children, the small, the misunderstood among us. The disciples missed out on some key moments of intimacy, blessing, sharing, and learning by letting fear and selfishness get in their way. May we learn from their mistakes and be open to what life-changing conversations may come our way so that we might be truly present in all of life, and most specifically in those moments that might change our lives. Amen. (Victoria Atkinson White)

Lectionary Commentary

Jeremiah 11:18-20

Our text falls in the midst of Jeremiah's lament to God about Israel and Judah breaking the covenant God made with their ancestors. Jeremiah feels as if nothing he has done has made a difference. He is at his wits end. Not knowing how to proceed, he turns his frustrations over to God and lays it all out in the open. Jeremiah is brutally honest and does not spare details. He was a lamb led to the slaughter. He was schemed against. He was threatened with death and with being forgotten. Rather than taking matters into his own hands and letting his emotions get the best of him, he puts it before God and essentially says, "I can't do anything about this; here, you take it." Jeremiah, while he may sound harsh and vengeful, is actually quite wise in his actions. God can handle his frustration. In fact, God invites our laments, just as God invites us to be in authentic and pure relationship with God at all times.

James 3:13–4:8

James comes down pretty harshly on his readers in this text. He does not mince words. He knows there is goodness among them (see v. 13: "good life" and "gentleness born of wisdom") but then spends the rest of the text berating bad behaviors and questioning their actions. If we look closely, however, we can also see glimmers of hope in the midst of these criticisms. James writes of pure and gentle wisdom and righteousness sown in peace and he reminds them that all is not lost. If we resist the devil, our temptations will fall away; if we draw near to God, God will also draw near to us. James is smart and strategic in his admonishing. This is not a pure lecture on wrongdoing. He reminds them of their prior goodness, their potential, and lets them know there is still hope and goodness in store for them if they cling to what they know is right. (Victoria Atkinson White)

Worship Aids

Invocation

Lord, in this time of worship, help us to better understand your ways. When we do not understand, guide our paths to where you would have us go, so we do not further drift from you. In this time, we bring to you our questions, our wonderings, and our whole hearts so that we might fully be present with you. Amen.

Pastoral Prayer

In your faithfulness, we bring before you the concerns of our hearts. Too often we burden ourselves with problems that are out of our control, which we should relinquish to your faithful hands. Help us to let go and trust in your goodness, wisdom, and mercy. Amen.

Prayer of Confession

God, you are our helper and the upholder of our lives. Yet we confess that we seek to control that which we should offer up to you. Forgive us when we get in your way; forgive us when we think our way is the best way. Guide us back to your path so that we may better live for you. Amen.

Words of Assurance

God hears; God forgives; God guides. Thanks be to God. (Victoria Atkinson White)

Breathing in Grace, Breathing Out Praise

Second in a Series of Four on Vital Elements of Christian Worship

Psalm 150

In the Hebrew language of the Old Testament, there is a wonderful word, *ruach,* which can be translated as breath, spirit, or wind. In Genesis 1:1, God's Spirit moves over the face of the watery chaos and brings forth life. In Ezekiel 37, God's Spirit is breathed into the valley of dry bones, and there is life. In the New Testament, the Greek word is *pneuma.* Jesus says to Nicodemus, "the wind blows where it chooses" (John 3:8). In John 20, after the Resurrection, Jesus comes to the disciples and breathes on them, and says, "Receive the Holy Spirit...." And in Acts 2, on the day of Pentecost, there is a sound like the rush of a mighty wind, and everyone is filled with the Holy Spirit.

God's Spirit dwells within us, as close to us as our next breath. To live is to breathe. The psalmist says, to breathe is to praise God. It is an imperative. We are created for the praise of God. The Westminster Shorter Catechism asks: "What is the chief end of [humanity]?" The answer: "To glorify God and to enjoy him forever." I think of the great hymn of Isaac Watts and John Wesley, based on Psalm 146, "I'll Praise My Maker While I've Breath." All of this leads to the climactic Psalm 150: "Let everything that breathes praise the Lord!"

To breathe in is to receive the grace of God. To breathe out is to offer praise to God with our words and with our lives. We inhale, and we exhale. There is a natural rhythm. In the same way that music has beats and measures, our lives are measured. There is evening and morning, each day measured. There are six days of work and one day of rest, each week measured. God has ordered our lives in such a way that we give and receive, work and rest, inhale and exhale.

This is God's intention. But our human temptation is to live outside God's will for us. We do not live measured lives. We do not live ordered lives. We sometimes live hurried and chaotic lives. Yet this is not God's purpose for us. We were created to receive grace and to offer praise. But at times we forget to praise. When Israel violated the Sabbath, the people sinned in two ways. They neglected their essential need to rest— Exodus 31:17 has been translated, "On the seventh day God rested and caught his breath" (Herman Gunkel and Mark E. Biddle, eds., *Genesis: Mercer Library of Biblical Studies* [Macon, Ga.: Mercer University Press, 1997], 116). They forgot that God had liberated them from slavery. Many of us, even the most sophisticated among us, can become enslaved to destructive patterns of living.

Years ago I read about the experience of a group of world-class climbers who had died on Mount Everest. An interesting comment was made by one of the expert guides in that field. "Most of the people who die climbing Mount Everest," he said, "make it to the top. They die on the way down. They discover, after they have made it, that they do not have enough oxygen to get down the mountain. Or they make bad decisions, critical errors, because of the lack of oxygen."

This is a parable of us. The spiritual life is our oxygen. We may get everything we want in this life and die in the process. Lack of spiritual insight may lead us to choose things that are not really important in place of what is nearest and life-giving to us. What is God's order and design for you? Listen to the way 2 Timothy 3:16 is translated by Eugene Peterson: "Every part of scripture is God-breathed and useful in one way or another—showing us truth, exposing our rebellion, correcting our mistakes, training us to live God's way" (*THE MESSAGE*).

In worship that is shaped by the Scriptures we begin to understand that praise is an essential experience for God's people. This has a number of practical implications for us. In worship we discover an order and a design for our lives that we ignore at our peril. If our lives are cluttered or overwhelmed, we need to reorient ourselves toward God, who grants each day to us as a gift. God wants us to have times of rest, renewal, catching our breath. In the wholeness of creation there is the rest of God. We were created to praise God. When our hearts and minds and spirits are oriented toward God, we are not so critical of others, not so weighed down by everyday life.

In our New Testament, our primary manual for worship is the Revelation. It is a like a doxology that gathers together all that came before it. Many misunderstand Revelation, or avoid it, but it is really the experience of John of Patmos, who is "caught up in the spirit on the Lord's day" (1:10). There John is given insight in the midst of great suffering. There is resonance between Psalm 23 and Revelation 7:17: "He leads me beside still waters, he restores my soul" (Psalm 23:2-3), and Revelation 7:17: "the Lamb at the center of the throne will be their shepherd, and he will guide them to springs of the water of life, and God will wipe away every tear from their eyes."

Because John has been shaped by the reading of Scripture, he sees the glory of God, which is finally the one and only purpose of worship. This also happens as we read the Psalms, intended to teach us that a life of praise occurs in the midst of very difficult experiences. The Psalms can be read as a long roadmap that passes through illness, loss of possessions, physical danger, depression, isolation, pain, fear, grief, and anger, on the way to this conclusion, this doxology, Psalm 150: "Let everything that breathes praise the Lord" (v. 6)! (Kenneth H. Carter Jr.)

Worship Aids

Call to Worship

This is the day that the Lord has made.
Let us rejoice and be glad in it!
Great is the Lord, who is worthy to be praised.
All: Let everything that breathes praise the Lord!

Words of Assurance

May the One who created you give you rest. May the One who redeems you give you assurance. May the One who sustains you give you peace. Amen.

Benediction

I want to invite you to pray and imagine that God is speaking to you:

"I have created you to praise me. I want you to know that praise is as necessary to you as your next breath. I want you to worship me. When you worship me, it is a foretaste of heaven. I have created you to receive and to give. I have formed you in such a way that you breathe in my grace and breathe out my praise. If you will breathe in and breathe out, you will discover the shape of your life.

"I did not create you for burnout. I did not create your pace of life. I want to do wonderful things for you. I want to shape you, mold you, fill you, use you. I want to breathe life into you. I am delighted when you accept the gift of my grace, and I am overjoyed when you offer to me the gift of your praise. That is why we have had this meeting today." Amen. (Kenneth H. Carter Jr.)

SEPTEMBER 30, 2012

❧❧❧

Eighteenth Sunday after Pentecost

Readings: Numbers 11:4-6, 10-16, 24-29; Psalm 19:7-14;
James 5:13-20; Mark 9:38-50

Life's Rewards and Reprimands Are Built In

Mark 9:38-50

For me, this is one of the oddest texts in all of Scripture. Even its order is strange. It starts with a conversation between Jesus and John about who is qualified to "do a deed of power" in the church. Jesus says that we shouldn't be interested in one's qualifications (in this instance, a member of a specific group) as much as we are in the motivation (out of love).

Then the conversation abruptly turns to focus on the children who are in Jesus' company. It goes from doing a kind act motivated by love of Christ to doing an unkind and hurtful act of making a child "stumble" or sin. Jesus uses an economy of words when talking about an act of kindness, then spends a lot of time explaining what happens to someone who commits a sin.

This episode in Mark's Gospel is fraught with questions for contemporary disciples. Why so much focus on the negative here? What is Jesus' reasoning behind this seemingly disjointed conversation? Was the writer trying to prove a point? When we do our homework regarding this text's history, we find that there is suspicion about whether Jesus may have even said these things. Maybe the writer was reflecting more of what the community wanted Jesus to say about sin and the consequences for the sinner. From a psycho-social perspective, do we not spend more time focusing on the negative than we do on the positive in life? After all, look at the media coverage of the human scene—what gets more attention? Doesn't murder get more coverage than someone saving a life? But this also raises the issue—how much time should we give to focusing on the negative? How much focus should we give sin versus grace? On and on the questions keep coming. Finally, the overarching question arises. What does this lesson from Mark offer us?

First, we are to focus on helping others. The genuine attempt to help another person is more important than the person who offers the help. Jesus is not interested in who gets the credit. Jesus is rather more focused on the recipient.

Second, any reward that comes with helping is embedded in the act of care; it doesn't come from the outside. A way to bring this to clarity is a story I once heard about a *Peanuts* cartoon. Schroeder is famous for his love of the piano. One day while he is practicing Beethoven's sonatas, Lucy stops by and asks what the prize is going to be for learning the sonatas. He tells her there is no prize. She is daunted by the answer and is beside herself because, for Lucy, there always has to be a prize or reward for doing anything. What Lucy fails to see is what we all fail to see when involved in God's realm, namely, the reward is the act itself. For Schroeder, the reward is learning the sonatas! The reward is built in.

Third, when gratification and punishment are built into our actions, we find another truth in Jesus' teaching. When gratification comes with the act itself, then we find that life is seasoned and tasty because of God's grace. When ulterior motives and selfish desire for gain underlie our actions, then we find life tasteless, graceless, and unrewarding.

Perhaps Jesus is trying to show us that, when we are motivated to help others based on what we can get out of it, we will often be dissatisfied or disappointed. That is the built-in punishment. The punishment can be a corrective process by which we are redirected and refocused so that we can behave out of genuineness and not ulterior motive. If we are motivated by the sheer desire to help without any reciprocity, then our reward is the sheer act of helping. Perhaps the litmus test, if you will, is that we seek to help those from whom we cannot possibly expect anything, including an acknowledgement of gratitude!

Perhaps this episode is not all that strange or scary. Actually, it can be a source of peace for us, especially when we are wearied by always trying to live life in terms of what we can get out of it rather than what we put into it. (Mike Childress)

Lectionary Commentary

Numbers 11:4-6, 10-16, 24-29

If ever there was a story in Scripture about being between a rock and hard place, this is it. On the one hand, Moses is lambasted by the people because God serves the same menu day after day. On the other hand, God is upset with the people for their indignation.

This is an excellent story for all leaders in the church who find themselves entangled in the drudgery of everyday parish life and dealing with the "ho-hum" day-to-day diet of sameness that comes with parish leadership. At wits end, Moses is iconic in his response to the cries of the people—he complains to God about them.

But this story has more to offer than whiners and those who are called to serve them. It is about God's way of openly, publicly, and honestly framing the realities of community life and then finding solutions. Note the process embedded in the story. Great leaders are good listeners. Even whining may have an underlying larger issue of value. God has Moses gather the community and get to the bottom of the matter. For church leaders, listening and hearing, followed by focusing on what is really the matter at hand, are essential components in finding workable solutions. What Moses learns is what we all seek to learn and employ as leaders, whether we are pastors, heads of church councils, boards, or committees. He learns that nobody's voice should be quieted. Everybody in the community has a vested interest in its prosperity and posterity. We would do well to learn this lesson.

James 5:13-20

In this passage, I imagine that the writer must be experiencing what the church has always had to face: a world that reacts to its surroundings rather than face life's issues with resolve, peace, and faith in God's providential care. The order in which the text is given is important. Each word is wisely and caringly chosen to reinforce and nurture faith among the people. For example, when trouble comes knocking on the door, it is time to respond with prayer, not react with wrenching of hands and whining about life's unfairness. When happiness and joy are experienced, the response of the faithful is not gloating and arrogant posturing; happiness and joy are to be shared by the community through song and praise to God. Illness and poor health are factors in every person's life. God's people are not spared from such things. When reactionary behavior overcomes the community, faith is victimized. When life's issues come knocking on life's door, the writer wants us to be prepared and respond to them with prayer, faith in one another, and faith in God's presence in and through all of life. Continually reminding ourselves of God's providential love will help us respond to life in ways that build up people and strengthen the community. In faith, such things as poor health, challenges, and devastating circumstances, with God's help, can become building blocks for faith rather than stumbling blocks. (Mike Childress)

Worship Aids

Call to Worship

Come into the presence of God, singing and praising God.
Praise God, our Creator,
for God is merciful and understanding.
Come into the presence of God, seeking wisdom and council.
All: All honor and glory be given to God,
our Savior and Redeemer. Amen.

Prayer of Confession

Lord, you teach us to see all people in need of your love, yet we play favorites and divide people into holy and unholy categories. Forgive us. Help us to seek and discern your image in every human being. When we seek to relate to one another in reciprocity or retribution, remind us that you have always sought us out of mercy, not merit. Amen.

Words of Assurance

Know that the mercy of God has healed you. Seek to share this kindness with your neighbor, knowing that the love of God seeks to save and redeem all who are lost. Thanks be to God. (Mike Childress)

Washing Your Hands

Third in a Series of Four on Vital Elements of Christian Worship

Mark 1:4-11

As a pastor, I visit in the hospitals, on average, a couple of days a week. Over the past years visiting in hospitals has changed. For one thing, people do not stay in the hospital for very long. When I began in the ministry twenty-five years ago, people would stay three to five days; now they are in and out in twenty-four hours.

There is also a great deal more privacy for a person who is hospitalized, which is good. Again, I can remember walking into the hospital and going down the list of everyone who was a patient. Federal laws prevent that from happening now. Another change, more subtle but just as significant, is the presence of hand sanitizers on the door of every hospital room. This has become the norm, I realize, although, until recently I had never given it much thought. That changed when I read an essay about washing your hands in the *New Yorker*. It later became a part of the book *Better*, by Atul Gawande (New York: Henry Holt and Company, 2007), a young physician in Boston, a Harvard professor, and a writer.

Last year two million Americans were infected with viruses in hospitals; 90,000 died. Can you guess what might be the single most powerful factor in preventing the spread of infections? Getting people who work in hospitals to wash their hands. Studies show that people who work in hospitals wash their hands about one-third or one-half as often as they need to (*Better*, 14–15). This is a problem that calls for a response. The solution lies not in a major scientific breakthrough or a profound intellectual idea. It is a simple, everyday ritual practice: washing your hands.

Christians believe that we live in a world that is infected, and the root issue is human sin. Theologians have argued about whether the infection is passed genetically from parent to child, or whether we are socialized into the environment of a sinful world. Christians differ about particular kinds of sins. The early church fathers even came up with seven deadly sins. But most agree that sin is a reality. Reinhold Niebuhr once remarked that "the doctrine of original sin is the only empirically verifiable Christian doctrine" (as cited in William H. Willimon, *Sinning Like a Christian* [Nashville: Abingdon Press, 2005], 10).

Because we are aware of the sin that is out there and the sin that is in here, we have worked on this problem in a variety of ways. Monks and nuns have been sequestered in cloistered environments to keep them away from the sins of money, sex, and power. But sin makes its way into the monastery. Some Protestants put their clergy on a pedestal; the laity get their hands dirty in the kingdom of the world, the clergy live in the kingdom of God. But scandal after scandal reminds us that this is not quite truthful.

We are all sinners, the apostle Paul tells us. But like those doctors and nurses who don't wash their hands as often as they should, we resist change. And yet, we are human beings; we as Christians have a deep need to change. The discipline of washing ourselves, cleansing ourselves, found its way in our most basic and fundamental practice: baptism.

It helps to remember the baptism of Jesus and its implications for our own baptisms. The baptism of Jesus is recorded in each of the four Gospels, and there are slight variations in each telling of the story. Matthew gives more of the details surrounding the baptism—John's sense of unworthiness, for example, but also John's conflict with the other religious leaders. John's Gospel links the baptism of Jesus to the confession that he is the lamb of God who takes away the sin of the world. Luke seems to connect the baptism of Jesus with his genealogy, traced back to Adam, as if to associate baptism and our need for cleansing with our common humanity. Characteristically, Mark's telling of the story is the briefest. John baptizes Jesus in the Jordan River. The heavens open, the light shines, the dove descends, the voice of God speaks, "This is my beloved son; I am pleased with him."

And so even the story of Jesus begins with a story about a washing; a cleansing. Of course Christians have also believed that Jesus was the One who was without sin, and this led to an appropriate question: "Why be baptized?" Well, Jesus was baptized for our sake; as he passed through the waters he stands with us, he identifies with us. He is fully divine but he is also fully human, the creeds affirm. In his baptism, Jesus gives us a practice, and in his entire life he responds to one of our greatest needs: to be washed, cleansed, renewed, all for the flourishing of life.

What helps us most may not be a tremendous breakthrough in research or the grasping of a complex insight, but a simple spiritual practice. This practice of washing our hands, of remembering our baptisms, can be profoundly helpful.

It can also be threatening. We are, all of us, in need of the cleansing grace of God. Christians around the world differ about who can eat at the Lord's table, who can be married, who can be a minister or a priest, and so on. Baptism is the one act that seems to place us, every one of us, on a level place. In our baptisms we are the same.

This was a powerful reality for the first Christians. At each point along the way God uses water to create us, to recreate us, and to sustain us. It really is what makes us different; not our spiritual superiority in relation to others, but our need for grace and renewal. To remember the baptism of the Lord and our own baptisms is as simple and profound a ritual practice as washing our hands. (Kenneth H. Carter Jr.)

Worship Aids

Call to Worship
The Lord be with you.
And also with you.

The Spirit of God is moving over the face of the waters.
All: Come, Holy Spirit, and renew the face of the earth!

Words of Assurance

When you pass through the waters, says the Lord, I will be with you. Let the healing mercies of God strengthen and sustain us in all things. Amen.

Benediction

May the God who created this world fill us with love. May Jesus Christ, the one who stands with us in the waters of baptism, fill us with joy. May the Holy Spirit, who descends upon us in our hours of need, fill us will peace. Amen. (Kenneth H. Carter Jr.)

OCTOBER 7, 2012

⛄⛄⛄

Nineteenth Sunday after Pentecost

Readings: Genesis 2:18-24; Psalm 8; Hebrews 1:1-4; 2:5-12;
Mark 10:2-16

Why Do We Like Getting in the Way?

Mark 10:2-16

For a long time after Jesus' earthly time, his disciples were commonly known as "people of the way." Their actions, their words, and their way of looking at life reflected Jesus' way of living in this world. They were people of the way; Jesus' way.

When I read stories like this one in Mark, I am persuaded that we differ little from Pharisees when we let questions about life get in the way of reaching people. In this instance, instead of seeing how divorce can be destructive and demeaning, the religious authorities focus on legalities. In Jesus' time, divorce was legal in the Jewish community. If a husband found his wife not pleasing, he could write out a document of divorce and dismiss her from his house (see Deuteronomy 24:1-4). In some cultures, it was lawful for men to divorce their wives for even simple and ridiculous reasons by simply saying three times, "I divorce you." Jesus addresses the divisive question of the Pharisees by removing the barrier that separates people from the ultimate question: what is it that separates people from God's love (what gets in the way)?

Today, we have to ask ourselves what issues get in the way of bringing people and God together. What about same-sex marriage? I won't even begin to address this issue, but it is dividing God's people. Who in the church is playing the Pharisees' role in trying to drive a wedge between God and those who find life commitment with someone of the same sex? What about health care? Some people in the church see health care as a privilege to be earned; others see it as the right of every human being no matter their station in life. What about waging war in the name whatever

307

reason we might justify as "God's will" and backing it up with scriptural proof-texting? The list of the ways we find to get between God and people is endless. There are no easy answers. Religious hyperbole and pulpit bullying only make it more difficult for people to know God, even impossible for some.

I am continually amazed that Jesus never wasted a thorny question. He never dismissed the character of the questioner with some judgmental or hateful epithet. I am continually agitated by the way the media, especially the cable news, constantly use vitriol and infectious accusations to destroy a person. This exchange between Jesus and the Pharisees begs us to reconsider how we get in the way of people getting to God by turning the kingdom of God into more of a talk show or "political pundit exchange" than a loving community of faith and acceptance.

The Pharisees who questioned Jesus had an agenda. Their intention was to trap him in some violation of the Jewish law, to catch him off guard and discredit him. Jesus models for us the spiritual and emotional maturity that such questions deserve, shifting focus from earthly squabbles to the love of God. The church tries its best to lay the hand of blessing on folks the way Jesus did to those children that day. That is the way of Jesus.

I appreciate Eugene Peterson's interpretation of verses 14-15: "Don't push these children away. Don't ever get between them and me. These children are at the very center of life in the kingdom. Mark this: Unless you accept God's kingdom in the simplicity of a child, you'll never get in" (*THE MESSAGE*). Jesus is speaking to all of God's children, which, by God's grace, includes those who are getting in the way of God's grace.

Why do we like getting *in* the way? Perhaps the answer lies in our penchant for making it all about us. When we are willing to make it all about God, we will again be people *of* the way, the way of Jesus. (Mike Childress)

Lectionary Commentary

Genesis 2:18-24

In biblical Hebrew there is no indefinite article. When the word for *man* is used it could mean human, or a man. This broadens the interpretation of the writer's intention in this text. This is further illustrated by use of the word *adamah* (adam), which means human, humankind, or humanity. Within the broader framework of God's creation, human beings are to have helpers or helpmates to carry out their stewardship of creation. This text deals with larger concerns than marriage, socioeconomic status, politics, or any other aspect of human need. God's intention is for people, regardless of gender (or any other qualifier) to work together.

This lesson is one that we should keep at the forefront of Christian teaching so that the separating forces of disunity do not isolate any of God's children. Therefore, when a concern surfaces and threatens unity in community, God would have us remember that we are not only human beings sharing a common planet, we are brothers and sisters, helpmates in stewardship of God's good creation.

Hebrews 1:1-4; 2:5-12

Jesus once asked the disciples what they were hearing people say about him. They had heard some saying he was Elijah while some were of the opinion that he was John the Baptist reincarnated (see Matthew 16:13-14). The writer of Hebrews responds to rumors that Jesus was an angel from God, not fully human. The danger was that Jesus would be treated as some divine being that looked human but was not subject to human temptations and concerns. The question of Jesus' humanity has been (and will continue to be) debated as often as his divinity.

The writer of Hebrews, a Jewish convert to the way of Jesus, reminds us not to make Jesus only a cosmic player in God's divine plan; we must not dehumanize Jesus even as we worship him as the Son of God, raised in glory through suffering. Jesus fully and completely related to others as a human child of God, called to serve God through gracious acts of kindness and mercy.

If we ask people today who they think Jesus was when he lived on earth, we will probably get as many different answers as the number of people we ask. If we ask the writer of Hebrews the same question, the answer is unequivocally: "Jesus is the one who is willing to call you and me brother and sister, no matter who we are." The writer gives a litany of evidence why this is so. (Mike Childress)

Worship Aids

Invocation

O God, we come into your presence singing and praising you as our Creator. With the company of heaven, we join the earthly choirs in giving glory to you and your Christ through whom all things exist. Today, we shout from the highest places your redeeming work, realizing that by your grace you invite us to participate in the work of salvation. Amen.

Pastoral Prayer

O God, we scarcely can imagine that you desire, even long for, our participation in your redeeming work. Today in our worship continue transforming our minds that we may think about your creation in terms of what we may give back to it. Transform our hearts that we may be stewards with a passion for your gifts to us, that we may share in the global church to further your realm in the world. Through Jesus Christ we pray. Amen.

Benediction (responsive)

Let us go forth in confidence,
    knowing that the still-speaking God is calling us into partnership
to be better stewards of this earth,
    our shared habitat for humanity.
We hear this call and,
    with God's help,
we will do on earth what is done in heaven! Amen.
    (Mike Childress)

Let Every Soul Be Jesus' Guest

Fourth in a Series of Four on Vital Elements of Christian Worship
(World Communion)

Hosea 11:1-11; Luke 15:1-2

The book of Hosea is a meditation on the love of God for God's people. But this is no typical love story. In this story, God commands that a prophet marry a prostitute and have children with her. The first three chapters describe the relationship between Hosea and his wife, Gomer, which is a parable for the relationship between the Lord and Israel. It is a long and rocky relationship, with anger, bitterness, and self-destruction. It is a miracle that the relationship endures; but relationships do endure. This is the story of a love that will not let us go.

In the eleventh chapter, the perspective shifts slightly from husband and wife to parent and child. Israel was adopted out of Egypt to be the Lord's child, Ephraim. We might think that Israel would display gratitude for this act of rescue and salvation; but no, Israel calls upon other gods, bows to idols, gives credit to other benefactors.

In the parable, God is somewhat bewildered. "Who taught Ephraim to walk?" God asks. "I did. I took them in my arms; I healed them; I was compassionate; I bent down to them; I fed them. Not those others. Me" (see vv. 1-4).

You can hear the resentment and the hurt; can't you? Ephraim represents the entire northern kingdom of Israel, God's own people. "They are determined to run away from me," God says, "backsliders. They've gone to the far country, Assyria, they have returned to Egypt where they were slaves." We can hear, in the parent's voice, if we listen closely, something deeper: "Why would they do this to me?"

If you were this parent, what would you do? The story of Hosea is a parable of God's relationship with God's people, and therefore, with us. Here are the words from the mouth of this bewildered parent: "How can I give you up, O Ephraim! How can I hand you over, O Israel! How can I make you like Admah? How can I treat you like Zeboiim [cities that shared the same fate as Sodom and Gomorrah]? (v. 8)?

Notice what has happened: The child turns away from the parent, but the parent turns toward the child. God turns toward us: "My heart recoils within me; my compassion grows warm and tender. I will not execute my fierce anger; I will not again destroy Ephraim, for I am God and no mortal, the Holy One in your midst, and I will not come in wrath" (vv. 8-9).

Keep this parable in mind as you consider a simple idea in the New Testament. Jesus is mixing with the people, all kinds of people, and the scribes and Pharisees are murmuring: "He welcomes sinners and eats with them" (Luke 15:2).

These two passages of Scripture lead us into the very heart of God, into the nature of salvation and the experience of grace. God's compassion grows as that of a loving parent. Jesus welcomes sinners.

The sign of God's compassion is that the relationship endures. The sign of Jesus' reception of sinners is that he eats with them. The sign of the relationship is the meal. A *sacrament*, defined in the early church, is an outward and visible sign of an inward and spiritual grace. How do we know that we are in a relationship? We come to this meal, we eat together, and it is grace.

Jesus' life and ministry was a gift of grace; we see this throughout the Gospels. Jesus takes the loaves and the fish and feeds the multitudes. He tells a story about a dinner party and those who respond to the invitation and those who do not. In his life and relationships, Jesus was always reaching out to others. At times some complained about this. The cultural idea was that the righteous associated with the righteous; the clean ate with those who were clean and did not associate with those who were unclean. But a physician goes to the sick, Jesus reminded them. The Son of Man came to seek and save those who are lost.

The core question is simple: how can a holy God be in relationship with an unholy people? How can Jesus (God forbid) eat with sinners? From a human point of view, it makes no sense. From a human point of view, there can be no relationship. But the prophet reminds us that God is God and not human; God promises not to destroy God's people in anger. (see Hosea 11:9). Holiness does not destroy sin; through compassion, it saves. Perfection does not destroy imperfection; through love, it heals.

I think God must wonder, "How do I get this message across to my people, that I love them, that I want this relationship to endure, that I am the One who gave them life—not those other gods—that I want the best for them?"

And God's answer comes to us through the life of Jesus: "We will sit down together at a meal. My son, Jesus, will preside. Jesus will eat not just with the worthy people but with the unworthy, not only with the righteous but with sinners, not only with the faithful but with the unfaithful, not only with the older brother who has done everything right, but with the prodigal son who has done everything wrong" (see Luke 15:11-32).

God seems to be saying, in the words of one of the faithful servants of God (Charles Wesley, who would come along much later):

> Come, sinners to the gospel feast,
> let every soul be Jesus' guest,
> Ye need not one be left behind,
> for God hath bid all humankind.
> ("Come, Sinners, to the Gospel Feast," st. 1)

Come, sinners to the gospel feast. Sinners—that's all of us. On this World Communion Sunday, we gather with all of God's people, sinners all of us, at the gospel feast. (Kenneth H. Carter Jr.)

Worship Aids

Call to Worship

Come, sinners, to the gospel feast!
All: Let every soul be Jesus' guest!

Invocation

Almighty God, whose power is over all thy works, and whose hand has provided for our every need. Draw near to us in thy grace, that we might be strengthened for every purpose and equipped for every good work. Through Jesus Christ our Lord. Amen.

Benediction

Now let us from this table rise to walk in newness of life, to the glory of God's name. The blessing and sustenance of God, Father, Son, and Holy Spirit go with you! Amen. (Kenneth H. Carter Jr.)

OCTOBER 14, 2012

꙳꙳꙳

Twentieth Sunday after Pentecost

Readings: Amos 5:6-7, 10-15; Psalm 90:12-17; Hebrews 4:12-16; Mark 10:17-31

Ruler or Ruled?

Mark 10:17-31

We all have heard the saying, "Everybody wants to go to heaven, but nobody wants to die." We have all grown up hearing children's sermons or Sunday school lessons that describe the Christian life as a journey to heaven. It's as if heaven is some place "out there," out of our reach or experience, but if we live good lives and are not bad boys and girls, when we die we will go to heaven.

The man in Mark's story is not talking about going to heaven. He's interested in how to experience eternal life in the here-and-now. Perhaps in exploring his profound question, we can lay to rest the notion that heaven or eternal life, whichever expression we choose, is a "place" or something outside and unreachable through human experience.

We are all conditioned by our environment. What have we kept since we were little children? As adults, we bring our histories, circumstances, and experiences with us. Our outlook on life is tied to this conditioning. Parents, teachers, friends, neighbors, work associates, and enemies have all contributed to who we are, what we think, and how we live. The man in Mark's story was also conditioned by such influences. He never murdered anyone, didn't run around on his wife, never stole anything from anybody, never told a lie, had not defrauded anyone, and had honored his parents. Wow! This fellow could be described as the preeminent community example of integrity. But there was one thing in his life that had taken complete hold of him—his possessions.

I am persuaded that Jesus never talked about "going to heaven." He talked about "experiencing heaven." As he said, "The kingdom of heaven

314

is among [or within] you" (Luke 17:21). He never talked about us being good in this life so we can get to heaven; he talked about heaven in this life. What the man in the story needs to do is what we all need to do—discern and discover how to allow ourselves to be claimed by the love of God. In doing so, we embark on a lifetime journey (now and eternal) of experiencing the goodness of God, the same goodness that claimed Jesus.

Unlike Luke's Gospel, Mark (and Matthew) avoids describing the man's position in the community. But we do know he had many possessions. Luke describes the man as a ruler (18:18) and perhaps this is significant. As a ruler, he would know what it was to have power over peoples' lives. Who better than this man to understand the power of possessions over one's own life? I believe this man leads us all to Jesus. We all have something that possesses, or rules, and interferes with us living life on God's terms. The man's question is our question: "What must I do to inherit eternal life" (Mark 10:17)? Let's pause and consider why he used the word *inherit*.

The word *inherit* in the text is *klironómisi* in Greek. One of its shades of meaning is "to share in." The man is essentially asking, "What must I do to share in God's blessings?" Jesus tells him that he needs to come to grips with the one thing that keeps him from sharing life on God's terms, namely, his wealth. It is clear from the man's response that he has much work to do. He realizes it will be nearly impossible for him to relinquish what he holds dear. It is his barrier to sharing in the blessings of God.

What must you and I do to share in the promise of God's blessings? What areas of our lives need some work so that we may share in God's life, life that is eternal? Based on Jesus' encounter with the man, God understands that we all have something in our lives that rules us. It is no accident that the writer notes Jesus' encounter is based on his compassion toward the man: "Jesus, looking at him, loved him" (v. 21). I believe Jesus' anguishing for forty days following his baptism included his own wrestling match with what sought to rule his life and mission as God's Messiah. The temptations were all things he had to face and deal with so that he was in command of them on God's terms, and they would not possess him. We follow one who completely understands how difficult—but not impossible—it is to rule over those things that would dominate us or rule us.

So, what are our "rulers"? What gets in our way of being Jesus' disciples? What sends us away shocked and grieving because we think we cannot live without them? Each of us must answer this question for ourselves. (Mike Childress)

Lectionary Commentary

Amos 5:6-7, 10-15

Amos is one of the Old Testament's minor prophets. A shepherd, he lived on the outskirts of Bethlehem. He was not formally trained as a prophet, but there was nothing minor about what he witnessed. Amos saw firsthand what can happen to a community when it turns a deaf ear and a blind eye to those victimized by greed and power. According to Amos, the community had become rotten to the core. Truth had been replaced with impropriety and honesty supplanted with duplicity.

Amos calls the people back to their spiritual moorings. He underscores his indictment with a plea: "Hate evil and love good, and establish justice in the gate; it may be that the LORD, the God of hosts, will be gracious to the remnant of Joseph" (v. 15).

Perhaps there is no better time than the present for Amos to step into the contemporary arena and speak to the injustice and atrocities that are happening in the world. Sometimes it is difficult to distinguish between injustice and grace in the church. Amos's words have a major contemporary ring to them.

Hebrews 4:12-16

The writer of Hebrews lays the reader wide open, as if he were a surgeon methodically and meticulously opening a wound and doing what is necessary to bring healing. Like a surgeon's scalpel that brings healing to a bodily wound, the Word of God brings healing to the human soul. If this metaphor has merit, then we can trust it in the hands of Jesus as God's great physician. Jesus' teachings and example can be trusted, for he fully and completely understands the human condition and the need for God's love and grace. We can trust Jesus to help us in our times of need; there is no aspect of the human condition for which Jesus is unable to administer care. (Mike Childress)

Worship Aids

Call to Worship

Come seeking the power of God's love for your lives.
We lay aside all that hinders us from worshiping God.
In Christ, the Holy Spirit calls us to be servants of the Most High God.
We bow before God in need of the power of God's grace. Amen.

Call to Confession

People of God, cling not to those things that diminish and demean the power of God's grace. Repent and be restored to the love that created you.

Confession

O God, week after week we find ourselves at the same place, wondering if your grace is sufficient. Forgive us. Reach down deep into our souls, and restore us to your merciful love. Heal our wounded souls that we might be the people you want us to be. Create in us hearts that seek to work with you and not against your will and purposes shown to us in Jesus Christ. Amen.

Words of Assurance

Hear the good news! God heals and restores our hearts and our will so that we may glorify God through Jesus the Christ. Amen. (Mike Childress)

Living in God's Dominion

First in a Series of Three on Stewardship: Managing God's Bounty

Genesis 1; Leviticus 25:23-24

The other day, while driving through some of the flattest land of eastern North Carolina, I suddenly encountered a large hill. There was a road leading to the hill with a gate and a big sign: "Landfill, Hours 7:00 a.m. – 7:00 p.m." It was not the first encounter I have had with a large mound in the middle of flat land. In Virginia Beach, Virginia, they have turned their large mound into Mount Trashmore Park, a sixty-foot-high landfill in a city barely above sea level. The United States has become the biggest polluter in the world, leading the way in greenhouse gases and other pollutants. God calls us, as Christians, to a higher standard as stewards of the world that God created for us.

This sermon series will look at our call to stewardship, and how we manage God's bounty. First, we will look at how the Bible provides commandment and covenant stories that charge humanity with the management of the earth and all of God's creatures. Next, we will discuss how humanity has treated the precious gift that God has granted to us to maintain. Finally, we will talk about what we need to do as faithful believers in Christ to renew our covenant with God to become better stewards of God's bounty.

"In the beginning when God created the heaven and the earth... (Genesis 1:1)." God is the creator of our earth. We are only passing through this world until we reunite with our heavenly Lord. This does not give us the right to mistreat or misuse the land and the creatures who reside in the land. We need to consider not only how we affect the earth while we are here but also how we leave it for those who come after us. This is God's world, not ours. Moses proclaims to Pharaoh in Exodus 9:29, "so that you may know that the earth is the Lord's." As I consider the ways we have polluted water, stripped land, and destroyed wildlife, I feel we have forgotten to whom the earth belongs. We are self-centered and have lost focus on the great Creator, our Lord.

In the United States, we believed it was our "Manifest Destiny" to populate the land from coast to coast. Wagon trains set forth to move people to the West, creating great cities along the way. Many of the early settlers believed that God was leading them to what were sometimes harsh lands so that they could set up lives for themselves and their families. As our country developed, we looked for more and more ways to make our lives less complicated. Resources seemed limitless. We became more dependent upon ourselves and less dependent upon God.

Many early settlers had the right idea; work the land and use what they needed for provisions—no less, no more. This reflects God's mandate in Genesis 1:26: "Then God said, 'Let us make humankind in our image, according to our likeness; and let them have dominion over the fish of the sea, and over the birds of the air, and over the cattle, and over all the wild animals of the earth, and over every creeping thing that creeps upon the earth.'" From the beginning, God has provided the means of food and shelter.

God also called the Hebrews to redeem the earth, to protect what nurtured them: "The land shall not be sold in perpetuity, for the land is mine; with me you are but aliens and tenants. Throughout the land that you hold, you shall provide for the redemption of the land" (Leviticus 25:23-24). The people of Israel were to work the land for six years and make the seventh year a Sabbath. Early North American settlers used this same principle. They knew that the soil would not remain fertile with continuous use. In our lifetime, we have begun to over-fertilize the soil, causing great environmental damage to satisfy our desire for more food at a cheap price. Farms have become more corporate and less family-owned. This is a rejection of God's call in Leviticus. We should not own the land in order to make a profit for humankind. We have forsaken biblical principles for our own gain.

Many people have interpreted the word *dominion* in Genesis 1:26 to mean "domination" as opposed to "care of" the earth and all of its creatures. I believe it is our God-given mission as human beings to serve the created order. We should not use up all the earth's resources and destroy species and their habitats in order to meet our wants.

Even if you believe that the Second Coming will be tomorrow, it is a misinterpretation of God's word to act as if it does not matter what we do to the world. Human service as protectors of the earth is part of our covenant with God. On the sixth day, God gives Adam seeds that produce plants, trees, and fruit in order that he should have food. After the Flood, God provides for Noah and his family, making covenant with them and their descendants (see Genesis 9). When we accept our relationship with Jesus Christ, we enter into a covenant to follow the ways of God and obey God's commandments. God calls people of faith to be guardians of God's earth and all the living creatures. Every day scientists discover new species of fish, reptiles, and mammals. We have only begun to understand the vastness of the creation that God has blessed us with.

God calls us throughout the Bible to protect the bounty that God has bestowed. We are responsible for our actions. Peter writes, "It is better to suffer for doing good, if suffering should be God's will, than to suffer for doing evil" (1 Peter 3:17). Think about it the next time you throw away the soda can, toss a water bottle into the trash, or even leave the water running while brushing your teeth. Tiny modifications in each of our lives can revolutionize the quality of our care for God's bounty. (John Mathis)

Worship Aids

Call to Worship

In the beginning, God created...
God created the world.
In the beginning, God created...
God created all the living things in the world.
In the beginning, God created...
God created us.
In the beginning, God created...
**God created us to be stewards of all the living things
in the world.**

Pastoral Prayer

Gracious Lord, give us the power to live as servants in your world. Grant us the courage to live as stewards of your world. Never let us forget that it is a world created by you in order to sustain us, not for us to abuse and misuse. Provide us ways to recreate your creation every day. Amen.

Offertory Prayer

O God, thank you for the world you have bestowed upon humanity. You have given us sustenance, clothing, and many resources for our well-being. Give us the power to give back a small portion of the plentiful bounty you have provided. As you have blessed each one of us, let us bless you with our gifts of gratitude. Amen. (John Mathis)

OCTOBER 21, 2012

❧❧❧

Twenty-first Sunday after Pentecost

Readings: Isaiah 53:4-12; Psalm 91:9-16; Hebrews 5:1-10;
Mark 10:35-45

A Suffering Servant

Isaiah 53:4-12

God struck him down. He was taken away by a perversion of justice. It was the will of the Lord to crush him with pain. Christians naturally think of Jesus when they hear these words. It didn't take long for the early church to apply this "Suffering Servant Song" to Jesus. But before we jump there, let's try to hear what Isaiah is saying. Let's go back at least 500 years before Jesus was born and imagine what it was like for the author to write these words.

There really is no good explanation for suffering. Certainly, theologians and philosophers have tried, but there is no way to reconcile our belief in a good and loving God with the fact that terrible circumstances happen. A wonderful family eagerly anticipates the birth of their daughter only to find out that she has a debilitating disease that will end her life after only a few years. They attend church regularly. They read their Bible and pray. And still God allows—or even worse, causes?—something like this to happen.

For some people, the answer is easy. When the earthquake devastated Haiti in 2010, popular televangelist Pat Robertson claimed the quake was God's retribution for some ancient misdeed. Many Christians were outraged at his assertion. The fact that thousands of the dead were children and the poorest of the poor made it impossible to consider this as God's revenge.

But several Old Testament authors would have had no problem with Robertson's claims. According to Deuteronomy, Israel's penalty for abandoning God was famine, war, torture, humiliation, and exile, going so far as to claim that God would send them back to slavery in Egypt "by a route that I promised you would never see again" (Deuteronomy 28:68). Does God go back on God's promises? Most of us would dismiss this text as hyperbole, but there's an angry force behind those words. When Israel did face famine, invading armies, and exile, the prophets shook their fingers at Israel and Judah: "You brought this on yourself," they said. "You turned your back on God. You failed to love your neighbor. Now it's time to pay the piper."

As the exiles left Jerusalem as prisoners, looking over their shoulders at the smoldering ruins of their temple, they must have wondered if they would ever see their homes again. They felt abandoned by God. Struck down. Afflicted. They must have wondered, "If we are God's chosen people, why have we been defeated by pagan armies? Is God unable to rescue us? Has God rejected us? Does God even care?" We can hear the same kind of anguish on the lips of the disciples in the boat on the Sea of Galilee. As the weight of the water begins to press the boat beneath the waves, they see Jesus, sleeping on a bench in the stern. "Teacher," they cry, "do you not care that we are perishing" (Mark 4:38)? Later, we see the same terror in their eyes when they flee from the scene of Jesus' arrest. Cowering in a locked room, they ask, "Is God unable to rescue him? Has God rejected us?"

Although she doesn't ask it aloud, I hear that question in the anguish of a mother whose teenage son is tortured by mental illness. Unable to draw him out of his invisible prison, she watches him fold into himself, peering out of eyes that do not see the same world she does. Her heart breaks. "Why is God punishing us? What have we done wrong?"

Our passage from Isaiah suggests that Israel has not been abandoned by God. The suffering of the people in exile may no longer be the consequence of their sin. It may be caused by the sin of other nations. Maybe it was the sin of the Assyrian Empire, a brutal regime that conquered other lands and tortured captives on a regular basis. Perhaps it was the sin of the Babylonians, the ones who actually carried them off, or the Edomites, who took the opportunity to kick their neighbor Judeans when they were down. Taking the role of an observer, Isaiah looks at the beaten people of God as a nation and makes a radical claim: yes, these people turned their backs on God, and God allowed them to be crushed (see Isaiah 53:5-6). But they are not abandoned by God; God sees their suffering in exile and uses their anguish to teach the world about faithfulness in adversity.

Historically, that's what happened. In exile, with no temple, no king, and no homeland to call their own, the people formed a new identity. It was not the land or the king that gave them meaning and purpose; It was God, and the story of God found in their Scriptures. Following God's law gave them their identity. "Out of his anguish he shall see light; he shall find satisfaction through his knowledge" (v. 11). Their renewed faith and belief in one God would, in time, reshape the entire world. Isaiah foresaw this when he wrote, "It is too light a thing that you should be my servant to raise up the tribes of Jacob . . . I will give you as a light to the nations, that my salvation may reach to the end of the earth" (49:6). It's no wonder that the early disciples saw a reflection of their own experience with Jesus. The cross did not mean that God had abandoned them or that Jesus was wrong. It showed the world that even when people are in defeat, in exile and despair, God is not finished with them. God has a greater work of salvation in mind.

I don't have a good answer for the mother whose son dwells in exile. There is no good answer for suffering. Her answer is, "God saves my tears in a bottle, and I believe one day, maybe even in this life, my son will be healed." I watch her walk to the chapel for her twice-weekly prayer meeting with other saints of the church. "I need prayer," she says. "It's like breathing." My faith and spiritual discipline are thin and weak compared to hers. This family's suffering is not just, and I cannot bring myself to say it is the will of the Lord to crush her family with pain. Yet out of her anguish, she sees light and brings the light of God into the world. God promises that even our pain and suffering can be redeemed, and this mother holds onto the hope that even in her feeling of defeat, even in her despair, God is not finished. God has greater things in store. (Dave Barnhart)

Lectionary Commentary

Hebrews 5:1-10

It doesn't get much heavier than this. The author of Hebrews is laying out a doctrine of the Atonement, wrestling with what, exactly, Jesus' death on the cross accomplished. The passage is filled with symbolism and metaphor that assumes the hearers familiarity with the obscure reference to Melchizedek from Genesis 14. The author puts a human face on all this theological language. Jesus is "able to deal gently with the ignorant and the wayward" (v. 2), because he himself has dealt with human frailty and pain. It is this gentle humility and Jesus' obedience to God that lead God to confer authority upon him. Likewise it is believers' obedience to Jesus that gives us access to Jesus as the "source of eternal salvation for all who obey him" (v. 9).

Mark 10:35-45

This account differs from the one in Matthew (20:20), where James' and Johns' mother makes the request of Jesus. Here, the brothers' request for special treatment isn't unusual; they are clearly part of the "inner circle" of Jesus. Peter is the only other disciple who witnessed the transfiguration (ch. 9). I find it interesting that while the disciples fume over the request of James and John, Jesus does not. He seems, if anything, touched. Jesus sounds almost sad that he can't grant it.

Jesus has already talked with them about greatness before (9:34-35), using almost the same words. Many books have been written for church and business leaders on the subject of servant-leadership. Apparently this was also an issue for the early church to whom this Gospel was addressed. Those early communities—and our own—needed constant reminders that leadership in the church should look very different from the leadership in the world. (Dave Barnhart)

Worship Aids

Invocation

Jesus, our great priest, our teacher, our friend, be with us today. Help us to see past the surface of things, to look at the world and our lives through the lens of the good news, so that we may see reality the way you see it, permeated with your love.

Prayer of Confession

Lord, we long to feel close to you. We sing about loving you and being near you, but we don't want to be so near that we have to drink the cup you drink or feel the pain you feel. Forgive us, Lord, for our false intimacy. We want to sit next to you at the great banquet. Help us to stand next to you as a servant. Amen.

Words of Assurance

Hear the good news. Christ knows and understands our human weakness and longing. The Holy Spirit accompanies us in our struggle to overcome. Thanks be to God.

Pastoral Prayer

We do not understand suffering. We wonder and throw up our hands in the face of illness, injustice, grief, and broken relationships. Why, God, we ask. But it is hard to complain to you as we see you hang on the cross. Help us to find grace in your suffering for us, that we may also find a measure of grace in our own. (Dave Barnhart)

Have We Been the Stewards We Are Called to Be?

Second in a Series of Three on Stewardship: Managing God's Bounty

Ezekiel 34:2-4

Throughout the Sriptures, the Lord calls us to be stewards of God's bounty. Therefore, we must ask if we have been faithful to this call throughout history. We could say that from the very beginning, when Adam and Eve partook of the fruit of the tree of the knowledge of good and evil, humanity has disregarded God's call. The Israelites constantly struggled with relying solely on God for provision. From the Gospels and the writings of Paul, we can see that early believers struggled to keep their priorities in order. As the population of the earth has exploded over the last century, we have discovered a multitude of ways to overuse, abuse, and destroy portions of the earth. The first step in becoming better stewards of God's bounty is admitting that we have sinned in our inability to put our needs before our wants and desires for cheaper energy, more convenient forms of food sources, and instant gratification. God calls us to use God's bounty for human need instead of human greed. We may ask, "What change can I make in my life to help protect the earth for the generations of the future?"

Through the prophet Ezekiel, the Lord tells the leaders of Israel that they have abandoned their sheep, the people of Israel, for their own selfish needs. God called them to be stewards of the people of God. Just as the leaders of Israel strayed from their covenant with God to care for the people of Israel and to care for God's bounty, we also have strayed from our covenant. We have taken whatever we could from the land, while many people go without; we allow people to die needlessly, and we disregard the stranger who enters into our midst. Our desire for comfortable lives leads to sins of omission. Child labor is a major problem all over the world, especially in Asia. We have to ask ourselves if it is better to protect the life of a child in a faraway land than to save five dollars on a shirt or blouse, a pair of shoes, or a video game. As God's stewards of the earth, we need to be willing to sacrifice to protect humanity from such exploitation.

Jesus told the parable of the dishonest manager to help the disciples sort their priorities: "No slave can serve two masters; for a slave will either hate the one and love the other, or be devoted to the one and despise the other. You cannot serve God and wealth" (Luke 16:13). I do not believe that God wants us to live a life of poverty and not provide for our families, but I do believe that God calls us to give generously out of our wealth and riches. This does not necessarily mean money. Perhaps it means using a God-given gift or talent to serve the Lord. When we live for our own personal success and glory and stop living for God, we lose sight of what should be our number one priority—God. First-century believers struggled with balancing their lives between God and the world just as we do in the twenty-first century. Jesus warns, "the cares of the world, and the lure of wealth, and the desire for other things come in and choke the word, and it yields nothing" (Mark 4:19). Sometimes we must sacrifice our own desires. God calls us to choose to live as good stewards of God's bounty.

Humanity has assaulted the earth, especially since the beginning of the Industrial Revolution in the eighteenth century. Corporations use strip mining throughout Appalachia in order to satisfy our need for cheaper coal. Strip mining increases the level of mercury in drinking water, pollutes the air, and causes vast ecological damage. The debate over global warming versus climate change rages on day after day. We can directly link the increase of greenhouse gases to our transportation needs and desires in the United States and throughout the world. Climate change affects humanity, the environment, and the creatures of the earth. Carbon dioxide, methane, nitrous oxide, and fluorocarbons are all greenhouse gases that have increased over the last hundred years due to human inventions. In our desire to dominate the earth, we have failed to fully protect God's bounty. There is hope that we can become better servants in this world, if we trust God to be our guide and seek changes in our lifestyle that lead to great changes in our lives. (John Mathis)

Worship Aids

Invocation

God of creation, allow us to enter this place of worship to bring a part of ourselves into the presence of the holy. We come with humble hearts, seeking your guidance and wisdom. We know that we sin. We know that you accept us as we are, sinful and not whole. Lord, make us whole. Take away the negative aspects of our nature and fill us with your Spirit to be proper stewards of your world. Amen.

Prayer of Confession

Almighty God, creator of heaven and earth, we have sinned. We put our own needs, our own desires in front of your will for our lives. We forgot the covenant you made with Adam and then with Noah. When we see a rainbow, do we forget the covenant you made with humanity? Forgive us. We know we are to be the stewards of your creation, but we struggle with our own desires. Help us, Lord. Amen.

Words of Assurance

Almighty God, grant us the wisdom and strength to be your caretakers in the world. You give us the courage to change. You give us the power to turn the smallest seed into the greatest tree. We can change because you are with us, leading our path and guiding our daily lives. Bless us and keep us. Amen. (John Mathis)

OCTOBER 28, 2012

❧❧❧❧

Twenty-second Sunday after Pentecost

Readings: Jeremiah 31:7-9; Psalm 126; Hebrews 7:23-28;
Mark 10:46-52

When the Poor Won't Shut Up

Mark 10:46-52

The disciples have been talking theology. They have been arguing about who is the greatest in the kingdom of heaven. They have listened to Jesus describe his mission, and they have been talking about churchy things. Their minds are occupied with cosmic ideas and big issues when they walk into Jericho, and they are not prepared for what happens there. Bartimaeus the beggar won't shut up. He keeps shouting to Jesus, demanding attention. He's distracting.

We know how beggars should act—most have learned to be quiet, to hold a cardboard sign with a scrawled message on it, and simply smile or say, "God bless you" when someone stops to give them money. The aggressive ones scare us. Some are cunning: "I need 68 cents for a cup of coffee," one asks, having learned that nobody will stop long enough to count out change but will hand over a dollar bill, or sometimes even a five. Sure, we know some people are legitimately poor, but others are just lazy and shiftless, and they make us uncomfortable. We who are not poor eye them with suspicion. Even worse are the poor who get uppity about their poverty, who demand attention and time as if they are entitled to it. The world could tolerate the poor if they would just be quiet.

So it's no surprise that the crowd tells Bartimaeus to hush. The people following Jesus are too busy to listen to his complaints. But Bartimaeus the beggar won't shut up. Bartimaeus keeps demanding attention.

Jesus halts. I imagine the people in front walk a few paces before they realize they are alone, and then they turn, puzzled. The whole crowd halts as Jesus refuses to budge. "Why are we stopping?" they wonder. Then

328

Jesus says, "Call him here" (v. 49). Jesus does not shout back to the beggar and summon him. Instead, Jesus gives his command to the people around him. The same people who had been shushing and scowling now turn, somewhat sheepishly, back to Bartimaeus. They try to look nonchalant, even gallant, as they say, "Take heart; get up, he is calling you" (v. 49). We hear the silent rebuke in Jesus' command. He bids his followers to welcome beggars, and in his words, we can't help but hear other things Jesus has said about the poor: "I was hungry and you fed me.... As you've done it to the least of these, you've done it to me" (see Matthew 25). So Jesus' followers have to stop their journey because their Savior won't budge until they pay attention to the beggar. Jesus will not allow the church to move forward until it hears the voice of the poor.

Stop a moment and listen to Jesus talk with Bartimaeus. Let the strangeness of this scene settle on you. Why does Jesus ask what Bartimaeus wants? Isn't it obvious? He's a beggar! He wants money! He is a useless member of society, unable to work or to be effective in any kind of employment. He wants a handout. But Jesus does not assume he knows what Bartimaeus wants. He asks. Many Christians and Christian organizations don't ever actually listen to the poor. In their zeal to set up a new ministry and do good, they start handing out food or running financial management classes without ever asking, "What do you want me to do for you?" One missionary group decided to address the fact that millions of women and children die every year from inhaling the smoke of their cook fires. They took it upon themselves to set up villagers in a developing country with modern wood-burning stoves and stovepipes. But they found that the families would remove the stovepipes and sell them as scrap metal. Anyone who works to alleviate poverty knows hundreds of examples of what happens when well-intentioned people fail to listen to those they are supposed to be helping. Jesus knows better than to assume. He treats Bartimaeus as a human being. Jesus asks Bartimaeus what he wants.

"Let me see again," Bartimaeus says in verse 51. "Restore my sight." Sometimes when churches make the effort to listen to the poor, they hear surprising things. "We need public transportation, a way to get to the grocery store." "I need daycare for my child so I can finish my degree." "I need a low-interest loan." These are not requests for handouts. They are requests for empowerment.

As Bartimaeus talks with Jesus, perhaps the listening crowd begins to recognize their own blindness. Bartimaeus is physically blind, and his disability has kept him poor. But the crowd has been blind to Bartimaeus, spiritually poor. They could not see him nor hear him, or at least pretended they could not. So when Jesus works his miracle on Bartimaeus, it is also a miracle for the crowd. Not only does Jesus give Bartimaeus the power to live a new life, he gives the crowd new eyes and new life as well.

When the crowd finally begins to move again, there is a new disciple among them. Bartimaeus chooses to follow Jesus. When Jesus tells him to go, Bartimaeus takes the command not as an order to go away but as freedom to take charge of his new life. He chooses to join the crowd. In this brief passage, we see a snapshot of potential salvation for the church. We began with the disciples arguing about who was the greatest among them, but now they have welcomed into their ranks one of the least, a beggar who has nothing to give but the joy of his new sight and the story of his healing. What would it be like if the church stopped to listen to the poor? What if it welcomed the poor as fellow disciples and empowered them to follow Jesus, instead of treating them as problems to be solved? One thing is sure: the church can't move forward with Jesus until it stops to listen. (Dave Barnhart)

Lectionary Commentary

Jeremiah 31:7-9

A woman hikes along the road with the returning refugees, huffing and puffing through her contractions. She is about to give birth, but she won't stop; going home is too important! It's the most striking visual image of this passage in which God gathers the scattered exiles. The author indicates how all-inclusive and immediate the restoration will be. The blind (who can't see the road), the lame (who can't walk it), the pregnant women (who are so eager they can't even wait a few months), and the ones who are giving birth (who can't even wait a few hours).

For anyone who has ever been an exile, literally or figuratively, it's a hopeful message. The crowd shouting "Save us, O LORD" (v. 7) is echoed in the shouts of "Hosanna!" to Jesus as he rides a donkey into Jerusalem (Mark 11:90). The joy is so intense it hurts, and they weep (v. 9). God's provision is so complete they never have to stop for water because the straight road will follow a straight river, and God will console them the entire way. It's a powerful image of hope, especially for those who feel alienated and who long for healing.

Hebrews 7:23-28

Priesthood is a difficult concept for most Protestants to wrap their heads around, especially in doctrines such as "the priesthood of all believers." Most Christians reading this passage simply shrug. Sure, Jesus is perfect and unlike human priests. But in the ancient world, the role of the priest was essential for the health of the community. In fact, the death of the high priest and the appointment of a new one reset the clock on the entire community. Numbers 35:28 specifies that someone guilty of manslaughter can leave a city of refuge and return home when the high priest dies.

Writing after the destruction of the temple in A.D. 70, the author of Hebrews makes the case that Jesus supersedes the old religious system. There is no longer any cosmic bureaucracy to navigate because Jesus has cleared it all away by doing perfectly what humanity had stumbled at for hundreds of years. (Dave Barnhart)

Worship Aids

Invocation

God who restores, who heals, who makes us whole, open our eyes to your work around us. Be in our praying, in our singing, in our proclamation, and in our silence. Open our eyes to see your kingdom coming into the world.

Greeting

Jesus has come to town.
Jesus, son of David, have mercy on us!
He invites us to join him on his journey.
Jesus, son of David, have mercy on us!
Come and be healed, and see with new eyes.
Hallelujah! Thanks be to God!

Benediction

Go as the church, as Jesus' entourage, following where he leads. Everywhere he goes he leaves healing and hope in his wake. Go, and listen, and learn, and love. Amen. (Dave Barnhart)

Hope for a Redeemed World

Third in a Series of Three on Stewardship: Managing God's Bounty

Mark 4:31-32

We saw that God calls us throughout Scripture to be caretakers of the earth. God challenges humanity to look at how we have treated the earth, and the question remains, "What are we going to do about it?" There is much hope for our world today if we are willing to make even a few small changes in our lives. An old proverb states, from a little acorn grows a mighty oak. An even older parable states,

> It is like a mustard seed, which, when sown upon the ground, is the smallest of all the seeds on earth; yet when it is sown it grows up and becomes the greatest of all shrubs, and puts forth large branches, so that birds of the air can make nests in its shade. (Mark 4:31-32)

As local congregations, we have much power as change-agents. Small changes we make in our own households can have tremendous effects on the world. We need to regain our trust in the Lord to help us renew our stewardship of God's bounty.

Each Sunday, parishioners look to the pulpit, waiting for a word, a sermon that will change their lives in even small ways. Do I speak words that inspire, comfort, or challenge? Global thinking regarding stewardship of God's creation requires a challenge. We need to change our worldview from self-centered to Christ-centered. Is our priority self-preservation, or are we concerned with humankind in the world today and in the future? Changes can be very simple. Instead of bulletins each week, use a standard order of worship and hymn boards and other items already available. Encourage church members to recycle and provide bins throughout the building to make the task a little easier. The church could become a central location for recycling within the community. Plant trees on the church grounds. These can be the basis for a memorial garden or a way to honor members of the congregation. There are many more ways that we can protect God's creation with tiny changes within the local church and become a witness to good stewardship for the world.

Changes need to occur in our households as well. We need to remember the three R's: reduce, reuse, and recycle. We need to reduce the amount of time we spend in the car and increase the time we use alternative transportation. I understand that sometimes this is not practical, but we need to stop and ask, "Could I have walked?" I spent three weeks in Spain one summer and was amazed at how I was able to get around with minimal use of cars. As a child, my friends and I would walk a mile or two to go to the local convenience store; now I hop in the car and drive, all in the name of saving time. We need to reduce the amount of trash we generate and place into the earth. We need to reduce the amount of water we use on a daily basis. Simple things like limiting the amount of times we wash our clothes, turning off the water while brushing our teeth or shaving, and double-checking to see that we have no water leaks in the house. We can reuse many items in our house and even the gifts that God provides for us to limit our waste. My neighbors collect rainwater in a barrel, which they use for their yard and garden. We also need to recycle. Just recently, the state of North Carolina passed a law prohibiting the trashing of clear water bottles. I applaud the state for its efforts, but the church needs to lead the way in protecting the creation that God has entrusted to humanity.

The question remains, "Do we want to be a part of God's plan for humanity and for creation, or will we continue to be selfish and concerned with our needs and desires?" These words may sound harsh, but God's creation is crying out for change; a change we must make in our lifetime. Through the Bible, God speaks to us, calling us to be stewards of this world that God provides. Yet we have acted selfishly throughout history in bringing God's earth to a point of crisis. We need to promote change in our local churches and all through our communities. People of faith need to be in the forefront in protecting the creation that God has so graciously bestowed upon us. (John Mathis)

Worship Aids

Call to Worship

God is calling us to redeem God's world.
**God grant us the wisdom to know where we need to change
in our lives.**
God is calling us to heal the planet.
God grant us the strength to make changes in our homes.
God is calling us to teach our children stewardship.
**God grant us the knowledge to bestow
upon future generations.**
God is calling us to protect our future.
**God grant us the strength to make changes
throughout your world.**

Prayer of Confession

Gracious God, we know that we need to make changes in our lives. We know that change is not effortless. We know that we must take old bad habits and weed them from our lives. We need to plant new habits of caring and preserving the world that you provide for us. God, take away our selfishness and instill in our hearts humility and a desire to join your plan for humanity to care for your creation. We seek your guidance to be the stewards that you created us to be. Amen.

Words of Assurance

Almighty God, grant us the wisdom and strength to be your caretakers in the world. You give us the courage to change. You give us the power to turn the smallest seed into the greatest tree. We can change because you are with us, leading our path and guiding our daily lives. Bless us and keep us. Amen. (John Mathis)

NOVEMBER 4, 2012

❧❧❧

Twenty-third Sunday after Pentecost

Readings: Deuteronomy 6:1-9; Psalm 119:1-8; Hebrews 9:11-14; Mark 12:28-34

The Cosmic Ritual
Hebrews 9:11-14

The crowd stands and sings the national anthem. Someone throws out the first pitch. People wear goofy outfits, take a seventh-inning stretch, sing "Take Me Out to the Ball Game," and buy overpriced hot dogs. Most of them will never know that what they are doing is religion.

A nonbeliever asked a friend of mine, "Why do Christians need to do all these rituals, like Communion? Why don't they just preach what they believe?" All I could think about was the ball game, and twenty thousand people or more singing, reciting creeds or pledges, and feeling a sense of unity—even with the opposing team—as they sing about buying "peanuts and Cracker Jacks." It must have been similar more than two and-a-half millennia ago, when the ancient Greeks gathered for the first Olympics, a series of games and rituals designed to give glory to their gods. Rituals are simply what human beings do. They make us feel close to one another and to God. They take away our guilt. They comfort us in times of stress. They remind people of what they believe, and teach them the values of their culture. Regardless of which team we root for, we love the game itself; and we don't care if we ever go back.

It must have been the same way in the temple. The psalmist says that one day in the temple courts is better than a thousand elsewhere, and he envies even the sparrow who makes its nest in a corner of the building (see Psalm 84). This was the place where people could come to formally wipe the slate clean, to start their relationships with God over again.

We are far away from the smoky slaughterhouse smell of the ancient temple, the sound of bells, and the bleating of sheep. Our Christian churches have a different smell: wood polish and flowers, carpet and

335

candles. So when the author of Hebrews starts talking about high priests, blood, goats, bulls, and sacrifice, some of us have a hard time relating. We're much more comfortable with baseball and the Olympics.

Blood has always been a symbol of both life and death. The ancient Israelites believed that a creature's life-force was in its blood, and therefore blood was holy to God. If someone was murdered, God was supposed to be able to hear their blood crying from the ground. If you killed an animal for food, you were forbidden to drink its blood; instead, you had to offer its blood back to God. When the Hebrews escaped from Egypt on the night of Passover, the Hebrews painted their doors with the blood of a lamb so that the angel of death would know which houses to avoid and pass over.

When we sing about fountains filled with blood and about being washed in the blood of the Lamb, it is best not to actually try to picture such things. A fountain filled with blood? It sounds like a scene from a horror movie! Yet we have hymns like, "Nothing but the blood of Jesus." This fascination with blood seems pretty grisly, but in the ancient world, blood was viewed as the divine source of life.

Actually we haven't come so far in our thinking. We still say someone is hot-blooded if they are passionate; we refer to a cold-blooded killer or a blue-blooded noble. We ascribe cultural attributes to blood: "He has Irish (or Native American or African) blood"; we speak of people having musical or athletic talent "in their blood." It's the stuff that beats through our hearts and fuels our passions. Abraham Lincoln had the audacity to stand up at the podium at Gettysburg and call a battlefield holy, because it had been hallowed with the spilled blood of fallen soldiers. Pouring out his life willingly, Jesus enacted an ancient ritual that changes who we are.

Sometimes Christians, hearing so often about how Christ takes our place on the cross, think that sacrifice and punishment are the same thing. It's important to remember that the animals slaughtered on temple altar were not being punished for the sins of the people. When we talk about Jesus as "the perfect sacrifice for our sins," it does not mean that someone had to be killed in order to appease an angry God's thirst for vengeance. It's something far deeper—a blood ritual that reminds us of where life comes from and where it goes.

Jesus' death on the cross was more than just a terrible injustice, says the author of Hebrews. It was more than just an inspiring act of nonviolent resistance. It was more than a ritual that makes us feel better. It was cosmic. It altered the very fabric of reality. Jesus' action of offering his own blood—that divine, life-giving substance—somehow made possible a new relationship between human beings and God. Our faith, says the author, is not in a set of rituals and dramatic actions that make us feel better. Our faith is in a God who has acted once and for all on our behalf.

So the author invites us to imagine Jesus as the cosmic priest, performing a glorious ritual outside of time. The cross becomes not merely an ugly upright pole upon which Jesus is nailed. It is an altar; crude but beautiful, surrounded with the smoke of incense. Although we may see Jesus bound, naked, and bloody; when we look through this author's eyes, Jesus wears the robe of a priest, and he ascends the steps to the altar of his own free will. The blood falling from his wrists, side, and torn back is no longer a reminder of pain and injustice, but the life-giving substance that Jesus offers back to God—his own essence and life-force—and by doing, so he purifies the world. Watching this spectacle are not only his mother and a few courageous followers but every human being who has ever lived and who will ever walk our planet. Like the crowd at the baseball game, root, root, rooting for their home team, those standing around the cross and watching the execution of Jesus have no idea that what they are doing is religion. (Dave Barnhart)

Lectionary Commentary

Deuteronomy 6:1-9

This passage is the *Shema*, from the Hebrew verb *hear*. Jesus calls it the greatest commandment: to remember that the God named "I am" is the only God, and to love God with all of one's inner self, and emotion, and force. The people of Israel are told to remember this law by teaching their children at every opportunity: on the road, in the morning before work, in the evening as they go to bed. They are also commanded to remember it in physical ways. When my wife and I moved into our first apartment, we found a mezuzah left by the former occupants. The mezuzah is a small container fixed to the front doorpost of a home, which contains a tiny scroll with the *Shema* written on it. Observant Jews today still fix it to their doorposts as a way of following the command in this passage. What physical reminders do we use to teach ourselves about God and pass that knowledge on to the next generation? What daily disciplines do we use to remind ourselves of the God we serve?

Mark 12:28-34

Jesus has already argued with the Pharisees and Herodians about paying taxes to Caesar, and with the Sadducees about the concept of resurrection. Now a scribe, overhearing their arguments and judging Jesus to be a smart cookie, poses his question. It's odd that Jesus gives him a straight answer instead of an object lesson (as when he asked for a coin from the Pharisees) or a counter-question. Perhaps he knows the scribe is asking a genuine question and doesn't have a hidden agenda? In Matthew's version (22:34-40) and in Luke's version (10:25-28), the questioner is a lawyer who is testing Jesus. Mark's scribe seems to be honest.

Mark's story is also unusual in that the scribe congratulates Jesus on giving a good answer, and that Jesus responds by saying, "You are not far from the kingdom of God" (v. 34). The Pharisees and Sadducees have just been shown up by a lowly scribe! He even gets in a dig at the Sadducees' focus on the temple, "This is much more important than whole burnt offerings and sacrifices" (v. 33). There is something touching in this encounter that offers hope to churches today. Despite those who try to control Jesus, to manipulate or discredit him, there is still hope for the few who come to him with genuine questions. (Dave Barnhart)

Worship Aids

Greeting

Hear, O people of God! The Lord alone is God.
We will love God with all our heart, and soul, and strength.
Recite it to yourselves. Recite it to the children.
We will love God with all our heart, and soul, and strength.
Bind it on your forehead, your hand, your home, your heart.
We will love God with all our heart, and soul, and strength!

Prayer of Confession

God, we get distracted so easily. The chatter of the television, the changing fashions, the bills at the end of the month, the tyranny of our calendars and to-do lists, and long lists of religious rules. You give us only two commandments, and it seems more than we can do to live up to them. We have not loved you, and we have not loved our neighbor. Forgive us, Jesus. Amen.

Words of Assurance

Jesus has taken care of the hard stuff. We have been purified from our sin and disobedience by his blood and his obedience. Hear Jesus' words: "You are not far from the kingdom of God." Amen. (Dave Barnhart)

Discovering Gratitude

First in a Series of Four on Relearning Christian Gratitude

Luke 17:11-19

You never know what you might see when you walk with Jesus. On this particular stroll along the border of Samaria and Galilee—the Mason-Dixon line of the first century—we see one of those unexpected scenes that characterize Jesus' life. A band of ten lepers, outcasts from society, call to Jesus, from a distance lest they spread their disease. They cry out, asking Jesus to have mercy on them. Jesus calls back to them, "Go and show yourselves to the priests" (v. 14). They set off to do what he says, and on the way they are healed.

That is amazing enough, but it is the next scene that makes the story so memorable. One person comes back to say thanks. One former leper returns to praise God for being given the great gift of his life back. This one—once required to stand at the margins, announcing to any who came near that he was both physically and spiritually unclean—can return to his family, to the comfort of human touch, to the warmth of life in the community. He is made whole and so overcome with gratitude that he throws himself at Jesus' feet. How could he do anything else?

Jesus, meanwhile, is taken aback—not by this man's dramatic show of thanks, but by the fact that just one returns. We, along with Jesus, are left wondering, "Where are the other nine? Why is there only one who really understands what just happened?"

It is a mystery. How could people who have suffered so much receive such a gift—the gift of a normal life—and not at least say thank you? Surely there's a reasonable explanation.

While it's possible that this is a display of extraordinary ingratitude, the kind that throws a gift back in the face of the giver, motivated by nothing but disdain, that seems pretty unlikely. Rather, it seems far more plausible that this was a case of benign neglect. Perhaps these now-cleansed lepers are celebrating with their friends and family, overjoyed by the return to the ones they loved. In the midst of the excitement, perhaps they forgot about Jesus, the one who had given them their lives back.

While the story shocks us, if we are at all honest with ourselves, we know that all too often we find ourselves living among the ninety percent who fail the gratitude test. We too are easily caught up in our own enjoyment of the great gifts of God that we forget their source. Oh, that the words of the doxology would become our very heartbeat: "Praise God from whom all blessings flow!" But the truth is that we are better at singing those words than living them.

So what about the grateful one who "gets it"? How is it that he responds when the others do not? We can only surmise, but it seems fair to say that somehow this person is moved with gratitude because he sees the situation rightly; he sees the magnitude of the gift and the goodness of God at the root of it. Perhaps Luke is hoping we will notice another detail that helps explain his unique reaction. The grateful leper is a Samaritan.

Since Jesus is walking along the border of Samaria, it is no surprise that one of the lepers he encounters was Samaritan—but it is a surprise that he is the only one who turns healing into an opportunity to worship. Jesus says incredulously, "Was no one found to return and give praise to God except this foreigner?"—reminding his hearers that those who are at ease in Zion might miss what God is doing in their midst because they simply aren't paying attention. This one, though, is well aware of his "otherness"—he has no sense of entitlement—and as a result he is capable of seeing the sheer gratuity of this miracle. He is able to recognize the gift as a gift simply because he doesn't think he has it coming to him. It is the resulting mix of humility and thankfulness that Jesus so appreciates.

At first glance, this story seems straightforward. We might be tempted to boil its meaning down to a maxim, "God loves an attitude of gratitude," or we might decide to extract from it an action item for our to-do lists: be grateful. But if we really contemplate the Samaritan leper's example, we realize that any of those responses would fall far short of the real depth of this encounter with Jesus. The message of this story is not the kind one finds in self-improvement literature; it does not simply encourage us to develop more pious manners toward God by saying thanks more often. No, in this story we can see something far deeper—we can see the roots of Christian gratitude within a profound awareness of God's grace. If we really understand who we are and what God has done for us, if we comprehend to the core of our being that every breath and even existence itself, is a gift, then how can we do anything but join the Samaritan leper at the feet of Jesus, overcome with gratitude? (Cameron H. Jorgenson)

Worship Aids

Call to Worship: (Based on Psalm 118)
"This is the day that the Lord has made." Ps. 118:24
Praise God from whom all blessings flow!
"Let us rejoice and be glad." Ps. 118:24
Praise God from whom all blessings flow!
"You are my God, and I will give thanks to you." Ps. 118:28
All: Praise God from whom all blessings flow!

Prayer of Confession
Our God, you have given us so many good gifts for which we ought to be grateful. But too often we are too busy, too distracted, too caught up with other things, and we forget to give you the thanks you are due. Today, may we be mindful. Give us eyes to see the enormity of your grace. Give us hearts ready to respond with true gratitude. Amen.

Words of Assurance
When we turn and run back to God in gratitude, be assured that God will already have forgiven us and stand ready to embrace us in new life.

Benediction
Go forth with glad and thankful hearts! Go in the peace of Christ who has given you every good and perfect gift. Amen. (Cameron H. Jorgenson)

NOVEMBER 11, 2012

❧❧❧

Twenty-fourth Sunday after Pentecost

Readings: 1 Kings 17:8-16; Psalm 146; Hebrews 9:24-28;
Mark 12:38-44

Emptying the Vessels

1 Kings 17:8-16

We often hear today about two groups of people—the haves and have-nots. Mostly we identify with the haves. The majority of us have plenty to eat, a roof over our heads, and shoes on our feet. Even when we look at the elite in society and begin to see what we do not have, it does not take us too long to realize that we still have abundance when compared to many people throughout the world.

Sometimes pride creeps in. We take pride in the fact that we have worked hard for our place on the socioeconomic ladder. We have worked hard, and we deserve all that we have. When we see a beggar on the street, we may feel more pity than compassion. As we offer a few coins or even a dollar bill, we may become frustrated, even angry, if the person says, "I'm hurting here. Can't you spare some more?"

1 Kings 17:8-16 is a story of haves and have-nots. We were introduced to Elijah in the first verses of chapter 8. It is a time of drought. Elijah has been living off of the land in a unique way—fed by ravens and drinking water from the wadi—through no sweat of his brow or work of his hands. When the wadi dries up, Elijah moves on at God's command and approaches a widow gathering sticks. He asks her for a drink of water, and before she even gets to the water, Elijah puts in another request, "Bring me a bite to eat." He does not say "please" or "thank you" (see vv. 10-11).

Let's think about this. If this was a story from our lives, and we were the widow, how would we respond? What would we say? Is it any surprise that the woman says, "I have no food prepared. Times are hard. I don't

342

have anything to spare. I'm going to fix what I have for myself and my son that we may have one last meal and die." (see v. 12).

Is the widow one of the haves or one of the have-nots? She has very little, but Elijah has even less and is dependent on her generosity. He urges her to fix a little cake for him before she makes something for herself. He even tells her that the Lord of Israel has said that the jar of meal and the jug of oil will not be empty until the day that the Lord sends rain on the earth. She does as he says, and all that he promises comes true.

We say that we put our trust in God. We pray, "Thank you, Lord, for our daily bread." But how many of us truly live each day? Do we have the faith of this widow? Do we have the faith of this widow to give our sustenance away? Do we have the faith of Elijah to trust God to provide?

We may overlook the fact that, according to verse 9, the Lord God commanded the widow to feed Elijah. It is also interesting to note that the widow has referred to God as Elijah's God, "As the LORD your God lives…" (v. 12). When the widow steps out in faith and gives food to Elijah, she is not a professed God follower. Yet the Lord God has commanded her to do something, and she does it. The Lord God commanded Elijah to go, and he went.

Do we have the kind of faith that, when God says, "Go," we go; the kind of faith that, when God says "Give," we give? If we don't, why not?

Perhaps we are selfish. Perhaps we believe that we deserve what we have. We don't see our food and shelter and clothing as gifts from God's hands. The Israelites were surrounded by people who worshiped the gods of Baal. The historians who recorded this story of Elijah are trying to help the people of Israel remember that God is in control. No other gods are in control. As hard as we may try to believe it, we are not in control. God is the great provider.

In my first year of seminary, I had the opportunity to learn about "mendicant spirituality." As a Baptist, I had never heard of mendicant spirituality, nor did I know much about the Franciscans and Dominicans. These orders live a life of simplicity and poverty of the spirit. They are beggars, fully depending on the generosity of others. They choose this lifestyle to empty themselves so they can be free to be more like Christ.

I don't know about you, but I can be full of myself. We need to learn to empty ourselves of the desire to have more and of the need to control. Only when we empty ourselves—just as the widow and Elijah did—will our cup overflow. We empty ourselves and stand with our hands open in need of God's grace and provision. We demonstrate our dependence on

God by letting go, moving, and giving all of what we have. We show that the Lord our God is sovereign by living out our faith. (Jessica Williams)

Lectionary Commentary

Hebrews 9:24-28

The writer of Hebrews is explaining how Jesus as high priest surpasses the tradition of high priests making sacrifices for the sins of the people. We do not need to wait for the high priests to make sacrifice on our behalf, day after day and year after year. Jesus' act of sacrificial love covers all, once and for all. We can live a life of peace and assurance knowing that Jesus' sacrifice covers all of our sins. We can live a peace-filled life knowing that Jesus, the Son of God who walked on this earth in perfection, has already appealed to God on our behalf.

Mark 12:38-44

Who are we in this familiar story, usually called the parable of the "widow's mite"? Are we the scribes (the rich people) or the widow? As human beings, it seems so natural for us to want positions of influence and prestige. Many of us want to be like the scribes, who walk around in their long robes and enjoy their prominence in society. We want the best seat. We crave attention.

But Jesus says "Beware!" Jesus warns that those who are motivated by selfish desires and social position will receive the greater condemnation. Why? Their motives are not pure, and they have taken advantage of the weak to get to their places of honor. What are our motives?

Jesus continues his teaching as he observes the crowd depositing their money into the treasury. The rich people give large sums, but Jesus commends the widow who gives nothing but two coins. She has given all that she has, not just her extra. What are we giving to Jesus, our leftovers or our all? (Jessica Williams)

Worship Aids

Invocation

Oh God, our Lord and our Provider, we ask you to meet us here. We have had a busy week, but as we pause in this moment, we remember that all of our energy comes from you. Allow this to be a time for us to refocus our hopes and desires. Let us praise you, for you are God! Amen.

Prayer of Confession

Lord, forgive us. We allow the world around us to influence our ambitions and our motives. Forgive us when we look to anything else but you as our God. Help us to empty ourselves, so we can be filled with your love and your presence. May we reflect you, God, in all that we do. Amen.

Words of Assurance

God waits in hope; God forgives; God fills us with new life. Thanks be to God. Amen.

Benediction

As we leave this fellowship, remember that the God who commanded Elijah to go and the widow to share continues to call. Know that God, the provider, will not take you into a situation where provisions have not been made. Now, go and live out your faith in the Lord God. (Jessica Williams)

The Deepest Thanks

Second in a Series of Four on Relearning Christian Gratitude

Luke 7:36-50

Dinner parties are full of potentially awkward situations. There's always the chance that somebody's bowl of soup will end up in a lap. Someone might misread the invitation and show up a day early, while you are still cleaning the house. Your scandalous neighbor might show up and start massaging your guest of honor's feet with perfumed oil. You never know what might happen at a dinner party, and that last catastrophic scenario is exactly what happens when Simon the Pharisee opens his home to Jesus.

You see, Simon is respectable; the woman is not. Simon is a pillar of the community; she is the talk of the town. Simon is the host; she is not even on the guest list. Nevertheless, having heard that Jesus was in town, she has a brilliant idea. She grabs her best perfumed oil and sneaks into the party, hoping against hope that she will have the opportunity to do some act of kindness for Jesus, perhaps anoint his head with oil, or at least give him a gift. Discretely, she makes her way to the place where Jesus reclines at the table. She stands behind him with the servants, hoping to hear him speak those words of life that have so stirred her heart. Perhaps, if she is honest, she even hopes that Jesus will take that self-righteous Simon down a notch.

As she attempts to listen without being noticed, she sees his feet. It is odd that they are still dirty from the day's journey; evidently no one washed them when Jesus arrived. Indignant, she wonders how Simon could have this great teacher under his roof and yet not extend the most basic hospitality to him. Perhaps this dinner is Simon's subtle way of interrogating Jesus, some attempt to figure out if he is a threat to the status quo. She wonders, "Is Jesus being set up?"

But again her gaze is drawn to Jesus' feet. She is transfixed. That dusty pair of feet have walked countless miles to deliver the message that the kingdom of God is at hand. Jesus reminds her of John the Baptist. They preach the same powerful message of repentance, but there is something different about Jesus, something different between the messenger and the message. She continues to stare, and the words of the prophet Isaiah run through her mind, "How beautiful upon the mountains / are the feet of the messenger who announces peace, / who brings good news, / who announces salvation" (Isaiah 52:7).

Before she is fully aware of what she is doing, she is doubled over Jesus' feet, weeping. Her tears flow freely. They are tears of anger at the rude reception Jesus has received at the hands of his ungracious host; they are tears of gratitude, because Jesus has given her a reason to live again; they are tears of compassion; she has been on the receiving end of Simon's judgment and knows how unpleasant it can be. Her weeping has left little streams on Jesus' feet, and without a second thought, she lets down her hair and begins to dry his feet with it.

She is vaguely aware of the stir she is causing, but she stays her course, if only to teach Simon a lesson on how a guest is to be received. Then she takes out her perfume and does the only thing she can think to do; she anoints those beautiful, gospel-carrying feet. As she does, she hears Jesus begin to speak, as if to answer a question that hasn't been asked. He tells a story, as he always does, this time about debts. Two debtors—one who owed a little, and another who was in way over her head—were both unable to pay a creditor and were both forgiven. Jesus asks, "Now which of them will love him more" (v. 42)?

She knows the story is about her. As far as sins go, she is a huge debtor, and everyone in there, including Jesus, knows it. The unexpected twist in the story is what the two debtors have in common; neither could pay up. Both had to be forgiven or face financial ruin. Jesus is talking about

Simon too!

She hears Jesus pointedly tell Simon that while he neglected his duties as host, she has welcomed Jesus with love and displays of hospitality. Then he turns to her and says, "Your sins are forgiven.... Your faith has saved you; go in peace."

She does not hear the murmurs of the other guests, grumbling at the audacity of Jesus forgiving sins. Filled with radiant peace, she covers her hair, now matted with road dust and sweet-smelling perfume, and she practically walks on air all the way home.

Her faith—her utter abandonment to the love of Christ, her grateful self-surrender to the source of all being—saves her. She is forever changed. (Cameron H. Jorgenson)

Worship Aids

Call to Worship

God is Spirit.
Those who worship him must worship in spirit and truth (John 4:24).
God is Love.
Those who abide in love abide in God, and God abides in them (1 John 4:16b).
God is gracious and merciful.
God will not turn away his face from you, if you return to him (2 Chronicles 30:9b).
O give thanks to the Lord, for he is good;
All: His steadfast love endures forever (Psalm 107:1).

Prayer of Confession

Lord, we know we owe you a debt of gratitude, but we are slow to pay. Worse yet, paying that debt can seem like a chore rather than a joy. We confess that our hearts need to be transformed by your love that they may freely give thanks. Renew our hearts, O God, that they might overflow with praise and thanks. Amen.

Words of Assurance

In the name of Christ, you are forgiven.
In the name of Christ, you are forgiven.

Benediction

Go in peace, knowing that you have been forgiven. Go forth in love, for those who have been forgiven much, love much! Amen. (Cameron H. Jorgenson)

NOVEMBER 18, 2012

❧❧❧

Twenty-fifth Sunday after Pentecost

Readings: Daniel 12:1-3; Psalm 16; Hebrews 10:11-14, (15-18), 19-25; Mark 13:1-8

Would Knowing the Future Change Anything?

Mark 13:1-8

If you could know the future, would you want to? I am sure that many of us have thought, "If only I knew tomorrow's lottery numbers, then I could be a millionaire." If you knew the future, then you could place a wager on the winner of the World Series or the basketball teams in the Final Four. Sure, it would be nice if you were a gambler to know the future. But it wouldn't really be gambling then, would it?

If you could know the future, not only the good but also the bad, would you want to? Would you want to have foreknowledge of who you were going to marry; if, when, or how many children you were going to have; or how you were going to die?

In our Gospel lesson from Mark 13, we join Jesus at the end of a long and arduous day. He has been debating with the Pharisees, Sadducees, and scribes. The sun is getting lower in the sky, and Jesus emerges from the temple with a group of his disciples. As they are walking, one of the disciples turns around, blocks the sun with his hand, taps Jesus on the shoulder, and motions for him to look at the temple. Pointing to the massive structure, the disciple says, "What large stones and what large buildings" (v. 1)! It's as if this disciple is asking Jesus to marvel at the magnitude of the temple. The stones were huge; many were the size of half of a semi-truck trailer. But the disciple is talking to Jesus. Would Jesus really be amazed by a bunch of stacked rocks? Before we scold the disciple too much, consider how often we find comfort in human accomplishments. Jesus replies to the astonished disciple, "Sure, I see it, but to tell you the truth, it will all crumble." There is a short pause, and the disciple's face drops. Finally, the two continue on their walk with the rest of the group.

Later, Jesus and the disciples cross over to the Mount of Olives, which faces the temple. Peter, Andrew, James, and John, the inner circle, are huddled up discussing the earlier statement. They begin to argue back and forth like a bunch of school boys. One of them eventually says, "Well, let's just go and ask him." The disciples rush over to Jesus and ask two questions. They not only want to know when the temple will crumble but also what signs will signal the event.

When is important to us. *When* allows us to plan and gives us a sense of control. *Signs* give us warning that our time is almost up. *Signs* are like the light that appears on my dashboard right before I run out of gas. I know that the tank will go only so far, but this light reminds me that the end is near. I cannot put things off any longer. Unfortunately, few things give us a fresh start like a tank full of gas.

Characteristically, Jesus does not give the disciples the answer they are looking for. Instead, he tells them to beware of false prophets and false signs. There will be wars, divided kingdoms, earthquakes, and famines, but these are not the signs to look for. Even today, some people associate wars and natural disasters with eschatological and apocalyptic times. According to some, the world as we know it will end this year.

I believe Jesus is simply telling the disciples, "You will hear a lot of bad stuff, but take courage and stay the course." Jesus knows the struggles that he and his disciples will face. Jesus knows that his struggles will lead him to the cross. Jesus knows that when the disciples accepted their call to follow him, he was signing their death warrants. Like a ship headed straight into a hurricane, Jesus calls his disciples to stay on track and keep the course. He doesn't promise that everything will be OK.

If you could know the future, would you want to? It's an interesting question to ask, but pointless. Jesus never discloses when the temple will be destroyed; he only gives examples of false signs. By warning the disciples of false signs, he was encouraging them to not give up or look for easy answers.

We cannot know the future. Jesus simply calls us to follow him. Jesus has called you and me to live as he did, regardless of life's circumstances. When false prophets appear, be close enough to God and Christ to know the difference. When there is war, find ways to make peace. When nations rise against nations, strive for reconciliation over revenge. During earthquakes and other natural disasters, help to heal and rebuild. During times of famine, help feed.

Jesus was right. These signs might be only the beginning of birth pangs, but the call to discipleship is still the same. All the foreknowledge in the world means nothing without strength and courage. As you go through life, walk in faith and have courage to stay the course. (Darren Williams)

Lectionary Commentary

Daniel 12:1-3

This short passage is packed full of theological implications. At the heart of the matter is the question of salvation. Michael is the protector and "everyone who is found written in the book" will be rescued (v. 1). For the original hearers and today's listeners, the message is a sign of hope and not condemnation. As a youth, I always heard that there was nothing I could to do for God to love me more and nothing I could do to make God love me less. We live in a culture, however, where people are continually judged by their actions. People today have a hard time believing that God's love never changes. I feared not making the cut or not being good enough to make the list. Then I realized something. If God is as amazing as I believe God to be, then my Creator and Sustainer knows me and everyone else well enough that no list is necessary.

Hebrews 10:11-14, (15-18), 19-25

The book of Hebrews is a reminder of hope. We are to approach God with confidence and "hold fast to the confession of our hope without wavering, for he who has promised is faithful" (v. 23). The early Christian community faced struggles that we can only faintly comprehend. Few of us face persecution or martyrdom for being Christian. Yet we often find it difficult to live out our faith to our full potential. As we read Hebrews 10, we should be encouraged to approach God in faith and worship, hold fast to our public confession of hope, and consider how we can help others in love. This is a threefold reminder of what it means to be Christian. We would do well to remember these on a daily basis. (Darren Williams)

Worship Aids

Invocation

All knowing God, we live in a world uncertain of what the day might bring. We fear the things we can't plan and try to protect ourselves from things too massive to stop. Give us faith to combat our fears and guidance to direct our paths. Amen.

Prayer of Confession

God, you have called us to follow you,
but we have found many other paths much easier to walk.
We confess our wandering and disobedience to you.
God, when you have told us to marvel at acts of mercy and grace,
we have been too busy taking pleasure in our own feats and
    accomplishments.
We confess our pride to you.
All: Forgive us, O Lord, and give us strength to follow you.

Words of Assurance

Hear the good news! God waits; God forgives; God strengthens.
Thanks be to God.

Benediction

Now may the God who called you give you faith enough to follow, courage enough to care, hope enough to hang on, and stamina enough to stay the course. You have been called. Go in peace and serve the Lord. (Darren Williams)

What Gratitude Does

Third in a Series of Four on Relearning Christian Gratitude

Luke 9:10-17

Jesus, knowing that it was time for the disciples to begin doing the work of the kingdom of God instead of simply hearing him teach about it, had sent his twelve most trusted disciples out on mission, full of the power of God. The results were tremendous. Lives were changed and great good was done. Now, it was time for a retreat. It was time to regroup, to recharge, and to rejoice for all that God was doing among them. So Jesus takes them somewhere near the town of Bethsaida to get away for a bit.

But the crowds won't have it. A rumor of Jesus' whereabouts is leaked, and soon the crowd gathers. It was quite a crowd, by any standard; five-thousand men were there, not to mention the uncounted women and children. As you might imagine, Jesus welcomes them. He speaks to them, encourages them, tells them all about the kingdom of God, and even heals anyone who needs it. Jesus welcomes the unexpected guests as if they are long lost friends.

Late in the afternoon, however, the disciples suggest that Jesus send them away to find food and lodging in the surrounding towns because there isn't much near their remote, improvised retreat center—certainly not enough to accommodate such a large mob of people. They have a point; the size of the crowd poses a real logistical problem. What do you do when your small picnic with friends has become a rock concert with thousands in attendance? I can't help but wonder, though, if there is a bit of resentment among the disciples toward all of these party crashers. These strangers, after all, are encroaching on their leadership summit, their "Kingdom-building Seminar," their reward of quality time with Jesus after a job well done. I can't help but hear within their question another, unstated one: "Jesus, can't you do something about all these needy people? We're trying to learn about your kingdom!"

But Jesus has something else in mind. They don't need another sermon. They don't need another motivational speech. They don't even need to go and preach a sermon on their own. What they need is to see the kingdom in action. So Jesus provocatively tells the disciples, "You give them something to eat." They reply, "We have no more than five loaves and two fish..." (v. 13). No more than. Only. Those are telling words, ones that Jesus would confound.

Jesus instructs the disciples to seat the crowd so its members will be easier to serve. He takes the loaves and fish, and "he looked up to heaven, and blessed and broke them, and gave them to the disciples to set before the crowd" (v. 16). It seems so simple to watch Jesus do it. Without fanfare, Jesus looks to heaven, and with a glad and sincere heart, he says thanks. On that day, everyone in the crowd eats their fill, leaving twelve baskets of food to spare.

With two millennia between now and then, we might be tempted to fault the disciples for their impatience and their "lack of faith." But if we put ourselves in their shoes, it is tough to throw stones. Who could have seen that miracle coming? Who would have guessed that so little could have fed so many?

There is something more at stake here than the issue of whether or not we believe that Jesus can do miracles. This story sheds light on how we approach our lives, especially in times of crisis. When the disciples faced the challenge of feeding thousands of hungry people, their immediate reaction was to turn them away to fend for themselves. They were so pre-occupied with the enormity of what they didn't have that they missed the significance of what was already in their hands. Jesus, taking the same modest lunch, thanked God for what he already had—and for what he would soon be given—and he began to give it away.

When we are consumed with the idea of scarcity, we begin to cling to the little we have in case it too suddenly disappears. But that is not the way of Jesus. Instead, Jesus looks to heaven and gives thanks, turning loose what he has, knowing that more will be given. In the space opened up by that thankful self-giving—the utter opposite of anxious hoarding—God is able to work.

Here we see something interesting in the life and work of Christ. We see that gratitude is far more than an internal feeling of thanks. It is more than an acknowledgment of kindnesses done to us by God or by others. Gratitude is a radical posture of openness to God and to others, based on the knowledge that God is a God of plenty. God is a God who provides. God may choose to use us to provide for someone else, and someone else may become God's provision for us. Gratitude is an acknowledgment of the goodness of God that takes us far beyond verbal expressions of thanks. It is something like faith, or hope, or love, because it is bound up in our lives with one another, exploding the myth that life is a game that are I can win only if another loses. Because it recognizes that God is a God of abundance, gratitude makes it possible to love our neighbors as ourselves. (Cameron H. Jorgenson)

Worship Aids

Call to Worship (Psalm 23)

"The Lord is my shepherd;
I shall not want."
God "makes me lie down in green pastures" and "leads me
    beside still waters."
God "restores my soul."
God prepares a table for me "in the presence of my enemies.
**Surely goodness and mercy shall follow me
    all the days of my life."**

Prayer of Confession

Lord, we confess that all too often we hold our lives in a tight grasp. We cling to the temporary as if it were permanent. We cling to what is ours as if it were ours alone. Teach us to love eternal things. Teach us generosity. Let our lives be transformed by gratitude to you, the source of all being. Amen.

Words of Assurance

God knows the longing of our hearts, and God hears our struggles to let go. God is with us. Thanks be to God.

Benediction

May the Lord bless you and keep you; may the Lord be your source and your guide; may the Lord be your peace on this and every day. Amen. (Cameron H. Jorgenson)

NOVEMBER 22, 2012

❧❧❧❧

Thanksgiving

Readings: Joel 2:21-27; Psalm 126; 1 Timothy 2:1-7; Matthew 6:25-33

When We Can Dream

Psalm 126

Are you able to dream for yourself, or are you in a time of wilderness and bondage waiting to be found, freed, and restored? The people of Israel remember when God delivered and restored them, but they find themselves in another difficult situation. They are grieving. They can only remember how it was when they laughed and shouted with joy.

There is something about the last part of verse 1 that is gripping to me: "We were like those who dream." The people of Israel are in such a difficult place in their community that they cannot even imagine dreaming. Have you been there? Have you been in the place where things are so bleak that it is hard to imagine a better day? Are you there today?

I can recall a span of several years when I disallowed dreams about my future as a minister. In 1998, I was a first-semester freshman when I first sensed God calling me into ministry. I applied to be a summer missionary with the North Carolina Baptist Convention. I looked over the opportunities and knew that I wanted to apply to be a youth and children's minister. Although several people told me that the convention would probably not place a freshman in that role and I would probably have to serve as a camp counselor, I was placed in a church in the middle of the state.

Within moments of being commissioned and heading out for my summer of ministry, I told my parents and my campus minister that I just could not do it. I was afraid of the unknown. I left the head person of summer missions the task of telling the church that they would not have a youth and children's minister for the summer. Although I thought I would feel relieved, I felt miserable. I had disappointed so many people.

For the next five years, I pushed the thought of going into ministry to the back of my head. I had my chance, and I blew it. God wouldn't count on me again. I had lost the ability to dream for myself. One could say that I had exiled myself.

But God didn't stop dreaming. God did not give up. Nine years later, after a few years as a public school teacher, I had the opportunity to be a campus ministry intern for the Cooperative Baptist Fellowship collegiate ministry at Clemson University. This time, I did not allow the opportunity to pass me by. As I prepared my last sermon as an intern and reviewed my year of ministry, I felt completely restored for the first time since the summer of 1998. I realized that although I sometimes act from a lack of faith, God is always faithful. I was able to allow myself to dream of God's ministry through me.

God was not the one suppressing my calling. I was. I inflicted my own pain. Of course, there are situations in which our pain is caused by others, by systems, by substances, by diseases, and by loss. We don't know exactly what the people of Israel were going through when Psalm 126 was written, just as I may not know what is causing heartache or despair that you may be encountering now. What we do know is that this psalm is a lament; the people of God were crying out. Know that you can cry out to God. Know that God continues to dream for your life, even when you can't.

Although we can hear the pain in the first verses of this song, we hear words of hope as the psalm grows to a close. "Those who sow in tears / reap with shouts of joy. / Those who go out weeping, / bearing the seed for sowing, / shall come home with shouts of joy, / carrying their sheaves" (vv. 5-6). Friends, even in our despair, we can be filled with hope that God listens to our cries, and we will be restored. We will laugh again, and we will again shout with joy, for the Lord God continues to do great things. (Jessica Williams)

Lectionary Commentary

Joel 2:21-27

In the verses preceding our text, we have the account of the plague of locusts, which was seen as divine punishment. But just as a parent disciplines children out of love, God does not stopped loving God's people.

Out of love, God calls the people to repentance. God continues to show love by promising deliverance. God is just and wants to repay the people for the years of locusts. God promises provisions of plenty to the point that the threshing floors will be full and the vats will overflow.

God is loving and merciful. Because we are God's people, we do not need to be afraid. God has promised good to God's children. We can be glad and rejoice, for the Lord has done great things and continues to do great things!

1 Timothy 2:1-7

If Christ died for all, and we are to be like Christ, then should we not pray for all? The writer of 1 Timothy gives the instructions to offer supplications, prayers, intercessions, and thanksgivings for everyone. There are different types of prayer that we can offer on the behalf of others. There is the prayer of supplication, which is the prayer that asks for God's help. There is the prayer of thanksgiving, and we give God thanks for the people in our lives and for abundance.

In seminary, my spiritual formations professor asked our class to think of intercessory prayer as taking others before Jesus and into his presence. When we take others into the presence of Jesus, our attitudes about those individuals are changed. Bitterness is replaced with sweetness. Disdain is replaced with deference. Hate is replaced with love. Perhaps this is why Jesus instructed his disciples to pray for those who persecute us and for our enemies.

Matthew 6:25-33

We should remember the context of this teaching from the Sermon on the Mount. Jesus' closest disciples are among the students for this teaching. The disciples abandoned their vocations to be with Jesus full-time, so they knew what it is like to depend on local hospitality for basic needs. During Jesus' day, the poor did not sow or gather, so how did they get by? They were dependent on wages as day laborers and on charity.

Jesus tells the poor, do not worry. God provides. You are precious in God's sight. Instead of God showering manna from heaven as God did with the Israelites, Jesus is saying that God will provide through human instruments. What about today? Does God provide for the hungry? Perhaps God has provided, but we, who have plenty to the point of waste, are just not sharing! (Jessica Williams)

Worship Aids

Call to Worship

We are people who have suffered hurts.
We remember when we were filled with laughter.
We are people who continue in despair.
We know that we will shout with joy.
All: For you, O Lord, have done great things!

Pastoral Prayer

Restoring God, we come as people with heartaches. We lift up our family, our neighbors, our leaders, those we don't even know, and ourselves. Hear our cries, O Lord. Bring restoration. Bring renewal. May those who weep now be with filled with laughter and joy. Amen.

Words of Assurance

When the people of Israel cried out, God heard their cries. When you, as the people of God, cry out, God hears your cries. Be assured that your weeping will be replaced with laughter, because the Lord our God restores! (Jessica Williams)

Giving Thanks around the Table

Fourth in a Series of Four on Relearning Christian Gratitude

Luke 22:14-20

Perhaps Thanksgiving is one American holiday that Jesus would have thoroughly enjoyed. Celebration with family and friends gathered around a table full of great food; those are some of the things that Jesus loved most!

We shouldn't underestimate the role of the table in Jesus' life. Countless times throughout Christ's story we see him at a table full of people, sharing life and talking about the kingdom of God. The sinful woman anointed Jesus during a dinner party thrown by Simon the Pharisee. The loaves and fish provided a meal for Jesus and more than 5,000 of his "closest friends." In today's passage, we see that Jesus chose to spend some of his last moments around the table with his disciples, sharing one last Passover meal before heading out to pray for the strength to endure the cross.

It was at this last supper that Jesus took bread and wine and radically reinterpreted them to be signs of the way he would give himself over entirely to God. The night before he died, Jesus said of the bread, "This is my body, which is given for you. Do this in remembrance of me" (v. 19), and of the wine he said, "This cup that is poured out for you is the new covenant in my blood" (v. 20). These are serious words—solemn declarations of holy intent. Think of how meaningful it is that just before offering the bread and the wine—his body and blood—he pauses first to say thanks.

The early church did not miss the significance of that prayer of thanks. In fact, the church began to call this meal of bread and wine simply, *Eucharist*, taken from the Greek term for "thanks." They were essentially saying if you want to capture the meaning of this act in a single word, it would have to be *thanksgiving*. Isn't that something? Every time we gather around this table as the family of God, the body of Christ, we are celebrating the great thanksgiving meal of the church, just as it has been done since the beginning.

But one might wonder, with his own death is looming, why does Christ give thanks? It is a puzzle. Who among us, knowing that such suffering was just around the corner, could say "thanks be to God" as we hand ourselves over to God as a gift? It is remarkable and so appropriate. Even in such a difficult situation, Jesus rightly understands the gratuity of life. He knows that each day, each breath, is a gift worthy of celebrating. Since he understands the love and grace by which that gift is given, he is able to respond by giving over his life as a gift in return. Jesus held his life with a loose grasp rather than anxiously clinging to it as a personal possession. His self-dedication to the purpose of God was his great act of thanksgiving.

We approach the table on slightly different terms. We too come in the spirit of thanksgiving, but we approach the table with the sort of gratitude that is appropriate of a guest. Hosts are thankful for the presence of their guests and for God's blessing that enables them to feed those around their table; guests are thankful to be there and to receive all that is set before them. As recipients of so many things freely given—a meal, a time of fellowship, even the gift of being welcomed to the table—being a true guest involves the practice of the disciplines of graciousness and thankfulness. This is no easy task. It is difficult to receive a great gift.

Imagine a young couple, soon to be wed. The invitations go out, wedding plans are made, and of course, the community gathers to shower the couple with wedding gifts with which they are to start their life together.

These days this shower is preceded by a new pre-marital ritual: wielding the scanning gun at various retailers to build the bridal registry, choosing dishes and dishtowels, sheets and shower curtains. While it is thrilling to be given the chance to identify any- and everything one could possibly want to receive, it is also a humbling experience. After opening a mountain of gifts at a shower, a couple may wonder, "Why did we ask for all of this stuff? Can we actually accept all of this? It is all just too much! If only we were rich, we wouldn't have to burden anyone with all of this!"

But, of course, these are burdens that the community gladly bears. Moments like these teach us an inescapable truth: whether the task is setting up house or raising a child, "it takes a village." Our illusions of independence are just that—illusions. We cannot make it on our own. There is an inescapable "given" in our lives that our existence is made possible only by the generosity of others.

Just as a young couple begins their journey together immensely indebted to the community that has nurtured them, we too are overwhelmed by the immensity of the gift offered to us as we approach this table. Questions of humility are demanded: can we accept so rich a gift as Christ's gift of himself? Will we humble ourselves enough to admit that we are in need? Can we admit to ourselves and to others that we must return to the source of all being to find newness of life?

If we do come with Jesus to the table, we will discover another surprising twist; somehow, when we share in Christ's body around this table, we become his body in the world. As a result we find that, just like Jesus, we too begin to offer ourselves as living sacrifices, giving ourselves to God and to others as a gift. We find ourselves bringing others to the table, inviting them to share in the same bread of life that has nourished us. Once we have learned the "table manners" that come from eating with Jesus, we find we are unavoidably drawn into the same habits of giving and receiving, of welcoming people to the table, and thinking together about the kingdom of God.

When we are fed at this table—participating in the Eucharist, the great thanksgiving of the people of God—how much better prepared are we for the other Thanksgiving feasts we encounter, even ones with candied yams and cranberry sauce? This is because with Christ we learn to count every moment as precious. Alongside him we learn to love those gathered around the table with us. We learn from the Master what it means to give thanks with all that we have and all that we are. Thanks be to God!
(Cameron H. Jorgenson)

Worship Aids

Call to Worship (1 Corinthians 10:17)

"Because there is one bread,
We who are many are one body,
All: For we all partake of the one bread."

Prayer of Confession

Lord, we are not worthy to sit at the table with you, and yet you welcome us, and this humbles us still more. You give yourself fully to us here; in return may we offer up our lives, our bodies, as living sacrifices. In light of your love and self-giving, this is our reasonable act of worship. May we be acceptable in your sight. Amen.

Words of Assurance

The good news is that while we are not worthy, we are welcome at the table of Christ. Thanks be to God!

Benediction

Go with hearts full of joy and gratitude, sharing the love given to you at this table with all who have need of it. Amen. (Cameron H. Jorgenson)

NOVEMBER 25, 2012

❧❧❧

Reign of Christ / Christ the King Sunday

Readings: Daniel 7:9-10, 13-14; Psalm 93; Revelation 1:4b-8;
John 18:33-37

King of Kings Forever and Ever

John 18:33-37

The last week of Jesus' life was an occasion of high drama, and its intensity increased exponentially each day. The days of that last week are so much of one fabric that it is difficult to separate one day from the next or to isolate one event from that which preceded or followed it.

It began with Jesus' triumphant entry into Jerusalem on Palm Sunday, when the masses would have crowned him king. But their concept of kingship was quite different from the kind of king Jesus came to be. Their history was permeated with hopes and dreams of a messiah who would bring them political salvation. They wanted a messiah-king who would deliver them from the political tyranny of Rome and restore the nation to the splendor and glory their forebears had known in the days of King David. Jesus had many characteristics that led them to believe he was that long-awaited savior. But he was king of a different domain, and they could never quite grasp why he could not be who they wanted him to be.

The power and influence of Jesus had become a serious threat to the religious leaders because they feared that he would upset the delicate balance of power that existed between the Jews and the Romans who occupied their country. This fear led to the arrest, trial, and execution of Jesus.

In the Gospel of John, the trial of Jesus before Pontius Pilate is a central feature in the larger drama. Once again the idea of Jesus as king takes center stage. The Gospel lesson for today takes us to the very heart of the matter.

Jesus has been hastily tried and convicted as a blasphemer by the Jewish court. This is a crime punishable by death, but under Roman rule the Jews were not permitted to carry out a death sentence, which in Jewish jurisprudence would have been death by stoning. They need the Roman procurator, Pontius Pilate, to affirm their sentence and carry out the execution.

They take Jesus to Pilate, but they will not enter lest they defile themselves and be unable to eat the Passover. (John is the only Gospel in which the trial of Jesus is described as taking place before the Passover meal.) Pilate begins to play political games with Jesus' accusers. He tells them to handle the case under Jewish law. They remind him that they can try Jesus, but they cannot carry out the death sentence. Thus begins the trial of Jesus before Pilate.

Pilate wants nothing to do with what he considers a religious matter, but the religious establishment maneuvers Pilate into taking jurisdiction. The religious leaders shift from the accusation of blasphemy to a charge of treason. Pilate summons Jesus into his headquarters to question him privately. He plunges directly into his main concern and asks, "Are you the king of the Jews?" Jesus parries the question with a question: "Do you ask this on your own, or did others tell you about me?" This matter is not going the way Pilate thought it should. You can almost hear Pilate snarl in reply: "I am not a Jew, am I? Your own nation and chief priest have handed you over to me. What have you done" (vv. 33-35)?

How should Jesus reply? Should he deny who he knew himself to be and try to save his own life, or should Jesus acknowledge his identity, knowing that it will be misconstrued by Pilate? Earlier in the week, the masses, including his disciples, had tried to make him into a king and political leader. Jesus had dealt with that situation by neither denying nor affirming their expectations. Now Pilate wants to know if he is the king of the Jews. What to do?

Jesus decides to identify the nature of his kingship, knowing full well Pilate will not understand. He begins by identifying the source of his kingship, but he does not describe any geographical realm. There is no doubt that Pilate fails to see this distinction. Jesus says: "My kingdom is not from this world. If my kingdom were from this world, my followers would be fighting to keep me from being handed over to the Jews. But as it is, my kingdom is not from here." Once again, you can hear the 'aha' in Pilate's response: "So you are a king?" Jesus answers: "You say that I am a king. . . . For this I was born, and for this I came into the world, to testify to the truth. Everyone who belongs to the truth listens to my voice." Jesus makes his identity clear. He is a king, but more than a king of some geographical realm. Jesus is the king of the world and beyond this world. If that assertion means anything to Pilate, it is not reflected in his question: "What is truth" (vv. 36-38)? Given the setting and the profound nature of Jesus' reply, Pilate's question is almost a *non sequitur*.

This story must not stop here. Pilate takes Jesus out to the accusers and makes four more distinct efforts to get Jesus out of his court. He says there is no case against him. He offers to release Jesus under the aegis of the Jewish custom of releasing someone at the Passover. The Jews ask that he release Barabbas, a bandit, instead of Jesus. Pilate then has Jesus flogged, and the soldiers dress him in purple and place a crown of thorns on his head. Thinking the Jews will have mercy on this pitiful, beaten and humiliated person, Pilate once again pronounces that there is no case against Jesus. The bloodthirsty Jewish leaders cry all the more for him to be crucified. All other attempts to mollify them are met by accusations against Pilate that if he releases this individual then he was no friend of the emperor. Pilate seems to delight in presenting Jesus to the Jews as "your King" (9:14)! This infuriates the Jews so much they finally speak the unthinkable words: "We have no king but the emperor" (v. 15). For John, this statement is pure irony.

Defeated in his efforts to free Jesus and get him out of his court, Pilate hands him over to be crucified. In doing this, he would have pronounced these words: "*Ibis ad crucem*" ("You will go to the cross").

Doubtless Pilate had uttered those words many times before, and no doubt, he would utter them many more before he was recalled to Rome to fade into obscurity. Yet never before or since have those words had a more profound influence on human history than when spoken to Jesus.

Perhaps Pilate thought he was putting a pitiful, radical Jew out of his misery, but instead he turned history upside down and crowned a new kind of king, who is King of kings forever and ever and ever, world without end. Amen. (Thomas Lane Butts)

Lectionary Commentary

Daniel 7:9-10, 13-14

Israel has suffered defeat, humiliation, and exile. When a people (or a person) has been stripped of the human means of resistance, when it is clear there are no conventional weapons with which to fight back, the mind devises resolutions to powerlessness. The answer to Israel's dilemma is not earthly power but trust in a divine solution. Apocalyptic literature is the source of hope for the hopeless. Daniel dreamed a solution. While he does not understand all that he sees in his "night visions" (v. 13), it is clear that help is at hand. He describes the powerful and heavenly appearance of "the Ancient One" (v. 13). When the court is seated, the books are opened. Judgment time!

As his vision continues, someone else, like a human, comes down from the clouds and is presented to "the Ancient One." This second one is given dominion, glory, and kingship. He is empowered permanently. "His dominion is an everlasting dominion that shall not pass away and his kingship is one that shall never be destroyed" (v. 14). This is messianic! Sounds like King Jesus. Everlasting and unshakable. Help is here.

Revelation 1:4b-8

John of Patmos is given a message to deliver to the seven churches in Asia. His message has the weight of divine authority. It is from God and graced with the testimony of Jesus Christ. This is Christian apocalypticism, but the same genre of literature as Old Testament apocalypticism. John uses the same form and pictures of the return as are used in Daniel 7. Old Testament apocalypticism is quoted or alluded to throughout Revelation. John is "marinated" in the Old Testament. It is natural that the language and form of what was sacred text to John should become the language and form for explaining the Christian message of hope and help.

The situation of Israel in the day of Daniel was very much like the predicament of Christians in the life and time of John. John was himself a victim of the enemies of Christianity. He was exiled to the Isle of Patmos, where he was doing "hard time" as a prisoner. He had witnessed the cruelty of Rome visited on a helpless people. When there was no earthly help, John pictured the power of the returning Messiah. "He is coming with the clouds. Every eye will see him, even those who pierced him; and on his account all the tribes of the earth will wail" (Revelation 1:7). Christians did not seem to have a chance in this world. They would be destroyed. But the enemy failed to factor God into the equation of reality. They had unwittingly pitted themselves against the Great God Almighty, the Alpha and the Omega—"He who is and who was, and who is to come" (Revelation 1:8b). Help is on the way! (Thomas Lane Butts)

Worship Aids

Invocation

Almighty God, father and mother of us all, we invoke your blessing on this worship occasion. We bring sins to be forgiven. We bring wounds to be healed. We have holes in our hearts. There is no other place to which we can go for the kind of help we need. So here we are. Touch our lives today. Amen.

Prayer of Confession

Dear God, we have old sins we have never confessed to you, and some sins we have never admitted even to ourselves. We have sins we have confessed and for which we have been forgiven, but we have relapsed and repeated those sins. We have sins in which we have participated as a community, and we cannot bring ourselves to say, "We have sinned." Hear our confession, O Lord; restore us and give us the resolve to go and sin no more. Amen.

Words of Assurance

God hears even the groaning in our secret hearts. God hears and forgives. Thanks be to God.

Benediction

I bless you today in the name of Jesus and pray that you will encounter no temptation this week that is beyond your power to resist. I pray that you will have dominion over obstacles you will encounter, and that you will find occasions of encouragement and hope and happiness along the way. Amen. (Thomas Lane Butts)

Hope: Watching and Waiting

First in a Series of Four on Advent

Luke 2:22-36

Have you ever had this conversation at your house? Children ask, "Can we go to the zoo again?" You answer, "Why, yes, we'll do that." Then they respond, "Promise?" As parents, we learn early the importance of keeping our promises, especially to our children.

God always keeps promises! What God says God will do, God does. We interpret the Old Testament prophets as God's promise of Christmas, made hundreds of years before the event itself. Isaiah spoke repeatedly of the coming messiah (for example, 7:14; 32:1-4; 53:1-5); Micah foretold the coming of a ruler as well (5:1-5). The Jewish people, whatever else they might have lost, kept alive this promise of a coming King of kings. Few, however, evidenced this in word and deed more than Simeon.

What was it that enabled Simeon to experience Christmas? He never gave up. He was watching and waiting for what the prophets had proclaimed 800 years before. Simeon was confident it would take place as God had promised.

Anticipation, when you think about it, is the heart of religion. Let's face it. To be cut off from your past is debilitating. However, to be cut off from the possibility of a future can be a disaster beyond compare. Without hope, life breaks down and becomes unbearable. Ask anyone who has been told there is no hope. In a world of cynics, the ancient prophet Simeon was an eternal optimist. He stood on tiptoe, waiting, hopeful.

The Scripture tells us he not only waited with expectancy, he waited with integrity. Simeon was "righteous and devout" (v. 25). Have you noticed that those whose lifestyle evidences commitment and dedication are first to "see the light?" To Simeon religion was not a game to play but a life to live. He called God "Lord" and lived the reality of that in his life.

There is another reason Simeon waited in anticipation; he was sensitive to God's leadership. We are told "the Holy Spirit rested on him" (v. 25). It was this Spirit who guided him to the temple. Being attuned to God's leadership, he followed God's direction. Can this be a lesson for all of us? Simeon was content to let God do things in God's way. Although most of Israel was expecting a conquering king on a white horse, Simeon sensed God at work in a poor mother with her baby. He could believe that Jesus was not just a baby to be cradled, but a Savior to be accepted. Most people in Jerusalem refused to see this. Simeon did.

Simeon recognized Jesus as the light of the world. Isaiah wrote, "I will also give thee for a light to the Gentiles, that thou mayest be my salvation unto the end of the earth" (49:6 KJV). There are at least two implications in Simeon's calling Jesus "a light." Jesus fulfilled the prophecy of Isaiah, and his coming prepared a way for the Gentiles.

We live in a dark world that needs a little amplification. The breakup or breakdown of the family is staggering. The use of drugs is appalling. The prevalence of abortion is mind-boggling. The growth of pornography is alarming. The persecution of Christians around the world is startling. The terrorist activity is frightening. Need I say more? We need that light!

We need to anticipate Christmas once again with expectancy, integrity, sensitivity, and insight. Christmas is more than a seasonal observance; it can be a life-changing experience. Our awareness as Christians of the true meaning of Christmas is not a secret to be held but an experience to be shared.

Just as in Simeon's day the majority of the people were not aware of the true meaning of Christmas, so it is in our day as well. If Christmas plays any part in the life of most people, it is within the realm of holiday parties, personal pleasure, the exchange of gifts, or days of vacation. In spite of the fact that the calendar itself notes the birth of Jesus (*anno domine* means "in the year of our Lord"), people who never expected it still do not recognize that God entered human history.

The hostility Herod shows at the birth of our Lord is still expressed by some. The religion of many nations and people remains indifferent to the coming of the Messiah. On the other hand, Mary's and Joseph's complete submission to the miraculous will of God inspires us. The worship of the magi and the adoration of the shepherds are lessons for us. Simeon's fulfilled hope challenges us.

May this Advent season cause us to anticipate the blessing of God among us as we celebrate Christmas and the Savior who made it all possible. (Drew J. Gunnells Jr.)

Worship Aids

Pastoral Prayer ("Come, Thou Long-Expected Jesus" by Charles Wesley)

Come, thou long-expected Jesus,
Born to set thy people free.
From our fears and sins release us,
Let us find our rest in thee.
Israel's strength and consolation,
Hope of all the earth, thou art.
Dear desire of every nation,
Joy of every longing heart.
All: May it be so this day in every heart. Amen.

Invocation

Lord, as we approach this Advent season, grant us sensitivity and appreciation for what you did that night in Bethlehem. May a childlike anticipation permeate this time of the year, and may we be aware of your continuing presence among us. Clear our minds and clean our hearts that we might see thee afresh. Send us a word of comfort and hope. Use this service to that end. In the name of Christ, we pray. Amen.

Benediction

Lord, in the spirit of this Thanksgiving season we express to thee our heartfelt thanks for the unspeakable gift of your Son to each of us who believes. While we look forward to Christmas as an event on the calendar, let us never forget to watch and wait for the return of our Lord, who is our eternal hope. In Jesus' name we pray. Amen. (Drew J. Gunnells Jr.)

DECEMBER 2, 2012

❧❧❧

First Sunday of Advent

Readings: Jeremiah 33:14-36; Psalm 25:1-10; 1 Thessalonians 3:9-13; Luke 21:25-36

Jesus Is Coming; Be Ready

Luke 21:25-36

The concept of the coming of a messiah, an anointed one, permeates the message of the Hebrew prophets. From the time of the fall of the kingdom of Israel, when the nation lost the stature experienced in the reign of David, the prophets spoke increasingly of the coming of a representative of God to restore Israel to its former glory and bring Israel home from exile. The idea of a messiah seemed to grow in intensity in direct proportion to the depth of despair in the nation. While the concept was not uniform in detail, it was somewhat institutional and universally religious. The primary theme of apocalyptic literature was messianic in nature. The concept was not only religious but also political and cultural.

Because the first Christians were Jews steeped in the idea of *messiah*, it was natural that the concept became prominent in early Christianity. Jesus came to be regarded as the Messiah. But Jesus was not the kind of messiah that fit the most popular Jewish model. He did not bring final judgment on the enemies of the Jews or restore the nation to its former glory. He was not a political messiah. His teachings, life, and death left undone so much that was expected of the Anointed One of God.

Jesus altered the general concept to fit a new understanding of the nature of God. He used messianic language and symbolism from the seventh chapter of Daniel, a human-like figure coming on a cloud from heaven and receiving authority from 'the Ancient One.' This same concept was subsequently used in Revelation 1:7.

In the Synoptic Gospels, the Messiah has come in the person of Jesus, but he will come again to finish the work of messiah. His appearance on

371

a cloud will be preceded by signs "in the sun and moon and the stars and on earth distress among nations confused by the roaring of the sea and the waves" (Luke 21:25). When these things begin to happen, get ready. "When you see these things taking place you know that the kingdom of God is near." Then Jesus says: "Truly I tell you, this generation will not pass away until all the things have taken place" (vv. 31-32).

Did the first generation Christian think that the second coming of Jesus would take place in their lifetime? It is clear that many of them did. The Second Coming permeates the letters of Paul. Certain members of the church in Thessalonica took this matter so literally that they quit work and started sponging off other members. Paul was compelled to modify this understanding of the immediacy of the Second Coming by decreeing that those who were unwilling to work should not eat (2 Thessalonians 3:10b). Luke's account leaves out the sentence from Mark 13:32: "about that day or hour, no one knows, neither the angels in heaven, or the son, but only the Father." Luke does deal with this matter in Acts 1 when the disciples come together just before the ascension of Jesus and ask, "Lord, is this the time when you will restore the kingdom of Israel?" Jesus replies, "It is not for you to know the times or the periods that the Father has set by his own authority" (vv. 6-7).

There has always been useless speculation about the Second Coming. There are those who have set dates and given unwarranted descriptions of what the end will be like. As dates and times expire, new calculations are made. Whole groups (denominations or cults) have beguiled thousands of people with such vain specifics concerning matters about which it is not ours to know.

How shall we understand these apocalyptic passages, some of which were spoken by Jesus? It is clear they are not timetables. These passages call us to be always alert and ready. Clearly the end comes for all of us at some time. That unadorned fact should lead us to value the significance of each new day. There is an expiration date on our lives. We do not know when and how it will come, but it will come. Two thousand years have come and gone, and Jesus has not yet returned. But the end has come for billions and will continue to come for all of us. In our most reflective moments, we know we are not here to stay, and we should make the most of the time we have. When the end comes, or when we reach the end, we will give account of our stewardship of life. While we may think we are indispensable, we should note that we are surrounded by cemeteries filled with indispensable people. Stay alert. Be ready to leave on the long journey, at the end of which there will be "a book" that is all about us.

A few years ago, my smart-aleck daughter put a plastic sign on my office doorknob that reads: "Jesus is coming, look busy." It is proper for us to remember that Jesus is coming, or at least that we will go to meet him. It is OK to "look busy," but it is very important that we be faithful. (Thomas Lane Butts)

Lectionary Commentary

Jeremiah 33:14-16

Jeremiah presents God's promise of hope for the future of Israel. Not only will Jerusalem be restored, but there will be a restoration of leaders who are faithful and just. Unjust and ungodly leadership has always been the beginning point for the defeat of the nation. Wicked and unfaithful leaders beget wickedness and unfaithfulness in the lives of those they rule. Influence runs downhill.

Jeremiah does not offer prophecy as a kind of magic that spells out dates and times and specifics. The word of the Lord is not to be understood as human discernment, but as divine decision to make known God's plan for the future. These are not manipulative claims that enhance the public stature of the messenger. It is God's announcement that "the days are surely coming when I will fulfill the promise I made to the house of Israel and the house of Judah" (v. 14). When it is understood that this is God's promise, specific details are not needed. Help is on the way. It sounds like messianic talk. If God says so, you can count on it.

1 Thessalonians 3:9-13

If ever there was a proper role-model for an itinerant pastor, it is Paul. He wants to be everywhere at the same time. He prays God will open up a way for him to get to the church (congregation) that needs him most. Letters become a substitute for his presence. Whenever Paul hears of a problem, he writes a letter if he cannot get there in person. You can almost hear him fussing with himself and his circumstances and saying, "Oh, dear, I have to write another letter!" Paul stays busy praying for churches he has started but at which he cannot stay. He cares about the needs of his converts, but he cannot stay to be a nursemaid for them. God is calling him to other places, but the new congregation's welfare is always on his mind. Paul praises and reproves them by letter and sometimes by sending word through a coworker, but he wants to be there with and for them.

There is not a clearer or more heartfelt affirmation than this of a dedicated itinerant pastor on a big circuit who cannot be everywhere at once. "How can we thank God enough for you in return for all the joy that we feel before our God because of you? Night and day we pray most earnestly that we may see you face to face and restore whatever is lacking in your faith" (v. 9). I would love having Paul as my pastor! Wouldn't you? (Thomas Lane Butts)

Worship Aids

Invocation

Dear God, in these days of Advent, when our expectations begin to rise, we invoke your blessings on our time of worship. You came once in time and history in the life of Jesus to set all humankind free for all time. Come again, Lord Jesus, to set us free from all the entanglements and conflicts we brought with us today when we walked through the door of this place of worship. Amen.

Prayer of Confession

Dear God, father and mother of us all, giver and sustainer of all life, we have many things on our minds we need to discuss with you today. An unabridged list of the sins we need to confess would fill a book. Sins we cannot forget play across the backdrop of our minds, but there are also sins we cannot remember because we have hidden them even from ourselves. Hear us as we confess our sin before you—at least as much of our sin as we can stand to say. Forgive us, restore us, and set us free in the name of Jesus. Amen.

Words of Assurance

God attends to the sins we confess and hears also those we are too ashamed to utter or think about. The good news is that God forgives all and calls us to new life. Thanks be to God.

Benediction

We do not know what challenges, temptations, or opportunities may cross our paths this week. We pray not to be delivered from any of them.

We pray for strength to meet them with faith and courage and to have dominion in your name. Go in peace. Amen.

Peace: The Peace of Christmas

Second in a Series of Four on Advent

Isaiah 11:1-10

I have had the privilege of taking many groups to the Holy Land, with one of the highlights of the trip being a day in Bethlehem, the town of Jesus' birth. Ironically this was the place the shepherds heard the angelic announcement about peace on earth and goodwill to people. I say *ironic* because today most visitors cannot go to Bethlehem to see the Church of the Nativity or visit the Shepherd's Field. Actually this area where peace was announced has been a battleground of wars and disputes for years.

On the second Sunday of Advent, with its emphasis on peace, we have to ask ourselves "Will peace ever become a reality?" Or must it always be an elusive dream? With troops in the Middle East, Jews and Arabs fighting over the Holy Land, and Bethlehem itself shut off due to violence in the streets, we might well ask "What is this peace and where can it be found?"

Isaiah spoke of peace in messianic terms. He was portraying the future of Judah and Jerusalem. "A shoot shall come out from the stump of Jesse, and a branch shall grow out of his roots" (v. 1). The appearance of David's son refers to the restoration of the Davidic dynasty. The prophet declares this ruler will rule with "righteousness" (v. 4)—judgment made on the basis of truth and honor.

In addition, a complete transformation of the world of nature and the world of the spirit will take place. Idealized conditions will prevail with the abolition of all hostility and killing—no more evil. Dangerous predators are mentioned: wolf, leopard, lion, bear, asp, and adder, coexisting with innocent creatures: lamb, kid, calf, fatling, cow, ox and finally, a nursing child and a weaned child.

Obviously this is a reference to the messianic age, not our present time. Not many of us want to run down to the zoo and throw open the doors. If we did, the animals would run the zoo! I believe it was Woody Allen who once said, "The lion and the lamb may lie down together, but the lamb won't get much sleep!" To enjoy this kind of peace, we need God to redeem us from this finite existence to that infinite existence!

We must understand that real peace does not imply the absence of conflict or an escape from reality. Failing to understand these truths is to forever look for something that does not exist. To know any real peace, we must move from the manger of Bethlehem to the cross of Calvary. Real peace is individual and communal, not national; internal, not external; more of an attitude than an act; a result, not a goal; a spiritual operation, not a human achievement.

Jesus' meal in the home of Simon the Pharisee (Luke 7:36-50) illustrates this salvation experience and the peace it provides. While Jesus dines in this Pharisee's home, a woman—portrayed in Luke as a "sinner"—breaches etiquette and crashes the party. As she stands at the Lord's feet, weeping, she washes his feet with her tears and then anoints them with ointment. The Lord forgives her sin and tells her, "Your faith has saved you; go in peace."

Paul makes the connection between the cross and peace as well. He writes to the church at Rome: "Therefore, since we are justified by faith, we have peace with God through our Lord Jesus Christ" (Romans 5:1).

Many of us want peace in some other way. We want to feel good without being good, to get adjusted without getting converted, or to have sins explained away by some counselor rather than washed away by the blood of the Lamb of God.

Even the carols of Christmas connect the cross with real peace. Listen: "Hark! The herald angels sing, 'Glory to the new-born King; peace on earth, and mercy mild; God and sinners reconciled!' " (Charles Wesley, "Hark! The Herald Angels Sing," 1734).

In the beatitudes, Jesus blesses the peacemakers, who will be "called children of God" (Matthew 5:9). But we know how the world operates. As J. B. Phillips renders the beatitudes for the modern world, the pushers "get on in the world"; the "blasé...never worry"; the "slave drivers...get results"; the "troublemakers" get noticed (*Your God Is Too Small* [New York: Touchstone, 1952], 92–93).

The key to peace is obeying the Lord's command, "Follow me." In the prayer of Francis of Assisi, we see the steps to real peace:

Lord, make me an instrument of Thy peace;
where there is hatred, let me sow love;
where there is injury, pardon;
where there is doubt, faith;
where there is despair, hope;
where there is darkness, light;

and where there is sadness, joy.
O Divine Master,
grant that I may not so much seek to be consoled as to console;
to be understood, as to understand;
to be loved, as to love;
for it is in giving that we receive,
it is in pardoning that we are pardoned,
and it is in dying that we are born to Eternal Life. Amen.

This is the peace of Christmas. (Drew J. Gunnells Jr.)

Worship Aids

Call to Worship (John 14:27-28)

Peace I leave with you; my peace I give to you;
I do not give to you as the world gives.
**Do not let your hearts be troubled,
and do not let them be afraid.**
You heard me say to you, "I am going away, and I am coming to
you."
**If you love me, you would rejoice that I am going
to the Father,
because the Father is greater than I.**

Invocation

Dear Lord, on this day set aside for worship let us think again of the peace about which the angels sang at your birth and which you later promised your disciples. May we see this peace not as an illusion but as a sacred promise. Remind us even now that we are the spiritual heirs of that promise. Help us to accept this gift with thanksgiving. Amen.

Benediction

Now may the God of peace be with you all. Amen. (Drew J. Gunnels Jr.)

DECEMBER 9, 2012

Second Sunday of Advent

Readings: Luke 1:68-79; Philippians 1:3-11; Luke 3:1-6; Malachi 3:1-4

What Is Your Role in God's Dream?

Luke 1:68-79

The winding road by which Jesus came upon the scene as the Messiah is foreign to the modern mind. We expect everything to be immediate. We push a button on the computer and find immediate information. We are assured by the plethora of television advertisements from the drug industry that we can have instant relief from all our ailments. Each ad ends with a healthy person confidently telling us to "ask your doctor if this medication is right for you." Patients show up in doctors' offices with proposed "cures" for their illnesses, some new medication they learned about on television last night. All the doctor needs to do is scribble a prescription that will authorize them to pick up that quick cure at their local pharmacy. Patients with emotional problems stroll into the offices of therapists expecting an immediate cure for a long-term problem. "Put my marriage back together." "Make my children behave." "Restore my broken relationship with _____." The expectation is "do this now!" There is more, but you get the gist of the expectations of immediacy.

The modern mind is impatient with the winding road that leads to the arrival of Jesus; and we tend to be no less understanding of how it all turned out. Oh, we can get rather enthusiastic about the Resurrection on Easter, but we do not want to be bothered by the details of how we got there.

In this passage, Zechariah is filled with the Holy Spirit as he exults over the role that his baby son, John, is to play in the historical drama that will culminate in the arrival of the long-awaited Messiah. In his divinely inspired vision of reality, he can see that his son will grow up to be a prophet and forerunner who will prepare the way for the Messiah. He will, in fact, introduce the Messiah and then step off the stage and fade into the background when his mission has been fulfilled.

In what is known as the *Benedictus*, Zechariah recites the historical context in which the role of the forerunner will take place. He connects this event with the holy covenant that God made with Abraham, who promised that "we, being rescued from the hands of our enemies, might serve him without fear, in holiness and righteousness before him all our days" (vv. 74-75). He traces the evolution of that covenant through King David and all the holy prophets of old who gave voice to God's promise.

I can see this old man, who thought he would die childless, looking down at his baby son as he says, "And you, child, will be called the prophet of the Most High; for you will go before the Lord to prepare his ways, to give knowledge of salvation to his people by the forgiveness of their sins" (vv. 76-77).

I suppose every parent looks at their newborn and wonders what he or she will become. We wonder and dream, but by the inspiration of the Holy Spirit, Zechariah knows what his son will be. He will play a unique role in an endless line of splendor, and what he does will not end with him. Through the unfolding drama of which Zechariah is unaware, "dawn from on high will break upon us, to give light to those who sit in darkness and in the shadow of death, to guide our feet into the way of peace" (vv. 78-79).

Neither Zechariah nor his special son, John, would live to see how it all turns out. But in their view of reality, knowing the details of the final outcome is not necessary. The God of Abraham and the prophets of old had been faithful. They know God will continue to guide the course of history. Faith makes it unnecessary for them to "know." All Zechariah knows is that God has given him who has a role in God's plan. That is enough. God's plan is not completed. Pray God to show you the role you have to play, for surely you have a role! Find it. (Thomas Lane Butts)

Lectionary Commentary

Philippians 1:3-11

If you have ever wondered how Paul was able to keep a positive and growing relationship with so many churches over such a large geographical area, this passage will give you the answer. How could Paul keep the whole Christian enterprise together when there was such diversity within and between the churches? How was he able to hold things together when he spent so much time in prison? The answer is here.

Paul articulates his genuine love and concern for each congregation with no condescension. He reminds them that they are partners with him. Paul reminds them of how he longs to be with them. He thanks God for all they have done and will do. He expresses confidence in their growing understanding of who they are in Christ. Trust begets trust. Genuine love overcomes barriers, even those of prison walls.

Paul reminds them continually of his wish to see them. His letters are a substitute for his presence, but he thinks about them all the time. When my daughter was about eleven years old, she brought a framed copy of her elementary school picture to my office and said to me, "Daddy, keep this picture where you can see it, and think about me all the time." And I did. Thinking about my dear daughter was a bond of love that bridged the absences between us. Paul's letters were pictures of him that the churches could see and feel. This bond of faith and love represented Paul's genius of leadership.

Luke 3:1-6

Luke was systematic in all that he wrote, carefully connecting the present with the past, and projecting the significance of the meeting of past and present into the future. To Luke, the arrival of John the Baptist was an important event that connected the past to the present. He introduced the event in such a way that future readers will know exactly when and where John arrived on the scene. He recites the names of political and religious leaders who were in power when the word of God came to John. While these were important people at the time, and the documentation of their presence on the scene was important for the purpose of dating an event, they would fade into relative insignificance in comparison to the one whose ministry was dated by their reign. They are remembered only because of how they related to John and Jesus.

Luke quotes from the book of Isaiah to show that the advent of John was not a random event in time but was something that had been anticipated as a significant event in the flow of God's plan. Through John and Jesus "all flesh shall see the salvation of God" (v. 6). God's plan is unfolding as predicted, and everybody will someday see it and have occasion to benefit from it.

Malachi 3:1-4

The idea of a "forerunner" to prepare for the coming of the Lord runs like a golden thread through Hebrew prophecy. There is little wonder that a forerunner plays a prominent role in the ministry of Jesus. It is not clear whether Malachi is predicting the coming of a forerunner or whether he sees himself in this role. Malachi certainly sounds very much like John the Baptist, with shades of Jesus on the margins. Traditional Christians have taken this passage in Malachi to be an historical prediction of the advent of John the Baptist.

Malachi alternates between two poles in terms of what news the forerunner will bring. He reflects some rather stern warnings, even for the righteous, who will be refined by what appears to be an uncomfortable process. He warns the good people that they are "not there yet," and that some parts of their understanding of reality will be treated as dross and cast aside. To all, especially the unfaithful, he addresses this rhetorical warning question: "But who can endure the day of his coming, and who can stand when he appears?" (v. 2). It sounds like John the Baptist's warning: "Even now the ax is lying at the root of the trees..." (Luke 3:9). To whatever audience and age this may be addressed, it means *prepare*.

Worship Aids

Call to Worship

This is the day that the Lord has made. Let us rejoice and be glad in it. This is the house of the Lord, a place to which we have come to confess our sins, receive forgiveness, and from which we will depart to serve. Let us now prepare to worship. Amen.

Prayer of Confession

Dear God of our forebears, we confess how often we have made you a relic of the past. We have acted as if you were unreal or at least irrelevant. By our inattention we have rejected you and the one you sent to teach us and save us. We are ruled more by fear than by faith, by hostility more than by peace, by a sense of failure more than by feelings of dominion and victory. Forgive our misuse of the precious time with which you have entrusted us. Let us smell the distant scent of victory in the air as we continue repositioning our lives to fit your intentions for us. In the name of Jesus. Amen.

Words of Assurance

God of past, present, and future waits in love, calls in hope, and sends us forth in faith. Hallelujah!

Pastoral Prayer

Dear God, father and mother of us all, we come today with expectant hearts, hoping for some fresh insight into your will for our lives and praying to be forgiven for all those times you have tried to show us the way and we looked the other way. We thank you for the church through which we experience the support of a community of prayer. We pray for our leaders of both church and state that they may be given the gifts and graces essential to those who lead. Grant us a common vision of ministry that will lift us beyond petty differences that endanger our unity in Christ. Save us from discouragement in our relationships. Save us from malignant pessimism. Lift our relationships above chronic criticism of those we love and with whom we live.

We pray for all who have suffered loss of something or someone dear. Increase our hope for a better tomorrow. Help us with our grief, even over those secret losses that others cannot see. We confess, O God, that we cannot anticipate or articulate the innermost needs of all the people around us. May the silent screams, the unseen tear, and unspoken need be heard and seen by you, O Lord, before whom the secrets of every heart are known. May the grace of this time together become bread for our souls. In the name of Jesus we pray. Amen. (Thomas Lane Butts)

Joy: For All People

Third in a Series of Four on Advent

Luke 2:8-20

In England there is always a joyous celebration whenever an heir to the throne is born. People gather at the gates of Buckingham Palace, bands play, fireworks explode, and guns are fired in royal salute. Thunderous applause erupts as the reigning sovereign arrives to make the official announcement.

It is in that same mood of joyous celebration that we read of the birth of Jesus. *The Living Bible* translates verse 10 this way, "I bring you the most joyful news ever announced, and it is for everyone!" Can you imagine the shepherds hearing this shocking, sudden, surprising message?

With the flocks inside the stone walls of an enclosure, the keepers of the sheep gathered around a fire, trying the break the chill of a night in the mountains. They might have been discussing the recent taxation imposed upon them by the Roman government. Suddenly, without any warning, there was the *Shekinah*, or glory of God, where there had been only darkness before and music coming from the heavens such as they had never heard before.

We tend to romanticize the shepherds, forgetting they were common folks who were not high on society's list of important people. They were certainly not part of the religious establishment, nor were they often seen at the synagogue or temple for worship. Because shepherds were not able to keep the elaborate rituals of ceremonial worship, orthodox people generally despised them. It is certainly not coincidence that this announcement, "good news of great joy for all the people" (v. 10) was made first to shepherds? The message they heard is the message each of us needs to hear again: "Fear not!"

Our age has been called the "Age of Anxiety." We have so many fears! Some are legitimate, and some are not. We fear the crime in our society. We fear for the lives of our children. As we grow older, we fear being a burden on the family or having the onslaught of some dreaded disease. We fear being left alone with no one to care for us. I learned quickly in flight training that fear brings on panic, and panic can mean death.

Paul's answer to fear can also be our answer: "neither death, nor life, nor angels, nor rulers, nor things present nor things to come, nor powers, nor height, nor depth, nor anything else in all creation will be able to separate us from the love of God in Christ Jesus our Lord" (Romans 8:35-39).

The reason we need have no fear is that the Messiah has brought eternal joy to all of us who believe. He was God's gift in the flesh, a mirror wherein we could see God and perhaps see ourselves more clearly. Some time ago I heard a helpful list of comparisons that is helpful as we look into the mirror of our Lord's life. This is how I remember it:

He was careless about himself, but we are careful.

He was courageous, but we are cautious.

He trusted the untrustworthy, but we trust only those who have good collateral.

He forgave the unforgivable, but we forgive only those who don't really hurt us.

He was righteous and laughed at respectability, but we are respectable and smile at righteousness.

He was meek, but we are ambitious.

He saved others, but we save ourselves as much as we can.

He had no place to lay his head and did not worry about it, but we fret over lodging and not having the latest convenience manufactured by clever science.

He took up the cross, but we neither take it up nor lay it down, we merely let it stand.

We have a problem because we cannot differentiate between happiness and joy. Happiness is superficial; joy is real. Happiness is transitory; joy is eternal. Happiness can be bought; joy is a gift. Happiness is often the thrill of a moment; joy is the thrill of a lifetime. Happiness is like a spring creek that flows only in season; joy is like an eternal spring welling up within us.

Joy is a special word in the New Testament—found at least fifty-six times in various books. We receive this joy at Christmas. The essence of it is in the Christmas carol, "Joy to the world, the Lord is come." You see, Christmas means God is not an absentee; God is ever with us. The divine name, *Emmanuel* literally means "God with us."

I read about a woman who got so caught up in her Christmas preparations that she completely overlooked sending her Christmas cards. Without any hesitation she immediately went out, bought a set of cards, addressed and stamped them, took them to the post office, and mailed them. She really liked the card—it had a beautiful and peaceful scene of Bethlehem and the manger on front and "Season's Greetings" on the inside.

She finally got back home and sat down recalling the events of the day, pleased with herself that she had gotten so much done. She picked up one of the cards she had left and noted, to her horror, something she had failed to see. Down at the corner of the card were the words, "A gift is on the way!" Forty of her friends were now expecting a gift!

Our gift has come. We have received it! Paul said it, "Thanks be to God for his indescribable gift!" (2 Corinthians 9:15). John said it as well: "And the Word became flesh and lived among us" (John 1:14). The angels were right when they announced this good news of great joy; a Savior had been born! Joy! Joy! Joy! (Drew J. Gunnells Jr.)

Worship Aids

Call to Worship (Luke 2:8-14)

In that region there were shepherds living in the fields,
    keeping watch over their flock by night.
Then an angel of the Lord stood before them,
    and the glory of the Lord shone around them,
    and they were terrified.

But the angel said to them, "Do not be afraid; for see—
    I am bringing you good news of great joy for all the people:
    to you is born this day in the city of David a Savior,
        who is the Messiah, the Lord.
This will be a sign for you:
    you will find a child wrapped in bands of cloth
    and lying in a manger."
And suddenly there was with the angel
    a multitude of the heavenly host,
    praising God and saying,
"Glory to God in the highest heaven,
    and on earth peace among those whom he favors!"

Pastoral Prayer

As we look forward to Christmas, Lord, we prepare our hearts to take our place among the shepherds of bygone days. Make us ready for that music and message of old. May we have the joy and excitement of those gathered on that hillside. Grant that the hope your people have envisioned through the ages be rekindled in each of us. May the light of your glory flood our hearts, the wisdom of your Spirit fill our minds, and the joy of the angels be ours today! Amen.

Benediction

Lord, What will we do with your gift—the gift of your Son? May we celebrate this Christmas by accepting you into our hearts. This is, after all, the only gift you expect of each of us. Amen. (Drew J. Gunnells Jr.)

DECEMBER 16, 2012

❧❧❧

Third Sunday of Advent

Readings: Zephaniah 3:14-20; Isaiah 12:2-6; Philippians 4:4-7;
Luke 3:7-18

Jesus and John

Luke 3:7-18

We have gotten a glimpse of John from Elizabeth, his mother, and from the Spirit-filled pronunciation of his father, Zechariah, who while John was still an infant identified the role and destiny of his son. We have John at some early stages in his life. He retreated to the desert and lived an ascetic life of contemplation and self denial. He was clothed with camel's hair and a belt and ate locusts and wild honey. We do not know at what age he took on this life of asceticism, but John emerged from the desert just before Jesus began his ministry at the age of thirty. John was born a few months before Jesus, so we know that he was past thirty when he appeared on the scene.

Here we have the message of John to the people. At no place does the difference between John and Jesus stand out in such clear relief. By comparison, you could not call the message of John a gospel of good news. He preached a gospel of repentance for the forgiveness of sin with such charismatic intensity that people from Jerusalem and the countryside were coming out in droves to hear him. John said to the crowds who came to be baptized: "You brood of vipers! Who warned you to flee from the wrath to come?" (v. 7). Matthew's Gospel has John address this scalding message directly to the Pharisees and Sadducees who came to him for baptism. Luke says that this was directed to the crowds at large. To whomever he addresses the message, John says: "Bear fruits worthy of repentance. Do not begin to say to yourselves 'We have Abraham as our ancestor'; for I tell you God is able from these stones to raise up children to Abraham" (v. 8). He admonishes them to verify the genuine nature of repentance by their fruits, not their roots. He tells them that their racial heritage means nothing before God. John warns them that every tree that does not produce good fruit will be cut down and thrown in the fire.

The crowds are mesmerized by this preaching. They do not want to be cut down and burned, so they ask John, "What then should we do?" He says, "Whoever has two coats must share with anyone who has none, and whoever has food must do likewise" (vv. 10-11).

The tax collectors ask the same question, and he tells them to collect only the taxes due. The soldiers ask his advice, and he tells them not to extort money by threats or false accusations and to be satisfied with their wages. John's message is direct, scathing, and cuts no slack for anyone.

Have you heard John preach? I have. I grew up hearing "John" preach every Sunday and for four weeks of revival meetings in the two little churches in our rural community each summer. John told his converts that he baptized with water that there was one more powerful than himself who was coming and who would baptize "with the Holy Spirit and with fire" (v. 16). John said that he was unworthy to untie the thongs of the sandals of the one who was coming. He then characterized the one who was coming as having "his winnowing fork . . . in his hand to clear the threshing floor and to gather the wheat into his granary; but the chaff he will burn with unquenchable fire" (v. 17). This is the preaching I heard during the first eighteen years of my life. I heard "John" speak of the one who was to come, but I never did hear very much of the gospel of that one—Jesus.

John's message never included the good news of the grace of God. John prepared the way but did not live to blend his ministry with that of Jesus. He never did get to hear Jesus say, "Whoever has seen me has seen the Father" (John 14:9). Jesus was baptized by John, but Jesus did not use the method and mood and emphasis that characterized John's message. He calls his hearers to repentance and to lives that bear "good fruit," but his message was dominated by love. I have wondered what John would have thought of the life and teachings of Jesus.

There is an interesting report in Matthew 11:2-6 and Luke 7:18-23 of John the Baptist's last message. While in prison John hears a report of the ministry of Jesus. He summons two of his disciples and sends them to ask Jesus, "Are you the one who is to come, or are we to wait for another?" Jesus tells them to "Go and tell John what you have seen and heard: the blind receive their sight, the lame walk, the lepers are cleansed, the deaf hear, the dead are raised, the poor have good news brought to them. And blessed is anyone who takes no offense in me." To modern ears this may seem an evasive answer, but it would have been quite clear to John as quotations from the prophecy of Isaiah. When John was beheaded on Herod's order, I don't think he had any doubts as to the identity of Jesus.

The teachings of Jesus opened up a whole new and enlightened understanding of the nature of God. It is difficult for those of us who have inherited two thousand years of theological explanation of the Incarnation to realize what an incredibly joyful surprise it must have been to the first disciples of Jesus to hear him say, "He who has seen me has seen the father" (John 14:9b). In Christ Jesus, we have the wonderful insight that not only is Jesus like God, but God is like Jesus and always has been.

It does not appear that John the Baptist had that insight before he died, but it is clear that whatever John did or did not understand, he prepared the way for the one who gave us that insight. John had a special role in God's drama of bringing salvation to all humankind. (Thomas Lane Butts)

Lectionary Commentary

Zephaniah 3:14-20

Zephaniah prophesied during an unusually dark time in the history of Israel. There was corruption and indifference everywhere—in religion, government, and the general population. Zephaniah begins with "both guns blazing." There are no opening niceties. He takes the condition of frail Israel and universalizes the punishment in the coming "day of the Lord." He sees no hope of restoration and reformation. He draws hope from the idea of a righteous remnant surviving the devastation. Our text reflects a sharp turn in the temper of Zephaniah. Here, finally, dawns some hope. The Lord has withdrawn judgments. The presence of the Lord in their midst will help Israel to rise like a phoenix from the ashes.

We can apply the sentiment of this brief book to contemporary society. When religion grows cold, leaders corrupt, and the people are indifferent, the result—internal decay—is predictable. Most great nations self-destruct before being toppled by an enemy. There is an element of hope that arises from the humiliation of destruction. In our despair and repentance, we find "The Lord in our midst." Where there is a remnant, there is hope when the Lord is in our midst.

Isaiah 12:2-6

It is natural that a hymn of thanksgiving should follow Isaiah's prophecy of the return of the exiles. When we have been lost and then are found, the natural response is to sing out. Singing is the response of hope. When the earthquake struck Haiti in 2010, thousands of people gathered where their homes and churches had been to sing hymns of praise and thanksgiving.

This new exodus can be compared to the experiences of all exiles. Beautiful and inspiring "Negro spirituals" were born in the hope of liberation of black slaves. One of the greatest sources of spiritual power during the Civil Rights movement was singing. "We Shall Overcome" stirred the hearts of those who marched against segregation, and it frightened the oppressors to hear the oppressed people sing. We sing not only when we have been saved but also on our way to being saved. When we trust in our own powers, we do not sing, we boast. When we find God "in our midst" leading us through the storm to salvation, we want to sing.

Philippians 4:4-7

More often than you might imagine, people reach the highest level of spiritual insight while undergoing the most painful experiences. This was certainly true of Paul. He is languishing in prison, knowing that he will not likely survive, and he is telling the church at Philippi to rejoice and let their gracious gentleness be obvious to everyone. Paul is commending characteristics of the Christian life that he is practicing. He reminds them that "the Lord is near" (v. 5). This is said to have been the "watchword" of early Christians. It could mean that Jesus would soon return, or that in all things the Lord is with us. That hope was and is a great comfort.

When Paul urges them not to worry, he is certainly not calling upon them to ignore difficulty. Paul means to keep anxiety in its proper place—secondary to hope. Concern about legitimate matters is human, normal, and healthy. But worry becomes a lifestyle for some people. It takes a degree of intentional effort to put anxiety in its place. This can be done not only by intentional effort first but also by faith in the power of God through prayer. When we have done our best in taking care of some matter, it is proper to leave it in the hands of God through prayer. The result of living like this, writes Paul, is that "the peace of God, which surpasses all understanding, will guard your hearts and minds in Christ Jesus" (v. 7). (Thomas Lane Butts)

Worship Aids

Prayer of Confession

Dear God, we come before you today with many of the same sins you have heard us confess before. We had resolved to go and sin no more, but temptation was beyond our power to resist. We do not claim to be perfect, but we pray for the strength of intention to do better. Forgive us for living lifestyles not in keeping with your will for our lives. Forgive us for lying to ourselves about what we do and think when we wander off course. For these sins and for the sins we do not see, we pray for your forgiveness. In the name of Jesus we pray. Amen.

Words of Assurance

Our God is patient and persistent. God hears our plea and offers us peace that passes all understanding through Christ Jesus. Amen.

Pastoral Prayer

Dear God of all ages, you give meaning to our hopes, struggles, and strivings. Without you, our lives are empty, and we are lost. O Lord, we do not ask for a life of ease. We pray that you will teach us and empower us to be uncomplaining and unafraid, though not unfeeling. In our darkness, help us to find your light; in our loneliness, help us to discover the many spirits in this world that are akin to our own. Give us strength to face life with hope and courage, that even in times of discord and conflict we may find meaning and blessing. Help us understand that we are called not merely to enjoy the richness of the earth but to exult in the heights attained after the toil of climbing.

Let our darkness be dispelled by your love that we may rise above fear and failure. May our steps be guided and sustained by faith. You give meaning to our lives, O Lord; you are our support and our trust. Give wing to our spoken and unspoken prayers, so that we may feel in our hearts that we have been heard. Deliver us from the grasp of all evil, and bring us to everlasting life, through Jesus Christ our Lord. Amen.

Benediction

In the name of the Lord, Jesus, we pray God's special blessings on you as you walk back out into the world. We pray that you will not be led into irresistible temptation or encounter evil people or circumstances. May the love of God grace your lives and give you power and peace. Amen. (Thomas Lane Butts)

Love: Unwrapping Christmas

Fourth in a Series of Four on Advent

Isaiah 7:14

"Dear Santa, Are you having a happy vacation? Me and mommy are writing an e-mail to you and where are you going on your vacation? Do you know? What else are you doing right now? Are your elves still helping to clean up from Christmas, or are they having fun playing with the toys from last Christmas?" The mother in this instance was the editor of *Good Housekeeping* who asked her daughter why she wanted to write Santa Claus a letter in the summer. The child looked up and said: "I want him to know that I don't just think about him at Christmastime." (Rosemary Ellis, *Good Housekeeping*, December 2009, 39).

Children can teach us, can't they? Any unwrapping of Christmas reveals that it lasts all year. A real understanding of the birth of Christ has lasted from Creation and will last until consummation, from the first coming of our Lord to the Second Coming. Therefore, as the little girl intimated, we should not just think of Christ at Christmastime. The more we unwrap God's gift, the more we understand the redemptive nature of the event.

It all began when the carpenter Joseph, and his wife, Mary, had a baby. They had journeyed from Nazareth to Bethlehem to register for the census demanded by Caesar. While they were there, Mary had her firstborn, a son, wrapped him in swaddling clothes, and laid him in a manger. Joseph and Mary named their boy Jesus. We are told that shepherds came to worship Jesus and later, magi came from the East bringing gifts fit for a king.

How much Mary knew and understood about this child is debatable. A beautiful song has been written about this. Did she know that he would work miracles like walking on the water, healing the sick, calming a storm, giving sight to the blind and hearing to the deaf? Did she know this child was the Lord of all creation? Did she know that her baby boy would someday rule the nations?

We know! We know this baby boy was the Son of God who would give his life for sinful humankind. After death, he would rise from the grave and ascend to the Father. As Paul Harvey used to say, we know "the rest of the story."

As we further delve into God's gift, we are amazed that the religious community of Jesus' day did not recognize his birth as unique. The prophets had spoken repeatedly of the coming of the anointed one, even about his birth: "Therefore the LORD himself will give you a sign. Look, the young woman is with child and shall bear a son, and shall name him Immanuel" (Isaiah 7:14). Truth is, the Jewish nation was saturated by a God-haunted history.

Their problem centered on faulty expectations. They didn't expect a baby of peasant parentage with no royal pedigree. They didn't expect an itinerant preaching, from Nazareth of all places! They expected a warrior, another David, a charismatic leader to bring back the days of grandeur. The Jewish people expected one thing and received something else.

What they received was a love gift. In his conversation with Nicodemus, Jesus made that clear. In a verse often referred to as "the gospel in a verse" we find this truth. "For God so loved the world that he gave his only Son..." (John 3:16).

If you keep looking at the package, you will see how unique this was. Jesus taught us that God is not a tyrant ruling over us or an angry dictator trying to bring us into submission or a despot trying to deceive us. God loves us so much that God sent God's one-of-a-kind Son to die in our place.

God did not want us to respond to this gift of love out of fear but out of faith. In fact, a predominant message in the Christmas story is, don't be afraid. Mary was frightened; Joseph was frightened. The shepherds were terrified. The heavenly message to all of them was "Fear not!"

Some years ago I heard about a Christmas pageant in which a child muffed his lines but made the pageant. His line was, "Fear not! For, behold, I bring you good tidings of great joy which shall be to all people." What he actually said was, "Don't be scared! I've got good news for everybody." What an insight!

I was in Branson, Missouri, two years ago and witnessed a spectacular Christmas presentation. What I saw in that drama symbolically pictured biblical truth. The nativity scene unfolded in a lowly stable. Joseph and Mary gently placed the newborn baby boy in a straw-filled feeding trough—a manger. A brilliant star shown overhead, but gradually the shadow of a cross fell over the scene. A crimson glow flowed from that cross like a river, from the base of the cross to the sleeping babe. The baby stirred, and Mary lifted him to her shoulder. As she did so, the tight wrappings around him loosed into a garment ,and your eyes were drawn to the band of crimson linen at the hem, a picture of his sacrificial life. Any unwrapping of God's Christmas gift will ultimately reveal this child who will bring salvation to all who believe. Jesus' coming was redemptive.

Reality points from the manger to the cross. God's gift of love is not merely the words or liturgies or vows of our worship. *Emmanuel* says it all—"God with us!" God loved us enough to die in our place. Jesus was not just a baby in a manger but the Lord of the universe giving his life for us all. This kind of love is not only greater than we can imagine; it is greater than we can ever fully know.

Let's unwrap Christmas, thank God for the unspeakable gift of love, and then sing with Christians of every generation, "Hallelujah! What a Savior!" (Drew J. Gunnells Jr.)

Worship Aids

Responsive Reading (John 3:16, Romans 5:8; John 15:13; 2 Corinthians 9:15)

For God so loved the world that he gave his only Son, so that everyone who believes in him may not perish but may have eternal life.

But God proves his love for us in that while we still were sinners Christ died for us.

No one has greater love than this, to lay down one's life for one's friends.

Thanks be to God for his indescribable gift!

Pastoral Prayer

Heavenly Lord, as we look forward to Christmas Day, remind us that the birth of your Son was the most momentous and meaningful gift we, as your people, have ever received. Give us a deeper understanding of the gift, that we might appreciate even more your indescribable love for each one of us. May our joy abound during these days as we unwrap Christmas and renew our thanksgiving and appreciation for your goodness. Bless us with a consciousness of your presence so that we, like the shepherds of old, might truly worship and leave with our heads high and our hearts full. In Jesus' name we pray. Amen.

Children's Sermon

Bring a wrapped Christmas gift to use as an illustration. Let the children help you unwrap the gift. Include something in the gift for all the children. Talk about the importance of expressing our appreciation for the gifts we receive at Christmas. Close with the need to express our love to God for God's Christmas gift to each one of us and discuss ways to do this. (Drew J. Gunnells Jr.)

DECEMBER 23, 2012

❧❧❧❧

Fourth Sunday of Advent

Readings: Micah 5:2-5a; Psalm 80:1-7; Hebrews 10:5-10;
Luke 1:39-45, (46-55)

Mary's Song

Luke 1:39-55, (46-55)

Today we see the meeting of Mary and her relative Elizabeth, who is wife to the priest Zechariah and six months pregnant with John the Baptist. Today we hear Mary's song.

Let us take a moment to appreciate the beauty of this Scripture passage and the beautiful example of Mary's humble servanthood and her willingness to answer God's call. Then we will take a closer look or closer listen, perhaps, to the song Mary sings, which is often described as "revolutionary." The passage is called the *Magnificat*, for that is the first word of the passage in the Latin Vulgate.

In the passage immediately preceding this, the angel Gabriel informs Mary that she has found favor with God, that the Holy Spirit will overshadow her, and that she will bear a child who will be called the Son of God. The angel also tells her that her relative Elizabeth, thought to be barren, has in her old age conceived a child and is six months along. Mary's answer is, "Here am I, the servant of the Lord; let it be with me according to your word" (1:38).

Try to imagine yourself a young teenaged servant girl in Nazareth, perhaps as young as thirteen or fourteen, and betrothed to Joseph, a carpenter, whom we guess was somewhat older—perhaps in his twenties or thirties. Gabriel appears and gives her the news. Remember that you may lose your betrothal. Remember that if Joseph accuses you, you will be stoned to death. And yet Mary does not ask, "Who will protect me?" Or "Can you explain this thing to Joseph?" She does ask, "How can this be, since I am a virgin?" which seems a reasonable question and is not interpreted by the angel as doubting what she has been told. Like Abraham when God called him to leave his home, Mary responds, "Here am I," adding, "the servant of the Lord." She is not reluctant, like Moses or others called in the Old Testament. She is more like those called by Jesus, who drop what they are doing and follow. In that sense at least Mary is an example for us, a model of loving obedience; it is not surprising that some call her the first disciple.

We don't exactly know why Mary travels to spend time with Elizabeth, but this account of their meeting is really remarkable. We have to remind ourselves that in ancient times, a meeting and conversation of two women would not likely be recorded in writing and given prominence in an important text. What women had to say would not have been valued by men, and yet this scene was written by a male writer and survived many centuries of male scribes and male editors who were, for the most part, writing and editing for a male audience. The importance of the conversation is helped by Zechariah's muteness, his punishment for doubting the angel's news that he and Elizabeth would have a child in their old age. Joseph seems to have stayed behind in Nazareth. Thus the stage is cleared for two pregnant women to share news.

When Mary enters the house and Elizabeth hears her greeting, she feels her child leap in her womb, and suddenly she is filled with the Holy Spirit and begins to exclaim that Mary is blessed among women. Elizabeth questions how she is so blessed as to receive a visit from "the mother of my Lord" (v. 43). In response to Elizabeth's greeting and insight, Mary breaks forth in song, glorifying the Lord and recognizing her great blessing from God.

Scholars point out that Mary's song recalls and echoes to some extent the song of Hannah in 1 Samuel 2. Mary's song is reminiscent of Hannah's and yet is not the same—indeed, if it were, it would be sung by Elizabeth, for she, like Hannah, is advanced in years and childless and then is granted a child by God.

That leads us to the other main point that we need to acknowledge and deal with in our understanding of this passage and of the Christian faith, and that is the revolutionary tone of the rest of Mary's song. The *Magnificat* is described with words like "revolutionary" and "bombshell," and is referred to by some commentators as the Christian "manifesto."

Notice that she is prophesying here, and she is using the past to talk about future acts of God as if they have already happened. After saying how God has blessed her and "has looked with favor on the lowliness of his servant" (v. 48), she sings:

> He has shown strength with his arm;
>   he has scattered the proud in the thoughts of their hearts.
> He has brought down the powerful from their thrones,
>   and lifted up the lowly;
> he has filled the hungry with good things,
>   and sent the rich away empty.

What are we to take from Mary's rejoicing and prophesying in song? Clearly there is radicalism at the heart of Christianity. Is this a political call on our lives? No, today's lesson is not about political parties. As Christians, there are just some things we need to accept. God expects us to help the poor. Period. The Old and New Testaments give us ample opportunities to learn that God cares about the poor and expects us to help them. God expects us to care for widows and orphans—that is, for those who are disadvantaged in ways that make them unable to completely take care of themselves or who are unable to obtain justice without help or intervention. Jesus does not categorically reject those with money, for although there are cautionary passages—such as the story of the rich man and poor Lazarus, or the rich young ruler (these stories go to the difficulty of being wealthy and still loving God and loving one' neighbor as oneself)—there are also moments when Jesus dines in the house of a Pharisee, and we have to assume that Joseph of Arimethea had some wealth to have been able to purchase a tomb and give it to Jesus. Whatever our party or ideology, we just need to work into it that our God expects us to help the poor.

How can we respond in our community? You already have, if you support a community food pantry. We could always do more in the way of missions. We could, for instance, provide support to a missionary already at work in a third-world country. Or perhaps we could round up a group from our congregation and go on a mission trip to, for example, Central America. Those are a couple of ways we could respond to the song of Mary—perhaps one of you has a better idea.

We are now in the last week of Advent, on the verge of another Christmas celebration, learning from Mary to welcome the coming of God in Christ and the hope that is represented by the child in her womb. Let us remember that there are millions in the world who are drawn to the celebration but without expectancy and with little hope.

Christ is our hope, and we need to let Christ in us bring reasons to hope to those who have not had as much reason as we. We need to take the example of Mary and say yes to God. We need to say, "Here am I, the servant of the Lord. Let it be me with me according, not to my will, but to thine." (Harris Worcester)

Lectionary Commentary

Micah 5:2-5a

The writer of this passage speaks of a time when, once again, the house of David will bring forth a great ruler. This shepherd, sent by God, will care for the people, and they shall live in peace and security.

Hebrews 10:5-10

While the passage does not specifically mention Christ's birth, it does explore the meaning of the first coming of Jesus into the world, of his time on earth (v. 5). This epistle reading includes Psalm 40:6-8, which the writer seems to be attributing to Christ (vv. 5-7), who informs us that it is his body, his life given as the sacrifice. Verses 7 and 9 remind us of Christ's prayer in the garden of Gethsemane (Mark 14:36). (Julie Worcester)

Worship Aids

Call to Worship (adapted from Luke 1:44, 46, 53; Micah 5:2-5)
My soul magnifies the Lord!
Behold! Our ruler comes.
My soul magnifies the Lord!
We leap for joy for the Lord has blessed us!
My soul magnifies the Lord!
Let us rejoice for the Spirit has filled us with great things!

Words of Assurance
When we are tired, when we are afraid, when we shed tears, when we doubt, God comes to lift us up and strengthen us. May the light of God shine on you, refresh your soul, and restore you to a life of peace.

Benediction (from Luke 1:48; Hebrews 10:10)
Go forth rejoicing in the Spirit, for you have been looked on with favor. Go forth as one restored, for God has saved us. Go forth as one who has been sanctified through the offering of the body of Jesus Christ once and for all. Amen. (Julie Worcester)

Our Fascination with End Times

First in a Series of Three on the Practicality of Eschatology

Luke 21:25-36

Surviving the end of the Mayan calendar is reminiscent of Y2K. Fear of the worst has evolved into relief. Our fascination with end times focused attention on predictions of destruction that accompanied the 5,125-year Mayan calendar. The movie *2012* heightened the fear. The movie portrays the earth's core temperature increasing rapidly. Earthquakes create cracks in the earth's surface. A tsunami sinks the USS John F. Kennedy. A new beginning emerges as some escape in an ark. Predictions of earth's end are as old as the human race. Christians tend to couch the discussion of end time around the second coming of Christ.

William Miller, using Hebrew apocalyptic literature in Daniel, first projected 1843 as the date of Christ's return. He later recalculated the date to 1844. Jehovah's Witnesses expected the establishment of Christ's kingdom in 1914, then again in 1925 and 1975. Human beings have long been interested in an end time that would reverse the ills of the present.

The theological term for the doctrine of the end time is *eschatology*. The Hebrew understanding of end time was tied to the nation of Israel. A theology around eternal life for an individual is primarily a Christian concept. While our contemporary understanding of eschatology quickly moves to God's judgment and the hope for a new kingdom, our understanding of the future tends to shape the way we live in the present.

Living with intense expectations has an impact on the way we live. Paul Tillich suggested that in waiting, we already in some way possess that for which we wait. "He who waits," said Tillich, "in an ultimate sense are not that far from that for which he waits. He who waits in absolute seriousness is already grasped by that for which he waits" (Paul Tillich, *The Shaking of the Foundations* [New York: Charles Scribner's Sons, 1948], 151).

The gospel of Luke suggests the eschaton will be identifiable by cosmic signs that will illicit fear. "People will faint from fear and foreboding of what is coming upon the world, for the powers of the heavens will be shaken" (v. 26). Jesus says we will be able to recognize the end times as we recognize the fig tree's response to changing seasons.

Humorist Roger Welsch reflects on how people on the Plains interpret weather signs. When it comes to telling wind direction, says Welsch, "'People don't bother with weather vanes. They just look out the window to see which way the barn is leaning" (Charles Kuralt, *A Life on the Road* [New York. Ballantine Publishing Group. 1990], 265).

We can find signs of the end time in almost any era of human history, including today. Looking at the consequences of global warming, terrorism, or social decay, we could make a case for these being the biblical signs. The Second Coming is imminent. The "fear and foreboding" has come to our world.

Our understanding of the end time is in large part a product of our social circumstances. First-century Christians expected Christ's return in their generation, and persecutions heightened their desire for the *parousia*. The nuclear age has created an era of anxiety with the possibility of total destruction. Contemporary Christians may presume less urgency about Christ's imminent return than their first-century ancestors, but the violent apocalyptic images are as powerful today as ever. For many, an understanding of eschatology is centered on a judgmental God.

The primary concern of Christian eschatology is the establishment of the kingdom of God. Jesus believed the kingdom was initiated through him, and the invitation is tendered to all people. There are consequences for the unrighteous, and that is what most end-time scenarios emphasize. However, God's grace is the centerpiece of eschatology.

Luke is offering words of hope to people who are anxious about their future. The text was written some fifty to sixty years after the resurrection of Jesus Christ. The event described is likely the destruction of the temple in Jerusalem, which happened in 70 C.E. Luke's words are not about destruction. They remind the church that the future is in God's hands.

The apocalyptic interpretation of this text suggests that an absent God will return in judgment. If the images refer to the fall of the temple, Luke emphasizes the hope that emerges from the temple's destruction. God has been present all along, and the future remains God's future.

The Christian is free to understand that the God who created is the God who sustains. God has always been present and will continue to renew us, and God is our hope for the future. That is the practicality of eschatology. (Dan L. Flanagan)

Worship Aids

Call to Worship

We are in the midst of the God who created, and who still creates.
May we hear words of hope from our God of hope.

We are in the midst of a God of the future, and a God of the present.
Thanks be to the God of Abraham and Sarah, our God today, and the God of our descendants.

Opening Prayer

Some of us live in fear of the future and even in fear of God. We know that things change and that life will end. We pray for peace in our hearts, O God, as we seek reassurance. Our world seems so violent and unstable. It is hard to see signs of hope. And yet, we know your creative Spirit is at work. Open our hearts to your presence. Help us to know of your grace and to live with anticipation rather than in fear. Amen.

Benediction

Go into a world that is ever changing, but a world that is shaped by God. Go into the world to share the good news and to serve those who are in despair. May the peace of Christ be with you! (Dan L. Flanagan)

DECEMBER 25, 2012

❧❧❧

Christmas Day

Readings: Isaiah 52:7-10; Psalm 98; Hebrews 1:1-4, (5-12);
John 1:1-14

The Santa Controversy

Psalm 98

Advent and Christmas are always beautiful, but one of my fondest memories is of celebrating the season with my new spouse in our new church home, First United Methodist Church. The lovely sanctuary was made even more beautiful by the greenery adorning the windows, the walls, and the chancel area. Children's eyes sparkled as they gazed upon the beautiful Christmas tree and heard stories behind the hand-stitched symbols and stories of the saints. One of the few decorations in the sanctuary that was not greenery or Christmas candles was the small statuette of Santa kneeling at the manger. It sat atop the church's organ. It was so unique, so different, so appropriate, and it piqued my curiosity. I asked the organist and some fellow choir members about the statuette following worship the Sunday prior to Christmas and was surprised by the varied responses. The comments ranged from, "I know, don't you just love it?" to "Humph!" to "Yea, well...," and my favorite—"We don't talk about it."

Don't talk about it? What was so controversial? Instead of laying the issue aside, I pressed on in search of an answer. I asked church members and our pastor.

I first found out that those who knew who purchased it would not divulge the identity of the family for protective measures. Some in the congregation felt Santa had no place in church, some felt it childish, for some it didn't matter one way or another, some liked it but were bullied by factions that didn't like it. Those wonderful congregational disagreements; I know, another sermon for another time.

401

It took me almost ten years to find out the story of the statuette. The purchase was made by a fellow choir member. She and her husband had happened upon the statuette during a vacation in New Mexico. The purchase was made because this couple felt that Santa should be in the church. It's where Santa began and where Santa served. Church was most definitely where Santa belonged and where he should have been all along.

As I gazed upon the kneeling Santa at the manger, my fellow choir member and dear friend, who, like me, was a Christmas baby, sat with me, and we began to share our stories and trivia about Santa Claus, and how he had been a servant of God and went by another name, Nicholas of Myra.

Nicholas was born in the port city of Patara in Myra—formerly known as Lycia, located in present day Turkey—around 275 C.E., to wealthy merchant parents. Nicholas' parents were Christian and the family worshiped in a congregation that was begun by the Apostle Paul toward the end of his third journey (see http://forum.kusadasi.biz/thread1962html).

Legend says that Nicholas' parents were childless for most of their married life. They prayed every day for a child, and in later life their prayers were answered by the arrival of a son whom they named Nicholas, which means "God is victorious."

Life as a happy family was short lived. By the time Nicholas was thirteen years old, he was an orphan. The plague claimed the lives of his parents. With no other family, Nicholas turned to God and the church for solace. Nicholas gave his entire inheritance to the Roman Catholic Church and became a priest. He was appointed Bishop of Myra at the age of twenty-four and lived a life of service to others.

The young bishop was respected and beloved by his congregation and his community for his many acts of generosity. A superhero for his time, Nicholas fought for truth, justice, and the Christian way. The gifts that Santa Claus brings are meant to be representative of the gifts and acts of kindness demonstrated by Nicholas for those in need, be it money for dowry, money to help a family pay their taxes to Rome that kept a child out of slavery, arguing before the Emperor Constantine for lower taxes on behalf of a community and region, or saving the lives of those who had been wrongly accused.

Nicholas died in 345 C.E., but within one hundred years of his passing the Santa we know today began to take shape. The stories of the Bishop of Myra spread to all parts of the Roman Empire, including present day England, France, Germany, Switzerland, and the Netherlands. Over time the bishop's robe, staff, mitre, and Bible were replaced with toys and other treats as symbols of St. Nicholas. His name even began to change, as his fame spread to various countries: *Sinterklaas*, Father Christmas, *Papai Noel*, *Niklaus*, *Père Noël*, *Winter Grandfather*, and *Christkindl* (see www.stnicholascenter.org). Sadly, as the legend of Nicholas became commercialized, he began to be seen as childish instead of being associated with people of all ages and all walks of life.

Would Nicholas, Bishop of Myra, approve of the changes? No. This pastor and priest would have insisted that the focus be returned to God. Nicholas would have been directing our attention back to the manger of our Savior where his present-day likeness kneels. Like the good bishop, we should be pouring over God's holy word and worshiping the One who came to this earth, fully human and fully divine, who was sent to free us, and who would give us salvation by dying on a cross and rising from a tomb.

If we look around, we will find that the kneeling Santa is us. As servants for Christ, we, the modern day Santas, present ourselves to God and kneel before our king with open hearts and open minds in search for opportunities to help those in need. As disciples of Christ, we should not limit who and when and how many times someone should be helped, and we should seek justice for those who have no voice. We can accomplish all these things because of God's amazing grace.

Years after I first saw the kneeling statuette, my children presented me with an ornament very much like it. As I gaze upon that ornament hanging on my tree, I discover that, like Nicholas, I have been transformed. I have knelt before the manger and left as a new creation because of the grace and forgiveness found in Christ the King.

Like Nicholas of old, and the kneeling Santa of today, may we abide always in Christ and strive to live as the Spirit leads us, and may the Prince of Peace and Wonderful Counselor be with you and your families this coming new year. (Julie Worcester)

Lectionary Commentary

Isaiah 52:7-10

This lection from Second Isaiah is beautifully written, reminiscent of a song. Using the image of a king returning victorious from a battle and the victory being announced by a messenger causing the sentinels to sing with joy, the prophet here says that God is redeeming Jerusalem before the eyes of all nations. The people's joy at this event, God's return to Jerusalem after the exile, reminds us of our joy as we celebrate the incarnation.

Hebrews 1:1-4, (5-12)

The lesson from Hebrews celebrates our Christian confession and states a number of claims about Christ, demonstrating his superiority to angels. Christ is "the reflection of God's glory and the exact imprint of God's very being, and he sustains all things by his powerful word (v. 3)." The author writes here in the same spirit as the author of John's Gospel.

John 1:1-14

We look to the other Gospels for nativity stories and narrative presentations of the Incarnation, how Jesus came into our world a human baby, fully human yet fully divine. John takes another approach in this familiar Bible passage, the beginning to John's Gospel. Rather than stables and angels, magi and shepherds, John begins with the beginning, with Jesus as *Logos* (Word), clearly presenting him as co-creator with God. Even without the familiar nativity elements, this passage bears reading aloud as we transition from Advent to Christmas. (Harris Worcester)

Worship Aids

Call to Worship (Isaiah 52:7, Psalm 98, John 1:14)
Beautiful are those who bring the good news!
God reigns!
Let all God's creation rejoice!
For the Word is among us, full of God's glory, grace, and truth!

Words of Assurance
Immanuel dwells among, and where he is there is no darkness. God has come to set us free, forgive us our sins, and set us upon a path of peace.

Benediction (John 1:8, Hebrews 1:2, Isaiah 57:7)
Go forth as one who lives in the true light. Go forth reflecting the glory of God. Depart from this place filled with the Spirit and ready to proclaim that your God reigns! Amen. (Julie Worcester)

Jesus' Concern with Eschatology

Second in a Series of Three on the Practicality of Eschatology

John 16:16-24

A Harvard astronomer was giving a lecture entitled, "The Expanding Universe" in which he pointed out that some galaxies are moving away from us faster than the speed of light. In essence, they are falling off the edge of the universe. A woman appeared noticeably upset by this revelation. "Professor," she asked, "what are we going to do about all of those galaxies we're losing?" "Let them go, Madam," came the reply. "Let them go!" (*Parables, Etc.*, [Vol. 8, No. 5, July 1988], 2).

We have all experienced anxiety over future expectations; it is neither healthy nor practical. Jesus speaks of an end time of chaos surrounding his return, but no one knows when it will happen. Throughout the Gospels, Jesus urges us to prepare ourselves in the present and not to be anxious. "Do not worry about your life, what you will eat or what you will drink, or about your body, what you will wear.... [C]an any of you by worrying add a single hour to your span of life" (Matthew 6:25, 27)? God's gracious nature should motivate us to live the kingdom in the present.

Jesus understood God's kingdom to be a present reality. Matthew's Gospel says Jesus' ministry centered on the proclamation, "Repent, for the kingdom of heaven has come near" (4:17). Jesus sends his disciples out with a similar message, "As you go, proclaim the good news, 'The kingdom of heaven has come near'" (10:7). As he wept for the city of Jerusalem a few days before his crucifixion, Jesus predicted judgment upon the city "because you did not recognize the time of your visitation from God" (Luke 19:44). Jesus understood himself to be the fulfillment of law and prophecy. The kingdom of God could be experienced in this person, Jesus of Nazareth, the Son of God.

The early church interpreted Jesus' prediction "there are some standing here who will not taste death until they see that the kingdom of God has come with power" (Mark 9:1) to mean that Jesus would return within their lifetimes. Jesus may have been referring to his death and resurrection. The church's subsequent frustration with its expectation of the Second Coming created a crisis among the faithful.

It is clear from our lesson that Jesus believed he would be returning. "A little while, and you will no longer see me, and again a little while, and you will see me" (John 16:16). While this probably refers to the Resurrection, Jesus believed he would be returning:

"In my Father's house there are many dwelling places. If it were not so, would I have told you that I go to prepare a place for you? If I go and prepare a place for you, I will come again and will take you to myself, so that where I am, there you may be also" (John 14:2-3).

Jesus did not return to the first-century Christians, but the church adopted the Second Coming as a doctrine. We affirm it at each Eucharist, "Christ has died; Christ is risen; Christ will come again."

Christ expected to return, but his primary concern was with the present. Jesus consistently references his generation as evil and adulterous. Jesus' call was to proclaim the good news of a kingdom that was unfolding before their eyes, and he used earthly images to describe it: yeast, a mustard seed, or finding fine pearls. All are to be invited to God's kingdom; the consequences of refusing the invitation will be judgment. "I tell you, many will come from east and west and will eat with Abraham and Isaac and Jacob in the kingdom of heaven, while the heirs of the kingdom will be thrown into the outer darkness..." (Matthew 8:11-12).

Through stories, such as a thief coming in the night, Jesus taught vigilance. Jesus' treatment of eschatology is more prescriptive than descriptive. Jesus speaks of the destruction of the temple and of cosmic changes associated with the *parousia*. His concern, however, is with the present generation, who fails to see the presence of God before them.

The Gospels are addressed to persecuted Christians and a generation who has witnessed the destruction of the temple in 70 C.E. It was an anxious time in the new church, and Jesus' words about the future were healing. Christians were living through an Armageddon, but they had experienced the grace of God. The future is not worth worry because God is present. According to Matthew, the final words of Jesus to his disciples were "And remember, I am with you always, to the end of the age" (28:20).

In a *Peanuts* comic strip, Linus and Lucy are standing at the window looking out at a terrible rain storm. Lucy raises concern about a worldwide flood. Linus, resident biblical scholar, reminds her of God's promise to Noah in Genesis 9, the promise symbolized by the rainbow. Lucy expresses her relief, and Linus affirms that "sound theology" is always reassuring.

A sound eschatology points to the present. Jesus spoke of the future, his coming again, and events that might happen if the world fails to repent. Jesus' concern, though, was the kingdom of God, which was emerging before the eyes of his generation, deserving their total attention, and ours. (Dan L. Flanagan)

Worship Aids

Call to Worship

We live in the mystery of God.
Sometimes that leaves us frustrated and anxious.
Come to worship with an open mind and learn of a God of hope.
We are eager to hear the word and to celebrate with hope.

Opening prayer

Prepare us, O Lord. Prepare our hearts for the coming kingdom. We hear the invitation through Jesus the Christ, and yet we worry about the future. Grant us peace that we may be confident in your grace and motivated to live a life worthy of the kingdom. The Scriptures are filled with images of destruction to come. We live in a turbulent world. Help us hear words of hope today that we may leave with an assurance of your continuing creative presence. May the power of new life in Jesus Christ be ours today. Amen.

Words of Assurance

Jesus taught us not to worry. We know not what it brings, except that it will be a future that God creates. It is a future unfolding before our very eyes. (Dan L. Flanagan)

DECEMBER 30, 2012

❧❧❧❧

First Sunday after Christmas

Readings: 1 Samuel 2:18-20, 26; Psalm 148; Colossians 3:12-17; Luke 2:41-52

Jesus at Twelve

Luke 2:41-52

We, my wife and I and our two small children, were attending a Fourth of July observance in a city park that has a river running through it. Our daughter was two years old. An in-law of a friend offered to watch our daughter while my wife and I ate lunch. Minutes later, we heard the friend ask where our daughter was, and with a surge of panic we realized that no one knew. With my heart in my throat and my legs becoming useless, I looked at the crowd, and then I turned and looked at the river.

The cliché does not do it justice: "every parent's worst nightmare." Try though I might, I cannot forget my introduction to that part of parenthood.

My wife took the crowd, and I took the river. We ran up and down calling her name. Then came word—our friend's husband had found her waiting in line to use one of the portable bathrooms, oblivious to the panic she had caused.

Surely it would have been similar for Mary and Joseph. They had taken Jesus to the Passover festival in Jerusalem and afterward had walked a day's journey back toward Nazareth with the same group of friends, family, and neighbors with whom they had traveled down. A twelve-year-old boy would have been free to roam among that group. Stopping for the night, they would have called Jesus and asked everyone if they had seen him, and then they would have realized to their horror that he was not with them. Thus begins this one and only story from the childhood of Jesus, a story told only by Luke.

In ancient times, one story from a great person's childhood would have served as an adequate foreshadowing of what sort of greatness that person would grow up to exhibit. The Gospel writers would not have shared our modern-day obsession with every last detail of great people, including their childhoods; the writers focused on the time of Jesus' ministry, brief though it was. Why then, our question becomes, did Luke choose this story to represent the childhood of Jesus, being the only episode from the time the family returns from Egypt until he begins his public ministry?

Jesus is twelve years old, which in that day meant that he was preparing to move from childhood into official adulthood. He would be trained in the law and would then be accountable for keeping the law. In our culture, Jesus was on the verge of becoming a teenager.

If you have children—and probably even if you don't—you have figured out already that if Mary and Joseph did not know that Jesus had stayed behind in Jerusalem, it is because Jesus had not told them. If this story demonstrates one thing clearly, it is that Jesus, fully human, had to learn things just as humans do, including the lesson so many teens learn after having failed it; that is, to inform their parents of where they are, where they are going, where they are staying, for how long, who will be there...in other words, communication. Now of course we have cell phones, which give our children one less excuse to use and give us one more thing to be annoyed about.

After three days, Luke tells us, they find Jesus in the temple. John Wesley theorized that these three days were spent in Mary and Joseph traveling a day's journey away, taking another day to return, and then spending a day searching. The important thing to note here is the symbolism. They find Jesus on the third day after Passover, the same day as those who seek him after the Passover of the Crucifixion will find him.

Jesus is in the temple, sitting among the teachers, listening, and asking questions. Luke says, "And all who heard him were amazed at his understanding and his answers" (v. 46). All through Luke's Gospel, people will be amazed at what Jesus has to say. Jesus is, at least, a precocious student, with emphasis on the word *student*. In other words, this episode underscores the full humanity of Jesus. It depicts him learning about the law and asking questions, discussing Scripture with the temple "faculty," with, of course, understanding beyond his years.

When they find him, Mary, as every parent would, vents her concern and frustration. "Child, why have you treated us like this? Look, your father and I have been searching for you in great anxiety" (v. 48). Her phrase, "in great anxiety," is such a gentle portrayal of what she and Joseph must have gone through, worried not only that their son Jesus was missing, but that the son about whom God had spoken to them through the angel was missing. If it were not so painful, it would seem comical. This is a tense moment in this loving family, and Jesus' answer seems colored by that tension. "Why were you searching for me? Did you not know that I must be in my Father's house" (v. 49)?

We see Jesus begin referring to God as "Father," as he does through the rest of the Gospel, and yet in this context, that almost seems like a rebuff to his mortal parents. Why would you be searching for me, he seems to say, as if I were some kid? As if I were your kid! I am in my Father's house, the temple. There seems to be just a touch of teen testiness in that response. But immediately, they return to Nazareth, and Jesus is obedient. Luke ends this account by observing, "And Jesus increased in wisdom and in years, and in divine and human favor" (v. 52). Perhaps my impression of his response is false, and Jesus is merely reminding them that he will increasingly be giving his time and his life to God's plan for him. Perhaps he is using that method of responding to a somewhat hostile question with another question, which we see him use to great effect later.

We have seen a portrait of Jesus as a preteen in his family, a loving and very human, very humble family, enjoying an upbringing that had apparently been foreseen and deemed by God as appropriate for the raising of the Son of God. That is an impressive endorsement of the righteous and loving human family.

Certainly, Mary and Joseph must understand from this experience that they will need to let go of their son as he comes of age, to release him to God's plan and God's call on his life. Jesus' lack of communication seems like a typical teen learning situation, but his staying behind in the temple to pursue God's plan for his life can be seen as a universal lesson for us as parents. As a father, I find myself identifying with Joseph at the end of this reading, for as our children grow in wisdom and years, in their relationship with God, and in their faith walk, they become, in effect, children of God in a way that preempts my parenthood. Just as Joseph may have had to remind himself that God was truly the father of Jesus, I may have to remind myself that God is parent to my children just as God is my parent. If God's call on their lives takes them away from me and out into a mission or a task that God has laid out for them, then I must accept it. Like Mary, I will treasure that in my heart. (Harris Worcester)

Lectionary Commentary

1 Samuel 2:18-20, 26

Young Samuel, an answer to his mother's prayer, serves in a priestly role. Although Samuel was given to God and raised in the temple, we find that Samuel's mother and father, Hannah and Elkanah, are still active and devoted parents. Eli offers blessing to both Elkanah and Hannah each year when they visit, praying that the Lord will bless them with additional children. Verse 21 tells us that the Lord saw Hannah's devotion ("took note," v. 21), Hannah who followed through with her promise to return her son to God, and the couple are rewarded with five more children.

Colossians 3:12-17

This passage reminds the reader that he or she is special, chosen, holy, and dearly loved (v. 12). This passage also shows qualities of a Christ-like life. The writer encourages us to live a life of thankfulness and gratitude. (Julie Worcester)

Worship Aids

Call to Worship

Come and worship!
For the Lord is among us!
Come and worship!
**Let us give praise to the One who conquers sin
and delivers us!**

Words of Assurance

Angels, shepherds, and wise ones proclaim the arrival of the humble king who has come to set us free. The King of kings has come to conquer sin and to save us. For this Christ was born.

Benediction (Colossian 3:12, 17, Psalm 148:14)

Go forth as God's chosen ones, holy and beloved, clothed with compassion, kindness, humility, meekness, and patience. Go forth praising the Lord, for God has lifted you up and brought you close. Go forth dwelling in the Word, and may all you do reflect God's glory. (Julie Worcester)

A New Heaven and New Earth

Third in a Series of Three on the Practicality of Eschatology

Revelation 21:1-7

The book of Revelation is a primary source for Christian eschatology, and for many it is the most controversial book in the Bible. This twenty-first chapter captures the writer's understanding of God's final chapter of human history. The earth's end time will evolve into a new heaven and a new earth. The God who has been absent from an earth in turmoil creates a new home "among mortals" (v. 3) without pain and suffering. The eternal will become the real as death has finally been conquered. "I am making all things new" (v. 5).

This pastoral letter is addressed to Christians in first-century Turkey, who are experiencing a kind of Armageddon. They are a persecuted minority. Nature is erupting with earthquakes and volcanoes. Even the imperialist Roman government is under attack. The whole world seems unstable. The writer of Revelation addresses the pain of the early churches with assurance that God has a plan of redemption. Evil will not prevail.

Contemporary end-time scenarios have been developed from Revelation, from some of Jesus' end-time sayings in the Gospels, and from some Hebrew texts, such as Daniel. Like Tim LaHaye and Jerry Jenkins, authors of the *Left Behind* series, some people have developed a worldview in which faith rests primarily on eschatology. While the interpretations differ on the order of the end-time events, the common elements include "rapture," a time of tribulation, a battle between Jesus and Satan, and a new creation. It is all seen as God's judgment, a way of separating the sheep from the goats (see Matthew 25).

Our view of history has consequences for the way we live our lives. The early Christian church expected Christ to return in its lifetime, which led many people to give up jobs and family. Those in our time who focus heavily on God's judgment may miss the grace available in the present. Some live in fear of God's retribution and judgment. Others pray for it to come soon, believing they will be among the chosen and not left behind. In his final days, Jesus wept for Jerusalem because "you did not recognize the time of your visitation from God" (Luke 19:44). Too much focus on the end time causes us to fail to see God's presence today.

British poet Thomas Carlyle apparently once said, "Our main business is not to see what lies dimly at a distance, but to do what lies clearly at hand." Jesus taught, as does Revelation, that heaven and earth will pass away, "but about that day and hour no one knows" (Matthew 24:36), so why worry?

While Jesus understood that judgment would be the consequence of continued sin, he did not understand God to be absent. For Jesus the kingdom of God is not a future concept but something unfolding before our very eyes. The kingdom of God is "near" rather than some mysterious event in the future. God is active, not passive or absent, and part of God's activity is through the Christ. "And remember," says Jesus as he departs his disciples for the last time, "I am with you always, to the end of the age" (Matthew 28:20). Jesus spoke of the eternal now, not of a 2012 Armageddon. In fact, isn't the lack of such endtime events evidence of God's grace rather than judgment?

An Englishman recalls his experience of the bombing of London during World War II. He remembers his dismay as he watched bombs destroy the buildings of London and clouds of black smoke arise. The sky was darkened as the apocalyptic images came to life. He had images of a lost war and the loss of all the values of Western Civilization. What he remembers most though is the moment a breeze separated the clouds of smoke. His first view was of the cross atop St. Paul's Cathedral. He remembers a surge of hope that rushed through him. God was still in charge.

The writer of Revelation offers a word of hope to the early Christian church. God is in charge, and out of the pain and suffering of the early church will come a new beginning.

Our eschatological framework reflects our understanding of God and influences our actions. Eschatology based on tribulation, spiritual battles, and "rapture" creates fear and spiritual arrogance. If we understand God to be ever present, as Jesus promised, and constantly creating a new heaven and new earth, we have chosen to accept the grace that God offers. We have accepted Christ's commission to "proclaim the good news, 'The kingdom of heaven has come near'" (Matthew 10:7). Our hope is in an ever-present God demonstrated in the life, death, and resurrection of our Lord Jesus Christ. Christian eschatology is about the kingdom of God initiated in Jesus Christ, and it continues to unfold today. The kingdom's fulfillment is an act of divine grace to be celebrated rather than judgment to be feared. (Dan L. Flanagan)

Worship Aids

Call to Worship

We come to worship God who is ever present.
A God who was revealed in Jesus Christ.
We have come to worship a God of grace.
Our God is patient and kind in inviting all to the kingdom.

Opening Prayer

Gracious God, fill our hearts with expectation and with hope. While we may be in pain, we know that hope abounds. You are not finished yet, and we look forward with anticipation to the new heaven and the new earth. Your creation is unfolding before us daily. We are here to celebrate and to live with the joy of your promise to be with us always. May our lives be an expression of that joy, as we share the good news of the gospel. Amen.

Words of Assurance

In the life, death, and resurrection of Jesus Christ we are assured that evil will not win. God is patient and kind. God calls us to live in hope! (Dan L. Flanagan)

III. APPENDIX

CONTRIBUTORS

Chuck Aaron
First United Methodist Church
Farmersville, Texas

Tracey Allred
Birmingham, Alabama

Guy Ames
Chapel Hill UMC
Oklahoma City, Oklahoma

Chris Andrews
First United Methodist Church
Baton Rouge, Louisiana

John Ballenger
Woodbrook Baptist Church
Baltimore, Maryland

Dave Barnhart
Birmingham, Alabama

Scott Bullard
Tuscaloosa, Alabama

Thomas Lane Butts
First United Methodist Church
Monroeville, Alabama

Kenneth H. Carter Jr.
Providence United Methodist
    Church
Charlotte, North Carolina

Mike Childress
Salisbury, North Carolina

Dan R. Dick
Wisconsin Annual Conference
Sun Prairie, Wisconsin

Neil Epler
St. Luke's United Methodist
    Church
Enterprise, Alabama

Dan L. Flanagan
Saint Paul's United Methodist
    Church
Papillion, Nebraska

Travis Franklin
Salado United Methodist Church
Enterprise, Alabama

Drew J. Gunnells Jr.
Mobile, Alabama

David Hockett
Forest Hill United Methodist
  Church
Concord, North Carolina

Dock Hollingsworth
McAfee School of Theology
Atlanta, Georgia

Cameron Jorgenson
Lillington, North Carolina

Wendy Joyner
Fellowship Baptist Church
Americus, Georgia

Gary G. Kindley
Dallas, Texas

Mike Lowry
Central Texas Conference of
  The UMC
Forth Worth, Texas

John Mathis
Charlotte, North Carolina

Ted McIlvain
William C. Martin United
  Methodist Church
Arlington, Texas

David N. Mosser
First United Methodist Church
Arlington, Texas

Timothy Owings
Augusta, Georgia

Amy Persons Parkes
Maple Grove United Methodist
  Church
Oakville, Ontario, Canada

Carl L. Schenck
Manchester United Methodist
  Church
Manchester, Missouri

Thomas R. Steagald
Lafayette Street United Methodist
  Church
Shelby, North Carolina

Mark White
Richmond, Virginia

Victoria Atkinson White
Mechanicsville, Virginia

Jessica Williams
Trinity Baptism Church
Seneca, South Carolina

Darren Williams
Seneca, South Carolina

Ryan Wilson
Trinity Baptist Church
Seneca, South Carolina

Julie Worcester
Cross Plains, Texas

Harris Worcester
Cross Plains, Texas

Sandy Wylie
University United Methodist
    Church
Tulsa, Oklahoma

Brett Younger
McAfee School of Theology
Atlanta, Georgia

SCRIPTURE INDEX

❧❧❧

NOTE: *Page numbers in italic refer only to pages on the CD-ROM.*

Old Testament

Genesis

Exodus

Leviticus

Numbers

Deuteronomy

Joshua

1 Samuel

1 Kings

2 Kings

Job

Psalms

New Testament

The *Abingdon Worship Annual 2012* offers fresh worship planning resources for pastors and worship leaders.

A trusted planning resource for traditional and contemporary worship... Now includes interactive CD!

Using a Theme Idea based on the lectionary readings, each week's offering of prayers and litanies follows a basic pattern of Christian worship: Invitation and Gathering, Proclamation and Response, Thanksgiving and Communion, Sending Forth. Alternative ideas for Praise Sentences and Contemporary Gathering Words are offered for those who work in contemporary worship settings. Includes a number of Communion liturgies in response to reader requests.

Now more than ever, *The Abingdon Worship Annual* is a must-have sourcebook offering countless opportunities for planning meaningful and insightful worship.

"Commendations to Abingdon Press for offering two fresh ecumenical resources for pastors."
For *The Abingdon Preaching Annual*—
"Anyone who dares proclaim a holy word week in and week out soon realizes that creative inspiration for toe-shaking sermons quickly wanes. Multitasking pastors who are wise seek out resources that multiply their own inductive initiatives."
For *The Abingdon Worship Annual*—"Not only the sermon but also the whole service dares to be toe-shaking... and the *Worship Annual* is a reservoir of resources in that direction."
—The Rev. Willard E. Roth, Academy of Parish Clergy President, *Sharing the Practice: The Journal of the Academy of Parish Clergy*

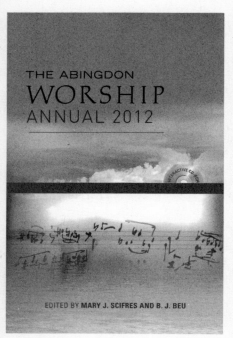

THE ABINGDON
WORSHIP
ANNUAL 2012

EDITED BY **MARY J. SCIFRES AND B. J. BEU**

Abingdon Press

WWW.ABINGDONPRESS.COM